SECULAR CYCLES

SECULAR CYCLES

Peter Turchin and Sergey A. Nefedov

PRINCETON UNIVERSITY PRESS PRINCETON AND OXFORD

Published by Princeton University Press, 41 William Street,
Princeton, New Jersey 08540
In the United Kingdom: Princeton University Press, 6 Oxford Street,
Woodstock, Oxfordshire OX20 1TW

Library of Congress Cataloging-in-Publication Data

Turchin, Peter, 1957–
Secular cycles / Peter Turchin and Sergey A. Nefedov.
p. cm.
Includes bibliographical references and index.
ISBN 978-0-691-13696-7 (hardcover : alk. paper)
1. Population—Mathematical models. 2. Demography—Mathematical models.
3. Business cycles—Mathematical models. 4. Economic development—
Mathematical models. I. Nefedov, S. A. (Sergei Aleksandrovich) II. Title.
HB849.51.T87 2009
304.6—dc22
2008050576

British Library Cataloging-in-Publication Data is available

This book has been composed in Janson

press.princeton.edu

10 9 8 7 6 5 4 3 2 1

Contents

Units and Currencies

Unit	*Abbr.*	*Explanation*
Metric		
1 hectare	ha	10,000 m^2 = 0.01 km^2
1 quintal		100 kg
1 hectoliter	hl	100 liters (l) = 0.75 quintals of grain[a]
England		
1 acre	ac.	0.4 ha
1 virgate (yardland)		30 acres =12 ha
1 quarter	q	8 bushels = 2.9 hl = 2.18 quintals of grain[a]
1 bushel	bus	0.352 hl
1 pound	£	20 shillings
1 shilling	s.	12 pence (d.)
1 penny	d.	1.33 g silver in 1300; 0.72 g in 1500; 0.46 g in 1700
France		
1 sétier		1.56 hl
1 livre tournois	l.t.	67 g silver in 1300, 21.7 g in 1500, 7.65 g in 1700
1 livre		20 sou
1 sou (sol)	s.	12 denier (d.)
1 denier	d.	
Rome (and Egypt)		
1 modius		8.62 l
1 iugerum		0.25 ha
1 pound (Roman)		327.45 g
1 as (libral)		1 Roman pound of bronze (before 220 BCE)
1 as (sextantal)		2 ounces or one-sixth pound of bronze (ca. 200 BCE)
1 denarius		3.9 g of silver (second century BCE)
1 sestertius	HS	0.25 denarii
1 medimnos		52 l
1 artaba		4.5 modii
Russia		
1 desyatin		1.09 ha
1 vyt'		15 desyatins
1 pud		16.4 kg
1 quarter (chetvert)		4 puds in 16th century, 6 puds in 17th century, 8 puds from end of 17th century
1 yuft'		1 quarter of rye plus 1 quarter of oats
1 ruble		67.5 g silver in 1535, 24.7 g in 1700, 18 g in 1900
1 denga		1/200th of ruble

[a] Throughout the book we use the conversion factor of 0.75 between the volume and weight of wheat (that is, 1 hl = 0.75 quintals). This is a very rough approximation, because the conversion factor varies with the grain variety, and thus between historical regions and periods.

Chapter 1

Introduction: The Theoretical Background

1.1 Development of Ideas about Demographic Cycles

The modern science of population dynamics begins with the publication in 1798 of *An Essay on the Principle of Population* by Thomas Robert Malthus. Malthus pointed out that when population increases beyond the means of subsistence, food prices increase, real wages decline, and per capita consumption, especially among the poorer strata, drops. Economic distress, often accompanied by famine, plague, and war, leads to lower reproduction and higher mortality rates, resulting in a slower population growth (or even decline) that, in turn, allows the subsistence means to "catch up." The restraints on reproduction are loosened and population growth resumes, leading eventually to another subsistence crisis. Thus, the conflict between the population's natural tendency to increase and the limitations imposed by the availability of food results in the tendency of population numbers to oscillate. Malthus's theory was extended and further developed by David Ricardo in his theories of diminishing returns and rent (Ricardo 1817).

According to the Malthusian argument, the oscillation in population numbers should be accompanied by systematic changes in certain economic variables, most notably food prices. Fortunately, data on prices are reasonably abundant in historical sources, and it is possible to construct time series documenting price fluctuations over very long periods of time. Compilations of price trends appeared as early as the sixteenth century. For example, Ruggiero Romano (1967) reports that a time series of grain prices between 1500 and 1593 appeared in an appendix of *La Patria del Friuli Restaurata* by Jacopo Stainero, published in 1595 in Venice. The data on prices in medieval and early modern England were made available to historians by Thorold Rogers (1862). By the 1930s the empirical material had accumulated to the point where it became very clear that European prices had gone through a number of very slow swings between 1200 and 1900 (Simiand 1932, Griziotti-Kretschmann 1935, Abel 1980).

A most important and lasting contribution was Wilhelm Abel's *Agrarkrisen und Agrarkonjunktur*, the first German edition of which was published in 1935. Abel compiled a rich data set containing time-series information about prices, wages, rents, and population movements in Western and Central Europe from the thirteenth to the twentieth centuries, ensuring that the empirical importance of his work would remain high to this day. The most striking pattern to emerge was the wavelike movement of grain prices (expressed in terms of grams of silver). There were three waves or "secular trends" (Abel 1980:1):

1. An upward movement during the thirteenth century and early fourteenth century, followed by a decline in the late Middle Ages
2. Another upsurge in the sixteenth century, followed by a decline or apparent equilibrium (depending on the country) during the seventeenth century
3. A third increase during the eighteenth century, followed by irregular fluctuations during the nineteenth century, eventually converging to an early twentieth-century minimum

The twentieth century saw another (fourth during the last millennium) period of price inflation (Fischer 1996).

On the basis of the observed patterns, Abel argued that the fluctuations in the circulation of money could not adequately explain the long-term trends in the price of grain. By contrast, population moved more or less in the same direction as the food prices and in an inverse ratio to wages (Abel 1980:292–93). Abel concluded that the Malthusian-Ricardian theory provided a better explanation of the data than the monetarist theory. Furthermore, the Malthusian-Ricardian theory predicted that an increasing population would result in a specific progression of effects. Rents would rise first, with grain prices lagging behind rents, the price of industrial goods lagging behind grain prices, and workers' wages bringing up the rear. The evidence showed that this was precisely what happened (until the whole system was dramatically changed in the nineteenth century).

Abel's conclusions were soon supported and extended by other historians, with the most influential contributions made by Michael Postan, working in England, and Emmanuel Le Roy Ladurie, in France. In a talk given in 1950, Postan rejected a monetarist explanation of long-term price movements during the Middle Ages and firmly asserted the primacy of the demographic factor (Hilton 1985). Le Roy Ladurie was an even more consistent follower of Malthus. In *The Peasants of Languedoc*, first published in French in 1966, he argued that southern France went through a great agrarian cycle lasting from the end of the fifteenth century to the beginning of the eighteenth (Le Roy Ladurie 1974:289). Although Le Roy Ladurie did not completely ignore the social and political aspects of the cycle, his explanation of the causes underlying the cycle was firmly Malthusian. Speaking in 1973, he said, "it is in the economy, in social relations and, even more fundamentally, in biological facts, rather than in the class struggle, that we must seek the motive force of history" (quoted in Hilton 1985:4).

Such a radical Malthusian position could not but provoke a reaction from scholars working within the Marxist tradition. Although some Marxist historians doubted the very fact of a drastic and prolonged population decline from 1350 to 1450 (Kosminsky 1956), others accepted it but preferred to explain it as the "crisis of feudalism." In an influential book first published in 1946, Maurice Dobb argued that the cause of the crisis was the inefficiency of feudalism as a system of production, coupled with the growing needs of the ruling class for revenue (Dobb 1963:42–47). The "feudal lust for expanded revenue" was a result of two processes: growth in the size of the parasitic class and the increasing extravagance of noble consumption. These two tendencies, working synergistically, resulted in an intensification of feudal pressure on the peasantry to the point where it destroyed the goose that laid the golden eggs. Dobb's theory occasioned an extensive discussion. One interesting contribution to the theory was Paul Sweezy's proposition that the growing extravagance of the feudal ruling class was a result of the rapid expansion of trade from the eleventh century onward, which brought an ever-increasing variety of goods within its reach (Sweezy et al. 1976:38–39). Thus, Sweezy sees the root cause of the fourteenth-century crisis in the impact of this exogenous force on the structure of feudalism (Sweezy et al. 1976:106).

Robert Brenner's 1974 critique of Postan's and Le Roy Ladurie's theories might be regarded as a continuation of the Dobb-Sweezy debate of the 1950s (the "Brenner debate" papers are collected in Aston and Philpin 1985, Hilton 1985). Brenner did not deny that the Malthusian model had a certain compelling logic (Brenner 1985a:14). However, its attempt to explain long-term trends in economic growth and income distribution was doomed from the start because it ignored ("abstracted away") the social structure, the most important part of which was the surplus-extraction relationship between the direct producers and the ruling class (Brenner 1985a:10–11).

One deficiency of the Malthusian theory, according to Brenner, was the empirical observation that different societies within Europe, starting from similar demographic and economic conditions obtaining after the Black Death, subsequently followed divergent trajectories. For example, serfdom completely disappeared from certain Western European countries (England, France) while making a strong comeback in Central Europe (Poland, Prussia). Thus, different property structures (the landholding system) and different balances of power (the cohesiveness and organization of the ruling class) could result in different paths followed by societies after the demographic catastrophe.

The second and even more damaging argument against the Malthusian model is the observation of continuous stagnation of most of the traditional European economies in the late medieval period (Brenner 1985a:18). For example, the Black Death removed about one-third of the English population in the mid-fourteenth century, and by the end of the century the population had been further reduced to one-half of its 1300 peak. According to Malthusian logic, such a drastic population decrease should have led to higher agrarian productivity, low food prices and high real wages, and the resumption of vigorous population growth. Indeed, the dynamics of prices and wages were largely in line with the Malthusian predictions. Yet population stagnated for more than a century, with growth resuming only in the late fifteenth century. Brenner argued that such episodes of long-term stagnation could only be understood as the product of established structures of class relations (Brenner 1985a:18). A decline in the number of direct producers reduced the income of the lords. To maintain their income, the lords attempted to extract a greater amount from each peasant, as well as trying to dispossess one another (via brigandage and internal warfare). The result was the disruption of production, leading to a further demographic decline, rather than a return to equilibrium as the Malthusian model would predict (Brenner 1985b:224).

In their responses to Brenner's critique, Postan and Le Roy Ladurie were unable to effectively account for the prolonged post–Black Death depression phase within the Malthusian theory. Postan and Hatcher acknowledged the problem: "Indeed the reason why the recovery was so belated and so sluggish is still one of the incompletely resolved difficulties inherent in the medieval hypotheses Brenner disagrees with" (1985:69). On the other hand, the extreme version of the Marxist thesis (perhaps found in the purest form in Sweezy), which assigns class relations the all-determining role in the economic development of medieval and early modern Europe, would also fail to account for empirical facts. For example, such a purely class-struggle-based theory is unable to explain the secular cycles in population, prices, and wages, as well as why exploitation of peasants also fluctuated cyclically.

In the end, the critique of Brenner and certain others, most notably Guy Bois (1984), played a constructive role by pointing out that the Malthusian model neglects an important explanatory variable. What we need is a synthetic theory that encompasses both demographic mechanisms (with the associated economic consequences) and power relations (surplus-extraction mechanisms). In the dynamical systems framework, it does not make sense to speak of one or the other as "the primary factor." The two factors interact dynamically, each affecting and being affected by the other. We pursue this idea in the next section.

It is curious that both sides in the Brenner debate almost entirely ignored the role of the state. This omission is understandable. The Marxists tend to treat the state as merely a vehicle for conveying interests of the ruling class, while the Malthusians' focus has been on the economic variables.

There is, however, a significant movement among historical sociologists "to bring the state back in" (Skocpol 1979). States are not simply created and manipulated by dominant classes; they are agents in their own right, and they compete with the elites in appropriating resources from the economy.

Historians have long recognized that there were recurrent waves of state breakdown and political crises in European history: the "calamitous" fourteenth century (Tuchman 1978), the "iron century" of 1550–1660 (Kamen 1971), and the "age of revolutions" of 1789–1849 (Hobsbawm 1962). Each of these periods was preceded by a period of sustained and substantial population growth. In a pathbreaking book, Jack Goldstone (1991) argued that there is a causal connection between population growth and state breakdown. The seeds of this theory were already contained in the work of Malthus. Goldstone, however, does not argue that population growth is a direct cause of state collapse (in fact, he carefully distances himself from the strict Malthusian doctrine). Instead, population growth causes social crisis indirectly, by affecting social institutions, which in turn affect sociopolitical stability. For this reason, Goldstone refers to his theory as demographic-structural: *demographic* because the underlying driving force is population growth, *structural* because it is not the demographic trend itself that directly causes the state crisis but its impact on economic, political, and social structures (Goldstone 1991:xxvi). We discuss this theory in more detail in the next section, but here we should mention that the verdict on Goldstone's work among historical sociologists has been highly positive (see, e.g., Collins 1993, Wickham-Crowley 1997, Li 2002).

To summarize, it is becoming increasingly clear to specialists from very diverse fields—demographers and historical economists, social historians, and political scientists—that European societies were subjected to recurrent long-term oscillations during the second millennium CE (Braudel 1988, Cameron 1989, Fischer 1996). Furthermore, the concept of oscillations in economic, social, and political dynamics was not discovered by the Europeans. Plato, Aristotle, and Han Fei-Tzu connected overpopulation to land scarcity, insufficient food supply, poverty, starvation, and peasant rebellions (Parsons 2005). The Chinese, for example, have traditionally interpreted their history as a series of dynastic cycles (Reischauer 1960, Meskill 1965, Usher 1989, Chu and Lee 1994). The fourteenth-century Arab sociologist Ibn Khaldun developed an original theory of political cycles explaining the history of the Maghreb (Inayatullah 1997). Are these phenomena, which at first glance seem very diverse, actually related? In this book we examine the hypothesis that secular cycles—demographic-social-political oscillations of very long period (centuries long)—are the rule rather than the exception in large agrarian states and empires.

1.2 A Synthetic Theory of Secular Cycles

The brief review in the previous section focused mainly on the controversies between advocates of various processes as dominant influences. In the heat of the debate, however, the opposing sides tend to simplify and caricature the views of each other. For example, it is clear that neither purely demographic nor purely class conflict explanations of secular cycles work very well when confronted with data. On the other hand, a synthetic theory that incorporates both of these (and some other) processes may provide us with a viable hypothesis that can be tested with data. The idea is that secular cycles can only be understood as a result of the interaction between several interlinked variables—economic (including demography), social structure (particularly, how the elites interact with the producing population and the state), and political (state stability or collapse). In the following paragraphs we sketch the outlines of such a synthetic explanation. Our explicit focus is on agrarian societies, that is, those in which more than 50 percent of the population (and typically above 80–90 percent) is involved in agriculture.

The Demographic Component

The demographic component of the theory is based very much on the original insights of Malthus and Ricardo, further developed by neo-Malthusians such as Le Roy Ladurie and Postan. The key variable is the population density in relation to the carrying capacity of the local region. The concept of *carrying capacity* was developed by ecologists in the context of the logistic model, invented by Paul Verhulst and popularized by Raymond Pearl (Pearl and Reed 1920). Carrying capacity is defined as the population density that the resources of the habitat can support in the long term (for an excellent discussion of human carrying capacity from an ecologist's point of view, see Cohen 1995). *Resources* usually refer to food, although in some environments the limiting resource may be the availability of water or fuel. Carrying capacity thus is an upper ceiling on population growth. From the point of view of economics, this limit arises because labor inputs into production suffer from diminishing marginal returns.

It is clear that the carrying capacity of a specific region is strongly affected by its physiographic features (the availability of land suitable for agriculture, water supply, soil characteristics, length of the growing season, and so on). It is also affected by year-to-year fluctuations in the temperature and the amount of rainfall, as well as by gradual changes in the climate. In other words, carrying capacity is a variable that changes in both space and time. Finally, and most important, carrying capacity is affected both by the existing level of agricultural technology and by how this technology is employed. As Ester Boserup (1966, 1981) famously argued, population growth can have a positive effect on economic innovation.

Although Boserup is widely regarded as being anti-Malthusian, both her insights and those of Malthus can be comfortably combined within the same general theoretical framework (Lee 1986, Wood 1998). Thus, adverse effects of population growth on the standard of living can provide strong inducements for the adoption of new means of production. However, in agrarian societies, economic change can win only a temporary respite from marginal immiseration (Wood 1998, Clark 2007a). For example, a society that approaches the current limits of population growth can invest in clearing forests, draining swamps, irrigation, and flood control. All these measures will result in an increase in the carrying capacity. However, at some point there are no more forests to cut or swamps to drain, and if the population continues to grow, eventually it will again begin pressing against the Malthusian limits.

As population density approaches the carrying capacity, a number of related changes affect the society. There are shortages of land and food, and an oversupply of labor. As a result, food prices increase, real wages decline, and per capita consumption, especially among the poorer strata, drops. Economic distress leads to lower reproduction and higher mortality rates, resulting in a slower population growth. Should population density reach the carrying capacity, there would be just enough food to sustain and replace one individual; birth and death rates would equalize, and population density would be at an equilibrium. At least, this is what simple models such as the logistic predict; in actuality, other factors not taken into account by a purely demographic model would preclude the emergence of a stable equilibrium.

Population growth in excess of the productivity gains of the land has a fundamental effect on society's structures. The typical changes accompanying population growth are high rents and land prices, increasing fragmentation of peasant holdings or high numbers of landless peasants, and increased migration of landless peasants to cities. Urbanization (measured by the proportion of population inhabiting towns and cities) increases. Cheap labor results in a flowering of trades and crafts. The demand for manufactures increases, because the elites profit from high rents on land and lower labor costs. Increased urbanization and conspicuous consumption by the elites promote regional and international trade. The gap between the well-to-do and the poor grows. In rural areas overpopulation means that no food reserves are available in case of crop failure. Accordingly, years of poor harvest that would hardly be noticed in better times now result in significant mortality and, at worst, in catastrophic famines. Chronic undernourishment creates conditions conducive to the spread of epidemics.

The cities accumulate landless peasants and jobless artisans, who join the growing ranks of paupers and vagrants. Food riots and wage protests become frequent. Eventually, deepening economic misery leads to peasant and urban uprisings. However, as long as the elites are united and the state maintains control of the military, such popular uprisings have small chance of success. This fundamental point was recently reiterated by Jack Goldstone:

> It is a profound and repeated finding that the mere facts of poverty and inequality or even increases in these conditions, do *not* lead to political or ethnic violence (Gurr 1980, Goldstone 1998, 2002b). In order for popular discontent or distress to create large-scale conflicts, there must be some elite leadership to mobilize popular groups and to create linkages between them. There must also be some vulnerability of the state in the form of internal divisions and economic or political reverses. Otherwise, popular discontent is unvoiced, and popular opposition is simply suppressed. (Goldstone 2002a)

Social Structure: Commoners, Elites, and Social Mobility

One important consequence of the law of diminishing returns is that the amount of surplus produced by cultivators is nonlinearly related to their numbers. Surplus is the difference between the total production and what is needed for subsistence (that is, the minimum amount of resources needed to support and reproduce each peasant household multiplied by the number of households). The amount of resources needed for subsistence increases linearly with population, while the total product grows slower than linearly as a result of the law of diminishing returns (figure 1.1a). As a result, at a certain critical population density, which we have defined as the carrying capacity, the two curves intersect. This is the point where the surplus becomes zero (and should population increase beyond the carrying capacity, the surplus becomes negative, with the consequence that peasant households do not get enough resources to reproduce themselves, and population density must decline).

The curve relating the amount of surplus produced to population density crosses zero both where population density equals zero and where it equals carrying capacity, and there is a hump somewhere between these two critical points (figure 1.1b). Thus, when population increases from a low level, initially the amount of surplus increases (more peasants means more surplus). At some intermediate density, however, the surplus reaches a maximum: this is where the effects of diminishing returns on labor inputs into agriculture begin to be felt. After that point, the surplus begins to decline.

The surplus produced by peasants is not made available to the elites (and the state) automatically; left alone, peasants would happily consume

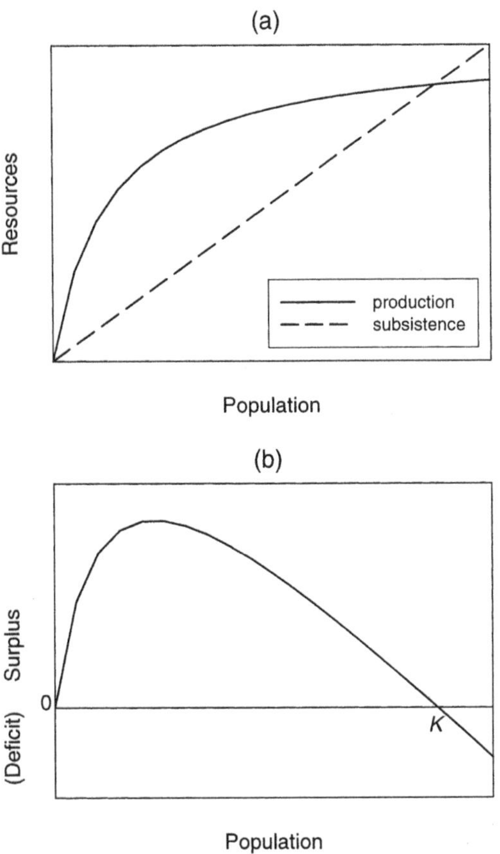

Figure 1.1 Effect of population growth on (a) total production, subsistence needs, and (b) the production of the surplus. K is the carrying capacity.

it themselves (or simply work less, "consuming" it as extra leisure time). How much of the production ends up in the hands of the elites depends on many economic and political factors. One important dynamic is that the elites are usually able to extract a larger amount of surplus during the late stages of population growth. Specific mechanisms depend on the landholding system. For example, an oversupply of rural labor elevates rents and therefore increases a landowner's profits. In a serfdom-based system lords can set the level of extraction almost arbitrarily high, because oppressed serfs have nowhere to flee—the whole surrounding landscape is at the saturation level, and the only alternative is the life of a vagabond or a bandit, which has always been brutish and short. Thus, most serfs have no realistic alternative to submission.

Prospects are equally bleak for free but landless laborers who must secure employment to support themselves and their families. Oversupply of labor leads to depressed wages and chronic unemployment or underemployment for a substantial part of population. On the other hand, employers, both rural and urban, profit greatly from this economic situation.

These considerations suggest that during the late stages of population growth, when commoners are already suffering from economic difficulties, the elites are enjoying a golden age. Both the reproduction of the existing elites and the recruitment of new elites from commoners will be fastest when the amount of extractable surplus is greatest. The expansion of elite numbers should take place during the "stagflation" phase (see below for the definitions of the phases of a secular cycle), when fast-rising prices and land rents offer the greatest opportunities for rapid accumulation of wealth by current and aspiring elites, and when state fiscal problems lead rulers to increase the sale of privilege and rank; both factors tend to accelerate social mobility into the elite ranks. As a result, the peak of elite numbers often lags behind that of the general population (the important exception of societies with widespread polygyny is discussed in section 1.3).

Such a happy state of events (for the elites) cannot continue for long. First, expansion of elite numbers means that the amount of resources per elite capita begins to decline. This process would occur even if the total amount of surplus stayed constant. But, second, as general population grows closer to the carrying capacity, surplus production gradually declines. The combination of these two trends results in an accelerating fall of average elite incomes.

The dynamic processes described above also have a sociopsychological aspect. During the good times the elites become accustomed to, and learn to expect, a high level of consumption (this is the "growing extravagance of noble households" of Dobb and Sweezy). An additional element, as pointed out by Sweezy, is the ever-increasing quantity and variety of goods available to the elites as a result of urbanization, the growth of crafts, and the expansion of trade (factors that are themselves a consequence of population growth). Modern studies of consumption level expectations suggest that people generally aim at matching (and if possible exceeding) the consumption levels of their parents (Easterlin 1980, 1996). Thus, what is important is not the absolute level of consumption but the level in relation to the previous generation. In other words, expected "living standard" is a culturally determined *inertial* variable (inertial because it changes slowly, on a generational time scale). If we can extrapolate results obtained by studying modern consumers to preindustrial elites (at least, this may be a reasonable working hypothesis), then we would predict that during the good times the elites would easily become accustomed to elevated levels of consumption, and this expansion would occasion little social comment. By contrast, should their level of consumption decrease in relation to the previous generation's, the elites would be expected to react vehemently to this development. This argument suggests there is no contradiction between the bitter critique of the elites for their luxurious and wasteful way of life by contemporary social commentators and the equally bitter complaining of the elites themselves about their poverty and indebtedness.

The deteriorating economic conditions of the elites during the late stagflation phase of the secular cycle do not affect all aristocrats equally. While the majority are losing ground, a few lineages, by contrast, are able to increase their wealth. The growing economic inequality results from the operation of what some sociologists call the "Matthew effect" (Merton 1968). Poor aristocratic lineages tend to get poorer because they attempt to maintain their elite status on an inadequate economic basis. This forces them into growing indebtedness, which eventually has to be addressed by selling some of their assets (such as land). A wealthier lineage, by contrast, can maintain the level of consumption necessary for preserving its elite status and have some resources left over to acquire land from its impoverished neighbors. As a result, the poor get poorer while the rich get richer. The same dynamic operates on peasants during the stagflation phase. During periods of economic hardship, poor peasants must sell land or starve. As a result, at the same time that the majority are sliding into absolute misery, a small percentage of thrifty, hardworking, or simply lucky peasants are able to concentrate increasing amounts of land in their hands. At some point, such successful peasants usually attempt to translate their wealth into higher social status. This demand for upward social mobility is an important factor contributing to the elite overproduction that develops towards the end of a prolonged period of demographic expansion.

During the stagflation phase, thus, economic inequality increases within each social stratum—peasants, minor and middle-rank nobility, and the magnates. Growing inequality creates pressure for social mobility, both upward and downward. Increased social mobility generates friction and destabilizes society. The growing gap between the poor and rich also creates a breeding ground for mass movements espousing radical ideologies of social justice and economic redistribution.

Dynamics of Surplus Extraction

The declining incomes of the majority of aristocrats have two important consequences: intensifying oppression of the peasants by the elites and increasing intraelite competition for scarce resources. The elites will attempt to increase the proportion of resource extracted from the producers by whatever means that are available to them, both economic and extraeconomic (coercive). Their success will depend on the structural characteristics of the society: the relative military strength of the elites with respect to the producers and the state, legal and cultural limits on surplus extraction, and so forth. If successful, elites may not only deprive the commoners of the surplus but may also cut into the subsistence resource, resulting in a negative growth rate for the commoner population. "Thus the lord's surplus extraction (rent) tended to confiscate not merely the peasant's income above subsistence (and potentially even beyond) but at the same time to threaten the funds necessary to refurbish the peasant's holding and to prevent the long-term decline of its productivity" (Brenner 1985a:31). It appears that this stage in the secular cycle may be what is known among dynamicists as a "bifurcation point," a point at which the system may follow one of several alternative trajectories. A classic example of such divergent trajectories is the disappearance of serfdom in post-medieval England and France and, during the same period, the rise of new serfdom in Prussia and Poland. Which of the alternative trajectories the system follows may depend on its structural characteristics or may be a result of a chance event. We are essentially rephrasing, in dynamical systems terms, the point made by Brenner in his critique of the Malthusian theory.

This thesis is illustrated by the recent study of Stuart Borsch (2005), which compared the effects of the Black Death in England and Egypt. In post–Black Death England wages rose, rents and grain prices dropped, unemployment decreased, and per capita incomes grew. Although the economic recovery of England occurred later than would be predicted by the Malthusian model, by the year 1500 it was in full swing. The consequences of depopulation in Egypt were profoundly different. Wages dropped, land rents and grain prices rose, and unemployment levels increased. No economic recovery was anywhere in sight by 1500. In fact, agricultural output declined between 1350 and 1500 by 68 percent. Borsch argues convincingly that the persistent stagnation of post–Black Death Egypt is explained by structural factors. After 1250 Egypt was ruled by a particularly cohesive and militarily capable group of elites: specialized slave-warriors known as Mamluks (as evidenced, for example, by their success at repelling the Mongol invasions in the second half of the thirteenth century). English peasants could resist elites by hiding in the hills and forests, of which there was an abundance in a depopulated England. Additionally, the longbow negated the advantage in military power usually enjoyed by the elites. By contrast, Egypt's narrow strip of arable land between uninhabitable desert left no room for evasive tactics. After the Black Death, Mamluks were able to use their tremendous coercive power to maintain the preplague level of resource extraction from a greatly diminished rural population. Extremely high levels of exploitation of individual peasants precluded any demographic revival. The system, thus, was caught in a "vicious equilibrium" that was apparently stable with respect to internal perturbations; it was finally destroyed by external conquest (the Ottomans in 1517).

The second consequence of plunging elite incomes is increased intraelite competition. The forms that this competition takes will depend (again) on the structural characteristics of the society. Probably the most important factor is the capability of the state to suppress overt violence. Here we consider the forms of intraelite competition in the presence of the state when internal order is maintained. The situation after the state collapses or is seriously weakened is considered later.

One recourse for elites facing declining incomes from agriculture was to seek employment with the state or church bureaucracy. Because training improved one's chances, a curious side effect of increased competition for such positions was the "credentialing crisis" (Collins 1979)—a rapid expansion of enrollments at the educational institutions (at least in those societies that offered formal training to aspirants for elite positions). Thus, we can use trends in higher education as an index of intraelite competition (Goldstone 1991:123). Another useful index of intraelite conflict is the level of civil litigation (Goldstone 1991:120).

Impoverished elites could also improve their incomes by attaching themselves to the retinues of powerful magnates. In fifteenth-century England this trend resulted in what is known as "bastard feudalism" (Dyer 1989:35). A large retinue was necessary to advance the lord's interests in government, litigation, and even civil war. However, limits on available land, civil and ecclesiastical offices, and royal patronage lead to increasingly polarized factional battles between patron-client groups for available spoils (Goldstone 1991:119). As a result, the elites tend to lose their unity and split along numerous fission lines: new elites versus old, one religious faction against the other, regional elites against the center, and so on. Because there are not enough resources for everybody, certain segments of elites, or groups aspiring to elite status, inevitably end up as the losers. We refer to them as the counterelites, or dissident elites. Usually, the counterelites do not constitute a true sociological group, because there is little that unifies them apart from hatred for the existing regime and a burning desire to bring it down. Incidentally, we are not implying here that the motivations of the counterelites are purely economical. The late stagflation phase, as we argued above, is typically characterized by a harsh oppression of the productive segments of the society and extreme social inequality, offering ample ideological justification for revolutionary action.

State Breakdown

Social trends resulting from demographic growth—declining surplus production, popular immiseration, and intraelite competition—have a profound impact on the ability of the state to maintain internal order, or even to survive (Goldstone 1991). Population growth leads to expansion of armies and bureaucracies, resulting in rising state expenditures. An increased number of aspirants for elite positions puts further fiscal strain on the state. Thus, states have no choice but to seek to expand taxation, despite resistance from the elites and the general populace. Yet the amount of surplus production declines (as discussed in the previous section), and the state must compete for this shrinking surplus with increasingly desperate elites. As a result, attempts to increase revenues cannot offset the spiraling state expenses, and even though the state is rapidly raising taxes, it is still headed for fiscal crisis. Note that declining *real* revenues may be masked by persistent price inflation, and it is therefore important to express all fiscal flows in real terms.

As we discussed in the previous section, population growth leads to rural misery, urban migration, falling real wages, and an increased frequency of food riots and wage protests. After a certain lag time, the negative effects of population expansion begin to affect the elites, who become riven by increasing rivalry and factionalism. Another consequence of rapid population growth is the expansion of youth cohorts. This segment of the population is particularly impacted by lack of employment opportunities. Finally, growing economic inequality, elite competition, and popular discontent fuel ideological conflicts. For example, in early modern Europe, dissident elites and dissatisfied artisans were widely recruited into heterodox religious movements.

As all these trends intensify, the end result is state bankruptcy and consequent loss of the military control, elite movements of regional and national rebellion, and a combination of elite-mobilized and popular uprisings following the breakdown of central authority (Goldstone 1991:25). Internal war among political factions is only one aspect of increased interpersonal violence. A breakdown of social order is also accompanied by increased banditry, homicides, and other kinds of violent crimes. On the ideological level, the feeling of social pessimism is pervasive and the legitimacy of the state authority is at its lowest point. The society approaches a condition that may appropriately be called "Hobbesian" (Hobbes himself lived during such a period). We refer to these conditions collectively as high sociopolitical instability.

The Effect of Sociopolitical Instability on Population Dynamics

In the previous sections we focused on the manifold effects of population growth on various structures of the society, including a bundle of variables that we call sociopolitical instability. Here we consider the feedback effect: how does instability affect population dynamics? We can envision two general (and, actually, interrelated) ways: by affecting demographic rates and by affecting the productive ability of the society (Turchin 2003b:120–21).

Most obviously, when the state is weak or absent, the populace will suffer from elevated mortality due to increased crime, banditry, and internal warfare (civil war). External war may also play a role. Although external warfare between states has been a constant feature of agrarian states, its effect on demography should change with the phase of the secular cycle. When the state is strong, warfare is directed outward, and the areas that suffer most are the state frontiers, as well as areas outside, which are targeted for conquest. Collapse of the state and the ensuing civil wars reduce the resistance of the society to external invasion. As a result, internal warfare and external invasions by groups ranging from small bands of raiders to rival great powers can become hard to separate (this is, for example, what happened during the Hundred Years' War in France). Warfare has also an indirect effect on mortality, because movements of rebel or invading armies spread epidemics.

The times of trouble also cause increased migration: refugees flee from war-afflicted areas or areas whose productive potential has been destroyed. Migration has several effects. First, it can lead to emigration (and we can simply add that to mortality). Second, people on the move cannot afford to have children. Thus, birth rates decline. Third, migration leads to epidemics. Increased vagrancy spreads the disease by connecting areas that would stay isolated during better times. For example, in Ireland during 1810–44 (the period just before the Great Famine), harvests failed or partially failed in fifteen years out of thirty-five. These failures did not lead to starvation, but they were followed by outbreaks of "famine fevers"—typhus, dysentery, scurvy, cholera—which were spread throughout the isle by beggars and vagrants seeking charity and employment (Grigg 1980:138).

Additional factors facilitating the spread of disease are the movements of armies and the expansion of international trade. The latter factor should be qualified by noting that international trade expands in the precrisis period (stagflation phase) and then gradually declines after the society has descended into anarchy. Thus, the rise of widespread epidemics—pandemics—is most probable during the late stagflation phase. In fact, the arrival of a pandemic is one of the most frequent triggers of the demographic-structural collapse.

On a more local scale, vagabonds and beggars aggregate in towns and cities, increasing their population size. This may tip the local population density over the epidemiological threshold (a critical density above which a disease spreads and below which it dies out).

Finally, political instability causes lower reproduction rates, because personal consumption plummets as a result of lowered production capacity. In the absence of organized ways to store surplus, peasants are unable to weather short-term subsistence crises. What stores are accumulated by individual households are easy prey to the marauding armies and other predators. In addition, during times of uncertainty people choose to marry later and to have fewer children. Incidentally, people's choices about their family sizes may be reflected not only in birth rates but also in the rates of infanticide. Thus, family limitation practices may be disguised as increased infant mortality.

The second and perhaps even more important effect of sociopolitical instability is on the productive capacity of the society (the carrying capacity). Vigorous states often invest in increasing the agricultural productivity by constructing irrigation canals and roads, implementing flood control measures, clearing land from forests, organizing the colonization of underpopulated regions, and so on. The end result of these measures is mainly an increase in cultivated area, although some measures also increase the productivity of land.

The other general mechanism is that the state offers protection. In a stateless society, people can live only in natural strongholds or in places that can be made defensible, such as walled cities. For example, at the height of the Roman Empire the overwhelming majority of the Italian population was to be found in the lowlands, where the most productive land was concentrated. After the collapse of Rome, settlements were moved to hilltops (Wickham 1981). An even more striking illustration comes from the Wanka hill fort chiefdoms in the Mantaro Valley of Peru (Earle 1997). Prior to Inka pacification of the region, the Wanka lived in crowded hilltop fortresses. After the conquest, the population moved down to lower elevations, where the best agricultural land was located. As a result, the diet and life span of both elite and commoner were dramatically improved (Johnson and Earle 2000:327).

The third example comes from *Histoire de Charles VII* by the Norman bishop Thomas Basin, who described northwestern France during the 1420s, after a particularly virulent outbreak of the Hundred Years' War:

> a state of devastation such that from the Loire to the Seine, and from there to the Somme, the peasants having been killed or run off, almost all fields were left for a number of years not only uncultivated, but without people. . . . All that could be cultivated at that time in that region was only around and inside towns or castles, close enough so that, from the top of the tower or watchtower the eye of the lookout could perceive the attacking brigands. Then, with the sound of a bell, or horn, or some other instrument, he gave all those working in the fields or vineyards the signal to withdraw to the fortified place. (quoted in Dupâquier et al. 1988a:368)

In other words, lack of effective suppression of internal violence by the state imposes a "landscape of fear," in which a large proportion of agriculturally suitable lands is abandoned because they are too far from a place of security. By contrast, the strong state protects the productive population from external and internal (banditry, civil war) threats, and thus allows the whole cultivable area to be put into production.

Elite Dynamics during the Depression Phase

Sociopolitical instability affects elite numbers in a fashion that is similar to its effect on commoners, although the relative importance of specific mechanisms can be quite different. Thus, the elites may be little affected by subsistence crises. They also tend to escape more lightly the effect of epidemics. This is partly due to their better nutrition and the likelihood of getting better care during disease, but even more important is their higher mobility. Urban elites could withdraw to their country estates at the first sign of incipient epidemic (as in Bocaccio's *Decameron*). Higher nobility with estates in multiple provinces could similarly avoid an epidemic striking a particular region.

On the other hand, by virtue of their more active participation in politics, the elites ran a much higher risk of violent death. The death toll in some conflicts was extraordinary. For example, Dupâquier et al. (1988a:342) quote an estimate by Philippe Contamine that around 40 percent of the French elite may have been slaughtered in the Battle of Poitiers (1356), and the same proportion at Agincourt (1415). During the Wars of Religion in the late sixteenth century, 20,000 Huguenots were killed in just one day, the St. Bartholomew's Day massacre (Kamen 1971:39).

Loss of life or elite status could also result from state purges. For example, the first Ming emperor purged 100,000 Chinese officials (Tignor et al. 2002:62). Sulla's proscriptions eliminated a third of the Roman ruling class, senators, and another third was eliminated by proscriptions following Caesar's death (see chapter 6).

A much less spectacular but perhaps ultimately more important process reducing the elite numbers is downward mobility. The plunge in elite incomes, which begins in the precrisis period and is greatly exacerbated by the general population decline, affects most strongly the status of the lowest noble stratum. A specific example is given by Christopher Dyer for late medieval England. An esquire or gentlemen living on £10–20 a year who was employing only three servants and lived in one house, and whose meals were devoid of much luxury in terms of wine and spices, had little room to maneuver when his income plunged by up to 50 percent in the mid-fifteenth century: "They must have cut back, or even cut out completely, their occasional wine-bibbings, and avoided travel whenever possible, but too many economies of this kind might force them to drop out of the aristocracy and accept yeoman status" (Dyer 1989:108).

In summary, a number of social mechanisms exist by which elite surpluses can be reduced: (1) deaths resulting from civil war, (2) deliberate purges of elites by new rulers, (3) limitations imposed on heir production (celibacy, primogeniture), (4) downward social mobility, voluntary or forced by the state, (5) increased material resources resulting from conquest or improvements in agricultural productivity, and (6) the development of a new political order that directs a greater share of resources to the elites. Several such mechanisms are usually operating in combination; the specific mix depends on cultural peculiarities of societies and historical accidents.

End of Instability and the Beginning of the New Cycle

Because the three main factors driving the rise of sociopolitical instability are general overpopulation, elite overproduction, and state insolvency, all these trends must be reversed before the disintegrative phase can end. Such trend reversal can occur in a variety of ways, depending on the characteristics of the society, its geopolitical environment, and various other exogenous factors. As a result, the last stages of the secular cycle are particularly rife with bifurcation points, and the sociopolitical trajectory can behave in a very nondeterministic fashion.

The problem of overpopulation is usually "dealt with" during the crisis phase. One of the most common proximate mechanisms of population collapse is disease, but not all population declines are accomplished by catastrophic epidemics. Prolonged periods of civil war can also cause drastic drops in population levels, although typically requiring more time. Finally, the external conquest of a disunited society often results in a demographic catastrophe.

An alternative to population collapse is an increase in the carrying capacity—after all, overpopulation results not from the absolute numbers being too large but from too high a population density in relation to the carrying capacity. The carrying capacity can increase as a result of technological progress. This is probably what happened in early modern England. During the crisis of the seventeenth century, the English population hardly declined, while the average yield of grain per acre probably doubled. The end result was a twofold decline in the population pressure on resources.

The carrying capacity may also increase as a result of the conquest of new underpopulated territories. An example is the conquest of the Kazan and Astrakhan khanates by Muscovy in the sixteenth century, which opened up vast areas along the Volga for Russian colonization during the succeeding centuries. Theoretically, the carrying capacity can also increase as a result of a substantial amelioration of the climate, although at this point we cannot point to a well-documented, convincing example of this mechanism in action.

The processes leading to the reduction in the elite numbers and appetites were discussed in the previous section. The manner in which elite overproduction is abated depends very much on the military strength of the aristocracy. A nonmilitarized ruling class can be expropriated en masse by warlords, such as rebel generals or even peasant bandits. A rapid and comprehensive elite turnover results in a relatively short period of sociopolitical instability that follows state collapse. This is apparently what happened on several occasions during the Chinese imperial period, where the ruling class was dominated by the literate administrative elites rather than by military specialists. A rapid elite turnover can also result when there is a ready external source of potential elites, as was the case in the Maghreb described by Ibn Khaldun (we discuss Ibn Khaldun cycles in the next section).

A ruling class that enjoys a preponderance of military power over both internal and external rivals can be reduced only by internecine fighting between various elite factions. This can result in very prolonged periods of sociopolitical instability, or "depression" phases, in our terminology.

Thus, for a new secular cycle to get going, the pressures of the general population on resources and of the elites on commoners must be substantially reduced from their precrisis levels. There is also a third condition. Not all societies are capable of the broad-scale cooperation that is required to construct a functioning state, and some societies with a previous imperial history can also lose this ability with time (Turchin 2003b, 2006). Thus, it is entirely possible for the civil warfare to gradually die out but a centralizing, integrative trend nevertheless failing to take hold. In this case, the area in question may persist indefinitely (or until it is conquered from the outside) in a fragmented state as a collection of small-scale polities. The potential explanations of this failure to build a functioning state lie beyond the scope of our book. Here we simply indicate that it is yet another possible bifurcation point.

Phases of the Secular Cycle

Oscillatory dynamics do not go through truly discrete phases with clearly marked breakpoints, but for convenience in talking about each secular cycle, we need to divide it in phases. Our classificatory scheme is given here with the understanding that transitions between phases are rarely abrupt, so that any particular year that we designate as an end to one phase and the beginning of another is to some degree arbitrary (for this reason, we usually round the date to the nearest decade).

Most broadly the cycle can be divided into two opposite trends. In the literature these are sometimes called the positive "A phase" and the negative "B phase," but we prefer the more descriptive terms *integrative* and *disintegrative* trends. Politically the integrative phase is characterized by a centralizing tendency, unified elites, and a strong state that maintains order and internal stability. Internal cohesion often results in the vigorous prosecution of external wars of conquest, which may result in the extension of the state territory (assuming there are weaker neighbors at whose expense the state can expand). The disintegrative phase, by contrast, is characterized by a decentralizing tendency, divided elites, a weak state, and internal instability and political disorder that periodically flare up in civil war. External wars of conquest are much more difficult to prosecute during the disintegrative phase. If they happen, they usually take place during the intervals between civil wars and at the expense of equally weak opponents. More frequently it is the external enemies that profit from the internal weakness of the state and society, resulting in an increased frequency of raids, invasions, and loss of territory.

The population tends to increase during the integrative phase and decline or stagnate during the disintegrative one. Climatic fluctuations, epidemics, or being overrun by an external enemy can cause short-term (if significant) population losses. However, vigorous population growth resumes as soon as such exogenous forces stop acting. During the disintegrative phase, by contrast, population losses due to epidemics, famines, or wars are not made up by sustained population growth. Even when the proximate Malthusian forces (epidemics, famines, and wars) are in abeyance, the population often fails to increase, despite being much below the carrying capacity.

It is useful to further divide the broad integrative and disintegrative periods into subphases. Population growth is particularly vigorous during the first, *expansion* phase of the integrative trend. This is a time of relatively stable prices and modest real wage declines (if any). However, as the population density begins to approach the limits set by the carrying capacity, price increases or wage declines accelerate—this is the "stagnation" or "compression" or even more descriptively *stagflation* (stagnation plus inflation) phase. Although the majority of commoners experience increasing economic difficulties during the stagflation phase, the elites enjoy a golden age, and their numbers and appetites continue to expand.

The stagflation phase (and the overall integrative trend) is succeeded by a general crisis. Whereas expansion grades smoothly into stagnation, the transition between stagflation and crisis is often (but not always) abrupt. Discrete events signaling the arrival of crisis can be pandemics, extreme episodes of famine, or state collapse followed by intense civil war (or any such events in various combinations). The crisis phase in our terminology is not a discrete, brief event (which is one meaning of the word *crisis*) but an extended period that can last for one or more human generations. The decline of population numbers during a crisis results in a situation of plentiful per capita resources. However, this does not necessarily end the disintegrative trend, because there are usually too many elites and elite aspirants, and intraelite conflict continues to generate internal instability. Thus, the crisis grades smoothly into a *depression* phase, characterized by endemic civil warfare. The population may grow during the intervals between intense civil wars, but such increases typically do not last and are followed by declines (although not as a catastrophic as those typical of the crisis phase). The depression phase ends when the ranks of elites are pruned by internal conflict to the point where the disintegrative trend can reverse itself, and a new secular cycle begins. Alternatively, if no functioning state can get going, then the depression phase grades smoothly into an *intercycle* of indeterminate length.

We wish to emphasize again that the classificatory scheme we propose is an ideal type. It is helpful to be able to indicate the rough state of the dynamical system with a single word. However, there is considerable variation in the trajectories followed by actual societies. Thus, the boundary between various phases should be taken as "fuzzy" rather than "hard." An early reader of the book manuscript even suggested that, instead of dividing the timelines of the societies that we study too neatly, we could allow phases to overlap. There is some merit to this suggestion, because different phases are dominated by different kinds of social processes, and these processes often overlap in time. For example, the onset of political crisis does not always coincide with the shift from population growth to population decline, and therefore the dating of the stagflation-crisis transition may be problematic. In the end, we chose to stay with nonoverlapping phases, because doing otherwise would be too confusing to our readers. But we do not impose these discrete phases on each case study in a procrustean manner.

1.3 Variations and Extensions

Factors Affecting Characteristic Lengths of Secular Cycles

Our exposition and illustration of the general theory of secular cycles in section 1.2 was Western European–centric, but the theory should, in principle, be applicable to any agrarian society. In this section we discuss how certain structural and cultural characteristics of societies should affect the demographic-structural dynamics, with a focus on one of the most important characteristics of oscillatory dynamics, the average period of a cycle.

Secular cycles are not periodic in the strictly mathematical sense, in which each succeeding cycle repeats exactly the preceding one. Although the secular rises and falls are generated endogenously by interactions between various components (subsystems) of the agrarian state, macrosocial dynamics of agrarian states cannot be strictly periodic. There are at least three reasons for that. First, nonlinear dynamic feedbacks can in theory generate not only strictly periodic (cyclic in the mathematical sense) dynamics but also aperiodic chaos—erratic-looking behavior that is nevertheless produced entirely by internal, endogenous reasons. The more complex the system (the more components it has) and the more nonlinear the interactions between the components (such as the presence of threshold responses), the greater is the likelihood that its dynamics will be characterized by sensitive dependence, the hallmark of chaos. Social systems are complex and feedback loops are nonlinear, so the possibility of chaos cannot be discounted (Turchin 2003b).

Second, the dynamics of agrarian states are affected not only by their internal workings but also by exogenous forces, such as changes in their geopolitical and ecological environment. Exogenous factors, unlike endogenous ones, are those that are not part of feedback loops (Turchin 2003a): they affect societal dynamics but are not themselves influenced by societal dynamics.

Finally, individuals possess free will and can act in unpredictable ways. In principle, even the act of a single person, if it takes place in the right place at the right time, may be able to influence the trajectory of a whole society. For lack of better theoretical approaches, we can model actions of individuals at the microlevel as a stochastic process, a kind of Brownian motion that also results in erratic, unpredictable changes in the macrosocial trajectory.

For all these reasons, we do not expect a strict periodicity in secular dynamics. Instead, dynamics should have an average period, a characteristic time scale, with a substantial degree of variation around this average. The mean period of a single—boom and bust—secular cycle is determined by the characteristic lengths of its phases, which in turn depend on various social, economic, and political parameters. Thus, the typical length of the expansion phase is primarily determined by (1) the per capita rate of population increase and (2) the population density in relation to carrying capacity at the beginning of the cycle. For example, if population grows at the rate of 1 percent per year, it takes seventy years for it to double. This is not a bad estimate of a typical expansion phase.

Expansion phases are also affected by geopolitical environment. States enjoy the greatest ability to mobilize the society for a war of external conquest during the middle parts of integrative secular trends. Abnormally long expansion phases result from successful territorial conquest, especially when it is accompanied by colonization of conquered territories, which serves to reduce population pressure in the metropole.

The length of the crisis phase is much less predictable, because while there is a definite biological limit on how fast a human population can grow, there is no comparable limit on how fast it can decline. Depending on the agent of change, population can decline very rapidly, as in a pandemic, or more slowly, due to incessant civil warfare. Furthermore, pathogens afflicting historical populations varied in their lethality. A relatively mild pathogen could drive population down slowly (perhaps as a result of recurrent epidemics), resulting in a long decline phase. A severe epidemic, on the other hand, would lead to a very short period of drastic population decline, and also to a deeper degree of social disintegration and longer depression phase (as happened in post–Black Death Europe).

The characteristic lengths of the stagflation and depression phases depend more on the state and, particularly, on elite dynamics than on what the general population does. In particular, the military strength of the elites has a large effect on the length of the depression phase, or even if there is such a phase at all. Models tailored to the characteristics of Western European societies (largely monogamous elites enjoying a preponderance of military power over their internal and external enemies) suggest that the typical periods of secular cycles in these societies should lie in the range of two to three centuries (Turchin 2003b:138).

Ibn Khaldun Cycles

A very different situation obtains in certain Islamic societies. The paradigmatic example is the sociopolitical dynamics in the medieval Maghreb, brilliantly described by Ibn Khaldun (1958). From the point of view of the demographic-structural theory, the Maghrebin states differ from Western European states in two important respects: (1) these Islamic societies permitted polygyny and (2) there was a ready source of militarily powerful counterelites nearby.

Polygyny is important because the number of wives is the most significant predictor of male reproductive success in humans (Betzig 1986). Because aristocratic males could afford to support several wives and concubines, the rate of elite population growth in Islamic societies was (and is today) much greater than that for elites in Christian societies. It is true that some degree of elite polygyny was practiced in Western Europe, where aristocrats often increased their biological fitness by having multiple mistresses and then acknowledging their bastards. Nevertheless, the fact remains that the biological reproduction rate of Islamic elites was several times higher than that of Christian elites.

The second factor is the location of Maghrebin societies in the rather thin strip of arable land squeezed between the Mediterranean Sea and the desert. The "desert" (or rather dry steppe and semi-desert zone between the agrarian societies of the Mediterranean littoral and the extremely arid central regions of the Sahara) was occupied by nomadic pastoralists, primarily the Berbers. These desert chiefdoms were not a significant military threat as long the agrarian states maintained their internal cohesiveness. But as soon as a Maghrebin society experienced state collapse, it became extremely vulnerable to conquest from the desert.

When demographic-structural models are modified to account for these two factors they exhibit very different dynamics (Turchin 2003b). High reproductive rate of the elites means that they increase much faster than the general population. Elite numbers, in fact, increase so rapidly that the commoner overpopulation plays a much lesser role or even no role in bringing about the state collapse. As a result, the integrative trend of the secular cycle is over much faster than in the standard model, developed for the Western European situation. Once the collapse occurs, there is usually no lengthy depression phase, because it does not take much time to organize a coalition of desert tribes to pick up the pieces and establish a new dynasty.

As a result of a shortened integrative trend and a missing depression phase, models predict a much faster secular cycle for Maghrebin-type societies, on the order of one century, rather than the two to three centuries for Western European states. This prediction is in agreement with the observation of Ibn Khaldun that the dynastic cycle in the Maghreb extends, on average, over four generations (a generation time in humans is typically twenty to thirty years). Note that this is a true theoretical prediction: models were not fitted in any way to the Maghrebin data. The shorter cycle period follows directly from the structural assumptions of the models of a faster elite reproductive rate and rapid elite turnover after state collapse.

Not all Islamic polities are predicted to exhibit Ibn Khaldun cycles. The key parameter, identified by the theory, is the rate of growth of elite numbers. Islamic societies that controlled the elite growth rates in one way or another are predicted to exhibit slower cycles, with periods similar to those observed in Western Europe. For example, in the Ottoman Empire the sultans had access to an essentially unlimited supply of wives and concubines. However, when the old ruler died, only one son was allowed to replace him; all others were killed. Furthermore, top levels of bureaucracy and army leadership were recruited not from native elites but by means of devshirme. In other words, the state, not biology, controlled the size of the high-ranking elite stratum. Only lower-rank landed elites were permitted to increase "biologically," and, being not very wealthy, they could not afford too many wives. As a result, we can predict that secular cycles in the Ottoman polity should be much longer than those in the Maghreb.

An even more extreme case is the Mamluk polity in medieval Egypt. Its ruling class was recruited entirely from the slave markets. Children of Mamluks could not be Mamluks, and thus automatically dropped out of the ruling class. In principle, this arrangement should have stopped dead the Ibn Khaldun's dynamic and, barring exogenous perturbations, should have led to a stable equilibrium.

The Fractal Nature of Historical Dynamics

In general, different social processes operate at a variety of temporal scales. The shorter scales include daily, weekly, monthly, and annual cycles. Beyond that we have human generations, processes occurring on the time scale of centuries (including secular cycles), and longer-term phenomena such as social and biological evolution. As an example we can consider the stock market, as measured by the Dow-Jones Industrial Average (DJIA). The DJIA fluctuates on a variety of scales: daily (because the stock exchange shuts down at night), weekly (no activity on weekends), annual (fiscal year accounting affects trader behavior), multi-annual (business cycles), and multidecadal (the Kondratieff cycle, although not all economists accept the reality of such long cycles). The DJIA trajectory looks "fractal" because the amount of fluctuation depends on the time scale at which the trajectory is viewed.

If we are interested in understanding the effect of the business cycle on stock prices, we really do not care about short-term fluctuations. We certainly should ignore price movements within a single day, and probably even within a week. Thus, the time series with which we would want to investigate multi-annual oscillations would probably use DJIA values averaged for each week. Averaging is the simplest kind of smoothing, so what we have done is essentially smoothed away all "uninteresting" short-term fluctuations—uninteresting, that is, from the point of view of the main question of analysis. On the other hand, if we want to know how holiday periods affect stock price movements, we would certainly want to retain within-week fluctuations, and perhaps go down to hourly movements (to see how trading patterns behave during the short preholiday days). Now the variation due to the business cycle becomes a nuisance, and it might be a good idea to remove the effect of multi-annual and longer-term fluctuations by detrending. The point is that different questions require approaching an analysis at different time scales.

Turning now to population dynamics, we observe that population changes also occur on a variety of scales: monthly (female menstrual periods), yearly (subsistence and epidemic cycles), generational (somewhere between two and three decades), and secular (one, two, or three centuries, according to the theory of secular cycles). If we are interested in the dynamics of childhood diseases, then the appropriate time scale would be weeks or months, to capture the within-year course of each epidemic (the incidence of measles, for example, begins to increase after children are brought together at the beginning of the school year, gradually building up to a peak in winter).

If we want to understand how secular cycles unfold, on the other hand, we certainly do not need to know how mortality fluctuates on a weekly or monthly time scale, or that there may be a deficit of births nine months after Lent as a result of devout Christians avoiding sexual intercourse. All such within-year or even year-to-year fluctuations are irrelevant for the purposes of our investigation. The appropriate time step is one human generation, and we need to average over smaller-scale fluctuations. We also need to do something about very long trends driven by social evolution. This requires some kind of removal of millennial trends (Turchin 2005:153), for example as was done for the early-modern English population (see appendix to chapter 3). By smoothing within-decade fluctuations and removing millennial trends, we retain two temporal scales of interest. The longer one is the average period of the secular cycle—this is what needs to be explained. The shorter one is the human generation time—this is the time step of the dynamical process that is postulated to be the explanatory mechanism of secular cycles.

It is important to remember that population numbers are a dynamic variable that has a lot of inertia on temporal scales shorter than a human generation. This is particularly true with respect to population increase: it can occur only slowly as babies are born and raised to enter the adult population. Even under ideal conditions, the human population needs at least one generation to double. On the other side of the demographic balance, mortality, it is theoretically possible for a population to collapse to a very low level (or even to go extinct) in a very short time. However, most typically annual variation in death rates, due for example to crop failures, can be quite substantial but is largely smoothed out—buffered—at the level of total population numbers.

This buffering ability of total population numbers is important in understanding how climate variability affects population dynamics. Annual variation, even if quite extreme, may have little effect on population change. If the population is well below carrying capacity, peasants may have sufficient stores to weather a year or two of bad crops without any demographic effect. In contrast, a long-term cooling, even if by less than one degree centigrade, may have a much more substantial effect on population dynamics by lowering carrying capacity. (This argument is just an illustration of why temporal scales are important; in the real world, the effect of climate change depends on the phase of the cycle, the alternative crops that peasants can switch to, and many other factors.)

Generation Cycles

The preceding discussion should make it clear that we are far from adopting a monocausal view of human history. The main hypothesis of this book is that demographic-structural processes are very important in historical dynamics, but we would be the last to argue that they are the only thing that goes on. However, it is not a good research strategy to include everything one can think of in the model. The history of science shows, over and over again, that an attempt to incorporate too many explanatory factors into theories is self-defeating. As Albert Einstein once said, a theory should be as simple as possible, but no simpler than that.

One particular process that is not part of the demographic-structural theory but has to be taken into account when studying secular cycles is the "fathers-and-sons" dynamic (Turchin 2003b, 2006). This mechanism operates during the prolonged disintegrative secular trends that are characteristic of secular cycles in Europe. The empirical observation is that disintegrative trends are not periods of continuous civil war; in fact, there are periods when sociopolitical instability is particularly high, interspersed with periods of relative pacification.

To illustrate this dynamic, during the disintegrative trend of late medieval France ("the Hundred Years of Hostility"), good reigns alternated with bad ones. The reign of John II (1350–64) was a period of social dissolution and state collapse, while that of his son Charles V (1364–80) was a time of national consolidation and territorial reconquest. The next reign, that of Charles VI (1380–1422), was another period of social disintegration and collapse. It was followed by a period of internal consolidation and national resurgence under Charles VII (1422–61), which finally lifted France out of the late medieval depression. This is a general dynamical pattern of alternation between very turbulent and relatively peaceful spells that is observed again and again during the secular disintegrative phases. A possible explanation of such swings in the collective mood lies in the social psychology.

Episodes of internal warfare often develop in ways similar to epidemics or forest fires. At the beginning of the conflict, each act of violence triggers chains of revenge and counter-revenge. With time, participants lose all restraint, atrocities become common, and conflict escalates in an accelerating, explosive fashion. After the initial explosion, however, violence drags on and on, sometimes for decades. Sooner or later most people begin to yearn for the return of stability and an end to fighting. The most psychopathic and violent leaders are killed off or lose their supporters. Violence, like an epidemic or a forest fire, "burns out." Even though the fundamental causes that brought the conflict on in the first place may still be operating, the prevailing social mood swings in favor of cessation of conflict at all costs, and an uneasy truce gradually takes hold. Those people, like the generation of Charles the Wise, who directly experienced civil war become "immunized" against it, and while they are in charge, they keep things stable. The peaceful period lasts for a human generation—between twenty and thirty years. Eventually, however, the conflict-scarred generation dies off or retires and a new cohort arises, people who did not experience the horrors of civil war and are not immunized against it. If the long-term social forces that brought about the first outbreak of internal hostilities are still operating, the society will slide into a second civil war. As a result, periods of intense conflict tend to recur with a period of roughly two generations (forty to sixty years).

These swings in the social mood may be termed "generation cycles" because they involve alternating generations that are either prone to conflict or not. Another example of such social mood dynamics has been noted, for example, by Arthur M. Schlesinger Jr. (1986). Furthermore, generation cycles keep cropping up in other contexts. The birth rates in twentieth-century America oscillated with a period of approximately fifty years (Easterlin 1980, Macunovich 2002). Many economic indicators oscillate with roughly the same period, a phenomenon known as the Kondratieff cycle (Kondratieff 1984). The Kondratieff and Schlesinger cycles may be related to each other; at least, they often seem to oscillate in synchrony (Berry 1991, Alexander 2002). The Kondratieff wave may also be correlated with the war cycle (Goldstein 1988). Our understanding of Easterlin, Schlesinger, and Kondratieff cycles is very deficient, and many researchers doubt the reality of these dynamics. This is not the place to try to make sense of this vast and confused topic, and in the rest of the book we focus only on the dynamics of sociopolitical instability. Even that focus is forced on us by the need to understand why disintegrative phases in certain types of societies tend to have multiple peaks of sociopolitical instability.

Exogenous Forces

The standard demographic-structural model of section 1.2 focuses on endogenous forces representing internal feedbacks between such structural variables as population, social structure, and instability. Real-life social systems are also affected by many exogenous factors that are not an explicit part of the model. We have alluded to some of them in this section; here is a more systematic discussion of the important external forces (see also the discussion in Turchin and Hall 2003).

- Geopolitical environment. Strong and aggressive neighbors may take advantage of internal weakness of the state during the disintegrative phase of the cycle. Such predation may deepen the degree of societal collapse. In the worst case the state may be conquered and annexed to a nearby empire (a very powerful expansionist empire, such as that of Chinggis Khan, may simply roll over the studied state and obviate its endogenous dynamics). Alternatively, the presence of weak neighbors may permit external conquests that could relieve population pressure in the metropole and provide an outlet for surplus elites, thus lengthening the integrative phase.

- Disease environment. Some pandemics, such as the Black Death, originate in distant parts of Eurasia and then spread over the whole continent. Such pandemics arose repeatedly within Eurasia (Turchin 2008). Their effect depends on the phase of population growth. For a population in the early stages of growth, the arrival of an epidemic could mean a minor interruption of the course of expansion. By contrast, a dense population is highly vulnerable to a pandemic, and a severe drop in population numbers could result in a longer and deeper cycle of disintegration.
- Social evolution. Of primary interest is the growth of agricultural technology that affects the carrying capacity of the environment. Significant increases in crop yields, by elevating the carrying capacity, will have the same effect on food prices and consumption levels as substantial population declines.
- Global climate. Its effects are similar to those of social evolution, inasmuch as long-term fluctuations in temperature and rainfall affect the productivity of crops and the carrying capacity. A society whose population is already pressing on its resources may be tipped into crisis by a significant worsening of the climate.
- In addition to the recurrent exogenous factors discussed above, we often need to take into account singular events, or historical accidents that may have significant long-term consequences. A good example of such a singular event is the discovery and colonization of the Americas by Western Europeans, which resulted in torrents of precious metals flowing into Europe starting in the sixteenth century. American silver acted as an amplifier that created a stronger and more inflationary growth cycle in the sixteenth and early seventeenth centuries. In other words, the "price revolution of the sixteenth century" had two causes, monetary and demographic (Fischer 1996:74).

1.4 Empirical Approaches

The main goal of this book is to determine how well the predictions of the demographic-structural theory map onto empirically observed patterns in the studied historical societies. The synthetic theory, described in section 1.2, has four fundamental variables: population numbers (in relation to the carrying capacity), social structure (specifically, the numbers and consumption levels of the elites), state strength (typically measured by its fiscal health), and sociopolitical instability. These variables are fundamental in the sense that it is the reciprocal interactions among them that generate secular cycles (in the parlance of dynamical systems theory, these are the endogenous variables). In each empirical case study our aim is to collect data describing how each of these variables changed during the period of study.

Ideally, we wish to have time-series data—accurate measurements of a particular variable collected at regular time intervals (the ideal time step is one decade, but a human generation—twenty to thirty years—serves almost as well). This ideal is rarely approached in historical applications. First, there is usually a substantial degree of measurement noise. This is not a fatal problem, because we can use statistical methods to estimate how much useful information is contained in the data. Even the worst case, when we lack quantitative data and all that we can say is that a variable is increasing, decreasing, or staying roughly constant, can be quite useful as a test of model predictions.

Second, we may have reasonable quantitative measures, but only for a few irregularly spaced points in time. Again, such data can be quite informative, especially if they are supplemented with qualitative indications about the dynamics of change between the "anchor points." Reconstructions by knowledgeable historians can be surprisingly accurate, as happened in the case of estimates of population dynamics in early modern England that were later confirmed by the formal population reconstruction methods. Incidentally, there are statistical methods for time-series analysis that can help us utilize data to their utmost, even when they are irregularly spaced, although we do not employ them in this book.

It is frequently the case that although we lack direct measurements of some variable, with a little ingenuity we can come up with another one that could serve as a proxy for the variable of interest. For example, climatologists made great strides in reconstructing past climate variations by studying such proxy variables as tree rings, varves in lake deposits, and isotope compositions of air bubbles trapped in ice.

A very useful source of information is archaeological records (e.g., Morris 2005). Certain kinds of archaeological data, such as estimated numbers of dwellings during different time periods, can be quite good indicators of population dynamics. The population history of Novgorod is revealed by the density of leather shoe remains in cultural layers (Nefedov 2002). Such archaeological data often cannot tell us what the absolute level of population was (in people per km^2). But having quantitative data on the relative fluctuations of a variable is almost as good for testing theory. In fact, it is much better to have a time series on relative fluctuations than an excellent absolute estimate limited to one point in time. The demographic-structural theory is about dynamics, that is, change with time, and it is impossible to measure change with a single time slice.

Many quantitative data sources are available for testing theories about historical dynamics, and few of them have been systematically exploited. For example, the intensity of public building, especially of temples or churches, shows remarkable fluctuations in time. This index may reflect the amount of resources at the disposal of the state, the elites, or both, depending on the specific arrangements prevailing in the society.

Another underutilized indicator is the temporal distribution of coin-hoard finds. In 1969, Michael Crawford suggested that there is a close correlation between concentrations of coin hoards and periods of internal war and disturbance in the Roman Republic (see Crawford 1993:162). Another study documented a similar pattern in the late Carolingian period (Armstrong 1998).

Proxy variables have to be used carefully, because they may not be perfectly correlated with the variable of main interest. Thus, we expect that the number of people per building or per room should vary with time. As a result, in order to estimate the total population within a certain area, the estimated number of rooms obtained with archaeological methods needs to be multiplied by the average number of people per room, which is usually unknown. Similarly, the number of coin hoards per decade is affected not only by instability but also by the degree of monetization of the economy and by how much time has passed since the period when the hoards were interred (the farther this is in the past, the more chances that the hoard would have been found before modern times).

Although proxy variables need to be treated carefully, it would be madness to completely ignore them, because they are often the best quantitative information that we have about historical dynamics. One way to make sense of the proxies is to build an explicit model of the various factors that may affect them, estimate the model parameters, and then "impute" the values of the variable of interest. Statistical methods for doing this have been developed and applied to many natural science problems. After all, even in physics we usually cannot measure directly a quantity of interest, such as temperature; we have to infer temperature by a proxy variable, such as the expansion of a small amount of mercury in a glass tube. In complex geophysical applications, such as locating underground oil, nothing can be measured directly but has to be estimated by building a complex model of the underground geological layers. We will not be attempting such exercises in this book, but it is certainly something that can be tried in the future.

There are many other endogenous variables in addition to the fundamental ones and their proxies. Endogenous variables are those variables that are part of the various feedback loops postulated by the theory. Their dynamics are largely determined by other endogenous variables (but there also can be an element of noise), and they in turn influence how other endogenous variables change with time. Exogenous variables, by contrast, are those that affect the state of the dynamical system but are not themselves affected by the state of the system. An example of an endogenous variable is the real wage. According to Malthusian-Ricardian theory, the real wage is primarily determined by the population numbers in relation to the productive capacity. It can also be influenced by other variables. For example, intense internal war may disrupt grain production and drive up food prices, with a deleterious effect on real wages. Real wages in turn influence other variables, such as demographic rates, which then affect the rate of population change. The point is that endogenous variables as a set describe the various feedback loops that drive the complex dynamics of the social system. A number of such variables, and predictions of the demographic-structural theory on how they should change with cycle phases, are given in table 1.1. In the chapters that follow our goal is to document the dynamics of as many as possible of these variables.

TABLE 1.1
Empirical predictions of the demographic-structural theory

	Integrative Secular Trends		*Disintegrative Secular Trends*	
	Expansion phase (growth)	*Stagflation phase (compression)*	*Crisis phase (state breakdown)*	*Depression/intercycle*
Fundamental variables				
Population dynamics	Population increases from nadir; rate of growth accelerates	Population is high and continues to increase but rate of growth decelerates	Population declines from the peak; the rate of decline accelerates	Population is low; it either declines at a decelerating rate or stagnates; periods of increase possible but do not lead to sustained growth
Elite dynamics	Low to moderate numbers; decline in elite/commoner ratio; modest consumption levels	"Golden age": increasing numbers; increased competition for elite positions; conspicuous consumption by some segments; appearance of counterelites	High numbers; factionalization and conflict; high corruption; high income inequality; impoverishment of service elites	Reduction in elite numbers as a result of civil war and downward mobility; collapse of elite consumption levels
State strength and collective solidarity	Increasing; social unity among the elites that may extend to commoners	High but declining	Collapse; social disintegration	Periodic attempts to restore state, followed by repeated breakdown
Sociopolitical instability	Instability decreases to a low point	Instability is low but increasing	Instability increases to its peak	Instability is high but begins declining
Other endogenous variables				
Number of rural settlements	Increases	Slow increase or stagnation	Decline; settlement abandonment	Lack of increase
Land, cultivated	Increase; assarting	Slow increase or stagnation	Decline; settlement abandonment	At a low equilibrium
Land, free	Initially abundant but decreasing	In short supply	Increasing	Abundant
Land to peasant ratio	High but declining	Low	Low, increasing	High
Land prices	Low, increasing	High	Falling	Low
Grain prices	Low	Increasing	High, very variable	Decreasing, variable
Real wages	High	Declining to the lowest point	Increasing, but with much variability	High, but variable; contingent
Rents	Low	High; high exploitation by the landowners	Declining, but with fluctuations	Low, but variable; contingent
Personal consumption; subsistence level	High; infrequent crop failure incidents have no lasting effect	Declining; poverty, misery, vagrancy	Subsistence crises	Contingent (depends on instability levels)
Grain reserves	High	Declining	Nonexistent	Variable
Urbanization	Low	Increasing, growth of cities	High	High but declining

TABLE 1.1 *(continued)*

	Integrative Secular Trends		*Disintegrative Secular Trends*	
	Expansion phase (growth)	*Stagflation phase (compression)*	*Crisis phase (state breakdown)*	*Depression/intercycle*
Artisanship and handcrafts	Low	Increasing; landless peasants become artisans	High	Declining
Trade	At a low level, local trading networks	Increasing in volume and spatial scale	Declining, variable, interrupted by political unrest	Local; long-distance networks disrupted
Usury	Absent	Increasing peasant indebtedness	High	Declining
Large private landownership	Absent, low, or medium	Increasing	High concentration of land in the hands of few large landowners	Declining
Economic inequality	Low	Increasing	High	High but declining
Incidence of epidemics	Rare; population bounces right back	Increasing; postepidemic population increases sluggish	Often catastrophic; population does not make up losses	High but declining
Internal peace and order	Increasing; a golden age	High but gradually unraveling; increasing resistance to taxation	Crisis: peasant uprisings, urban uprisings, interelite conflicts, regional/nationalist rebellions	Recurrent civil war, political fragmentation; high susceptibility to external invasions
Incidence of coin hoards (an indicator of sociopolitical instability)	Declining to low levels, unless there is a catastrophic external invasion	Low, unless there is a catastrophic external invasion	Rapidly increasing to a peak owing to state breakdown and civil war	Peaks when state breakdown and civil war recurs
State finances	Increasing revenues and stable expenditures, leading to budgetary surpluses	Declining real revenues, increasing expenditures due to growth of the army and bureaucratic apparatus	State bankruptcy loss of control over the army and bureaucracy	Finances generally in poor state, but high variability and contingency
Taxes	Increasing	Stagnant or even declining in real terms; heavy tax burdens on the peasantry	Tax system in a state of crisis	Variable; periods of high taxes alternate with collapse of the tax system
Ideology	Positive, optimistic ideologies rule the day	Growth of social pessimism; criticism of powers-that-be; ideological and social conflicts	Popular movements for social justice and abolishment of debts, and for land redistribution	Pessimistic ideologies; the cult of death
State policy	Internal policy is noninterventionist, laissez faire; externally, increased interest in conquest	Increasing attempts at social reforms, construction of irrigation and other infrastructure; colonization of borderlands; external aggression for acquisition of new territories	Social reforms, sometimes leading to social revolutions	Retrenchment; weakening of the state often results in external invasion

Chapter 2

Medieval England: The Plantagenet Cycle (1150–1485)

2.1 Overview of the Cycle

We bracket the secular cycle of medieval England by two periods of intense and prolonged internal conflict: the Anarchy during the reign of Stephen (1138–53) and the Wars of the Roses (1455–85). Because this period, roughly 1150–1485, was spanned by the Plantagenet dynasty (including its Lancastrian and Yorkist branches), we will refer to it as the Plantagenet cycle. The end of the cycle, which we assign to 1485, is probably uncontroversial, since most authorities agree that the population regime in England changed from stagnation to growth at the end of the fifteenth century. As to the starting point of the cycle, sustained population growth in England apparently did not get going until the end of the twelfth century. This is a more controversial point, and the empirical evidence supporting it is introduced later in this section.

In our discussion of each case study we use the following scheme. First we present the data on the dynamics of the major variables that lie at the heart of the demographic-structural explanation of secular cycles. We start with demographic and economic variables, then move on to social structure and elite dynamics, and finally to political aspects. Once the general outlines of the cycle have been established, we shift the focus to examining how these variables interacted with each other during each of the phases of the cycle (expansion, stagflation, crisis, and depression).

Trends in Population and Economy

The major features of population movements during this period are not in doubt (Hatcher 1977, Hallam 1988b, Hatcher and Bailey 2001, Dyer 2002). There was a period of general population growth up to the late thirteenth century, a peak around 1300, a slow decline during the early fourteenth century, which accelerated to a population collapse associated with the Black Death of 1348 and its aftershocks, and a depression phase

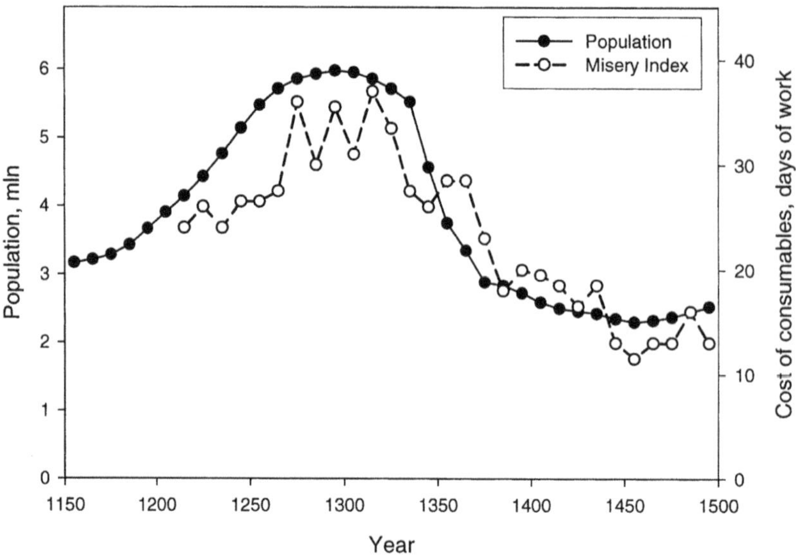

Figure 2.1 Population numbers and the "misery index" in England, 1150–1500. Population data from Hatcher (1977) and Hatcher and Bailey (2001), modified to show slower growth during the twelfth century, following Hallam (1988b:537). The misery index is the inverse real wage, here measured as the number of days of work needed to purchase the standard basket of consumables (data from Farmer 1988: Table 7.11 and Farmer 1991: Table 5.11).

during most of the fifteenth century (figure 2.1). The first signs of population recovery made themselves known around 1480, and there was a sustained increase during the sixteenth century (which belongs to the next cycle). However, although the outlines of the demographic cycle are clear, we know much less about the quantitative details (such as the precise magnitude of the peak in 1300) and, more important, when the period of sustained growth began.

The starting point of reconstructing the dynamics of English population is the Domesday Book census of 1086. The census lists about 275,000 persons (Hatcher 1977:68) who were either males of working age or heads of households (Harvey 1988). This number needs to be converted into total population. Additionally, allowance must be made for the omission of four northern countries and two major cities from the survey, and for the likelihood of unrecorded subtenants and landless men (Hatcher 1977:68). One important source of uncertainty is the multiplier that should be used to convert the number of heads of households into a total population figure. Russell (1948), using a multiplier of 3.5 per household, estimated the population of England in 1086 as 1.1 million. By contrast, Postan (1966) argued

TABLE 2.1
Population of England and Wales

Year	*Population (mln)*	*Implied per capita growth rate (% per yr)*
1086	2.00	—
1149	3.42	0.85
1230	4.96	0.46
1262	6.20	0.70
1292	6.52	0.17
1317	6.30	–0.14

Source: Estimated by Hallam (1988b:537).

for a figure of 2.5 million. Currently, a multiplier estimate of 4.5–5 appears more plausible (Harvey 1988:48), and the most often quoted number for the population of England in 1086 lies in the range of 1.75–2.25 million (Hatcher 1977:68).

The second anchoring point is the 1377 poll tax, which indicates there were between 2.5 and 3 million people in England at that time (Hatcher 1977:68). Between 1348 and 1377 the population probably dropped by 40–50 percent. Additionally, there was some decrease from 1300 to 1348. On the basis of these considerations, Hatcher estimated the peak population in 1300 as 4.5–6 million, "with the balance of possibilities pointing to the higher reaches of this range" (Hatcher 1977:68).

A similar number was estimated by Hallam (1988b) working forward from 1086. Using the information about the number of holdings recorded on various manors between 1086 and 1350, and assuming that the household size was 4.7 people and the 1086 population was 2 million, Hallam (1988b:537) generated the estimates shown in table 2.1. These figures indicate that population and settlement expanded in an uneven manner during the period of 1086–1300. Earlier (in 1956) Michael Postan had suggested that population expansion was most rapid to 1130, while between 1130 and the closing quarter of the century population stagnated (Postan 1973:276). More recently, the same conclusion was reached by Langdon and Masschaele (2006:63).

In fact, even this conclusion may be too optimistic. Certain data, although admittedly fragmentary, suggest that the population may have declined during the middle of the twelfth century as a result of the civil war between the adherents of Stephen and Matilda. Thus, *Gesta Stephani* speaks of villages "standing lonely and almost empty" and of fields unharvested because the peasantry had perished or fled (Miller and Hatcher 1978:x). Furthermore, the amount of taxes collected during the early years of Henry II reign shrank by 25 percent compared to 1130. This decline was not due simply to the disruption of revenue collection resulting from the civil war. Officials reported that many previously productive lands were now "waste." Furthermore, the fiscal machinery of the English state had fully recovered by 1165, yet it was only at the very end of Henry II's (1154–89) reign that his revenues matched those enjoyed by Henry I. Thus, it is very likely that the general population declined during Stephen's reign. Rapid population expansion resumed at the end of the twelfth century and continued during most of the thirteenth century. The sudden appearance of inflation during 1180–1220 (Harvey 1973) is indirect evidence of the changed population regime.

Both Hatcher and Hallam estimate peak population to be in the vicinity of 6 million people, and that estimate is reflected in the curve in figure 2.1. The case for lower peak numbers—4.25 million—continues to be made by Campbell (2005). Our inclination is to accept the higher estimate, but whichever point of view prevails in the end is not important for our main argument, because it relies on relative population changes, which are noncontroversial.

The final signpost is the tax returns and muster certificates of the 1520s, which suggest that the population of England around 1522–25 was in the range of 2.25–2.75 million (Hatcher 1977:69). There is a good reason to believe that by this time, the population had recovered from the lowest point in the mid-fifteenth century. Hatcher suggests that at the population nadir, England contained between 2 and 2.5 million people. Thus, the English population increased by a factor of three from 1086 to 1300, but by 1450 had declined to a level scarcely above that of Domesday England (Hatcher 1977: Figure 1).

The movement of prices mirrored faithfully population dynamics (figure 2.2). Prices rose from the low level of 1.5 shillings (s.) per quarter of wheat (11 g of silver per quintal, 1 quintal = 100 kg) in the mid-twelfth century to more than 6 s. (44 g S/quintal) in the early fourteenth century. Overall, between 1180 and 1330 there was a four- to fivefold rise in prices (Farmer 1988:718). After 1350 the price of a quarter of wheat continued to fluctuate around the level of 6 s. When expressed in silver, however, the price of wheat declined more than twofold (to 20–25 g S/quintal).

Nominal wages did not exhibit a cycle but grew fairly monotonically. Thus, a building craftsman's wage increased from 3 pennies (d.) per day in the late thirteenth century to 6 d. per day in the early sixteenth century (Phelps-Brown and Hopkins 1955). Real wages, by contrast, exhibited an oscillation, driven by the cycling movement of prices (figure 2.3). The "rural wage" in figure 2.3 is the farm laborer's wages, recently compiled by Clark (2007b). The "urban wage" is the average of real wages of laborers and craftsmen in London and Oxford (Allen 2001). Both curves show similar dynamics. Real wages declined during the thirteenth century, reaching

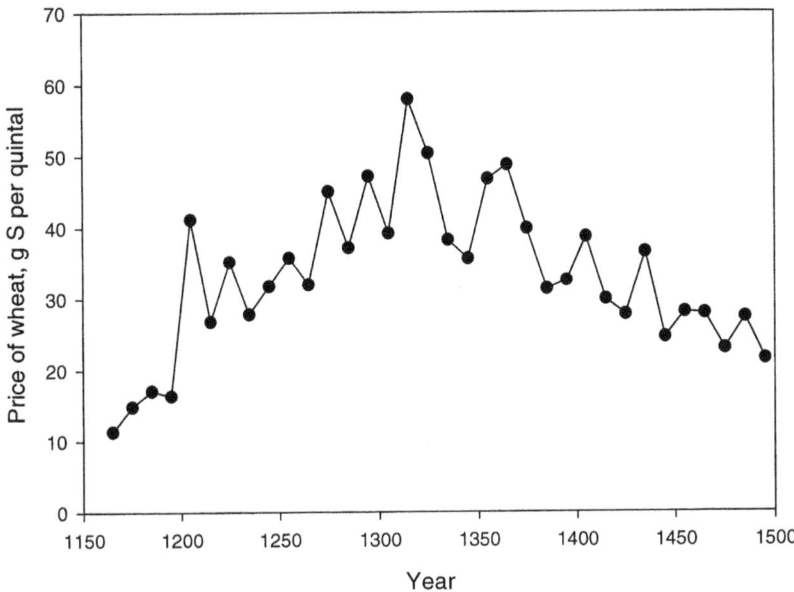

Figure 2.2 The price of a quintal (100 kg) of wheat in grams of silver (data from Farmer 1988: Table 7.1 and Farmer 1991: Table 5.1).

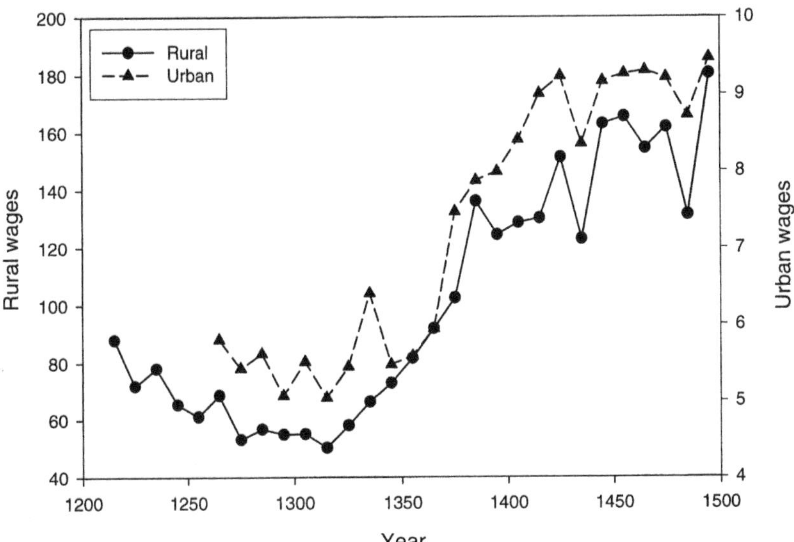

Figure 2.3 Real wages: rural (Clark 2007b) and urban (Allen 2001). Units are arbitrary.

TABLE 2.2
Foodstuffs (by value, in percentages) consumed by harvest workers at Sedgeford, Norfolk

Year	*Bread*	*Meat*	*Year*	*Bread*	*Meat*
1256	41	4	1353	31	15
1264	48	4	1368	19	25
1274	49	7	1378	15	24
1286	47	14	1387	14	30
1294	48	8	1407	17	28
1310	43	8	1413	20	—
1326	39	11	1424	15	28
1341	34	9			

Source: Dyer (2000:82).

an absolute minimum during the second decade of the fourteenth century. After that they grew continuously, apart from short-term fluctuations, until the 1430s. During the rest of the fifteenth century they stayed at an approximately constant high level. One interesting difference between city and country is in the overall magnitude of increase: just under twofold in the urban wage, but over threefold in the rural wage. (One possible explanation is that relative depopulation was more pronounced in the countryside; see the later discussion of urbanization dynamics.)

Peasant consumption patterns were also affected by population movements. During the second half of the thirteenth century the peasant diet was dominated by bread, with very little meat consumed (table 2.2). The proportion of bread in the diet started to decline after 1300 and decreased to less than 20 percent after the Black Death. Meat consumption increased from 4 percent in the 1250s and 1260s to 30 percent at the end of the fourteenth century.

Social Structure and Elite Dynamics

Turning to the social composition of the population and how it changed during the cycle, we first focus on the magnates, the upper elite stratum. In 1166 there were 133 baronies in England, defined as any tenure in chief with five or more knights' fees (Painter 1943:26). In 1200 this number increased to 160 (Painter 1943:170). By 1300 the baronage may have included well over 300 families. According to Matthew Paris, Henry III (d. 1272) could recall the names of 250 English baronies, and there were actually even more "barons" because of partition among heiresses, since the holder of a portion of a barony was still regarded as a baron (Pugh 1972:117). However, not all "barons" may be considered magnates. The question of whom to include in the top stratum of English society is further

TABLE 2.3
Numbers and incomes of English magnates

Year	*Number of magnates*	*Average income*
1086	170 barons	£200
1166	133 barons	£200
1200	160 barons	£200
1300	220 greater barons (196 peers)	£668
1436	73 peers	£881

Source: Data from Painter (1943) and Given-Wilson (1987)

complicated by shifting definitions, since the decades around 1300 were a period of transition from the tenurial to the parliamentary baronage (Painter 1943:173). The best guess is that there were 200–220 magnate families in England around 1300 (Painter 1943, Given-Wilson 1987). R. J. Wells (cited in Given-Wilson 1987:188) identified 217 families belonging to the greater baronage in 1300. This number is not very different from the 196 heads of noble families summoned to a parliament in the period of 1295–1325 (McFarlane 1973: Appendix B). To summarize, the numbers of magnates increased between 1166 and 1300, but this increase probably did not match the general population increase (table 2.3).

The dynamics of the magnate stratum after 1300 can be followed using the data presented by K. B. McFarlane (table 2.4). Until 1350 the nobility increased or stayed roughly constant (depending on whether we focus on the numbers at the start of the period or on total numbers). The size of the stratum started to decline after 1350, plunged during the first half of the fifteenth century, and then leveled off by the end of the century. The number of peer families was still around sixty in 1540, well into the next secular cycle (see the next chapter).

The extinction rates calculated by McFarlane tell a similar story: a general increase up to 1400–1425 and a decline after that. However, an even more important factor was a drastic drop in the number of new families summoned to parliaments. Thus, the reduction in the peerage around 1400 was accomplished both by enhanced extinction rates and by lowered upward mobility, while the equilibrium of the post-1450 era was a result of continuing low upward mobility and decreased extinction rate.

We should also comment on the fairly high average extinction rate, which fluctuated between 25 percent and 35 percent per quarter-century. The average rate of 28 percent implies that more than 70 percent of families went extinct each century. This result is in part due to the technical definition of extinction used by McFarlane, which somewhat inflates

TABLE 2.4
Numbers of noble families in England during the fourteenth and fifteenth centuries

Period	*Number of families at the start of the period*	*New families summoned during the period*	*Total families*	*Extinctions during the period*	*Extinction rate (% per 25 yr)*
1300–1325	136	60	196	51	26.0
1325–50	145	47	192	45	23.4
1350–75	147	29	176	50	28.4
1375–1400	126	17	143	41	28.7
1400–1425	102	11	113	40	35.4
1425–50	73	25	98	25	25.5
1450–75	73	22	95	24	25.2
1475–1500	71	10	81	20	24.7
1500–	61				

Source: (McFarlane 1973: Appendix B).
Note: Noble families are defined as those whose head received at any time after 1295 a writ of summons to a parliament.

the real rate. But the conclusion is still inescapable: the English nobility of the later Middle Ages was characterized by a poor replacement rate. For comparison, we can use the statistics compiled by R. J. Wells (cited in Given-Wilson 1987:188). According to Wells, of the 206 baronial families in 1216, 77 (37 percent) had gone extinct or suffered derogation by 1300. These numbers imply a 13 percent extinction rate per twenty-five years for the English magnate families during the thirteenth century; a rate that is half that for the succeeding two centuries. This difference is so strong that the qualitative conclusion should remain unchanged even when we take into account the different definitions of extinction used in these two studies.

To gain some understanding of the numerical dynamics of the broader elite strata, we turn to the remarkable data on inquisitions post mortem analyzed by J. C. Russell (1948) and reanalyzed by T. H. Hollingsworth (1969). The data deal with some 8,000 tenants-in-chief, that is, persons who held land directly from the king. The sample includes both magnates and some individuals holding minute amounts of land but is dominated by middle-rank landowners, so it should give us a good idea of what was happening to the elites as a whole. The replacement rate (following recalculation of Russell's data by Hollingsworth) is plotted in figure 2.4. It shows that the numbers of elites continued to expand right up to the Black Death (the replacement rate is above one). During the next century the pattern is of one of almost uniform decline, with the worst period around 1400. Only after 1450 does the curve break above the replacement rate,

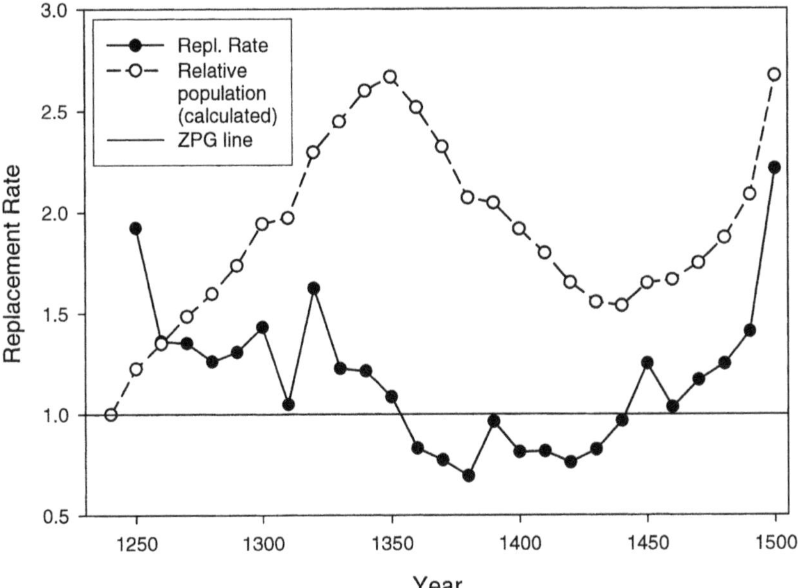

Figure 2.4 Numerical dynamics of landed elites. Solid line indicates replacement rates calculated from inquisitions post mortem. Dashed line indicates relative numerical dynamics calculated from the replacement rates, assuming a generation time of 32 years. "ZPG" line denotes zero population growth, when the replacement rate is precisely one. Data from Hollingsworth (1969).

and the rapid population growth, last seen during the thirteenth century, resumes only at the very end of the fifteenth century.

The pattern of the replacement rate curve shown in figure 2.4 has interesting implications for the dynamics of the lord-peasant ratio during the fourteenth century. As previously noted, it is generally agreed that general population started declining soon after 1300. The numbers of the landed elites, on the other hand, continued to increase for another fifty years. We can estimate the magnitude of this increase by calculating the relative population of elites, starting with one in 1240 and then using the replacement rate to project the population change one step forward. The calculated relative population increases by 40 percent between 1300 and 1350. Naturally, we cannot conclude that the elite numbers increased by the same amount, because elite dynamics are governed not only by the biological reproductive rate but also by upward and downward social mobility. Nevertheless, it seems likely that during the first half of the fourteenth century elite numbers continued to increase while commoner numbers declined. As a result of both these processes, the lord-peasant ratio must have grown substantially on the eve of the Black Death.

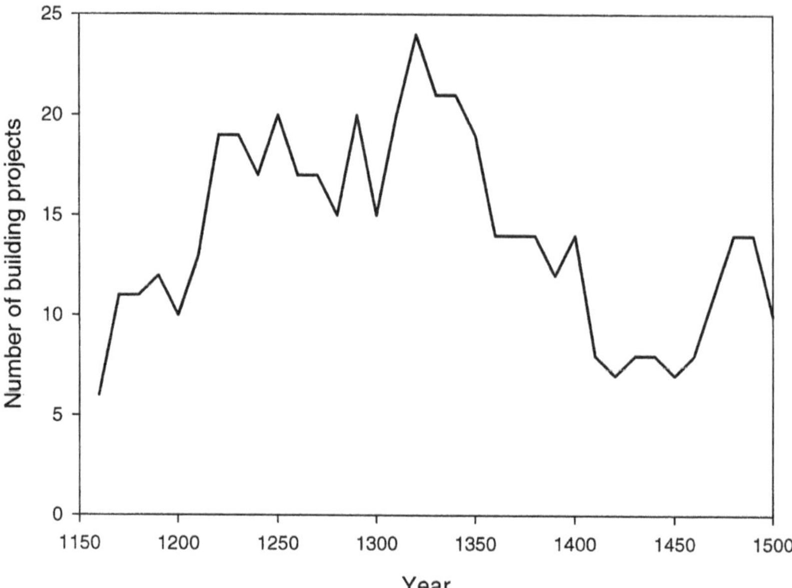

Figure 2.5 Number of major building projects in progress in each decade, 1150–1500 (after Morris 1979: Figure 7).

As a useful indicator of elite consumption patterns, we can look to the dynamics of ecclesiastical building. Generally speaking, public building can be funded both by the state and by the elites, but in medieval England the state played a minor role in church building. Funds to build churches were provided by a broad spectrum of elites—ecclesiastical, lay nobility, and the urban rich. When we look at the church-building activity dynamics (figure 2.5), we observe a steadily rising trend that reaches a peak during the first half of the fourteenth century, then collapses to a minimum during the first half of the fifteenth century. If church-building activity is a reasonable index of economic prosperity of the elites, this pattern suggests that elite replacement rates responded directly to elite economic prosperity.

State Finances

The English state in the Middle Ages derived its revenues from a bewildering variety of sources, for which only fragmentary documentation has been preserved, making the reconstruction of state budgets a very difficult task. Nevertheless, various types of revenue can be grouped in three general classes: the Crown lands ("the farms"), taxation, and feudal sources. The relative importance of these sources fluctuated during the period of interest. In 1086 the Crown held around 18 percent of the landed revenues of the kingdom, valued at approximately £11,000 per annum (Dyer 2002:82).

The royal estates contributed 60 percent of the total state revenue. In 1165 the farms were still responsible for 61 percent of the total revenues, 23 percent was raised from taxation, and judicial and other payments contributed 16 percent (White 2000:160). However, from that point on the contribution of the Crown lands exhibited a declining secular trend (although there were several short-term fluctuations around this trend). Around 1300 the farms yielded £13,000–14,000 (Dyer 2002:115), a major decline in real terms compared with the times of William I. At this time the contribution of Crown lands to the total state revenues dropped to 20 percent. Another way of looking at this number is to note that the king's share of the overall landed income had fallen to 2 percent (Dyer 2002:115). During the reign of Edward III (1327–77) the farms contributed only 5 percent of the total income (Madge 1938:30).

Ramsay (1925) used Exchequer accounts (the pipe rolls) to trace the history of royal revenues for the period up to 1400. His calculations have been much criticized, for a variety of technical reasons. However, we are interested not in specific numbers for any particular year but in the overall dynamics of royal finances, and for that purpose Ramsay's numbers can serve as a rough guide. When expressed in real terms (deflating them by the price of wheat), we observe that real revenues declined steadily during most of the thirteenth century at a time when population was increasing (figure 2.6).

The thirteenth century's pattern of revenue decline was reversed in two spurts, the first one under Edward I (1272–1307) and the second one under Edward III (1327–77). Since by the reign of Edward III the farms had fallen to a very minor part of royal revenues, the main new source of revenues was taxes, both direct and indirect (Ormrod 1999). The rise (and fall) of medieval English taxation can be traced in the data compiled by Patrick O'Brien (figure 2.6). These data indicate that after a peak achieved in the late fourteenth century, tax revenues went into a decline that was reversed only after 1485 with the start of a new cycle.

Sociopolitical Instability

England during the Middle Ages was racked by periodic baronial rebellions, which seemed to recur at intervals of fifty to sixty years (figure 2.7 and table 2.5). However, during the thirteenth century, internal warfare was not as protracted and intense as during the fourteenth century and, especially, the fifteenth century. This trend can be measured, for example, by the treatment of defeated high-status enemies. "Between the later eleventh and the early fourteenth century, defeated political opponents of high birth were rarely dispossessed and scarcely ever maimed or killed in cold blood" (Bartlett 2000:60). Internal wars during the fourteenth century and, particularly, the fifteenth century were much more sanguinary. This point

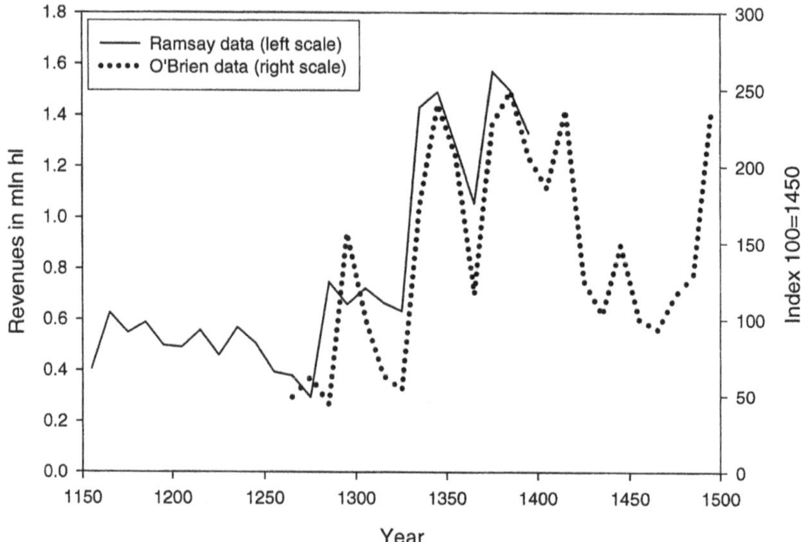

Figure 2.6 English real revenues, 1150–1400, based on data from Ramsay (1925) (solid line). Units are millions of hectaliters. Revenue from taxation (1260–1500): decadal averages, indexed to 1450 = 100%. (Based on O'Brien's data from Richard Bonney's European State Finance Database, files \obrien\engm009.txt.)

is best illustrated by the fates of royal losers: the deposition was followed by murder in prison (or at least death under suspicious circumstances) for Edward II (1327), Richard II (1400), Henry VI (1471), and Edward V (1483). Finally, Richard III was killed on the battlefield (1485).

The temporal distribution of coin hoards supports this interpretation (figure 2.7). After a peak in the mid-twelfth century, hoards dropped off to the early thirteenth-century minimum. The thirteenth and fourteenth centuries saw a gradual (and uneven) rise, culminating in a peak around 1370. Another great peak during the second half of the fifteenth century closely tracks instability associated with the Wars of the Roses. In fact, there is a general correspondence between the peaks in the instability index, constructed by counting years in civil war or rebellion per twenty years, and the temporal distribution of hoards (figure 2.7). The only significant mismatch is between the major peaks of 1370 in hoards and 1400 in instability index. We should note, however, that this comparison relies on a very inadequate hoard data. We had to rely on the compilation by Thompson (1956), which is fifty years out of date. We know that many more English medieval hoards came to the attention of numismaticists or were discovered with the aid of a metal detector, but we were unable to find any compilations updating Thompson's data.

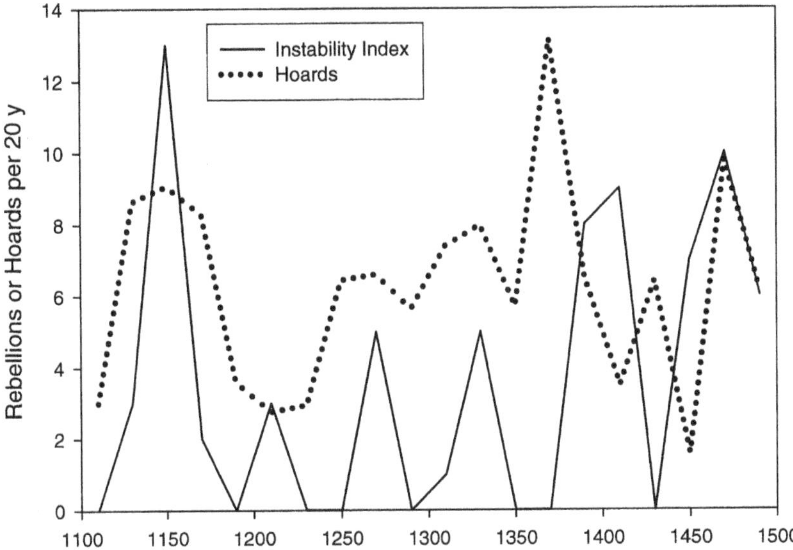

Figure 2.7 Sociopolitical instability in England, 1100–1500: incidence of rebellions and civil wars per 20 years (solid line) and the number of hoards per 20 years (dotted line). Instability index is calculated from the data in table 2.5; coin hoard data are from Thompson (1956).

This concludes our overview of general trends during the Plantagenet secular cycles. In the next sections we turn to a more detailed discussion of demographic-structural dynamics organized by cycle phases.

2.2 The Expansion Phase (1150–1260)

We lack direct estimates, but lasting population growth must have started soon after the end of Stephen's anarchic reign and the establishment of stability under Henry II. Indirect evidence of this growth is provided by the persistent inflation in the prices of wheat from 1160 (see figure 2.2). Other signs of overpopulation include evidence of fragmentation of peasant holdings. In a classic paper on the Somerset manor of Taunton, J. Z. Titow (1961) showed that in 1248, the land-to-peasant ratio was 3.3 acres (1.33 ha), while in 1311 it was 2.5 acres (1 ha) at best.

Political instability during this period achieved the lowest level of the whole medieval period (table 2.5 and figure 2.7). Nevertheless, this period was not conflict-free. There were three major political crises: the rebellion of 1173–74, the civil wars at the end of John's reign, and the troubles of 1258, leading into the "barons' wars" of 1263–67 (Mortimer 1994:77). The

TABLE 2.5
Occurrence of rebellions, coups d'état, civil wars, and other instances of internal war in England, 1100–1500

Period	*Description*
1138–53	Anarchy (civil war between Stephen and Matilda/Henry)
1173–74	Widespread rebellion against Henry II
1215–17	Civil war between John and the barons (resulting in the Magna Carta), then royalists against rebels
1263–67	Civil war between "reformer" and "conservative" barons; Simon de Montfort defeated and captured Henry; defeat and death of de Montfort at Evesham
1315	Civil disorders (private wars in several southern counties) during supremacy of Lancaster (1314–22)
1321–22	Civil war; baron uprising in the western counties; Edward II defeated Lancaster at Boroughbridge and beheaded him
1326–27	Rebellion of Isabella and Mortimer; abdication of Edward II, followed by his murder in prison eight months later
1330	Coup of Edward III against Mortimer (hanged in 1330)
1381	Peasants' Revolt
1387–88	Insurrection of the "Lords Appellant"
1391	Coup d'état of Richard II
1397–99	Events leading to the deposition of Richard II (1399): Richard, furious at a parliamentary demand for financial accounting, had the mover (Haxey) condemned for treason (not executed). In the next parliament, three of the lords appellant were convicted and executed for treason. The conspiracy of Henry of Bolingbroke; Richard forced to abdicate, thrown into the Tower, and later died (was murdered?) in prison (1400)
1400–1408	Glyn Dwr rebellion
1414	Lollard plot against the king's life
1448–51	Domestic disorders: Henry VI, declared of age (1437), was unfit to rule; the council continued in power, and factions and favorites encouraged the rise of disorder. The nobles maintained increasing numbers of private armed retainers (livery and maintenance) with which they fought one another, terrorized their neighbors, paralyzed the courts, and dominated the government
1450	Jack Cade's rebellion
1455–56	Wars of the Roses, 1st phase; Battle of St. Albans (1455): Somerset defeated and killed

TABLE 2.5 *(continued)*

Period	*Description*
1460–65	Wars of the Roses, 2nd phase; battle of Northampton (1460): Yorkists defeated the royal army and took Henry VI prisoner; Richard's son Edward defeated Lancastrians at Mortimer's Cross (1461) but was defeated at the 2nd battle of St. Albans (1461); London admitted Edward to the town, and after his victory at Towton acclaimed him king (1461); civil war continued intermittently; Henry VI finally captured (1465) and put in the Tower
1467–71	Wars of the Roses, 3rd phase: Edward's victory at Barnet (1471), where Warwick was killed; Henry VI died (in all probability, was murdered) in the Tower
1483–85	Wars of the Roses, 4th phase: Richard III aborted a rebellion conceived by Morton, bishop of Ely, and led by the Duke of Buckingham; the latter was beheaded; the landing at Milford Haven of Henry, Earl of Richmond; Henry defeated Richard II on Bosworth Field (Leicestershire), where Richard fell
1489	Rebellion in Northumberland
1495	Rebellion of Perkin Warbeck
1497	Insurrection in Cornwall on occasion of imposition of a tax by parliament; insurrection was suppressed by defeat at Blackheath (June 22, 1497), and leaders were executed (Flammock)

Source: Following Sorokin (1937), supplemented by Stearns (2001).

troubles of 1173–74 started in Normandy and then spread to England, where several disgruntled earls were in revolt (centered in the Midlands). The kings of France and Scotland invaded, but were defeated by royal loyalists. The next serious conflict, forty years later, was a politico-constitutional struggle between the feudal barons and John Lackland that eventually led to the Magna Carta. Both civil wars of 1173–74 and 1215–17 were fairly mild conflicts (by medieval standards), mostly conducted by maneuvering and sieges. The civil war of 1263–66 and conflicts after it are discussed in section 2.4.

2.3 Stagflation (1260–1315)

Rural Population

Population growth continued to 1300, but at a slowing rate, as overall population numbers in England and Wales approached the six million mark. In some regions growth apparently ceased altogether.

This period saw the development of the classic signs of overpopulation, as postulated by the Malthusian-Ricardian framework. Prices reached a

TABLE 2.6
Rents, 1000–1450

Period	*Rent (d./acre)*	*Location*	*Reference*
1000	0.3–0.6	England	Dyer (2002:39)
11th C	1	East Anglia	Miller and Hatcher (1978:45)
11th C	1	Kent	Miller and Hatcher (1978:45)
1251	2–4	Cambridgeshire	Bolton (1980:187)
1251	4–6	Norfolk	Miller and Hatcher (1978:45)
1299	12.5[a]	Bishopric of Worcester	Dyer (1980:72–73)
1300	12	Cambridgeshire	Bolton (1980:187)
Early 14th C	8–28	Huntingdonshire	Miller and Hatcher (1978:45)
Early 14th C	33	Yorkshire	Miller and Hatcher (1978:45)
Early 14th C	30–36	Northumberland	Miller and Hatcher (1978:45)
1370–90	10.75[b]	Norfolk	Bolton (1980:214)
1437	10.5	Warwickshire	Fryde in Kaeuper (2000)

[a] Average rents and dues per acre.
[b] This is the open market rate. For customary land where services were commuted landlords demanded 24 d. but could not find takers.

secular peak in the 1310s (see figure 2.2), real wages declined (see figure 2.3), and land rents increased (table 2.6). Entry fines paid on taking up tenancy were another means by which landlords could extract income from land. Evidence for fines prior to the mid-thirteenth century is scarce, but what there is suggests they increased even more steeply than the rents (table 2.7).

An analysis of the Hundred Rolls of 1279–80 suggested that rent per acre depended on the size of the holding, whether the tenant was free or unfree, whether landlords were church or lay, and land fertility, among other factors (Kanzaka 2002). Some of the variation in fines was probably explained by differential land fertility, the circumstances of the prospective tenant, nearness to markets, and access to nonagrarian employment (Miller and Hatcher 1978:46). It is also possible that some lords used entry fines as a way to increase returns on land where they had no flexibility in raising rents, for example. The great amount of variability exhibited by rents and fines precludes precise quantitative statements, but the overall trend is unmistakable: the ability of landowners to extract surplus from peasants increased during the stagflation phase.

Peasant holdings became increasingly fragmented during this period. Here are some numbers, brought together by Grigg (1980:68). On the bishop of Worcester's estate, the proportion of peasants who held a yardland (thirty acres or 12 ha) declined from 33 percent in 1250 to 25 percent in 1300. At Kempsey, the number of smallholders tripled between 1182 and 1299. The average holding on a manor in Taunton was 1.3 ha in 1248,

TABLE 2.7
Entry fines, 1200–1450

Period	*s./virgate*	*Location*	*Reference*
1214	1–1.67	Wiltshire	Miller and Hatcher (1978:46)
1250	13.3–20	Ramsey estates, Hunts	Miller and Hatcher (1978:46)
1296–97	30 (range 2–113)	Earl of Cornwall estates, various counties	Miller and Hatcher (1978:46)
1277–1348	8–47	Wiltshire	Miller and Hatcher (1978:46)
1283–1348	39	Oxfordshire	Miller and Hatcher (1978:46)
1283–1348	109	Taunton	Miller and Hatcher (1978:46)
1300	60	General estimate	Dyer (2002:141)
After 1300	> 60	Ramsey estates, Hunts	Miller and Hatcher (1978:46)
Early 14th C	20–30 (max = 100)	Northamptonshire	Dyer (1980:47)
Early 14th C	800–1600[a]	Somerset	Miller and Hatcher (1978:46)

Note: One virgate is 30 acres.
[a] These are exceptionally high.

TABLE 2.8
Distribution of peasant land holding ca. 1280

Land	*Free*	*Villein*	*All*	*Percent*
Over virgate[a]	521	173	694	3.2
One virgate	904	3,940	4,844	22.6
Half virgate	1,083	5,724	6,807	31.8
Quarter virgate	775	1,378	2,153	10.0
Smallholders	2,251	4,687	6,938	32.4

Source: Kosminsky (1956).
[a] One virgate = 1 yardland = 30 acres = 12 ha.

declining to 1 ha in 1311. By the end of the thirteenth century, on a sample of estates owned by various ecclesiastical lords, 33 percent of the population had less than 1 ha. The minimum size of a farm needed to provide subsistence to a family has been estimated by various authorities to lie in the region of 4.5–6 ha. By 1300 the majority of peasants in England had less than this amount of land and could not survive without some alternative source of income (Grigg 1980:68). The distribution of landholdings (table 2.8) in the late thirteenth century suggests that holdings of a half virgate were both the median and the mean.

Various estimates of peasant budgets around 1300 have been made by economic historians (Titow 1961, Hilton 1966, Hollingsworth 1969, Hallam 1988a, Dyer 1989). There is a general agreement among these authorities that a typical peasant in 1300 holding a half virgate of land was

TABLE 2.9
Estimated peasant budget

Assumptions	*Calculations*
Production	
Crop acreage, assuming 3-field system	10 acres
Sowing rate per acre	0.25 q
Total seed	0.25 q/acre × 10 acres = 2.5 q
Yield ratio	1:4
Crop harvested	10 q
Net (seed deducted)	10 – 2.5 = 7.5 q
Production in money (1 q = 6 s.)	7.5 q × 6 s./q = 45 s.
Extraction	
Tithe (10% of harvest)	0.1 × 10 q = 1 q = 6 s.
Rent (1 s. per acre)	1 s./acre × 15 acres = 15 s.
Other feudal exactions	1 s.
Taxes	1 s.
Death duties	
Heriot (best animal)	1 bull = 10 s.
Mortuary (another animal)	1 bull = 10 s.
Entry fee	40 s.
Total death duties	60 s.
same per year	60 s./20 y = 3 s.
Total extraction = (6 + 15 + 1 + 1 + 3) s.	26 s. = 4.3 q
Summary of peasant budget	
Total extraction	4.3 q
Remaining to the peasant	7.5 q – 4.3 q = 3.2 q
Minimum consumption	4 q
Deficit	3.2 q – 4 q = – 0.8 q
Deficit in money (1 q = 6 s.)	0.8 q × 6s. = 5 s.
Proportions	
Total production (assuming the deficit of 5 s. was somehow made up)	45 s. + 5 s. = 50 s. = 100%
Consumption (% of total production)	24 s. = 48%
Church tithes (% of total production)	6 s. = 12%
Landowner (% of total production)	19 s. = 38%
State (% of total production)	1 s. = 2%

Note: Assumes landholdings of one-half virgate = 15 acres (6 ha).
Abbreviation: q, 1 quarter of wheat (8 bushels = 64 gallons = 2.9 hectaliters = 218 kg)

barely making ends meet, if that. Let us retrace here the main points of this calculation.

The calculation in table 2.9 makes a number of simplifying assumptions. For example, peasants did not grow just wheat, as is assumed in table 2.9. However, the overall result is very similar when a more realistic mix of crops is substituted. For example, Dyer (1989:113) performed a more elaborate calculation, assuming that crops were split among wheat, barley, peas, and oats. Repeating his calculation with the assumption that only wheat was grown, we obtained a result that was less than 10 percent different from Dyer's. Another source of agricultural income that table 2.9 does not take into account is a cash income from animals. Dyer calculated that a peasant holding a virgate would derive additional income of 33 s. from this source. Unfortunately, he did not duplicate these detailed calculations for a half-virgater, but it is unlikely these peasants with more typical land holdings would derive much income from this source. They kept considerably fewer animals than full virgaters, and what they kept would have yielded very little cash surplus after tithes and personal consumption were taken into account. Perhaps it would be enough to cover the calculated deficit of 5 s., or perhaps the peasant had to rely on the garden or poultry, and the extra earnings by his wife (spinning) or family (sons hiring out as agricultural laborers) would become very important in meeting his obligations to the lord, church, and the state. "How he paid for clothing, cooking pots, or furnishings is not at all clear," concludes Dyer. The final note here is that the calculations in table 2.9 assume normal conditions. During times of even mild crop failure, the half-virgater would have had to go into debt to survive.

These calculations can also give us at least an order of magnitude of the estimated proportion of resources extracted by the elites and the state from the producers. Assuming that peasants could somehow make up the deficit of 5 s. through exploiting nonarable resources, their estimated total production rate would be 50 s. per year. Of this amount, the church took 12 percent (this is an underestimate that does not include the tithe on animals and garden produce), the lord took 38 percent (again, an underestimate, because it does not include labor services; also, various feudal exactions are probably underestimated at 1 s. per year), and the state took a tiny 2 percent, leaving the peasant less than half the product (and barely enough for basic subsistence).

While typical half-virgaters were balanced on the edge of survival, those few well-to-do peasants who had a virgate did much better. On the basis of his investigation of the manor of Bishop's Cleeve in Gloucerstership in 1299, Dyer (1989:117) concluded that "an average yardlander in a normal year was in a good position to make a cash surplus." By contrast, a smallholder in order to make ends meet had to find employment for 130 days per year. Since the numbers of such smallholders were very large, it is likely that only a small minority of them would have been able to secure full employment. The contrast between the economic position of different peasant strata can be further illustrated by the fact that around 1300 at Halesowen in Worcestershire, the wealthier peasants had on average 5.1 children, compared to the cottagers' 1.8 offspring (Dyer 2002:158).

One remarkable feature highlighted by the calculation of the peasant budget is how little—2 percent—of peasant-generated product went to the state. Our estimate of taxes equaling 1 s. per year follows Dyer (2002:258), who calculated that a peasant born in 1270 and acquiring a holding of twenty acres in 1293 would find himself paying direct taxes in every year in 1294–97 and then in an additional nine years between 1301 and 1322. His son, succeeding him in the mid-1320s, would pay in 1327, 1332, 1334, and 1336, and contribute to three subsidies in 1337–40. In all, the two generations would pay 60 s. over the period of forty-six years, or 1.3 s. per year. A half-virgater holding fifteen (instead of twenty) acres would probably pay a little less, say 1 s. per year.

The state, of course, had other sources of revenues than lay subsidies that affected peasants directly. However, Dyer (2002:257) estimated that in 1297 the Crown's taxes amounted to only 2 percent of the estimated gross domestic product. In sum, England of 1300 was a very undertaxed country, and the process of surplus extraction was heavily lopsided in favor of the elites. In fact, the crude estimates given above suggest that by 1300, elite extraction had started cutting into the bare subsistence minimum, and this tendency would only become worse during most of the fourteenth century.

The chief factor underlying popular immiseration in the late thirteenth century, however, was not surplus extraction by the feudal lords but the massive population growth during the preceding century. Furthermore, the effect of population growth was not just that it decreased peasant-to-land ratios on average but that it also resulted in growing inequality of landholdings. One-third of rural freeholders held an acre or less of land, while another third held between one and ten acres (Kanzaka 2002:599), not enough land to break even. By contrast, 10 percent of freeholders were very well off, with forty or more acres of land.

Urbanization

Keene (2001:196) speculated that in 1100 there were 20,000 Londoners, or 0.8 percent of the total population in the country. By 1300 the population of London had reached 80,000, constituting 1.3 percent of the total (Keene 2001:195). The poll taxes for 1377 indicate that 1.7 percent of the assessed population of England was found in London (Keene 2001:194), suggesting there were slightly under 50,000 Londoners. In summary, between 1100 and 1400 the urbanization index of England (defined as the proportion of the total population found in the capital) doubled.

The proportion of population living in large towns (over 10,000 people) also increased. In the eleventh century there was only one such town, London, while by the end of the thirteenth century there were between four-

TABLE 2.10
Changes in the social structure of the top strata, 1150–1450: Magnates

Year	*Numbers*	*Avg. income*	*Real income (hl)*
1166	133	£200	7,700
1200	160	£200	3,100
1300	200	£670	6,600
1436	70	£880	8,600

Source: Data from Table 2.3.

teen and sixteen towns with a population of 10,000 or more, which contained at least 5 percent of the population of England (Britnell 1995:10). Urbanization continued to increase during the fourteenth century.

In addition to the expansion of urban populations in established towns, new towns were founded during the twelfth and thirteenth centuries. For example, planned towns built in England and Wales reached a peak during the second half of the thirteenth century (Beresford 1967:366).

The increase in the proportion of population found in towns during the fourteenth century was clearly not a result of better demographic rates there compared to rural locations. In fact, everything we know about medieval cities suggests they were population sinks ("death traps"). Most English towns were decimated by outbreaks of the plague (Dobson 2001:276), but then made up losses as a result of immigration from rural areas. Direct evidence of this process comes from the spectacular increase in the recruitment of new citizens recorded in York's freemen's register (Dobson 2001:276). The population of some cities, such as Coventry, actually expanded during the second half of the fourteenth century despite the ravages of the Black Death (Phythian-Adams 1979:33).

The Elites

While general population growth slowed sometime during the thirteenth century, and eventually reached a peak around 1300, the elite numbers continued to expand throughout the stagflation phase and even beyond it (to 1350). In general, the elites did well economically during the thirteenth century. At the top, the number of magnate families expanded only slightly, from perhaps 160 to 200 families, but their average income grew from £200 to £670 per year, which represents more than a twofold increase in real terms (table 2.10).

The middle ranks also participated in this expansion: whereas there were perhaps 1,000 belted knights (substantial landowners holding land worth at least £10 per year) in 1200, by 1300 there were 3,000 knights and es-

TABLE 2.11
Changes in the social structure of the top strata, 1150–1450: Middle ranks and lesser elites

Year	*Designation*	*Numbers*	*Min. income*	*Real min. Income*[a]	*Reference*
(a) Middle ranks					
1100	Belted knights	1,000	£5	190	Dyer (2002:85)
1200	Belted knights	1,000[b]	£10	160	Painter (1943:172)
1300	Knights and esquires	3,000[c]	£20	200	Given-Wilson (1987:18)
1400	Knights and esquires	2,400	£20	180	Given-Wilson (1987:73)
1500	Knights and esquires	1,300	£20	190	Mingay (1976:4)
(b) Lesser elites (very approximate)					
ca.1100	Lesser landholders	7,000–8,000	£1	40	Dyer (2002:85)
ca.1200	Knights	4,500–5,000	?		Bartlett (2000:216)
ca.1300	Country gentry	18,000–20,000	£5	50	Denholm-Young (1969:16)
ca.1300	Gentry and clergy[d]	20,000	£10	100	Dyer (2002:152)
14th C	Gentry	9,000–10,000	£5	45	Given-Wilson (1987:72)
15th C	Gentry and clergy	10,000	£10	100	Dyer (1989:32)
15th C	Gentry	6,000–9,000	£5	50	Pugh (1972:97)
1436	Taxpayers with incomes < £40	6,200	£5	40	Gray (1934:630)
ca.1500	Gentry	5,000	£5	55	Mingay (1976:4)

[a] In hectoliters of grain.
[b] Assuming that the numbers of belted knights did not change much during the twelfth century.
[c] Of which 1,250 were knights.
[d] Households enjoying £10–100 per annum, including beneficed clergy.

quires with incomes of more than £20 per year, a rough equivalent in real terms of £10 in 1200 (table 2.11).

The numbers of lesser landholders also grew, although a precise numerical estimate of this increase cannot be given: Given-Wilson estimated the numbers of lords with income over £5 at 9,000–10,000 in the fourteenth century, while Denholm-Young proposed a number twice that (table 2.11). Dyer suggests there were 20,000 households that enjoyed incomes between £10 and £100 per year in 1300. This estimate, however, includes beneficed clergy, while excluding those lesser landowners whose incomes were between £5 and £10.

The truth probably lies between these extremes. In general, it seems likely that the numbers of landholders kept pace with the general populace (although with a lag), in which case they should have tripled from around 5,000 in the twelfth century to 15,000 at their peak in the fourteenth century. Inquisitions post mortem support this interpretation. The elite replacement rate was well above one during the whole period of 1250–1340. If the landed elites were a closed class whose size would change only as a result of births and deaths, then their numbers would have expanded by a factor of 2.67 during the century after 1250 (see figure 2.4). In reality, of course, elite numbers were also affected by upward and downward social mobility. There is no evidence, however, for massive downward mobility after 1250 comparable to that of the earlier period that resulted in substantial numbers of the lesser nobility slipping down the social scale in the years around 1200 (Given-Wilson 1987:16). Regional studies suggest that those losing ground were in the minority. For example, in a sample of thirty-one families from Oxfordshire, five families lost land, nine gained it, and seventeen remained in much the same position (Dyer 2002:152).

The size of the nonproductive class was greatly bloated by the huge numbers of the clergy. England of the thirteenth century was "swarming with clerics" (Jessopp 1892). There were an estimated 25,000 monks and nuns (Moorman 1946:258). As to the numbers of parish clergy, estimates range from 40,000 (Moorman 1946:53) to 2 percent of the population (Coulton 1907), which would imply a staggering figure of over 100,000. There were 9,000–10,000 parishes in thirteenth-century England (Moorman 1946:5) and around five ordained men per parish (Moorman 1946:55). For example, Hilton (1966:62) estimated there were 2,000 ordained clerics in the diocese of Worcester, which had 445 parishes. These numbers thus imply an estimate of 50,000 secular clergy in England in 1300, or 75,000, counting monks and nuns. And this figure does not include the huge "clerical or semi-clerical underworld" (Hilton 1966:62).

The foundations of elite prosperity were provided by the plentiful labor supply, leading to increasing rents and declining wages. As a result, the elite incomes from land kept pace with or even grew faster than inflation. Dyer (2002) suggests that "the main benefit for lords came from additions to the numbers of customary tenants who owed heavy burdens of labor service and cash payments."

The gap between the economic well-being of commoners and elites increased: while the incomes of peasants plummeted as a result of lack of land, increased rents, and decreased wages, the elite incomes increased both in absolute and in relative terms. This trend can also be seen in the dynamics of military wages. The rate of pay for elite soldiers (knights) grew faster than inflation, while the real wages of commoners (foot soldiers) declined (table 2.12).

The overall pattern in incomes up to 1300, therefore, was one of increasing inequality: the standard of living of commoners declined, gentry incomes generally outpaced inflation, while the magnates did best of all. In Henry II's reign few lords had an income exceeding £500 per year (Bartlett 2000:80). The highest income in Sidney Painter's list of fifty-four barons around 1200 was the £800 enjoyed by Roger de Lacy, constable of Chester, at his death in 1210. The ratio of maximum to average income among the barons was only 4:1. One hundred years later, the largest income in Paint-

TABLE 2.12
Daily rates of pay for soldiers in England

Period	*Knight*	*Foot soldier*	*Knight to foot ratio*
1060	4 d.		
1160	6 d.		
1165	8 d.	1 d.	8:1
1195	1 s.		
1215	2 s.	2 d.	12:1
1250	2 s.		
1300[a]	2, 3, or 4 s.	2 d.	18:1

Source: Harvey (1976:150) for 1060 and Contamine (1984:94) for the rest.

[a] Rates varied according to rank: between 2 s. for a knight-bachelor and 4 s. for a knight-banneret.

er's list of twenty-seven landholders was that of Edmund, Earl of Cornwall, who had an annual income of £3,800 at his death in 1301 (Painter 1943:174). Taking inflation into account, this represents an increase of 2.8 in real terms. An even greater landed income was that of Thomas, Earl of Lancaster: £11,000 in 1311 (Dyer 1989:29). The maximum to average income ratio was 16:1, compared to 4:1 one hundred years earlier. Six earls (including the Earl of Cornwall) enjoyed an income of more than £3,000 per annum (Dyer 1989:29). The largest known fortune in cash in late medieval England was that of Richard, Earl of Arundel, which amounted to £72,250 at the time of his death in 1376 (Bean 1991:565).

Another way to address the well-being of elites is to examine their consumption of luxuries. Wine consumption reached the medieval peak in the early fourteenth century, when the English imported 20,000 tuns from Gascony (Dyer 1989), worth wholesale £60,000 (Miller and Hatcher 1978:81). Assuming there were 20,000 elite households at that time, this represents two to three liters of wine per household per day.

2.4 Crisis (1315–1400)

Population Decline

The economic misery of the commoner population grew steadily during the stagflation phase, reaching a peak in the early fourteenth century. Peasants were squeezed from below by an insufficient land supply resulting from too many people competing for limited land and from above by an expanding (and increasingly rapacious) class of noble landowners eager to maintain the consumption levels to which they had become accustomed during the thirteenth century. There were important regional variations in how the social structure responded to population pressure. In East Anglia, for example, the freeholder stratum (the sokemen) progressively subdivided their land among heirs, which resulted in a proliferation of smallholders with tiny plots of land (Poos 2004). In the south, by contrast, manorial lords exerted a better control over land distribution, so that a substantial minority of peasants held from one-quarter to a whole virgate (between 3 and 12 ha), leaving the surplus population with cottages and garden plots. In both cases, however, most of the population did not have enough land to feed itself and had to rely on additional sources of income. Increasing misery also affected the amount of grain that peasants were able to store. Thus, in Colchester between 1295 and 1301, the median store of wheat per taxpayer slipped below one quarter (Hallam 1988a:822). Peasants were increasingly leading a precarious hand-to-mouth existence, with most having no protection against any fluctuations in the amount of grain brought in as harvest. As a result, a string of very poor harvests in England beginning in 1315 resulted in mortality rates that were nothing short of catastrophic.

The classic study of Postan and Titow (Postan 1973: Chapter 9) on the heriots paid on five Winchester manors allows us a glimpse into how the mortality rate fluctuated between 1245 and 1350 (heriots were paid when a tenant died and another replaced him). The average number of heriots more than doubled, from 47 per year during the second half of the thirteenth century to 106 during the decade of 1310–19. But most revealing are the dynamics of one category, money heriots, paid by the poorer villages who had few or no beasts, and by implication few or no acres of land (Miller and Hatcher 1978:58). The number of money heriots fluctuated around ten per year until 1290, then grew rapidly to a peak of almost sixty in 1310–19 and another peak in the decade just prior to the Black Death (figure 2.8). It is clear that the first to suffer from the dearth were the poorer segments of the rural society. Further evidence for this conclusion comes from the observation that high wheat prices were correlated with numbers of money heriots but not with animal heriots (the analysis by J. Longden in Postan 1973:179–185).

The period of severe harvest failures and livestock epidemics between 1315 and 1322 was a dividing line in the history of the medieval English countryside (Miller and Hatcher 1978:60). The poor harvest of 1314 was succeeded by two disastrous harvests in 1315 and 1316. Harvests improved after 1317, but a series of deadly epidemics affected cattle herds between 1319 and 1321. The agrarian crisis of 1315–21 resulted in a noticeable decline in the population. Direct evidence of this fall is fragmentary, but

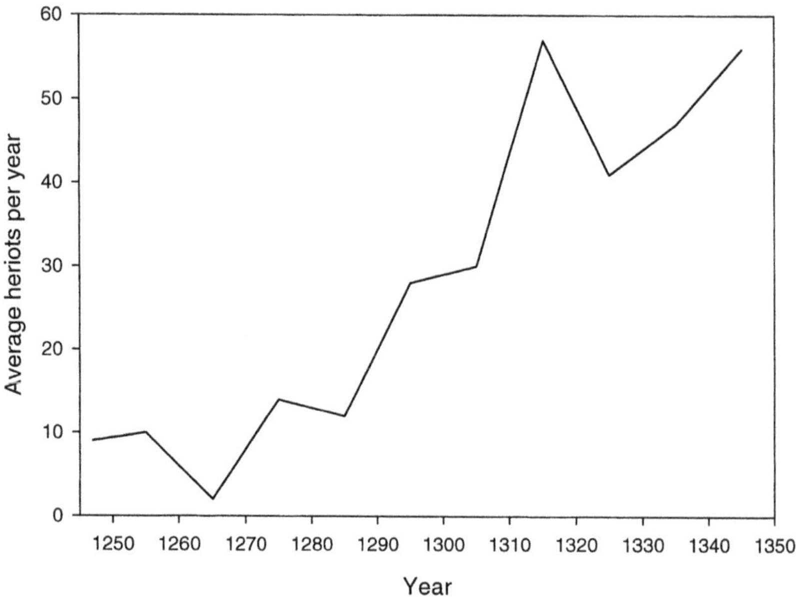

Figure 2.8 Number of money heriots paid on Winchester manor, 1245–1348. Data from Postan (1973: Table 9.2).

the tithing penny data from Essex parishes indicate that between 1300 and 1340 the number of tithingmen declined by 30 percent (Poos 1985). Indirect evidence of the population decline was a significant increase in the number of unwanted holdings, signaling the slackening of competition for land (Miller and Hatcher 1978:59). Wheat prices during the 1330s and 1340s declined to levels not seen since 1270 (see figure 2.2), and the secular trend was definitely down, although with significant fluctuations. By the 1340s the amount of uncultivated land had reached noticeable dimension in some counties, such as Sussex or Cambridgeshire (Miller and Hatcher 1978:61).

The disasters of 1315–21, however, soon paled into insignificance compared with what came next. In 1348 the Black Death arrived in England, and the number of cash heriots on Winchester manors jumped to 675 in 1349 (compared with less than 60 even during the worst decades of the early fourteenth century). The evidence of a drastic population collapse countrywide is abundant and is reviewed in, for example, Hatcher (1977). There is a broad agreement among the authorities that the first shock of the epidemic carried away 30–40 percent of the population, and that the aftershocks of 1361–62, 1369, and 1375 depressed the population to a level less than half its 1300 peak.

TABLE 2.13
Mortality rates (%) of various social strata in England during the years of plague outbreaks

	Year				
Stratum	*1349*	*1361*	*1369*	*1375*	*Reference*
Monks	45				Hatcher (1977:22–25)
Beneficed clergy	40	14	13		Hatcher (1977:22–25)
Tenants-in-chief	27	23	13	12	Russell (1948:216–18)
Bishops	18				Hatcher (1977:22–25)
Peers	8	19	6	5	McFarlane (1973:170)

The Effect of the Black Death on Social Structure

As we noted above, demographic rates varied widely among various social strata. Wealthier peasants had two to three times as many children as cottagers, and their death rates tended not to be affected by crop failures. Moving up the social scale, we also saw that while the general population in England probably declined between 1300 and 1348, replacement rates calculated for landowners (tenants-in-chief) suggest that their numbers continued to expand at a healthy clip throughout this period. What is known about mortality rates during the mid-century plague epidemics provides more evidence for the strong effect of socioeconomic status on demographic rates (table 2.13).

The highest mortality rates during the first and most severe outbreak of 1348–49 were observed among monks and beneficed clergy. Parish priests are of particular interest, because although they were better fed and better housed, which would tend to lower death rates, conscientious performance of their duties would tend to raise them (Hatcher 1977:23). Thus, their death rates provide a reasonable estimate of the death rates among the general rural population. In fact, abundant, although varying in quality, data from manorial records, reviewed by Hatcher (1977:22), suggest that the death rate of beneficed clergy is an underestimate of that of peasants.

If peasant death rates were over 40 percent, middle-rank elites suffered only 27 percent mortality, while the magnates escaped with even lighter losses of 8–18 percent (table 2.13). The privileged groups had a better than average chance of escaping infection because they lived in stone houses (rats preferred wooden houses) and they could flee the advancing plague (Hatcher 1977:23). However, the elites apparently paid the price during the next epidemic of 1361–62. Among the general population the death rates were much lower than during the first visitation of the plague in 1348–49. A numerical estimate is again provided by the death rates of the beneficed gentry (at least for the adult population; see table 2.13). The most likely reason is the build-up of resistance to infection among the population (which was a direct consequence of the removal of those who were most susceptible in 1348–49, leaving those who were more resistant). While the first epidemic struck mainly at people in the prime of life (Hatcher 1977:24), later epidemics had a disproportionate effect on the children. There was also a disproportionate effect on the higher ranks: the mortality rate of tenants-in-chief was hardly lower in 1361 than in 1349, while the death rates among the peers actually increased (table 2.13).

To summarize the numerical dynamics of the productive and elite strata during the phase of crisis, the numbers of peasants started declining no later than 1315 and plunged in 1348–49, while the numbers of elite expanded until 1348 and declined at a much milder rate between 1348 and 1380. A highly important consequence of these divergent dynamics from the point of view of the demographic-structural theory is that the elite-to-commoner ratio experienced a substantial increase during this period; the social pyramid became top-heavy. This development spelled problems for the elites. Of course, a twofold decrease in the size of the productive stratum did not translate into a twofold decrease in the society's productive capacity, because per capita productivity increased. Pre-1315 England had built up an enormous demand for land. Thus, many landlords were able to immediately rent out the land of tenants who died in the epidemic of the Black Death. However, on the estates of the bishop of Worcester, few new tenants could be found for the larger holdings in 1349–50, and the majority of them remained vacant. Surviving smallholders lacked the necessary animals or equipment or skills to embark on such large ventures (Fryde 1991:747). Subsequent epidemics in 1361, 1369, and 1375 disrupted productive capacity even more. Thus, in 1362–64, grain prices rose more than in 1349–51, and there was a severe famine in 1370 (Fryde 1991:745–46).

An even worse threat for the elite incomes was an indirect consequence of the post-1348 depopulation. Since the thirteenth century, landlords had become accustomed to the high supply of labor driving high rents and entry fines and low wages. This economic clout was lost after 1348, and ultimately resulted in a substantial reduction of per capita incomes enjoyed by the elites. Particularly badly hurt were the middle ranks and lesser landowners, who relied on personal servants and hired labor to farm substantial properties (Fryde 1991:755).

How did the elites deal with this threat? Apparently, they immediately recognized the enhanced bargaining power of peasants and took steps to legislatively fix the rents and wages at rates prevailing before 1348. The Ordinance of Laborers was vigorously enforced, although ultimately economically ineffective. It foundered on the "free-rider problem": it was to the benefit of each individual employer that others would be limited to lower wages, so that he could attract sufficient labor by offering a slightly better wage. Since everybody felt the same way, the limits on wages quickly unraveled. Characteristically, the employers (the gentry) were not prosecuted for offering illegal wages, while many laborers were punished for accepting them. The labor legislation, in general, was the focus of much popular hatred, and its enforcement was one of the important causes of the peasant revolts of 1381 (Fryde 1991:760). Another element of the "seigneurial reaction" was implemented by landlords in their private courts. Manorial courts increased their revenues after the Black Death, a remarkable achievement as the numbers of tenants had fallen drastically (Dyer 2002:286).

The magnates did better than the middle-rank and lesser elites, at least until 1380. The large landowners employed numerous retainers, whom they could and did employ to intimidate peasants to continue to accept the high rents and low wages that prevailed before 1348. In counties where their estates dominated, they also had a much better chance of locating runaway serfs and returning them to their land, or punishing them as an example to others. In short, they were able to use extraeconomic coercive means to stabilize their incomes, at least temporarily. In some (rare) cases, as on the Welsh Marches, lords were even able to increase their incomes by intensifying peasant oppression. For example, the Arundels increased their income from the lordship of Chirk in North Wales from £300 to £500 between 1320 and 1380. Henry the Bolingbroke used the occasion of his succession after the death of his father, John of Gaunt, to force the people of Cydweli to pay £1,575 (Dyer 2002:292). Such unpredictable and arbitrary exactions contributed to the Welsh uprising led by Glyn Dwr in 1400.

In general, the elites enjoyed a temporary success in postponing the effects of the depopulation brought about by the Black Death for about a generation. Wages rose gradually and reached their highest level only twenty to thirty years after the first epidemic (Dyer 2002:293). The incomes of lords declined, but not drastically. The aristocracy continued to enjoy a high level of expenditure to which they had become accustomed during the century around 1300. Another factor contributing to the well-being of elites was the initial success of the English in the Hundred Years' War. This is probably the explanation why the trade, industry, and towns continued to do well after 1348 (Dyer 2002:296).

In fact, the degree of urbanization of England increased in the late fourteenth century. In 1300 the population of London was estimated at 80,000, or 1.3 percent of the total English population. The poll taxes of 1377 indicated that the proportion of population living in London had increased to 1.7 percent. In other words, although the population of London declined to about 50,000, the rural population declined even faster. Several towns actually increased in size: Colchester from 4,000 to 6,000 and Coventry from 5,000 to 9,000. Larger towns such as Bristol, Norwich, Southampton, and York experienced a phase of prosperity at the end of the fourteenth century (Dyer 2002:296). Because towns suffered very much during the plague epidemics, and generally had a negative rate of population growth, we must conclude that rural population continued to flow to towns during the second half of the fourteenth century, even though the countryside had long ceased to be overpopulated. The most likely explanation for this seemingly paradoxical fact is the simultaneous push-pull conjuncture, where the push was the increased extraeconomic oppression of the rural population by lords and the pull was exerted by increased employment opportunities in towns aimed at satisfying the consumption of the same elite individuals.

Elites in Crisis

As it became clear that no more revenue could be squeezed out of the peasants, the elites increasingly sought other means of additional income. One avenue of advancement open to impoverished but ambitious individuals was to join the retinue of a great lord, or find employment with the royal government. Increased competition for such elite positions was manifested in the spread of literacy among the aristocracy. As Denholm-Young (1969:2) notes, during the fourteenth century the *miles literatus* ceased to be a rarity. (In the fifteenth century, when intraelite competition slackened, there was a decline in the student population of, for example, Oxford [Thomson 1983:351].) However, by far the most common employment was in the military.

The extent of aristocratic involvement in the war during the fourteenth century was remarkable, especially during the period 1338–61, when the English enjoyed a string of successes in France. For example, more than 900 knights served at Crécy and Calais, while 870 (of whom no fewer than 680 were English) participated in the royal expedition to France in 1359–60, and this was only a part of the mobilized forces, since England was fighting on several fronts at the same time (Ormrod 1990:149). To place these numbers in perspective, Denholm-Young (1969) estimated there were around 1,250 knights in England at the beginning of the thirteenth century.

Knights were paid at the rate of 2–4 s. per day, depending on the rank. Thus, two or three months of campaigning would add up to a substantial sum (£6–18), given that about £20 per year was needed to support a knight during the fourteenth century. Many archers were probably recruited from the ranks of impoverished lesser gentry (Powicke 1962). Although their rate of pay (2 d. per day) was relatively low, they could improve their fortunes by a windfall of booty or a ransom. In addition to wages, the spoils of war included plunder, ransoms paid by captured French noblemen, and indemnities paid by occupied fortresses and towns (*rachâts*). The order of magnitude of these cash flows is indicated by the Crown's portion: Edward III received more than £250,000 in ransoms for King John of France and King David of Scotland, and a similar amount from *rachâts* (Postan 1973:74–75). Finally, the conquests brought with them landed income. For example, when Normandy, Maine, and Anjou were conquered during a later stage of the Hundred Years' War, Henry V conferred lands worth about £30,000 on his followers (Bean 1991:566).

English medievalists have debated whether the Hundred Years' War paid for itself or resulted in a net loss (Postan 1973:63–80). Whatever the general answer, it is clear that for the elites it was a very lucrative enterprise, because the rewards went primarily to them, while most of the costs of the war (the bulk of taxation, purveyances, and so on) were borne by the commoners. Thus, according to the estimate by McFarlane, out of over £8 million in taxes levied for war purposes over the 120 years, half came from taxation on wool.

There is no question that the elites did very well out of the war, as long as it went well for the English. When Edward III returned to England in 1346, after the victorious battles of Crécy and Neville's Cross (where the Scots were defeated and King David II was captured), the rolls of parliament record that "all thanked God for the victory he had granted to their liege lord . . . and said that all the money they had given him had been well spent" (King 1979:157–58).

Eventually, however, the respite brought about by military successes in France was over. Anglo-French warfare broke out again in 1369, and during the 1370s the French were able to reconquer most of Aquitaine, leaving in English hands only a narrow strip of coastline between Bordeaux and Bayonne (Ormrod 1990:33). Social tensions had been increasing in the aftermath of the Black Death, and the poll tax of 1381 precipitated a major crisis, the Great Revolt of 1381 (Fryde 1991). Although the peasant revolts were speedily suppressed, they laid an indelible imprint on the landowner psyche. Parliaments became terrified that further taxes might provoke more risings, and for a time they refused to grant any more direct taxes. Thus, the Great Revolt of 1381 proved to be a turning point in the war with France, undermining the ability of the English to profit from the internal turmoil in France during the early years of the minority of Charles VI (Fryde 1996:5). It also accelerated the transition from direct domanial exploitation to the leasing of demesnes, which started in the late 1360s (Fryde 1991:762). During the first half of the fifteenth century, land incomes of the nobility continued to decline in value. Reductions of 20 percent were normal in southern and midland England, whereas in the northeast revenues fell by a third (Dyer 2002:337).

Squeezed by diminishing returns on the land and deprived of opportunities for overseas profits from conquest, the elites put more pressure on the state finances, resulting in a greater proportion of the Crown's income being diverted in their direction. If the annuity bill of Edward III in the 1360s was £13,000, by 1399 Richard II's bill was closer to £25,000 (representing a threefold increase in real terms). However, only a small proportion of the aristocracy could benefit from these funds, small relative to their numbers and appetites. A similar pressure from lesser gentry, coupled with the magnates' need for large retinues to defend their interests in parliaments, courts, and factional conflict, led to the development of what became known as "bastard feudalism." Mertes (1988: Appendix C) presents evidence that the average retinue of magnates (peers and bishops) increased from 50 during the first half of the fourteenth century to over 150 during the second half of the fifteenth.

The rise of huge baronial retinues was one of the outward manifestations of intense intraelite competition, the increasing factionalization of England's ruling class, and privatization of coercive power. It was one of the most important factors contributing to later civil wars, particularly during the Wars of the Roses period.

The Rise and Fall of State Finances

As we noted above, the demands made by the English state on the society during the thirteenth century were mild. Taxes stayed approximately constant or even declined in real terms before 1290, implying that the proportion of GDP going to the state plunged (since both GDP and population expanded greatly during the same period). Even during the local peak around 1300, after taxes were doubled, they were less than 2 percent of GDP. England was undertaxed and clearly could be made to yield more. What was needed, however, was a worthy cause that would unify the Crown, the aristocracy, and the commoners. This common cause was the war with France (King 1979:155).

Revenues of the Crown doubled during the early stages of the Hundred Years' War (figure 2.6). During the 1370s and 1380s, revenues stayed at roughly the same level, but since the population had been reduced by half, this represented another doubling of the tax burden. Additionally, the aim of the new poll taxes, first granted by Parliament in 1377, was to shift the burden of taxation toward the peasantry (King 1979:163).

Between 1369 and 1380 the English government incurred extraordinary expenditures amounting to more than £1.1 million (Fryde 1991:43). After some political struggle (the "Good Parliament" of 1376 rejected the Crown's requests for direct taxation, while the parliament of 1377 granted a direct subsidy in the novel form of a poll tax), the decision was reached to bring into the tax system a large segment of lower classes of the population that were previously exempt (Dyer 2002:284). Unprecedented taxes were imposed on the population in 1377, 1379, and 1381. In the first, everybody over age 14 was expected to pay 4 d., while the last demanded 12 d. from everybody over 15.

According to the calculations of W. M. Ormrod and Patrick O'Brien, the maximum yield from taxes (in real terms) was achieved during the decade centered on 1340 (1336–45). The general trend for the next century was down. This secular trend, however, was overlaid by shorter-term fluctuations, whose peaks (in 1300, 1340, 1380, and 1420) closely correlated with periods of intensified warfare against Scotland and France. Overall, between 1340 and the lowest point of 1460, the revenue from taxes declined almost threefold.

Rising Sociopolitical Instability

Popular immiseration, intraelite conflict, and the state's financial difficulties were the primary factors underlying the unraveling of the social order that was experienced by English society during the fourteenth century. However, the rise of sociopolitical instability between the early thirteenth century and the late fourteenth century (figure 2.7) was not a simple, unilineal dynamic. The rising secular trend was overlaid by a series of waves, which tended to occur every other generation. The most significant period of unrest during the thirteenth century was the crisis of 1258, leading into the "barons' wars" of 1263–67 (Mortimer 1994:77).

The next wave of internal war occurred in the 1320s, during the last half of Edward II's reign. It began with the unsuccessful rebellion of the barons of the Welsh Marches, the Battle of Boroughbridge, which the royal forces won, followed by the execution of the rebel leaders (1322). These events were followed by a successful rebellion of Mortimer and Isabella (1326), the deposition and murder of Edward II (1327), a rebellion led by Henry of Lancaster, which was put down by Mortimer (1329), the execution of Edmund, Earl of Kent, for plotting against the regime (1330), and finally the coup led by Edward III against the regime of Mortimer and Isabella, followed by the execution of Mortimer (1330). The regicide of Edward II marked a significant elevation in the intensity of intraelite conflict.

The reign of Edward III was relatively free of internal strife (except at its very end), because the focus of elite energy was directed toward the war against France, which initially met with great success. However, by the end of his reign, the French had reconquered most of the lands lost to the English, leading to the chain of events that eventually resulted in the Peasants' Revolt of 1381. Thus, the reign of Edward III's successor, Richard II (1377–98), was another period of enhanced sociopolitical instability in which strife between elite factions was accompanied by peasant uprisings. Between 1381 and 1405 at least five more popular revolts (in addition to that of 1381) broke out, or were averted only at the last moment. Most of these were regional in extent, with only the Cheshire rising of 1403 evolving into a major civil war (Fryde 1991:797). Serious elite infighting started with the uprising of the "Lords Appellant" in 1387–88, followed by the coup d'état in which Richard II regained control of the government (1391). The civil war reached its peak in 1397–99, when Richard II had three lords appellant convicted of treason and executed. The following year Henry of Bolingbroke deposed Richard II and had himself crowned Henry IV (Richard died or was murdered in prison in 1400). Finally, in 1400 there was a great uprising in Wales led by Glyn Dwr, which lasted eight years.

The Late Medieval Crime Wave

The fourteenth and fifteenth centuries were also a period of heightened criminal activity, the so-called "late medieval crime wave" (Dean 2001). Based on her analyses of the coroner's rolls, Barbara Hanawalt (1976, 1979) showed that the best explanations for changes in the pattern of crime in fourteenth-century England were economic changes and war. Economic crimes increased during the periods of scarcity. Thus, the number of burglaries increased enormously during the period of 1315–19 (figure 2.9) as a result of the Great Famine. Annual statistics on economic crimes followed very closely fluctuations in the price of wheat (see Hanawalt 1979: Figure 12).

Homicides tended to be primarily affected by political strife and war. This conclusion is supported by the more detailed analysis of criminal patterns focusing on each county (Hanawalt 1979:229–38). For example, Herefordshire was the scene of some of the major phases of the civil war that led to the deposition of Edward II, and the highest peak in crime in this county was achieved not during the famine of 1315–17 but during a civil war. The periods of Scottish wars (1314–19, 1322–23, and 1332–37) all coincided with rises in crime rates in Yorkshire. "War also contributed to the problems of the nobles' households and gang activity in general and correlated with increased murder. The Commons were undoubtedly correct in their complaints about the increased horrors of gangs and pardoned felons who were king's veterans" (Hanawalt 1979:238). As a result, homicide rates greatly increased from 1300 to 1348 (figure 2.9). The increased murder rate probably persisted during the second half of the fourteenth century, as suggested by data from rural Northamptonshire (table 2.14). The murder rate of fourteen to eighteen during 1360–79, compared to the average of eleven in 1300–29, implies that the homicide incidence

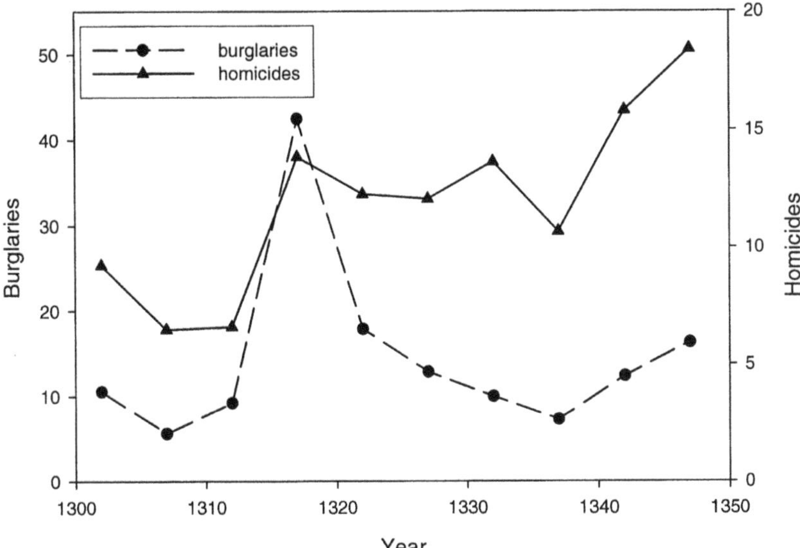

Figure 2.9 Number of crimes (burglaries and homicides) committed in eight counties of England during 1300–1348 (averages over the counties and five-year periods) (Hanawalt 1979: Tables 9 and 10).

per capita nearly tripled during the fourteenth century, given the post–Black Death population decrease.

Intraelite conflict took various forms, ranging from full-scale civil war to persistent infighting between noble factions down to small-scale feuding and individual-on-individual violence. In fourteenth century Gloucestershire, more than half the resident knights and esquires committed at least one felony or trespass (Saul 1981:174).

2.5 Depression (1400–1485)

As we stressed in the introductory chapter, all temporal breakpoints are to a greater or lesser degree arbitrary, and this applies with particular force to the year of 1400. There was no abrupt transition in that year, and in fact, outbreaks of civil war continued to arrive in a recurrent fashion.

General Population and Peasant Economy

During the fifteenth century the population numbers in England stayed relatively constant, in the range of 2–2.5 million. Some authorities depict the population trend as essentially flat (e.g., Dyer 2002: Figure 2), while

TABLE 2.14
Average number of homicides per year in rural Northamptonshire

Period	*Homicides*
1300–1329	11
1330–39	13
1340–49	21
1350–59	10
1360–69	18
1370–79	14

Source: Hanawalt (1976: 303).

others suggest that the population continued to decline toward 1450, although at a much slower rate than during the second half of the fourteenth century (Hatcher and Bailey 2001: Figure 3). Inasmuch as the replacement rates for both commoners and landowners tended to be below one before 1450, the second view is probably closer to the truth.

However, it is likely that regional variation and population redistribution were more important than whatever national trend obtained. People moved from rural areas to towns and from one village to another. Between 1370 and 1520 at least 2,000 villages were deserted in England (Dyer 2000:350).

Low population densities translated into greatly improved living standards. Real wages continued to increase during the first half of the fifteenth century, although at a slowing rate (see figure 2.3). Peasants ate less bread and more meat, fish, and dairy products. For example, bread accounted for about half the value of foodstuffs consumed by harvest workers in Norfolk in 1300. In the fifteenth century the proportion of bread in diet declined to 15 percent of the total. At the same time, the proportion of meat increased from 8 percent to 30–40 percent (Dyer 1989:82). Land-peasant ratios increased greatly. By 1500, one-eighth of rural householders in England held fifty acres or more, compared with the tiny proportion before the epidemics (Dyer 2002:358).

As we remarked in chapter 1, the great puzzle of late-medieval English demographic history is why excellent real wages, consumption patterns, land-peasant ratios, and low rents did not translate into renewed population growth. All these conditions were in place by 1400, yet population growth resumed only a century later. One possible cause of the lower birth rate could have been late marriage (e.g., Dyer 2002:276). Yet this hypothesis is not really satisfactory, because it does not explain why population growth resumed in the sixteenth century. What changed around 1500 that caused population growth to resume? We return to this question later when we discuss the role of sociopolitical instability.

Elite Dynamics

At the same time that the commoners enjoyed increasingly better incomes and consumption levels, the incomes of the landholding elites continued to decline. Bean (1991:579) points to 1420–70 as the period of a marked fall in landed revenue for many estates (while 1470–1500 were years of recovery). There was significant variation between different regions: reductions in land value of 20 percent were normal in southern and midland England. In Cornwall the lords lost less ground, while in northeast England revenues fell by a third (Dyer 2002:337).

The decline in aristocratic revenues was matched by decreasing consumption. Earlier we mentioned that around 1300, the English consumed 20,000 tuns of French wine. By the 1460s less than 5,000 tuns were imported, and wine imports did not recover until after 1490 (Dyer 1989:104).

> To sum up, the aristocracy as a whole expanded their consumption in the thirteenth century; they drank more wine, rebuilt their monasteries, cathedrals and castles, and surrounded their houses by moats. In the fourteenth and fifteenth centuries they experienced greater or lesser degrees of financial embarrassment. . . . Even those skilful and fortunate families who did add to their estates still had to cope with the fact that newly acquired assets were deteriorating in value. Cash incomes declined, and real incomes declined still further because of the operation of price scissors. The problem was first felt in the twenty or thirty years before the Black Death. After that catastrophe the aristocracy felt vulnerable but did not suffer drastic drops in income. The most serious decline came after 1400, and the worst was over by the 1470s or 1480s. (Dyer 1989:108)

Falling income from land meant that many aristocratic families could not continue to maintain their status. As a result, the balance between upward and downward mobility had to shift decisively in favor of the latter. This process affected all ranks (tables 2.9a–c). The numbers of magnates declined from around 200 barons in 1300 to 60 peers in 1500. There were 3,000 middle-rank aristocrats (knights and esquires) in 1300 and only 1,300 in 1500. Thus, the numbers of both the magnates and the middle-rank elites apparently declined by two-thirds. It is harder to quantify the numerical decline of the lower-rank elites, but it was probably on the same order of magnitude.

The reduction in elite numbers was a result of several processes working together. First, some lineages were extinguished when they backed the wrong side in the civil war or coup d'état. The intensity of this process tended to fluctuate in cyclical fashion. For example, of the sixteen new earls, marquises, or dukes created during the troubled reigns of Edward II and Richard II, at least fourteen were executed, exiled, or demoted within five years of their creation. Of the thirteen created by Edward III, on the other hand, not one suffered that fate (Given-Wilson 1987:54). Second, many noble lineages could not maintain status because of diminishing revenues. Thus, George Neville, Duke of Bedford, was quietly dropped from the list of peers in 1478, while the Marquis of Berkeley disappeared in 1492. Some lost their status temporarily, such as the lords Clinton, who dropped out from 1460 to 1514 (Stone 1965:53). Similar forces drove downward mobility from the middle ranks into gentry and from gentry to yeomanry. Finally, negative replacement rates between 1350 and 1450 (see figure 2.4) meant that many more lineages than before or after this period failed in the male line. Their fortunes were often merged with other lineages of the same rank, keeping the latter afloat in the face of the declining returns from the land.

The forces contracting elite numbers generated an enormous amount of social tension, because many members of the privileged class were not content to sink quietly into the ranks of yeomen. This was an important factor contributing to the civil wars of the fifteenth century.

Another factor undermining political stability was the growth of armed retinues associated with magnates. Henry Percy, Earl of Northumberland, was spending a third to a half of his total income of £3,000 on fees and annuities to supporters (Dyer 1989). Retainers were paid between £2 and £10 per annum, which would be a very welcome supplement to an income of £10–20 per annum.

State Fiscal Collapse and Onset of the Civil War

The reign of Henry V was another period of internal stability (apart from minor incidents of Lollard persecution) and successful warfare against France, similar to the middle years of Edward III. The years of Henry VI's minority were also relatively peaceful. However, in 1429 the English failed to capture Orléans (the city was relieved by Jeanne d'Arc), and their position in France began to unravel. In 1442 the French conquered Gascony (except Bordeaux and Bayonne), and during the years 1448–51 the English were almost completely expelled from France: the French reconquest of Maine (1448), Normandy (1450), and Bordeaux and Bayonne (1451) left only Calais in English hands at the end of the Hundred Years' War. This string of defeats triggered a series of events that had a remarkable resemblance to what followed English reverses at the end of Edward III's reign.

By 1433 the government was in increasingly dire fiscal straits (Pollard 2000:112): the accumulated debt was £168,000, and the income from all taxation voted and to be paid in the next two years was assigned. The annual

TABLE 2.15
Crown debts, 1290–1450

Year	*Debt (£000)*	*Reference*
1289	110	Raban (2000)
1307	200	Ormrod (1999)
1339	300	Ormrod (1999)
1433	168	Ormrod (1999)
1450	372	Ormrod (1999)

deficit on regular and domestic income and expenditure alone was over £21,000, while the defense of the possessions in France against the resurgent French required huge outlays. By 1449 the situation had become infinitely worse. The economic depression of the mid-fifteenth century (Hatcher 1996) meant that the landed revenue of the Crown had declined. Recession and a trade embargo with Flanders halved the income from customs and poundage. In addition, the reign of Henry VI saw a steady alienation of royal properties, many for terms of life or lives. Royal annuities cost the Exchequer around £30,000, accounting for close to a third of all royal revenues (Given-Wilson 1987:155). Parliament grudgingly voted a half subsidy in 1445 and none in 1447. In 1448 Crown jewels had to be sold. In 1449 the total Crown debt rose to the staggering sum of £372,000 (Pollard 2000:126).

This was the second time that the state debt had reached the unsustainable level (table 2.15). But Edward III, a century before, was saved by his military successes in France. Not the least factor in Edward's ability to weather financial crisis was the enormous ransom of John II, who was captured at Poitiers. In 1450 the military situation in France was reversed.

Henry VI was intermittently insane and unfit to rule. The government lost the last vestiges of legitimacy with the disastrous loss of all French possessions (with the sole exception of Calais), and now it was broke and could not even maintain internal order.

The general level of lawlessness and disorder increased during the 1440s and especially 1450s (figure 2.10). Royal justice came to be perverted for partisan ends, "particularly in East Anglia, Kent, and Sussex, where extortion, fraud, theft, violence, and intimidation . . . had not been witnessed on such a scale since the reign of Richard II" (Pollard 2000:125).

Private feuds, riots, and armed clashes reached such proportions between 1448 and 1455 that at least one-sixth of the peerage were at some time or another imprisoned for disreputable conduct (Lander 1976:20). The feuds of nobility gradually became private wars, and those in turn

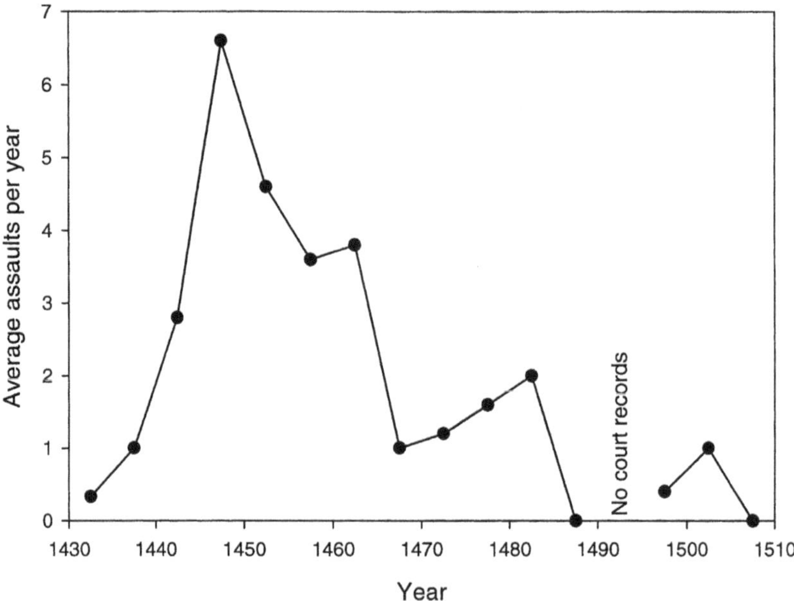

Figure 2.10 Average number of assault cases per five-year interval at Kempsey, Worcestershire (Dyer 1980:371).

merged into general civil warfare, later called the Wars of the Roses (Storey 1966).

Here is a list (probably incomplete) of counties affected by major elite quarrels around 1450, culled from Storey (1966). (1) The west (Cornwall and Devon, spilling into Somerset and Wiltshire): the feud of the Earl of Devon against Lord Bonville. At one point, the Earl of Devon led a private army of 5,000–6,000 retainers and allies. (2) The north (Cumberland, Westmorland, and Yorkshire): persistent guerilla warfare between the adherents of the Nevilles and the Percies. (3) Bedfordshire: the feud of Lords Grey and Fanhope. (4) Norfolk and Suffolk: the minions of the Duke of Suffolk against Sir John Falstoff and the Pastons. (5) Oxfordshire and Warwickshire: the quarrel between the Stafford and Harcourt families. (6) Gloucestershire: the Berkeleys against the Countess of Shrewsbury. (7) Southern Lincolnshire: the exploits of Sir William Tailbois. (8) Derbyshire: the Longfords against the Blounts.

The year of 1450 was the year of a major popular rebellion led by Jack Cade. In fact, the pressure in Kent had been rising for more than a decade: there were disturbances in that county in 1438, 1443, 1445, and 1448. The Cade rebellion spread widely across southern England. In Wiltshire a mob lynched Bishop Ayscough, and there were risings in Salisbury, Isle of Wight, Glocester, and Essex. Later in 1450 (August–September) there was another wave of risings in Sussex, Wiltshire, Essex, and Kent (Storey 1966). Jack Cade's Revolt was finally suppressed in 1451.

The collapse of royal finances in 1449 was followed by state breakdown. The parliament of 1449–50 impeached the Earl of Suffolk (he was murdered as he tried to leave the country). The ensuing struggle for power between Richard of York and Edmund Beaufort, Duke of Somerset, escalated into open warfare in 1455. The following year Somerset was defeated and killed in the Battle of St. Albans. Between 1459 and 1471 the civil war was fought between the factions led by Queen Margaret and by Richard of York. York was killed in 1461, but his son Edward IV was crowned the same year. Henry VI was captured and imprisoned in the Tower, where he died (most likely was murdered) in 1471.

The period from 1471 to 1483 was a peaceful lull, but when Edward IV died, he was succeeded by his son, Edward V, who was only twelve years old. Conflict erupted between two elite factions, one led by the king's maternal uncle Lord Rivers and the other by the paternal uncle Richard of Gloucester. Richard won, and Rivers and some other anti-Richard leaders were executed without trial. Edward V was deposed and, in all probability, later murdered in the Tower, along with his brother. Finally, in 1485 Richard III himself fell at the battle of Bosworth Field, and Henry Tudor became king of England.

Bosworth marked the end of the Wars of the Roses, and indeed, the intensity of internal warfare rapidly declined after 1485. There was a rising in Northumberland in 1489, a rebellion led by the pretender Perkin Warbeck in 1495–97, and an insurrection in Cornwall in 1497. The last aftershock of the troubles of the fifteenth century was a rather minor uprising in Yorkshire called the Pilgrimage of Grace (1536–37), after which England was to enjoy a century of internal stability.

The intensity of intraelite conflict during the Wars of the Roses was extremely high. Three kings were deposed and killed, and numerous magnates were executed, often without trial. Many ending on the losing side of a battle were simply made to kneel in the mud and were beheaded on the spot. However, its direct effect on the population of England must have been insignificant. It is unlikely that more than 50,000 (out of the total population of 2–2.5 million) ever took part in the battles of the civil war (Storey 1966). Military operations affected only a small proportion of the kingdom.

On the other hand, the direct losses of combatants in the battles of the Wars of the Roses were just the tip of the iceberg. It was not the struggle for the throne itself that damaged the fabric of the society but the general increase in sociopolitical instability during the period of 1445–85. Instability manifested itself in increased interpersonal crime, banditry, feuding, and factional infighting. The political struggles of the great lords were themselves a manifestation of this underlying social trend rather than its direct cause.

We argue that high sociopolitical instability during 1380–1485 (and within this period, particularly 1380–1410 and 1445–1485) damaged the productive capacity of the society (its carrying capacity). The specific mechanism was the establishment of a "landscape of fear." The most clear-cut case can be made for the peripheries, which were largely left to fend for themselves. In the north, persistent Scottish raids depopulated large swaths of the Borderlands. In fact, the north was essentially abandoned by the Crown to the Nevilles and Percies (who fought each other incessantly, taking opposite sides in the York-Lancaster conflict). The southern seashore suffered badly from the raids of the French pirates, and many coastal areas were abandoned as the population moved inland. In Wales, the Glyn Dwr rebellion and the following reconquest had caused widespread destruction (Pollard 2000:172). On a smaller scale, land was lost in East Anglia from inundation as a result of failure of flood control measures installed in the thirteenth century. All these abandoned lands could not be put to productive uses.

The situation in the central parts of the kingdom was not as dire as on the periphery, but the life of a cultivator was precarious there as well. As the list of intraelite conflicts, given above, indicates, the breakdown of law and order in the English countryside in the middle of the fifteenth century was the rule rather than the exception. Common people were very vulnerable to intraelite fighting. Many factions targeted the tenants of their rivals, or any others who were caught in the middle of conflict, for intimidation, extortion, robbery, and simple murder. For example, Bishop Lacy of Exeter recorded in his register that, during the private war between the Earl of Devon and Lord Bonville in 1451, some of his tenants at Clyst (east of Exeter) "dared not occupy the land" (Fryde 1991:193). Followers of Thomas Percy, Lord Egremont, even after his death in the battle of Northampton in 1460, continued to hold the castle of Wressle in Yorkshire against all comers, using it as a base for raiding and harrying the country nearby (Bohna 2000:94). It was impossible to cultivate land when you or your dependents could be robbed or murdered at any moment, your work horses stolen, and your house burned down around your ears.

Some areas were probably more secure because local elites maintained peace; others were less so. Strong places, such as walled towns, also created a zone of security around them. A landscape of fear came into being, which meant that a proportion of arable land could not be cultivated, thus lowering the overall carrying capacity, the number of people that the English soil could support.

The fifteenth century was a time of high population mobility. A facile explanation would be that fifteenth-century Englishmen and women were particularly footloose. Generally, however, people need weighty reasons to abandon places in which they have invested time and labor. In the fourteenth century such reasons could include economic oppression by landed elites, and in the fifteenth century a breakdown of law and order.

We also know that a great number of English villages were abandoned during the fifteenth century. Some were probably "murdered" by landlords who wanted to turn them into sheep pasture. Others—and this applies particularly to the smaller ones—could have been abandoned because they were too insecure.

Some migrants moved from one rural area to another, while others moved to towns. We know that the majority of towns continued to do well during this period. Since premodern towns were population sinks, the only way in which they could maintain their numbers was through a constant influx of immigrants. When the Tudor regime pacified the countryside, it removed an important reason for rural dwellers to move to the security of towns. As a result, during the early Tudor period most towns lost their population, and some of them simply withered on the vine.

2.6 Conclusion

The Major Predictions of the Demographic-Structural Theory Appear to Be Borne Out by the Data . . .

The great mass of data that we have reviewed in this chapter suggests that the Malthusian-Ricardian theory of Postan and Le Roy Ladurie works quite well in explaining the demographic, economic, and social dynamics of England up until the mid-fourteenth century. The most striking observation is the almost perfect inverse relationship between population pressure and the real wage (conversely, there is a very good correlation between population pressure and the misery index; see figure 2.1). Incidentally, strong dynamical patterns, such as the one documented in figure 2.1, support the idea that historical processes can be profitably studied using the theoretical and data analytical methods of nonlinear dynamics.

The "medieval depression"—a failure of population growth to resume once the aftershocks of the Black Death died out—is, however, a significant anomaly from the point of view of the crude Malthusian model. We have argued in this chapter that what is needed to understand the medieval depression is the elite- and state-centered perspective of the demographic-structural theory. The key factor preventing population growth during the period of 1380–1485 was high sociopolitical instability that manifested as the recurrent breakdown of law and order. In turn, law and order could not be established on a permanent basis until the numbers and appetites of the elites could be brought in line with the productive capacity of the society. In other words, population growth could not resume until the problem of elite overproduction was somehow solved.

For a variety of reasons, it took an unusually long time for this to happen. By 1485, however, economic hardship and internal warfare during the fourteenth and fifteenth centuries had pruned the size of the English ruling class to roughly one-third of what it was in the early fourteenth century. Thus, the numbers of magnates declined from about 200 barons to some 60 lay peers, the middle ranks (knights and esquires) shrank from 3,000 to 1,300, and the numbers of lesser gentry declined from perhaps 15,000 to 5,000 (see tables 2.10 and 2.11).

Another aspect of the same process was the decline of the extreme economic inequality that developed in England by 1300. At the lower end of the social hierarchy, population decline greatly increased land-peasant ratios and improved consumption patterns of even the poor. At the higher end, the huge fortunes of the fourteenth century, such as that of the earls of Lancaster (£11,000 in 1311) or the dukes of Lancaster (£12,500 in 1394), were gone by the fifteenth century. Thus, the maximum income assessed in 1436 (Gray 1934) was £3,230, belonging to Richard of York, well below that of even the earls of Cornwall of the early fourteenth century (£6,000 in 1300). The other incomes over £3,000 were those of the Earl of Warwick and the Duke of Buckingham. By contrast, around 1300 there were six earls who enjoyed an income of more than £3,000 per year. Later in the fifteenth century even these fortunes tended to disappear. The York inheritance was merged into the Crown as a result of Richard of York's son being crowned Edward IV in 1461. The Warwick fortune was absorbed by the Crown after 1471, when Richard Neville, Earl of Warwick, was killed in battle fighting against Edward IV.

. . . *But the Theory Does Not Capture All the Complexities of the Historical Process*

We need to stress two important qualifications to our generally positive assessment of the fit between the theory and data in the case of the Plantagenet cycle: the importance of exogenous factors, and the operation of other endogenous processes that are not, strictly speaking, part of the demographic structural theory.

One important exogenous factor was the influence of climate. The cold and wet years after 1315 apparently served as a trigger for the beginning of population decline. The global cooling following the medieval optimum probably depressed crop yields, and therefore decreased the carrying capacity of the medieval–early modern agrarian system.

An even more obviously important exogenous shock was administered by the arrival of the Eurasia-wide plague pandemic in England in 1348. Although it is likely that population would have continued to decline even in the absence of the Black Death, it would probably have declined much more slowly and not as deeply as it actually did.

The geopolitical situation of England with respect to its neighbors, Scotland and France, is another exogenous factor of great importance. As we argued above, it was the dealings with France that served to lengthen the disintegrative phase of the Plantagenet cycle.

Turning now to endogenous factors, we note that standard demographic-structural models predict continuous sociopolitical instability and a gradual numerical decline of the ruling class. Yet in actuality, instability waxes and wanes in waves, interspersed with relatively peaceful periods in between. This is a general occurrence during the disintegrative phases of many secular cycles and has been termed the "fathers-and-sons" cycle (Turchin 2003b, 2006).

In the case of Plantagenet England, there were three such fathers-and-sons cycles, which interacted in a repeatable way with changes in England's geopolitical environment. The essential dynamic of each cycle was (1) a centripetal phase, characterized by unified elites, increased taxation, and success in external wars, followed by (2) a centrifugal phase, characterized by state fiscal problems, intraelite competition shading into civil war, and loss of external conquests.

The basic dynamic was set during the reigns of Edward I (1272–1307) and his son, Edward II (1307–27). Edward I reversed a century-long decline in Crown revenues (see figure 2.6) and conquered Scotland, profiting from its collapse into civil war. Edward II, in contrast, presided over an increasingly fractious nobility and declining revenues. He experienced a disastrous defeat at the hands of the Scots at Bannockburn (1314) and lost Scotland. Finally, he lost his crown and his life as a result of the civil wars of the 1320s.

The next iteration of the same pattern came with the reigns of Edward III (1327–77) and Richard II (1377–99). Edward III unified the elites, achieved the highest rate of taxation in medieval English history, and conquered half of France. His successor, Richard II, alienated a major segment of the nobility (and executed some of them). His reign saw declining revenues and the refusal of parliaments to vote more taxes, along with widespread popular uprisings. Like Edward II, he was overthrown and later died, possibly murdered, in prison.

The last cycle was the combined Lancastrian and Yorkist period. During the reign of Henry V and the infancy of Henry VI, England experienced a period of national unification, relative fiscal stability, and successful conquest in France. Beginning in the 1430s, however, it gradually slid into state bankruptcy, intraelite conflict, territorial loss in France, and finally all-out civil war. The last battle of the Wars of the Roses in 1485 was not only the end of the third mini-cycle of fathers and sons, it was also the end of the grand secular cycle of Plantagenet England.

Chapter 3

Early Modern England: The Tudor-Stuart Cycle (1485–1730)

3.1 Overview of the Cycle

As the start of the cycle we take the year when the Tudor dynasty was established, marking the end of the long period of instability that culminated in the Wars of the Roses. The year 1485 is also a good candidate for a turning point in the population history of England, when the medieval population depression was succeeded by the first signs of demographic growth. The end of the cycle is harder to pinpoint. We chose 1730 because that was the last quinquennium of negative population growth in Wrigley et al. (1997) data, but another possible endpoint is 1750, since sustained population growth resumed only after that date. The secular cycle encompasses the Tudor, Stuart, and the beginning of the Hanoverian dynasties.

Trends in Population and Economy

The population trajectory of early modern England was dominated by two trends: sustained population growth between the early sixteenth century and the mid-seventeenth century, followed by population stagnation until the mid-eighteenth century (figure 3.1a). One factor that we need to take into account in order to interpret the observed pattern is the acceleration of scientific and technical progress, which eventually (after our period) culminated in the Industrial Revolution. The chief enabling factor of the Industrial Revolution was the great progress in agricultural productivity that began during the seventeenth century (figure 3.1a). Increasing average yields of an acre of cropland meant that English agriculture could feed more people. In other words, the carrying capacity began increasing soon after 1600.

The main variable in the Malthusian-Ricardian theory is not the total number of people but the number of people in relation to resources, or the population pressure on resources. Population pressure can be estimated by dividing actual population numbers by the maximum number that can be fed within a certain geographic region given current technology. The appendix at the end of this chapter calculates the carrying capacity of England

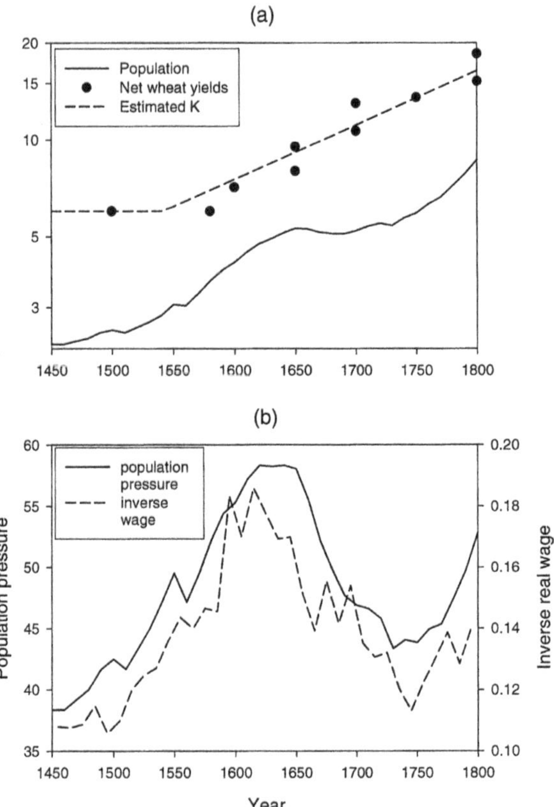

Figure 3.1 Detrending population trajectory for England (Turchin 2005, see also the appendix at the end of this chapter). (a) Population numbers (in millions), net yields (in bushels per acre), and estimated carrying capacity (in millions of people) in England, 1450–1800 (all variables plotted on a log scale). (b) Detrended population ("population pressure") trajectory (solid line) and inverse real wages (dashed line).

as a function of changing yields per acre of cropland, and figure 3.1b plots the dynamics of population pressure between 1450 and 1800.

We see that at the same time that population numbers stagnated, population pressure decreased substantially, owing to increasing agricultural productivity of cropland. As a result, between the late fifteenth century and the mid-eighteenth century, population pressure, but not numbers, traced out a typical secular cycle. To check on our calculations, we also plotted the "misery index" (inverse real wage) in figure 3.1b. The general parallelism between the two curves supports our procedure for estimating the population pressure.

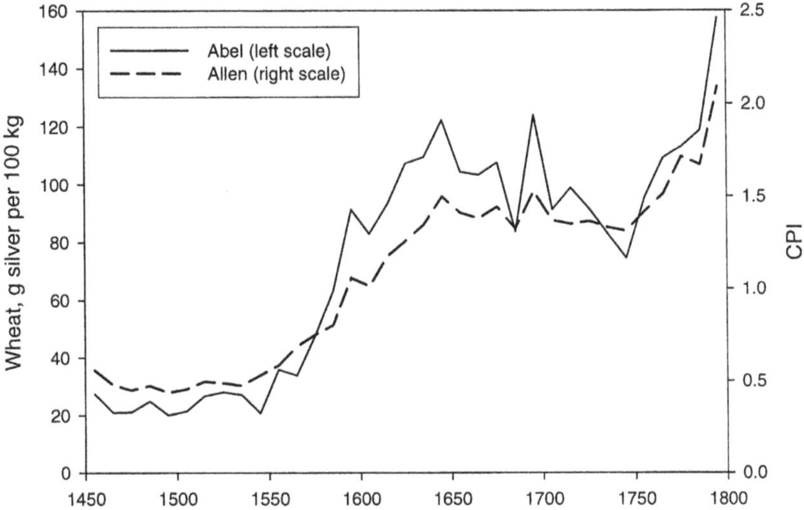

Figure 3.2 Dynamics of prices (decadal averages) in England,1450–1800. Solid line: the price of wheat in silver equivalents (Abel 1980). Dashed line: CPI of a basket of consumables (Allen 1992).

This period also saw a very rapid inflation, the famous price revolution of the sixteenth century (figure 3.2). Between the 1540s and 1600 the price of wheat quadrupled, from 20 to over 80 g of silver per quintal (100 kg). At its peak in the 1640s (and again in the 1690s), the price of wheat exceeded 120 g per quintal—a sixfold increase over the century since 1540.

Social Structure and Elite Dynamics

The apex of the social hierarchy in early modern England was occupied by the magnates—the lay peers (barons, viscounts, earls, and dukes), the spiritual lords (archbishops and bishops), top government administrators, and influential court figures. The number of peers during the Tudor cycle varied between fewer than 60 and 170 (table 3.1a). There were fewer than thirty bishops and no abbots after the dissolution of the monasteries in the 1530s. Not only did the numbers of the higher clergy decline after the reformation, but their social status was considered inferior to that of lay peers (Stone 1976:241).

The bulk of the middle-rank elites consisted of the county gentry—esquires, knights, and (later) baronets, numbering between 1,300 and 4,400 (table 3.1b). The numbers of the lesser elites, the "parish gentry," varied between 5,000 and 15,000 (table 3.1c). In addition to the landed gentry, the elite stratum included lawyers above the barrister level, the urban elites

TABLE 3.1
The numbers and average incomes of elites during the Tudor-Stuart cycle

Period	*Number*	*Avg. income (£)*	*Income (quarters)*	*Tons of wheat*
(a) Magnates (Peers)				
1500	60			
1540	60	400–1,400[a]	1,000–3,500	220–760
1600	55			
1615	81			
1628	126			
1640	160	6,000[b]	2,600	567
1700	170			
(b) Middle ranks (county elites)				
1500	1,300 county gentry (500 knights, 800 esquires)			
1524[a]	1,300 (500 knights, 800 esquires)	Knights: 120–200 Esquires: 50–80	320–520 130–210	70–115 28–46
1640	4,400 (1,400 baronets and knights, 3,000 esquires)	Knights: 500–1000 Esquires: 100–300	220–430 45–130	48–94 10–28
1700	3,000 (1,000 greater gentry, 2,000 lesser gentry)			
(c) Lesser elites (parish gentry)				
1500	5,000 gentlemen	17	64	14
1540	5,000 armigerous gentry			
1640	15,000 armigerous gentry	< 100	< 43	9
1700	10,000 country gentlemen	240	100	22

Sources: For magnates, Mingay (1976).
[a] Data for 1524 from Britnell (1997:191).
[b] Data for 1640 from Stone (1965:762).

(wholesalers, large-scale exporters, customs farmers, and financiers), and the parish clergy.

As to commoners, Stone (1976:240) describes a tripartite division: (1) the lesser and the more substantial yeomen, the husbandmen, the artisans, shopkeepers, and small traders; (2) the living-out laborers, both rural and urban, agricultural and industrial; and (3) the apprentices and living-in servants, and those dependent on charity (widows, the aged, and the unemployed).

Before 1540 the numbers of aristocrats of all ranks stayed flat (table 3.1). Between 1540 and 1640, however, elite numbers roughly tripled. Because the general population increased during this period by only 80 percent (from 2.8 million to 5.1 million), English society became significantly more top-heavy. After 1640, the numbers of middle-rank and lesser elites declined by about one-third, while the number of peers continued to grow, although at a much slower rate than before 1640.

The changes affecting lesser clergy were more complex. There were 9,000–10,000 parishes in medieval England (Moorman 1946:5). Toward the end of the Plantagenet cycle, however, a high proportion of parishes did not have a resident curate, or even a parish church. During the disturbed period of 1540–60 there was a sharp decline in the number entering ministry (Stone 1972:80). In the diocese of Canterbury, of 274 documented livings, 107 were without an incumbent in 1560. In the archdeaconry of Oxford the number of rectors, vicars, and curates declined from 371 in 1526 to 270 in 1586 (Stone 1972:80). After 1600, the numbers of local clergy increased very rapidly, and by 1640 there were not enough livings to satisfy the demand. In 1688, Gregory King estimated there were 10,000 clergy in England, an estimate revised to 12,000 by Lindert and Williamson (1982). Thus, the numbers of lesser clergy at least doubled since 1500. But the numbers do not tell the whole story. The quality and status, although not income, of parish clergy rose during the early seventeenth century. "The late medieval parish priest was little more than a semi-literate dirt-farmer of dubious morals: the Caroline minister of a parish had a university degree, strong religious convictions, a comfortable house, some books on his shelves" (Stone 1972:81). In other words, during the seventeenth century employment as a parochial clergyman became a "spillover reservoir" for surplus elites.

State Finances

In nominal terms the state revenues continued to increase throughout the cycle, with what appear to be minor fluctuations around the trend. When deflated by the price of wheat, however, the pattern of change becomes more complex (figure 3.3). During the first phase until around 1550, real revenues increased more than threefold. During the second half of the sixteenth century, the trend inverted, and the purchasing power of Crown revenues lost two-thirds of its value. This reversal was entirely due to the price inflation of the sixteenth century. Between 1600 and 1640 revenues fluctuated at a low level. Interestingly, because population continued to increase, on the eve of the Great Revolution per capita tax rates declined to half of what they were in the late fifteenth century.

The Revolution saw the first spurt of increase, followed by a slight decline under the Restoration. Finally, there was a great and sustained growth in real revenues in the decades around 1700, which finally took them to levels beyond the mid-sixteenth century peak (figure 3.3).

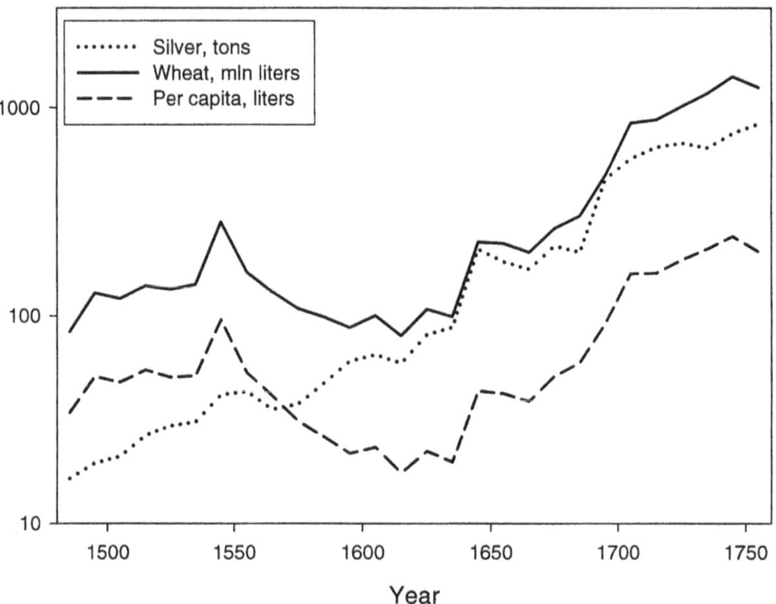

Figure 3.3 Total revenues of the English state, 1485–1755 (ESFDB 1995). Dotted line: revenues expressed in silver equivalent. Solid line: revenues in terms of wheat. Dashed line: real per capita revenues.

Sociopolitical Stability

The period between the end of the Wars of the Roses and the onset of the Great Revolution was quite peaceful (table 3.2). A partial exception was the two decades in the mid-sixteenth century, which were characterized by dynastic instability, religious strife, and financial difficulties—the so-called mid-Tudor crisis (Jones 1973). This instability, however, never escalated into a full-blown crisis (Matusiak 2005). A series of rebellions that flared up between 1536 and 1554 (the Pilgrimage of Grace, the Cornwall Rising, Kett's and Wyatt's rebellions) were regional in character, did not seriously threaten the central authorities, and were rapidly suppressed (Loades 1999:150–53, 173, 177–78, 193–95).

The period of 1640–60, by contrast, saw a full-scale state collapse, followed by a lengthy and bitter civil war. There was a relatively peaceful interlude during the Restoration, which was followed by a second period of instability, involving violent overthrow of the government, during 1685–92 (table 3.2). The eighteenth century was very peaceful, apart from two Jacobite risings in Scotland, which were rapidly suppressed.

The coin hoards' trajectory during 1500–1800 is dominated by the peak associated with the Great Revolution (figure 3.4). Two secondary peaks

TABLE 3.2
Occurrence of rebellions, coups d'état, civil wars, and other instances of internal war in England, 1500–1603, and England and Scotland, 1603–1800

Period	*Description*
1536–37	Pilgrimage of Grace (the Catholic rebellion in Yorkshire)
1549–50	Kett's Rebellion, Cornwall Rising
1554	Wyatt's Rebellion
1639–40	Scottish rebellion: the Bishops' Wars
1642–47	Civil War
1648–51	Second Civil War
1655	Penruddock rising in Salisbury
1660	Monk's coup; restoration of James II
1666	Revolt of Scottish Covenanters
1679	Revolt of Scottish Covenanters
1685	Monmouth and Argyll rebellions
1687–92	Glorious Revolution, with intervention by France
1715–16	Jacobite rebellion in Scotland
1745–46	Scottish rising (Jacobite pretender)

Sources: After Sorokin (1937) and Tilly (1993), supplemented by Stearns (2001).

are also present. One of them reflects the second period of sociopolitical instability, associated with the Glorious Revolution. Another one, in the mid-sixteenth century, probably has less to do with internal instability in England (although this period includes Wyatt's Rebellion) than with events outside it: the English-Scottish succession war and suppression of a major rebellion in Ireland.

3.2 Expansion (1485–1580)

General Population and Economy

After a long period of stagnation, the population of England began expanding sometime around 1500. Some scholars point to the 1480s as the time when the population started to increase, others to the 1510s (Hatcher 1977). Certainly by the 1520s the population was increasing briskly (Britnell 1997:246). We lack good population data for the period before 1540, but one indirect sign of expansion is the jump in the replacement rates detected in the inquisitions post mortem around 1500 (but these data primarily tell us what was happening with the landed elites). Another sign is the intense rebuilding activity by peasants of their houses, with a concentration of new construction in the period 1440–1520 (Dyer 2002:356). This was followed by a rebuilding of thousands of parish churches between 1480 and 1540 (Hoskins 1976:12). The final indication is the price inflation of

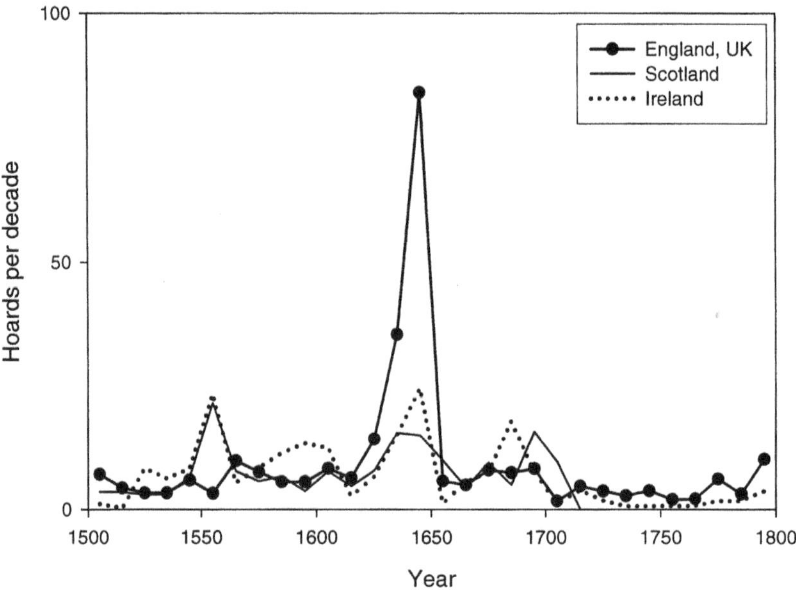

Figure 3.4 Number of coin hoards per decade in the British Isles, 1500–1800 (Brown 1971). Thick solid line: England (including Wales) until 1707, after that United Kingdom (includes Scotland). Thin solid line: Scotland (until 1707). Dotted line: Ireland.

1500–1530, accompanied by a sluggish response of the wages (Britnell 1997:244). In fact, 1500 appears to be the turnaround point when the misery index (inverse real wage) began a sustained ascent (figure 3.1).

An analysis of lay subsidies of 1524 and 1525 suggests a population of 2.3 million people (Cornwall 1970), which is the same as the estimated minimum during the fifteenth century. A later reevaluation suggests an even lower number (Campbell 1981), which is, however, difficult to reconcile with the firmer estimate of 2.8 million people in 1541. A population increase from 2.3 to 2.8 million between the 1520s and the 1540s implies a relative growth rate of 1 percent per year, which is somewhat above the growth rate after 1540 for which we have solid data: the backprojection suggests that the annual rate of population growth between 1541 and 1556 was 0.87 percent (Wrigley and Schofield 1981:566).

One important aspect of the early stages of population expansion was that it was accompanied by a significant shift in the urban-rural population balance. With the exception of London, it appears that all English towns lost population between 1400 and the middle of the sixteenth century. For example, Coventry, the dominant town of the Midlands, managed to expand its population between 1348 and 1450 despite the ravages of the

Black Death. In 1440 its population was over 10,000, and in 1500 only slightly less (8,500–9,000). However, in 1520 the population was only 7,500, and by the mid-sixteenth century it had collapsed to 4,000–5,000 (Phythian-Adams 1979:281). Coventry was not an unusual example. Other cities that lost about half their population between 1377 and 1525 were Winchester, York, Boston, Lincoln, and Lynn (Dyer 2002:300). Leicester, Norwich, Bristol, Southampton, Salisbury, and Hereford all shrank severely or experienced serious economic difficulties (Phythian-Adams 1979:283–84, Dyer 2002:300). The population of London, the only exception to this pattern, grew during this period, but slower than the overall population. A number of towns simply stopped being towns, either because their inhabitants deserted them or because they ceased to have an urban economy (Dyer 1980:301). This trend was particularly severe in the west and north of Britain.

The general dynamic underlying deurbanization was the reverse of the trend observed during the stagflation phase of the previous cycle. A shrunken elite stratum coupled with reduced consumption levels by an average elite household translated into a depressed demand for luxuries and manufactures. As a result, towns offered reduced employment opportunities to potential immigrants from rural areas. Meanwhile, rural areas became more attractive places to live as political stability returned under the Tudor regime. There arose new possibilities of expanding the carrying capacity by internal colonization of previously abandoned lands. Thus, both pull and push factors aligned to reduce the inflow of rural migrants to towns. As a result, urban populations shrank because of high mortality and the low birth rates prevailing in premodern towns. Incidentally, this redistribution of population between urban and rural locations may help explain why it is so difficult to directly document the early phase of population increase (1480–1540). Unlike urban shrinking, rural recolonization is not easily detectable (except by using indirect measures, such as peasant house construction and parish church rebuilding).

Whatever the timing and tempo of the early population expansion, by 1541 the total was 2.8 million (Wrigley et al. 1997), a substantial increase over the fifteenth-century level. Thanks to excellent research by the Cambridge Group for the History of Population and Social Structure, the population trajectory of post-1540 England is well-known. After 1540, population grew at an accelerating rate, which exceeded 1 percent per year in 1580. After 1580 population continued to grow, crossing the 4 million threshold in the early 1590s, but at a declining rate.

Rapid population growth during the second half of the sixteenth century, combined with torrents of precious metals from the New World, drove prices to unprecedented levels. At the same time, nominal wages increased at a much slower rate, with dire consequences for commoner standards of life.

In the early sixteenth century, before the price revolution, a laborer's wages provided for a standard of life that was modest but well above the starvation level. Assuming that a worker could find employment for 150 days a year and that the daily wage rate was 4 d., Hoskins (1976:113) estimated the annual income of 50 s. (master craftsmen would be paid 50 percent more, since their daily wage was 6 d.). Five quarters of wheat (14.5 hl, a reasonable index of food consumption for a family of five) would cost 30 s., and would take 60 percent of the annual income. Other expenses were much smaller. The typical rent was 5 s. per year. Working-class clothing cost 4 s. per person per year, but it is unlikely that laborers spent that much. Most clothing was probably made at home, and poor people wore others' cast-offs. A pair of shoes for "poor people" cost a shilling. Where woodland was within easy access, the poor collected wood for fuel. Where woodland was scarce, they burned the dried haulms of peas and beans and even dried cow dung (Hoskins 1976:116), or did not heat their dwellings at all. Life was not easy, but the laborer's wages were sufficient for food and basic shelter. Additionally, the wife and children could supplement the family income, either by working in the textile industry or by seasonal employment in agriculture.

During the sixteenth century wages grew slower than prices, collapsing in real terms. For example, the agricultural wage in southern England stayed constant at 4 d. per day until 1550, and then grew to 8 d. per day by the 1580s and 1590s (Thirsk 1967:864). The purchasing power of the wage rate, however, had declined by 50 percent by the 1590s (Thirsk 1967:865).

Land rents rose, but initially slower than prices, shifting the distribution of agricultural profits from the landlord to the tenant (Stone 1972:68). As we shall discuss below, during the stagflation phase rents increased faster than prices, and the direction of the flow of profits was reversed.

Elites

Until the middle of the sixteenth century the expansion of elite numbers lagged behind general population growth. Throughout most of the century, the numbers of peers fluctuated near 60 (Mingay 1976). The numbers of knights increased from 375 in 1490 to 600 in 1560 (Stone 1965:71), an increase of only 60 percent, while the population more than doubled.

In the mid-sixteenth century the elite fortunes were dramatically changed by the greatest land transfer in the English history after the Norman conquest—the dissolution of monasteries. The net yearly income of the church was estimated by Hoskins (1976:121) as £400,000, at least 60 percent of which passed to the Crown. During 1536–54 a large part of this land (valued at £1.1 million) was sold to the gentry (Stone 1972:154), creating the economic basis for the subsequent expansion of the elite class.

3.3 Stagflation (1580–1640)

Population and Economy

The population continued to grow, but at a decelerating rate, reaching 5.3 million during the 1640s (Wrigley et al. 1997). Thus, between 1480 and 1640 the English population more than doubled. "The doubling of the population in the 120 years before the civil war is the critical variable of the period, an event the ramifications of which spread out into every aspect of the society" (Stone 1972:67). Similar statements were also made by other authors (e.g., Russell 1990:1, Kishlansky 1997). One consequence of population growth was a drastic decline in the land-to-peasant ratio. For example, whereas prior to 1560 57 percent of landholdings were one acre or greater in size, after 1620 only 36 percent were in that category. Worse, the numbers of landless peasants drastically increased: the proportion of laborers owning only a cottage with garden or croft increased from 11 percent before 1560 to 40 percent after 1620 (Everitt 1967:402).

Overall the price of grain rose almost eightfold from 1500 to 1640 (in nominal terms; when expressed in grams of silver, the increase was sixfold). To investigate factors that were responsible for this inflation, Jack Goldstone (1991: Table 3) fitted a simple regression model with log-transformed population, an index of harvest quality, and time (the dummy variable for technical change) as independent variables to the data. The model explained 99 percent of the variance in the log-transformed prices and indicated that the most important factor driving inflation was population growth.

Expansion of the money supply as a result of the large-scale importation of bullion from the Americas also contributed to the price revolution of the sixteenth century. However, even in Spain, where the effect should be the greatest, sustained inflation started in 1540—before any substantial amounts of precious metals started arriving from the New World—and continued after 1620, despite declining bullion imports (Fischer 1996: Figure 2.09). Another clue suggesting that the primary mover behind inflation was population growth is the disparity between price increases of food and fuel versus manufactures (table 3.3). Whereas the price of grain increased almost eightfold, the price of manufactures increased only by a factor of three.

Another indicator suggesting that price inflation was driven primarily by population growth is real wages, which declined by more than 40 percent

TABLE 3.3
Relative increases in prices of food and fuel (grain, livestock, and wood) versus manufactures

Years	*Grain*	*Livestock*	*Wood*	*Manufactures*
1450–69	99	100	102	101
1470–89	104	101	102	101
1490–1509	105	105	88	98
1510–29	135	128	98	106
1530–49	174	164	108	119
1550–69	332	270	176	202
1570–89	412	344	227	227
1590–1609	575	433	312	247
1610–29	788	649	500	294

Source: Fischer (1996:74).

between 1500 and 1640 (Allen 2001). Land rents also increased at an accelerating rate (table 3.4). During the sixteenth century rents increased in line with prices, but after 1580 rents rapidly outpaced inflation. As a result, real rents stagnated during the expansion phase, so that the only way for landlords to increase their revenues was to get more land. During the stagflation phase, by contrast, real rents grew rapidly, and the landlords enjoyed a substantial increase in their incomes. For example, the standard of living of the average gentry in Warwickshire increased by nearly 400 percent between the 1530s and 1630s (Stone 1972:74).

Urbanization and Trade

During the sixteenth century the growth of the London population largely kept pace with the total population of England. As a result, London had between 2 and 3 percent of the total population. After 1600, however, the size of London mushroomed to the point where over 10 percent of the total population resided in it. During the second half of the eighteenth century and the early nineteenth century the growth of London's population again lagged behind that of the country (in 1830 London had 9 percent of the total population). In other words, urbanization exhibited the typical secular dynamics, with the peak of urbanization lagging substantially behind the population peak. Urbanization was dominated by, but not limited to, London. For example, between 1603 and 1670 the urban population of East Anglia grew by 50 percent, while the total population of the area rose by only 11 percent. The largest towns grew fastest: Norwhich increased from 12,000 to 30,000 during the seventeenth century (Clay 1984a:20).

The dynamics of trade and industry paralleled those of urbanization. Shipping owned in London rose from 12,300 tons in 1582 to 35,300 tons in 1629, and to about 150,000 tons by 1686 (Clay 1984a:202). Between

TABLE 3.4
Rents

Kerridge			Allen	
Year	*d./acre*	*Real rent*	*Year*	*Real rent*
1515	6.562	1.00	1462.5	1.1752
1525	6.235	0.75	1487.5	1.2217
1535	13.283	1.65	1512.5	1.0736
1545	13.796	1.37	1537.5	1.3542
1555	20.192	1.22	1562.5	0.7887
1565	22.902	1.33	1587.5	4.1571
1575	28.551	1.51	**1612.5**	**5.3031**
1585	21.577	1.00	1637.5	4.3822
1595	35.927	1.20	1662.5	4.2364
1605	44.070	1.54	1687.5	4.2230
1615	**54.405**	**1.67**	**1712.5**	**7.1223**
1625	45.867	1.36	1737.5	6.6528
1635	57.838	1.44	1762.5	6.1794
1645	42.572	0.99	1787.5	5.3608
1655	55.447	1.47	1812.5	5.3611

Source: Data from Kerridge (1953) and Allen (1992).
Note: Peaks in real rents are in boldface.

1622 and 1700 the value of imports of food and raw materials to London increased from £1 million to £3 million (Clay 1984b). The growth of industry can be illustrated with some numbers on iron production. In 1500 this was a mere 140 tons per year, but by 1600 it had grown to 10,000 tons per year. In 1660 total home iron production rose to 20,000 tons.

Elites

Between 1540 and 1640 the numbers of the various elite strata expanded much faster than the general population did (see table 3.1). Whereas the population grew by 80 percent (from 2.8 to 5.1 million), the elite numbers tripled (from 6,300 to 18,500 aristocratic families). The radical increase in aristocratic numbers affected all elite strata: the number of peers increased from 60 to 160, the number of baronets and knights increased from 500 to 1400, the number of esquires increased from 800 to 3,000, and the number of armigerous gentry increased from 5,000 to 15,000 (Stone 1972:72).

As the numbers of the gentry grew, so did their involvement in the local and central government. For example, the number of men appointed justices of the peace in four sample counties (Kent, Norfolk, Warwickshire, and the North Riding of Yorkshire) increased from 60 in the late fifteenth century to 96 in 1562, 166 in 1636, and 396 in 1702 (Heal and Holmes 1994:167)—a 6.6-fold increase. The membership of the House of Commons grew from 300 to 500, while the gentry component in it rose from 50 percent to 75 percent (Stone 1972:92), implying a 2.5-fold increase in the number of gentry MPs.

The expansion of the landed elites was accompanied by a rise of professions. The numbers of lawyers, doctors and other practitioners of medicine, and secretarial/administrative assistants showed a sustained and striking increase, generally peaking in 1640 (Stone 1976:34). For example, the number of attorneys enrolled in the Court of Common Pleas rose between 1578 and 1633 from 342 to 1,383. The numbers of the clergy also increased, starting in 1560 and reaching a peak in 1640 (Stone 1976:34).

The causal factors underlying the rise of the gentry are well understood. In the first phase, roughly 1540–60, the gentry profited from the massive land transfer of church property. In the second phase, after 1580, the gentry benefited from rising real rents. Additionally, as the Crown's finances worsened, it was forced to sell more land. The value of the Crown lands sold between 1589 and 1635 was £2.1 million (Stone 1972:154), and most of it ended up in the hands of the gentry.

The rise of the gentry was accompanied by ever increasing levels of conspicuous consumption, as well as by increasing degree of inequality:

> In 1485 most English people, even well to do, wore similar dress. Women wore plain, loose-fitting garments and men did likewise. Fine but simple linen was as acceptable in formal costume as ornate silk. . . . The third and fourth decades of the sixteenth century, however, saw an explosive growth in the consumption of expensive and ornate costume. Demand rose enormously, especially among the wealthy, who purchased expensive brocades, velvets, and silks for new and splendid costumes. . . . During the reign of Elizabeth, men changed their fashions entirely; their clothes became more elaborate and distinctive. . . . Women matched male attire with exquisitely decorated farthingales and fine damask gowns. . . . [T]he sixteenth century closed with a "wild orgy of extravagance," as the provincial gentry attempted to emulate the London *haute monde* by wearing extravagant costumes and hats with twelve-inch crowns. (Berger 1993:20–21)

At a certain point, however, the elite numbers increased beyond the "sustainable level." As a result, competition for jobs and patronage gradually intensified, with all the dire consequences for political stability of the English society. Goldstone (1991) proposed two ways to quantify intraelite competition. First, one can examine the data on university enrollments. University enrollments increased drastically during the second half of the sixteenth century, reaching a peak in 1640. This secular trend was not simply a part of the much longer ("millennial") increase in the general level of European literacy and education, because by the 1750s, when intraelite competition had greatly subsided, the enrollments had declined to pre-

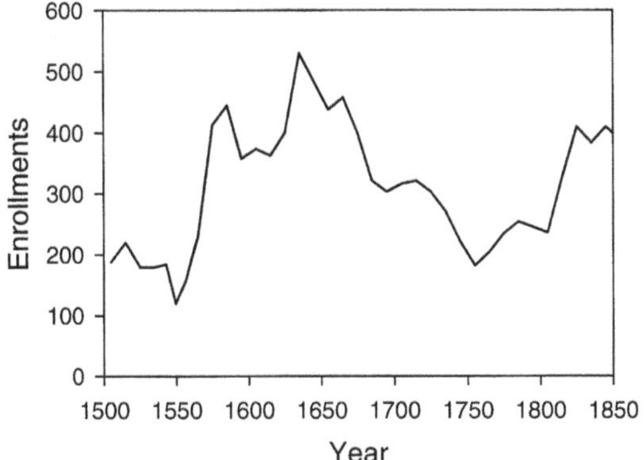

Figure 3.5 Enrollments at Oxford University, 1500–1850.

1600 levels (figure 3.5). "The universities were turning out an educated clergy and laity in excess of suitable job opportunities, and were thus creating a large and influential group of discontented 'Outs'" (Stone 1972:96).

The second indicator of intraelite competition was the amount of litigation among gentry. "In 1640, there was probably more litigation per head of population going through the central courts at Westminster than at any time before or since. But one hundred years later in 1750, the common law hit what appears to have been a spectacular all-time low" (Brooks 1989:360). For example, from 1640 to 1750, the number of gentry who appeared in the Courts of Common Pleas as plaintiffs or defendants dropped by over 65 percent (Brooks 1989). Thus, the increase in litigation was not simply a result of the rise of the modern society in England.

A third indicator of intraelite competition, in addition to the two proposed by Goldstone, was the veritable epidemic of dueling that afflicted the English aristocracy in the late sixteenth century. The number of duels and challenges mentioned in newsletters and correspondence jumped from five in the 1580s to nearly twenty in the 1590s, and then to a peak of thirty-nine in the 1610s (Stone 1965).

The rise of dueling coincided with (and perhaps was a part of) the crime wave that inundated the English society in the late sixteenth century and peaked in the early seventeenth. Data on homicides assembled by Eisner (2003) suggest that the general incidence of crime increased and declined in step with population pressure and inverse real wages (figure 3.6).

The State

The final major consequence of population growth was the increasing fiscal strain on the English state. The state revenues were strong under Henry VII and continued to increase until the mid-sixteenth century. After that point, revenues declined in real terms (see figure 3.3), while expenses con-

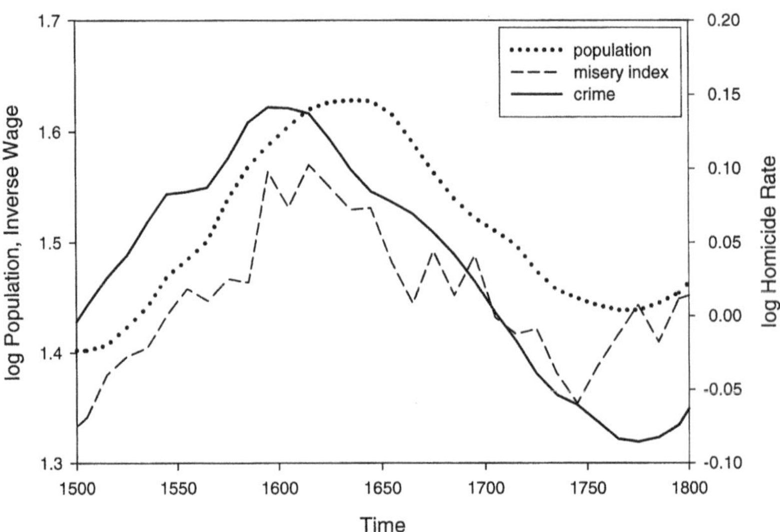

Figure 3.6 Homicide rate in relation to inverse real wages (misery index) and population pressure.

tinued to rise. The state's fiscal difficulties mounted during the sixteenth century and reached a peak on the eve of the Great Revolution (figure 3.7a). The basic problem was that the Crown's real expenses increased proportionately to population numbers, while real income declined. Additionally, the expanded elite numbers imposed greater patronage costs on the state. Increasingly, from the mid-sixteenth century on, the Crown was forced to sell assets, levy forced loans, and seek parliamentary grants even in peacetime (Goldstone 1991:93). By the 1630s, the Crown lands were largely gone, and the unpaid Crown debt reached the point where the interest on it was greater than the ordinary revenues. Furthermore, prior efforts to secure extraordinary revenues had alienated the elites to the point where they were unlikely to acquiesce to further fiscal demands or entreaties by the Crown.

Here are some numbers. The state debt grew from £400,000 in 1603 to £900,000 in 1618 (Hughes 1991:27). Under Elizabeth, "perks" of £8,000 per annum were distributed to the peers; under James I, this figure increased to £105,000 (Hughes 1991:151). By 1626 pensions had increased to £140,000 per year, or about a quarter of the total cash revenues of the Crown (Stone 1965:419). Some of these pensions were due to legitimate demands of government service, but an increasing part went to fuel "the growth of a parasitic court aristocracy preying upon the revenues of the Crown" (Stone 1965:419). In the 1630s more than half of government revenue was absorbed by official salaries (Clay 1984b:261).

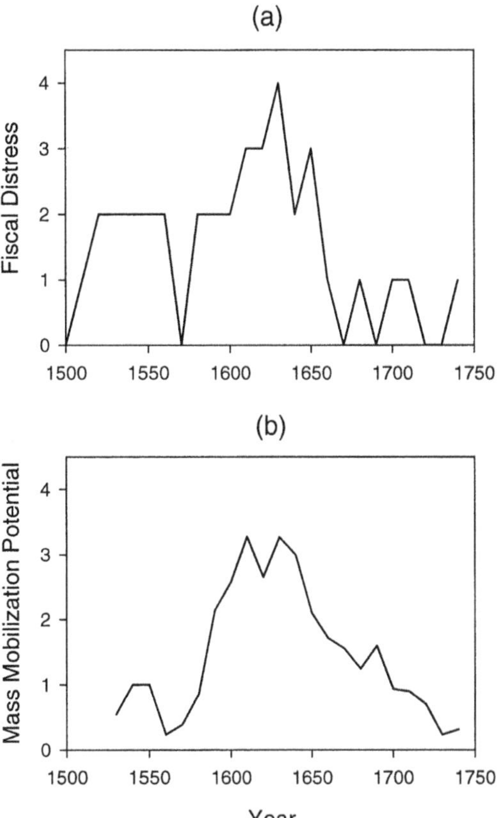

Figure 3.7 (a) Index of the state's fiscal distress, 1550–1750 (Goldstone 1991: Figure 4). Goldstone's index of fiscal distress varies from 0 (adequate income and credit) to 4 (total bankruptcy) (Goldstone 1991:105). (b) Mass mobilization potential in England, 1530–1750 (Goldstone 1991).

3.4 Crisis (1640–60)

The Onset of the Civil War

By 1640 the social pressure resulting from population expansion, elite overproduction, and growing state insolvency had reached the breaking point. In his seminal work, *Revolution and Rebellion in the Early Modern World*, Jack Goldstone (1991) used several social and political indicators to quantify the growing pressure.

The first index is the mass mobilization potential (MMP) of the general populace. One population group is of particular importance, the urbanized workers and artisans, especially in the capital, because they are located near the centers of power. Goldstone proposed three measurable components in the MMP: (1) the degree of misery affecting the urban masses by the dynamics of real wages, (2) youthful age structure, which increases the mobilization potential of the crowd, and (3) urban growth, which concentrates the poor young sons and other discontented commoners and thus should play an important multiplier role in amplifying the popular discontent brought about by increasing poverty. Goldstone proposed a formula combining the effects of these three mechanisms in one measure of mass mobilization potential. The estimated MMP for England during 1530–1750 is plotted in figure 3.7b.

An increased MMP by itself was not enough to cause the state collapse when the elites were unified and determined to prevent it. Thus, the second trend contributing to state breakdown was the loss of elite unity. A favorable economic conjuncture for landowners during the stagflation phase resulted in the massive expansion of elite numbers. However, the amount of surplus that could be wrung from the peasants stagnated and even declined after 1620. For example, real rents peaked during the first quarter of the seventeenth century and declined thereafter (table 3.4). The direct consequence of these two opposing trends was that the average income per elite capita declined on the eve of the Great Revolution. As usually happens, the pain was not spread evenly, and although many elite families were greatly impoverished, others continued to do well. Thus, not only was there a growing segment of elites who faced the prospect of downward mobility, there was also a visible rise in inequality. One avenue for preserving elite status was to seek employment with the state, church, or the magnates. But employment opportunities could not keep pace with the growing numbers of elite aspirants (most of whom had university degrees). "Limits on available land, civil and ecclesiastical offices, and royal patronage led to increasingly polarized factional battles between patron-client groups for available spoils" (Goldstone 1991:119). When one elite faction won, it attempted to completely exclude its rivals. This is what happened when the faction led by George Villiers, the Duke of Buckingham, managed to monopolize the court's patronage from about 1617 to his death in 1628. In the words of David Loades (1999:308), "the ascendancy of Buckingham . . . transformed abuse into a scandal of systematic exploitation."

The increasing clamor of the elites for positions aggravated the third trend, the fiscal difficulties of the state. The state finances were also under pressure from rising military costs from the military revolution of the sixteenth century. The revenues, however, ultimately failed to match the pace of increased outlays. In fact, real revenues declined during the second half of the sixteenth century, and stagnated from 1600 to 1640 (see figure 3.3). Thus, the ability of the state to raise revenue could not keep up with the increasing fiscal demands on it. The Crown used a variety of expedients to provide short-term relief—the sale of Crown lands, offices, and titles, debasement of coinage, and borrowing from the city of London and the international money market. By the 1630s, however, Crown lands were gone and the state debt had reached over £1 million. The state was on the brink of bankruptcy, and it took a very slight shock (the Bishops' Wars) to tip it over the precipice.

Economic Consequences of the Civil War

The civil wars started in 1642 and lasted with intervals until 1651, followed by a period of continuing political instability until the restoration of the monarchy in 1660. During this period of civil war and governmental confusion some 10 percent of the male population was killed. Towns such as Birmingham (1643), Bolton (1644), and Leicester (1645) were sacked. The castles and houses of the nobility and gentry were sacked or destroyed to prevent their use in future campaigns (King 1971:355). Local studies document the extent of property damage. For example, even though Gloucester remained under one side's control throughout the conflict, and its siege was not reckoned to be particularly destructive, a 1646 investigation found 241 houses destroyed, leaving 1,250 people homeless, and the suburbs were not rebuilt until the eighteenth century (Warmington 1997:78). The countryside suffered much more. Almost every village in Inshire (the area around Gloucester) was plundered at least once, and many repeatedly. The Tewkesbury region (also in Gloucestershire) was plundered in 1643, 1644, and 1645. As a result of pillage and heavy taxation imposed by both sides, land values declined so far that tenants refused to pay rents and abandoned their leases. Some villages were reportedly depopulated as a result of the war (Warmington 1997:77).

An enormous amount of land changed hands (although much of it was later reversed), including £3.5 million of Crown lands, £2.5 million of ecclesiastical lands, and over £1 million of royalist lands (King 1971:355). This transfer of land caused significant dislocation in the countryside. Purchasers of confiscated lands were anxious to secure quick returns, and tenants who could not produce written evidence of their titles were liable to eviction (Hill 1982:125).

The rural poor in England were almost entirely neutral during the 1640s and 1650s. The only serious intervention by the rural poor came in the form of assemblies of the "clubmen" who gathered in several counties during the latter stages of the war. These interventions were no more than desperate attempts by the rural poor to protect their fields, crops, cattle, and women from the depredations of both armies (Stone 1972:55)

To sum up, the civil war did enormous damage to the economic infrastructure of England. It appears that the only reason for the very slight population decline that the country experienced during the seventeenth century was rapidly increasing agricultural productivity. Thus, wheat yields increased by more than 50 percent during the seventeenth century, apparently compensating for the loss of cultivated land resulting from internal warfare.

Population

Thanks to work by Wrigley, Schofield, and co-workers on the population reconstruction of the early modern England, we have a firm grasp of the demographic machinery underlying population changes from the mid-sixteenth century to the nineteenth century. The temporal variation in the population growth rate was due to changes in both birth and death rates, but crude birth and death rates responded with different lags to changes in population numbers.

Wrigley, Schofield, and co-workers showed that a large proportion of variance in the crude birth rate could be explained by nuptiality. The proportion of the population never marrying increased from 5 percent in the mid-sixteenth century to over 25 percent by 1650, before declining back to 5 percent during the next hundred years (Wrigley and Schofield 1981:262). The average age at first marriage also increased between 1550 and 1650, which had the effect of reducing the average number of children per married woman by at least one (Wrigley et al. 1997:136).

The seventeenth century was an era of steadily worsening mortality that reached a maximum around 1680. There was an improvement around 1700, then another mortality peak during the 1720s, particularly affecting infants and children (Wrigley et al. 1997:283). The eighteenth century saw a gradual (and not always monotonic) improvement in the expectation of life. Migration began growing in 1550, peaked in 1650, and then entered a secular decline until the 1780s (Wrigley and Schofield 1981:220).

The explanations of the worsening demographic regime are provided by the "usual suspects" of famine, disease, and war. The worst famine of the period occurred during the years 1594–97, which saw the longest run of bad harvests of the sixteenth century (Clay 1984a:19). A generation later, in 1622–23, a rise in the price of grain coincided with a severe depression in the cloth industry, leaving many people without money to buy food. There is clear evidence from both periods of deaths from starvation, especially of vagrants, elderly widows, and pauper children. Other subsistence crises followed, but by the middle of the seventeenth century widespread famine seems to have become a thing of the past (Clay 1984a:19).

The plague, which relaxed its grip on the English population by the end of the fifteenth century, gradually increased during the sixteenth (Biraben 1975). The century between 1570 and 1670 was a period of recurrent plague epidemics, culminating in the great plague of London (1665). During the late seventeenth century the plague suddenly went extinct in England. However, the plague was not the only scourge during the seventeenth century. Typhus epidemics often flared up when internecine fighting intensified (for example, in 1648). The annual death toll of smallpox epidemics in London often exceeded 2,000 during the 1670s (Scott and Duncan 2001:40).

3.5 Depression (1660–1730)

Population Stagnation

The population of England declined from the peak of 5.4 million, achieved during the 1650s, to a trough of 5 million in the 1680s. The period after that was characterized by very slow and uneven growth. The population was still 5.4 million in 1730, and the next period of vigorous growth began only after 1750. The main factor explaining this prolonged period of stagnation appears to be mortality, because fecundity exhibited an increasing trend from 1650 on. However, detailed demographic investigation by Wrigley et al. (1997:298) indicates that adult mortality improved during the eighteenth century, but this improvement was offset until the 1750s by high infant and child mortality rates. Infanticide indictment rates in England peaked in the very late seventeenth century and slowly declined during the eighteenth (figure 3.8), suggesting that high infant mortality during this period may have been a result of a conscious (or unconscious) attempt at birth control. Thus, the demographic picture is murky and does not tell us much about the possible causes of population stagnation prior to 1750.

We believe that three factors, two endogenous and one exogenous, can help us understand this puzzling phenomenon (but not a unique one; a similar period of population stagnation occurred during the depression phase of the Plantagenet cycle). First, there was a strong negative effect of urbanization on population growth. As we discussed above, the peak of urbanization was considerably lagged with respect to the population peak. Between 1700 and 1750 London had 10 percent of the country's population, a fourfold increase from 1580 and slightly greater than the urbanization index of 1830 (9 percent). A high degree of urbanization during the depression phase of the Tudor cycle without doubt was an important factor contributing to the unfavorable demographic regime. E. A. Wrigley (cited in Clay 1984a:191) calculated that during 1690–1710 immigration to London (estimated at 30,000 per year, on average) absorbed half of the natural increase of the entire population of the country. The enormous losses that London suffered in the seventeenth-century plagues were made good by the second year after an outbreak. The dampening demographic effect of

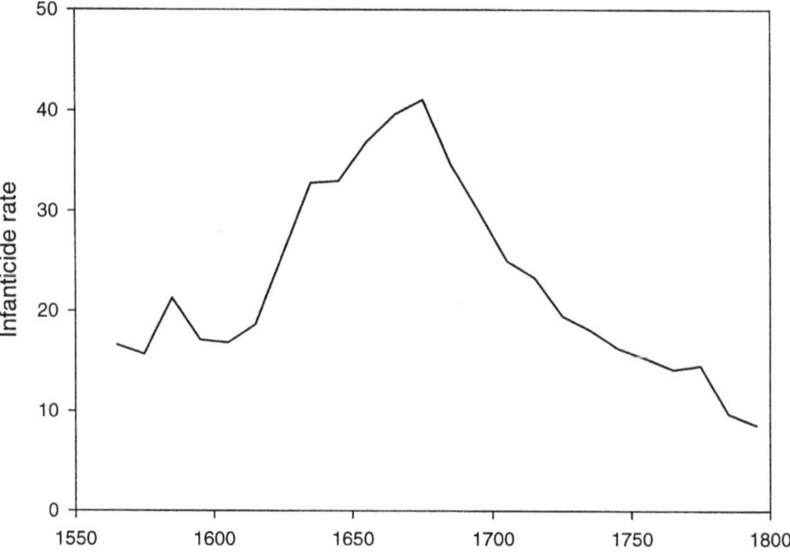

Figure 3.8 Infanticide indictment rates per 100,000, 1560–1800 (Roth 2001).

London was amplified by the fact that it disproportionately attracted female immigrants, who came in response to the great demand for domestic servants. As a result, there were fewer than ninety men for every one hundred women (Clay 1984a:209). The sex imbalance served to further depress the ability of population to increase.

Second, the data on rents collected by Robert Allen suggests that real rents jumped by 70 percent from the last quarter of the seventeenth century to the first quarter of the eighteenth century (Allen 1992:172). It is likely that, once the period of intraelite disunity was over, the elites were in a much better position to "turn the screws" on the peasants. Although the increased rent was partly compensated for by the increase in productivity achieved by English agriculture during the seventeenth century, it still must have substantially decreased the personal consumption of peasants. This is a very tentative interpretation, and not free of problems. For example, real wages during this period generally kept increasing (although they never reached their fifteenth-century maximum). But if peasants were overexploited, this should have spilled over into real wages, which we do not see. Perhaps increased rents simply retarded the growth of the rural population, thus contributing indirectly to slow population growth. This issue requires further investigation.

The third factor was the general worsening of the climate in the early eighteenth century (associated with the Maunder Minimum of solar activity). The climate cooling affected Europe from London to Moscow, causing a sequence of crop failures and famines. We know that populations of both France and Russia experienced declines during the first decade of the century, which are usually attributed to the exactions imposed by wars pursued by Louis XIV and Peter I, respectively. However, it is equally possible that the explanation for this pan-European population decline may lie in the exogenous factor of climate.

The Elites

The civil wars resulted in serious deterioration of the economic position of the landed elites. Particularly affected were the royalists, whose lands were confiscated and sold. The combined value of these properties was over £1.25 million. This land transfer was partially reversed because many royalists bought their estates back before 1660 (Hill 1982:126). However, most of them had to incur heavy debt to do so. Nearly £1.5 million was raised from some 3,000 royalists by the Committee of Compounding. On top of these and other exactions came heavy taxation. In order to pay composition fines after a long period of receiving no rents, royalists had to sell part of their lands, and these lands were not restored after 1660. Thus, although the bulk of royalist landlords retained their position, many were greatly impoverished in the process, and some lesser elite families had a stiff fight to keep their heads above water (Hill 1982:126).

During the last quarter of the seventeenth century almost all landlords experienced a further reduction in their incomes as a result of low agricultural prices and falling rents (Clay 1984a:162). On top of this, again, they had to bear a much great rate of taxation. For example, after 1692 taxes were absorbing one-fifth of the income of many gentry. Many of those at the lower fringes of the gentry had to part with their land (Clay 1984a:162). The declining economic fortunes of the gentry were reflected in their consumption patterns. Whereas the early seventeenth century witnessed a rapid expansion in the imports of luxury (Clay 1984a:26), after the civil wars there was significant change of ethos among the elites, leading to a reduction of conspicuous expenditure on houses, clothes, and entertaining (Clay 1984a:160).

The economic malaise affecting gentry extended into the eighteenth century. Thus, the average wealth of esquires in Norfolk and Suffolk was £700 in 1628–40 and then declined to £330 for the period of 1700–40, a drop of more than 50 percent in real terms (Overton 1996:39). The result was increased downward mobility, with an almost automatic descent by younger sons into lower social strata. For example, in Cumbria between 1680 and 1750 only one younger son of the gentry was able to purchase

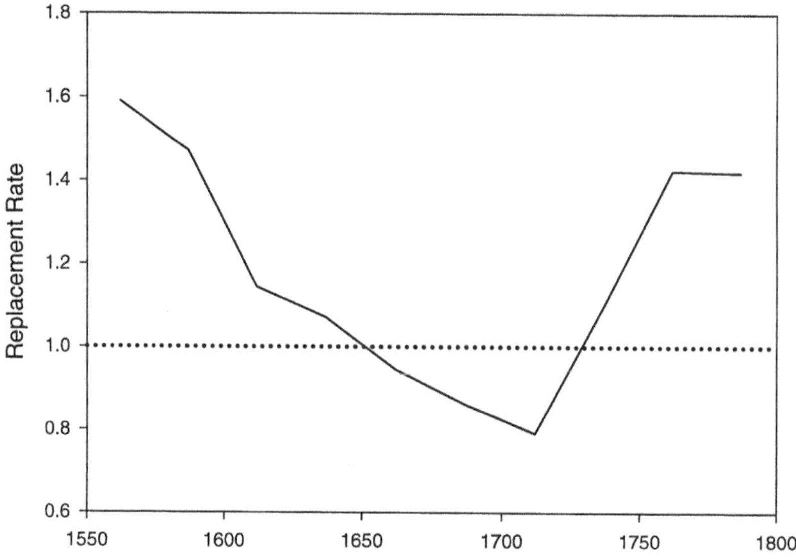

Figure 3.9 Replacement rates of peers, 1550–1800 (Hollingsworth 1964).

land and climb back up into the group (Beckett 1986:23). The upward mobility into the ranks of the gentry was similarly restricted. "With a few exceptions, the days when a man of fortune converted his wealth into landed acreage were already numbered by the end of the seventeenth century, and the practice had more or less disappeared by the mid-eighteenth century" (Beckett 1986:69).

The numbers of elites shrank from the late seventeenth century to the middle of the eighteenth century. Partly this was a result of diminished upward and enhanced downward mobility. Partly it was a result of the elite demographics (Hollingsworth 1964). The replacement rate (average number of adult sons per father) among the upper-rank elites declined below one after 1650, and kept declining (to below 0.8) until the first quarter of the eighteenth century (figure 3.9). During the next quarter century it increased to 1.1, but it was not until after 1750 that the replacement rate achieved the healthy level of 1.3–1.4 it was to have to the middle of the nineteenth century. "Collectively, the peerage, baronetage and knighthood totalled only 1075 by 1760, a fall of 30 per cent since the beginning of the century, and among the lesser gentry in the counties the position appears to have been much the same" (Beckett 1986:98). These numbers are given in table 3.5. Overall elite numbers declined from 18,500 to 13,000 (see table 3.1). As the number of landowning families shrank, the average size of estates tended to increase (Clay 1984a:158, 268).

TABLE 3.5
Numbers of upper rank elites

Year	*Peers*	*Baronets*	*Knights*	*Total*
1700	173	935	290	1,398
1710	167	924	180	1,271
1720	190	892	180	1,262
1730	189	836	150	1,175
1740	183	800	70	1,053
1750	187	738	70	995
1760	181	713	70	964
1770	197	706	110	1,013
1780	189	725	90	1,004
1790	220	747	160	1,127
1800	267	779	160	1,206

Source: Beckett (1986).
Note: There were also Irish and Scottish peers, not shown here.

Consequences of the Civil War: Changed Social Mood

When the civil wars began in 1642, the English could look back to a century of internal peace:

> The risings of 1549 were quelled without undue difficulty. . . . The overthrow of Somerset was accomplished without bloodshed. Northumberland's attempt to divert succession collapsed with only a hint of civil war. Mary's regime, although hardly popular, achieved most of its initial objectives and never looked, even at the end, in danger of being overthrown. The harvests of the mid-1550s and the mid-1590s inflicted terrible sufferings upon the poor, but nowhere in England set off the large-scale risings. . . . Elizabeth crushed the Presbyterian movement and effectively contained the Catholic threat, while Essex's revolt collapsed into black comedy in twenty-four hours. . . . [T]he succession crisis at the death of Elizabeth was solved dextrously and peacefully. (Williams 1995:22)

"The last peasant revolt serious enough to send gentry fleeing from their homes in terror had been in 1549 . . . [and] by 1640 two generations of gentry had gone by since the great fear, and memories had grown dim" (Stone 1972:76). Few among the elites could foresee the depth of the societal collapse that would result from their actions, and the intraelite conflict was allowed to escalate unchecked until it acquired a dynamic of its own.

The two decades following 1640 were the most protracted and intense period of sociopolitical instability in England since the Wars of the Roses. The following two decades (after the Stuart Restoration) were, in contrast, internally a peaceful period. This alternation between civil war and internal stability thus provides another example of a bigenerational cycle. Around 1680, however, social pressure began increasing again. Three parliaments came and went in rapid succession (1679–81). A reign of "legal terror" against Whigs and dissenters began in 1682. Several were executed, and others driven into exile (Hill 1982:169). When Charles II died in 1685, he was succeeded peacefully by James II, but the same year two risings took place. The Argyll and Monmouth rebellions were rapidly suppressed, but when William of Orange landed in England three years later, the rebellion quickly spread, and James II chose to flee England. As a result of this "Glorious Revolution" (1688–90, with aftershocks in Scotland and Ireland until 1692), the Stuart dynasty was abolished, and Parliament offered the crown to William and Mary jointly. One remarkable feature of this revolution was its relative bloodlessness. Whigs and Tories disagreed sharply on a number of issues, but these differences were patched up, largely as a result of "men's recollection of what happened forty-five years earlier, when unity of the propertied class had been broken" (Hill 1982:236). The compromise reached by the elites held up remarkably well throughout the whole of the eighteenth century and beyond. After the Glorious Revolution there were no major rebellions in Great Britain (as the union of England and Scotland was called after 1707), apart from two Jacobite risings, one in 1715–16 and another in 1745–46. These aftershocks followed the Glorious Revolution at roughly generational intervals: the first one was led by James II's son and the second by his grandson.

The Turnaround Point: The Mid-eighteenth Century

By the mid-eighteenth century, the last echoes of the early modern crisis had dissipated. Real wages increased throughout the early eighteenth century, reaching a peak around 1750. The last serious disturbance of internal peace in Great Britain was the Jacobite rising in 1745–46. The numbers of the elites reached a minimum sometime around the 1760s. The ruling class achieved an unprecedented degree of unity. After the stabilization of the political system in 1721, landowners drastically reduced the number of both electors and contested elections to Parliament (Stone and Stone 1984:14). The elite cohesiveness allowed them to tax themselves at an unprecedented rate for an early modern society, an ability that served England well during the century-long conflict with France culminating in the Napoleonic Wars. Thus, by the mid-eighteenth century, the stage was set for the astonishing demographic, economic, and territorial expansion England was to experience during the next century and a half.

3.6 Conclusion

The demographic, economic, political, and social trends in early modern England, from roughly 1485 to 1730, generally moved in ways that were consistent with the predictions of the demographic-structural theory. The case of the English Revolution fits the demographic-structural theory particularly well, as was argued earlier by Goldstone (1991). The three ingredients of the revolution were the financial crisis of the state, acute competition and factionalism among the elites, and the existence of a large body of disaffected commoners who could be mobilized by parliamentary leaders against the royalists in London. Measures of all these processes increased during the second half of the sixteenth and the early seventeenth centuries, peaking around 1640.

As in the previous case study of the Plantagenet cycle, we found that the operation of the demographic-structural machinery was influenced and modified by other factors. The geopolitical environment apparently played a minor role during this cycle. Although it was the invasion by the Dutch Statholder, William of Orange, that precipitated the Glorious Revolution, the success of it was entirely due to internal factors.

Long-term fluctuations in climate were probably important in contributing to population stagnation of the late seventeenth century to early eighteenth century. During this cycle there were no traumatic exogenous events comparable to the arrival of the Black Death in 1348. The increase in the incidence of epidemics during the seventeenth century was apparently an endogenous process.

The most important factor outside the core variables of the demographic-structural theory was the acceleration of social evolution that eventually resulted in the Industrial Revolution. Because of scientific and agronomic advances, crop yields began increasing shortly after 1600. During the seventeenth century yields doubled. As a result, the carrying capacity also doubled. We believe it was this dramatic increase in the carrying capacity that explains why population numbers in England did not collapse to the same degree as happened in, for example, Spain or Germany in the seventeenth century. When we divide the total population by the estimated carrying capacity, we observe that the resulting variable, the population pressure on resources, oscillates in a very similar fashion to what happened during the Plantagenet cycle (figure 3.10).

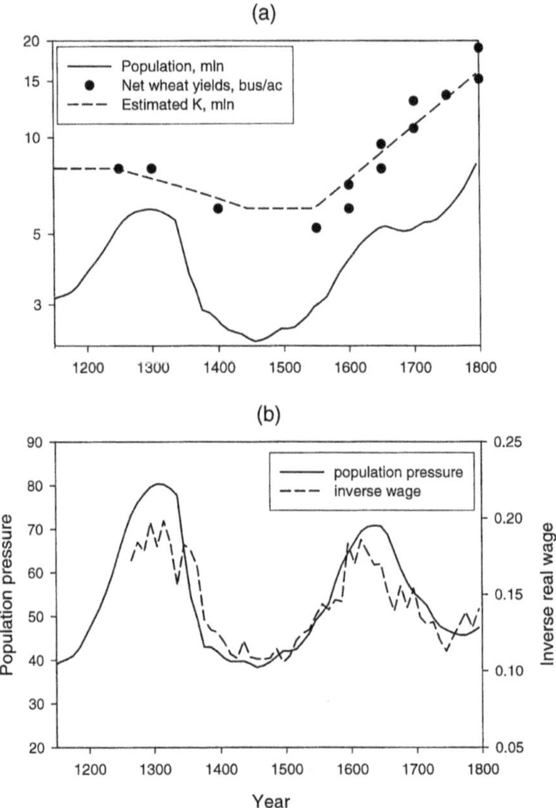

Figure 3.10 Population dynamics in England, 1150–1800 (see appendix to this chapter). (a) Raw population numbers, average yields, and estimated carrying capacity. (b) Population pressure (population numbers in relation to carrying capacity, in percent of *K*) and the misery index (inverse real wages).

Appendix to Chapter 3: Detrending Population Data (This material is reproduced from Turchin 2005.)

England 1450–1800: Population Data

Population numbers for the period 1540–1800 were taken from Table A.9.1 in Wrigley et al. (1997). The quinquennial data of Wrigley et al. were resampled at decadal intervals. For the period 1450–1525, population data were taken from Hatcher (1977), also sampled at ten-year intervals (all data analyzed here were sampled at ten-year intervals). The value for 1530 was interpolated. The population data show an increasing long-term trend.

Such nonstationarity violates one of the most important assumptions of nonlinear time-series analysis; thus, the data need to be detrended (Turchin 2003a:175).

Detrending the English Population Data

The agrarian revolution in England started during the seventeenth century (Grigg 1989, Allen 1992, Overton 1996). We can trace this revolution using data on long-term changes in grain yields (Grigg 1989, Overton 1996). Average wheat yields in the thirteenth century were around 10 bushels of grain per acre. Yields declined slightly during the fourteenth and fifteenth centuries to 8 bushels per acre (perhaps as a result of the worsening global climate). Even as late as the 1580s, the yields were still at their late medieval level. During the seventeenth century, however, yields began improving, increasing to ca. 15 in 1700 and 20–21 in the early nineteenth century (Grigg 1989:69). Net yields (subtracting seed corn) were lower. For example, the typical late medieval seeding rates were 2 bushels per acre; thus, the net yield was only 6 bushels per acre. Net yields from Grigg and Overton are plotted in figure 3.10a. To capture the rising trend, we fitted the data after 1580 with a straight line (see figure 3.10a, and note the log-scale). The linear relationship appears to be an adequate description of the trend (for example, adding a quadratic term failed to better the regression in a statistically significant fashion).

We can obtain an approximate estimate of the carrying capacity by assuming that it was proportional to the net yield. Assuming a total potentially arable area of 12 million acres (Grigg 1989) and that one individual (averaging over adults and children) needed a minimum of one quarter (8 bushels or 2.9 hectoliters) of grain per year, we calculated the carrying capacity of England shown by the dashed line in figure 3.10a (by coincidence, 1 bushel of net yield per acre translates exactly into 1 million persons of carrying capacity).

We can now detrend the observed population numbers by dividing them by the estimated carrying capacity. The detrended population, which can also be thought of as population pressure on resources, is defined as $N'(t) = N(t)/K(t)$. The critical assumption here is that K is proportional to the net yield, Y; since Y is the only quantity varying with time in the formula; other components (total arable area, consumption minimum) being constant multipliers, K will wax and wane in step with Y. In other words, the exact values of constant multiples do not matter, since we are interested in the relative changes of population pressure. The estimate of K is based not on the area that was actually cultivated (this fluctuated with population numbers) but on the potentially arable area. The latter quantity fluctuated little across the centuries (for example, as a result of some inundation of coastal areas during the Middle Ages or more recent reclamation using modern methods) and can be approximated with a constant without a serious loss of precision.

A test of the appropriateness of this detrending was obtained by regressing the estimated population pressure on real wages reported by Allen (2001). There was a very close inverse relationship between these two variables, and not a very good one if we were to use the nondetrended population numbers. As figure 3.10b shows, population pressure and inverse real wages fluctuated virtually in perfect synchrony.

Chapter 4

Medieval France: The Capetian Cycle (1150–1450)

4.1 Overview of the Cycle

The official start of the Capetian dynasty is dated to the accession of Hugh Capet to the French throne in 987. However, before 1200 the Capetian kings of France directly controlled a rather insignificant extent of territory, overshadowed by other north French polities, the most important of which were the Normans and the Angevins. The integrative trend set in gradually during the twelfth century. The important landmarks were the consolidation of royal lands under Louis VI "the Fat" (1108–37) and the activities of Suger, abbot of St. Denis, between 1122 and 1151. For this reason, we date the beginning of the high medieval cycle in France to 1150.

The century between 1150 and 1250 was the expansion phase, which saw a rapid growth of population densities and also an enormous expansion of the territory controlled by the French kings. The stagflation phase set in after the mid-thirteenth century, when population growth slowed down and gradually ceased altogether. The onset of the crisis was signaled by the famines of 1315–17 and reached a peak with the arrival of the Black Death, followed by military defeats, peasant uprisings, and the first civil war. A temporary stabilization was achieved during the 1360s, but it proved to be a very fragile one. The depression phase, characterized by high sociopolitical instability and the absence of sustained population growth, lasted until the mid-fifteenth century. It was around 1450 when the new integrative trend became obvious, so we take this date as the end of the medieval cycle and the beginning of the early modern one.

As before, our dates for the cycles and phases within cycles are provisional and subject to change should new evidence be forthcoming. They are also "fuzzy," in that a specific date had to be selected within a broad penumbra of events occurring in the ten or twenty years surrounding it. Thus, the date of 1450 really means 1440–60, or even 1430–70. Our division of a continuous cycle into discrete stages is a useful device for organizing the presentation but does not mean that transitions between successive phases occurred abruptly, in a single year.

The large and spatially heterogeneous entity of the kingdom of France offers further challenges to historical analysis. The country we know as modern France was, in the medieval period, an aggregation of different polities and cultural regions, which could and did move out of synchrony with one other. The chronology that follows, then, is primarily relevant to the territorial core of the French state, the region north of the Loire inhabited by the speakers of Langue d'Oïl (Planhol 1994:124).

Population and Economy

There were perhaps 6 million people in France around 1100, and close to 20 million in 1328 (Braudel 1988:137). Such a tripling of the population during the twelfth and thirteenth centuries (with the fastest growth concentrated in the century around 1200) was quite typical of Western European countries (Abel 1980). During the century after the Black Death, the French population declined to around 10 million people (figure 4.1a).

These numbers refer to the population within modern French borders. The peak population in the area controlled by the Capetians was smaller, perhaps around 16 million (Sumption 1991:10). In 1328 the officials of the royal treasury counted nearly 2,470,000 households (the great fiefs and princely appanages, not taxed by the king, were excluded).

The dynamics of food prices, when expressed in silver equivalents, exhibited a very similar pattern to population dynamics: a thirteenth-century increase, followed by a decline to a minimum toward the mid-fifteenth century (figure 4.1b). There are also shorter-term oscillations (of about fifty years) superimposed on the secular cycles.

Social Structure

At the top of the power hierarchy of France stood the great territorial magnates—lay lords (the king, dukes, counts, and barons) and prelates (abbots, bishops, and archbishops). Below them were the middle and lower rank elites, from the more substantial knights to the relatively poor country squires (Tuchman 1978). A view of the typical incomes of various elite substrata is provided by Edouard Perroy's (1962) study of the nobility of the county of Forez (south-central France) in the late thirteenth century. At the top of the local hierarchy stood the Count of Forez, with 12,000 *livres viennois* (l.v.) of annual income. Below him were two or three barons with incomes of between 1,000 and 2,000 l.v. per year. Twenty or so substantial knights, each with a castle, enjoyed incomes between 100 and 500 l.v. The holders of fortified houses were worse off, with incomes of 50–100 l.v. per year. At the bottom of the noble hierarchy were about a hundred lesser gentry whose incomes varied between 25 and 50 l.v. per year. To put this income in perspective, the basic minimum on which a single person could live in modest comfort at the time was 5 l.v. (this was the

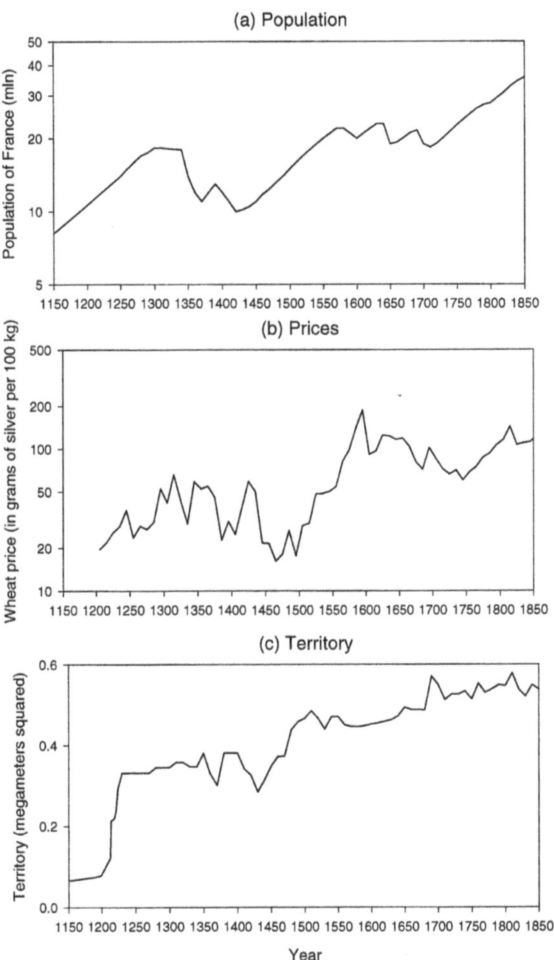

Figure 4.1 Demographic, economic, and territorial dynamics of France, 1150–1850. (a) Population within the modern borders of France (note the logarithmic scale) (after Braudel 1988 and Dupâquier 1988a). (b) Wheat price in grams of silver per 100 kg (data from Abel 1980). (c) Territory of the French state, in millions of square kilometers (Mm^2) (Reed 1996).

typical allowance provided to a young nobleman attending university or a pension to a widow of the lesser gentry). In other words, 25 l.v. per year was enough to maintain a family of four or five, but left no surplus for status-seeking. A sum of 25 l.v. at that time was equivalent to £5; thus, the minimum incomes of the lesser gentry in France and in England were essentially the same. The substantial knight in Forez with a minimum income of 100 l.v. had his counterpart in an English knight or esquire with £20 per annum.

The elite numbers changed dramatically during the cycle. Around 1300 the proportion of noble households in the population varied between 1 and 4 percent, depending on the region (Contamine 1997:50–52). The average was 2.4 percent, a figure that Philippe Contamine, however, has cautiously lowered to 1.8 percent (Contamine 1997:53). Assuming a population of 20 million and five persons per household yields an estimate of 70,000 noble families in 1300. A century and a half later, Contamine (1997:56) estimates, the proportion of nobles to the total population had declined to 1.5 percent. Assuming a population near the 10 million mark in the middle of the fifteenth century, this produces an estimate of 30,000 noble families at the end of the cycle.

Political Dynamics

The early Capetian kings ruled a tiny area centered on Paris and Orléans in northern France. The situation changed dramatically during the twelfth century (when the Norman state experienced protracted civil war and change of dynasty). Under Philip II Augustus (1180–1223), the territory directly controlled by the French state expanded enormously, so that in 1223 it was ten times as large as the territory controlled by Hugh Capet (figure 4.1c). During most of the twelfth century, thus, France was at war with England under first the Norman and then the Angevin dynasties, a period of conflict sometimes called "the first Hundred Years' War." "Pillage, murder, banditry, and insecurity were part of everyday life" (Braudel 1988:133).

This period of instability, associated with the Capetian conquest of France (which included such violent episodes as the Albigensian Crusades), is clearly reflected in the temporal distribution of coin hoards (figure 4.2). Once the boundaries of the kingdom expanded, however, the central regions began to enjoy the benefits of the peace. Most of the decades of the thirteenth century and the first half of the fourteenth century have yielded relatively few hoards (figure 4.2). There is a minor upward fluctuation during the second decade of the fourteenth century (perhaps associated with the baronial rebellion at the end of Philip IV's reign), but the next major peak of instability was brought about by the collapse of the state in the 1350s and 1360s (figure 4.2). Unfortunately, the third volume of Jean Duplessy's *Les Trésors Monétaires Médiévaux et Modernes Découverts en France* has not been published, and thus we lack information on this extremely useful indicator for the period after 1385.

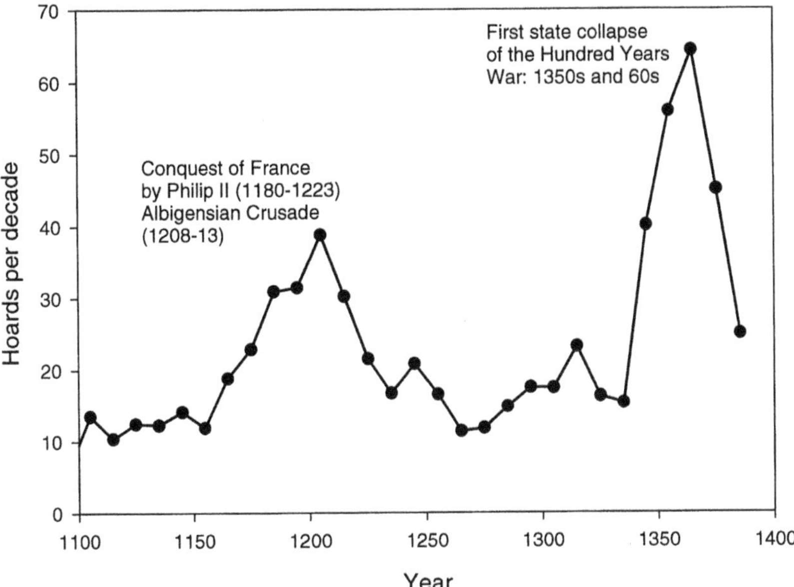

Figure 4.2 Temporal distribution of the French coin hoards, 1100–1385 (Duplessy 1985).

4.2 Expansion (1150–1250)

Demographic data are hard to come by for the medieval period. Table 4.1 gathers together several estimates on the number of surviving children in a family from various sources. This is a good statistic, because it integrates over fecundity and survival (to adulthood) and because it is directly related to the population growth rate. Cross comparisons of different localities and of different social strata are not valid, but temporal changes within each data set are in general agreement. There was apparently a slowing of population growth during the tenth and eleventh centuries (although the data are very crude). What is clear is that replacement rates tended to increase during the twelfth century (table 4.1).

During the twelfth and thirteenth centuries the population of France must have tripled from 6 million to 20 million (figure 4.1a). The economic base for this enormous population build-up had to come primarily from the expansion of cultivated lands. As a result of massive internal colonization, farmland expanded at the expense of heath, forest, and marsh. It is estimated that out of 26 million ha of forest cover in France in 1000, one-half was destroyed by 1300 (Braudel 1988:140). To appreciate the magni-

TABLE 4.1
Average number of children per family in France, 800–1500

Time period	*Number*	*Area*	*Source*
9th century	*2.5*	Polyptyque d'Irminon	Reinhard et al. (1968:65)
980–1050	4.5	The rich of Mâconnais	Dupâquier et al. (1988a:214)
10th century	*3.8*	Nobility, northern France	Reinhard et al. (1968:69)
1000–1050	4.2	Nobility, northern France	Reinhard et al. (1968:69)
1050–1100	*3.8*	Nobility, northern France	Reinhard et al. (1968:69)
1100–1150	5.5	Nobility, northern France	Reinhard et al. (1968:69)
1150–1200	**5.6**	Nobility, northern France	Reinhard et al. (1968:69)
1200–1250	4.9	Nobility, northern France	Reinhard et al. (1968:69)
1250–1300	5.1	Nobility, northern France	Reinhard et al. (1968:69)
1025	*3–4*	Nobility, Picardy	Dupâquier et al. (1988a:215)
1050	4–4.5	Nobility, Picardy	Dupâquier et al. (1988a:215)
1075	>4	Nobility, Picardy	Dupâquier et al. (1988a:215)
1100	5–6	Nobility, Picardy	Dupâquier et al. (1988a:215)
1075–1100	**5.06**	Nobility, Picardy	Dupâquier et al. (1988a:215)
1100–1125	4.52	Nobility, Picardy	Dupâquier et al. (1988a:215)
1125–1150	4.70	Nobility, Picardy	Dupâquier et al. (1988a:215)
1150–1175	4.92	Nobility, Picardy	Dupâquier et al. (1988a:215)
1175–1200	5.40	Nobility, Picardy	Dupâquier et al. (1988a:215)
1200–1225	**5.54**	Nobility, Picardy	Dupâquier et al. (1988a:215)
1225–1250	5.24	Nobility, Picardy	Dupâquier et al. (1988a:215)
1250–1275	5.08	Nobility, Picardy	Dupâquier et al. (1988a:215)
1275–1300	5.32	Nobility, Picardy	Dupâquier et al. (1988a:215)
1245–1300	**4.00**	Urban elite, Périgueux	Dupâquier et al. (1988a:302)
1300–1330	2.75	Urban elite, Périgueux	Dupâquier et al. (1988a:302)
1330–1370	1.91	Urban elite, Périgueux	Dupâquier et al. (1988a:302)
1370–1400	2.29	Urban elite, Périgueux	Dupâquier et al. (1988a:302)
1400–1430	*1.82*	Urban elite, Périgueux	Dupâquier et al. (1988a:302)
1430–1470	2.35	Urban elite, Périgueux	Dupâquier et al. (1988a:302)
1470–1500	3.55	Urban elite, Périgueux	Dupâquier et al. (1988a:302)
1350–1375	**1.81**	Arles	Dupâquier et al. (1988a:387)
1391–1395	1.75	Arles	Dupâquier et al. (1988a:387)
1471–1475	*1.03*	Arles	Dupâquier et al. (1988a:387)

Note: Maximum values are in bold, minimum values are in italic.

tude of this land clearance, the total arable land of modern France is 18 million ha (CIA 2002). It is difficult to estimate, though, how much new land was actually brought into production. Estimates of the increase range from a conservative 40 percent to a more optimistic 100 percent (Carpentier and Le Mené 1996:158). The increase in cultivated area was probably accompanied by increased yields per unit of area. Thus, Carpentier and Le Mené (1996:161) suggest that yields increased from 3–4:1 before the twelfth century and 4–5:1 toward 1180. This translates into a 40 percent increase in *net* yield.

An expanding population, coupled with growing productivity (or, at least, productivity not decreasing as a result of diminishing returns—and there is no evidence of diminishing returns prior to 1250), should have translated into healthy state finances. Indeed, the century around 1200 saw a great expansion of royal revenues. Accounts for the year 1202–3 suggest that the ordinary revenues of Philip Augustus were about 115,000 *livres parisis* (l.p.), and that these had increased by 72 percent since the beginning of his reign in 1180 (Henneman 1999:104). Gross receipts in 1202–3 (including revenue raised for the war against the Plantagenets) amounted to 196,327 l.p. (Hallam and Everard 2001:226). Louis IX's fixed annual revenue was probably between 200,000 and 250,000 l.p. by 1250 (Hallam and Everard 2001:311), twice that of Philip Augustus. Thus, real revenues grew substantially, since the price of grain increased between 1200 and the 1250s by only 20 percent (figure 4.1b). Increasing revenues underwrote state expansion, which brought in more potential taxpayers, in a kind of a virtuous cycle. This dynamic probably explains the explosive growth of the Capetian state during this period.

4.3 Stagflation (1250–1315)

Population and Economy

At some point during the second half of the thirteenth century, the rate of growth of agricultural production started to lag behind that of population. The reclamation of land ceased between 1230 and 1280 in most provinces (Braudel 1988:155, Carpentier and Le Mené 1996:331). Shortly thereafter—at some point between 1280 and 1315—the population reached its peak. There is mild disagreement among different authorities on the date of the peak. Most likely, different regions peaked at different times; there is no reason to expect a perfect synchrony. For example, Carpentier and Le Mené (1996:314) suggest that the population of the Midi may have continued to expand as late as 1340.

Population growth was reflected in the rise of prices (figure 4.1b). The price of wheat increased through the thirteenth century, but the worst period of inflation was from the 1250s to the 1310s, when the price of a quintal of wheat went from 24 to 66 g of silver (Abel 1980). There are no systematic wage data for medieval France, but pay rates for soldiers suggest that nominal wages increased, although they did not keep pace with inflation (table 4.2). What is interesting is that the real wages declined for both elite and commoner soldiers, but the commoners suffered more (we saw a similar dynamic in the wages of English soldiers; see chapter 2).

TABLE 4.2
Daily rates of pay for soldiers in France

Pay rate	*1202*	*1295*
Knight		
Nominal, l.t.	7 s. 6 d.	10 s., 12 s. 6 d., or 15 s.
In silver	25.1 g	41.8 g
In wheat	1.71 hl	1.06 hl
Foot soldier		
Nominal, l.t.	10 d.	12 d.
In silver	2.8 g	3.3 g
In wheat	0.19 hl	0.08 hl

Source: Contamine (1984:94).
Note: Units: l.t., *livre tournois;* g, gram; hl, hectoliter; s., sou; d., denier.

The pressure of population also translated into progressive fragmentation of peasant land holdings. In Dauphiné, 75 percent of peasants had less than 2 ha of farmland; in Hainault, 60 percent held 1 ha or less (Carpentier and Le Mené 1996:328). This amount of land was far below the level needed to feed a peasant family. Estimates of the production budgets of peasant holdings suggest that the minimum land allowing a comfortable leaving was around 6 ha (Carpentier and Le Mené 1996:340). Assuming a three-field system and an average harvest of 10 hl/ha, 6 ha should yield 40 hl every year. From this the peasant had to pay the tithe of one-ninth and *terrage* of one-seventh, leaving him with 30 hl. After reserving 8 hl for seed, the peasant and the family had at its disposal 22 hl (16 quintals) of grain for personal consumption, enough for a family of four to five people. However, only a small minority of peasants, less than 20 percent, had land of 6 ha or more (Carpentier and Le Mené 1996). Thus, the huge majority of rural households did not have enough land to feed themselves, and their very existence critically depended on securing outside employment. The result of this process was a vast and growing rural proletariat. In a vain hope of finding employment, many of the rural poor migrated to towns, further depressing urban real wages (Carpentier and Le Mené 1996:357), as well as fueling the remarkable urban growth.

As land became scarce, its price shot up. In Normandy an acre of land at the beginning of the thirteenth century cost 2 livres; a century later it went for 20 livres. In Picardy a price of a *journal* (approximately 0.4 ha) during the first half of the thirteenth century varied between 1 and 3, at most 4, livres. During the second half of the century, prices went above 4 livres per *journal,* and toward 1300 they fluctuated between 6 and 10 livres. There were some regional variations, however. At Beamont-le-Roger, for example, land prices rose until 1260 and then stagnated until 1313. In Beauce (near Chartres) there was actually a tendency for prices to decline.

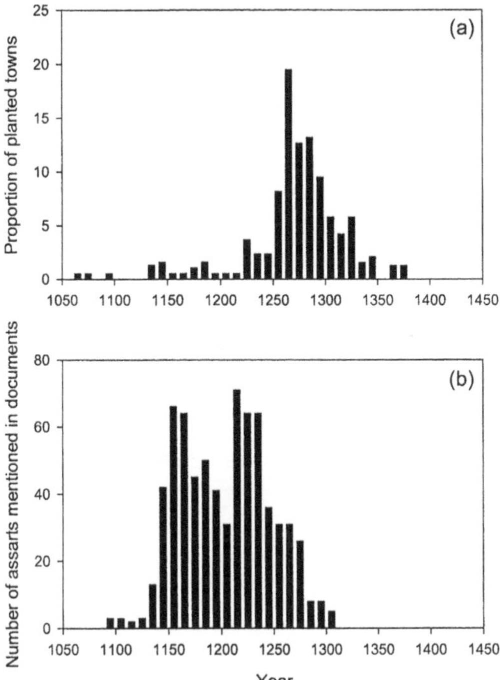

Figure 4.3 Distinct dynamics of urban and rural development. (a) Dynamics of planted towns (Beresford 1967). (b) Number of assarts mentioned in documents (Fossier 1968).

Land rents increased even faster than prices. For example, in just forty years between 1276 and 1316, rents around Lille increased fivefold (Carpentier and Le Mené 1996:334, 336).

While the rural population grew ever more slowly and eventually stagnated during this period, the urban population increased rapidly. Large numbers of new towns appeared during the thirteenth century, with a particularly frenetic pace of urban development after 1250 (figure 4.3a). Over 70 percent of planted towns in France outside Gascony appeared during the stagflation period (1250–1315) (Beresford 1967). Rural development, as measured by the number of assarts mentioned in the documents (figure 4.3b), thus preceded urban development. Rural land clearance was concentrated in the expansion phase, while the bulk of urban expansion fell within the stagflation phase.

During the thirteenth century the population of Paris doubled (figure 4.4a), and it kept on increasing during the next century. The number of cities having populations between 10,000 and 20,000 increased to twenty or so, and there were a dozen in the 20,000–50,000 range (Carpentier and

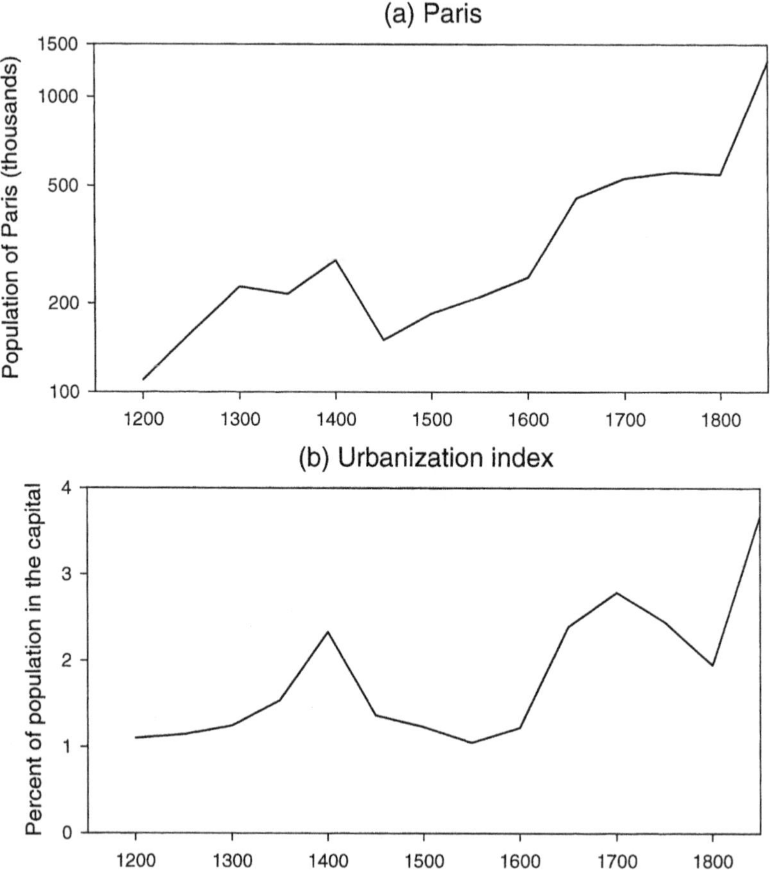

Figure 4.4 Dynamics of urbanization in France, 1200–1850. (a) Population of Paris (Chandler 1987). (b) An index of urbanization (defined as the proportion of the population in the capital).

Le Mené 1996:317). Cities grew partly because of the influx of migrants from rural areas, partly because of increasing trade and crafts. But city walls also offered protection, and as sociopolitical instability increased, growing numbers of rural dwellers abandoned exposed *plat pays* and moved to the relative safety of fortified towns and cities.

Elite Overproduction

There is abundant, although largely anecdotal, evidence of elite overproduction developing toward the end of the stagflation phase, summarized, for example, by Jonathan Sumption (1991:30–32). The main problem of minor noblemen was "the smallness of their holdings, the result of generations of pious bequests and family partitions. Primogeniture was never rigidly applied even in the west and north of France, where it was theoretically the rule of law. Elsewhere, it was not even accepted in principle. As a result, by the beginning of the fourteenth century the holdings of much of the lesser nobility had been reduced to barely workable parcels" (Sumption 1991:31). The situation was particularly dire in Ile-de-France. At least a quarter of the noble vassals of the Parisian abbeys and the Crown had an annual income of less than 10 livres (data of Guy Fourquin, cited in Sumption 1991:31). Many petty nobles mortgaged their land or sold it to rich peasants. "In the century to come the survivors of this pauperized gentry would turn to war for their living and finally to brigandage" (Sumption 1991:32).

The State

During the stagflation period royal revenues increased in nominal terms but could not keep up with inflation. Louis IX's ordinary revenues were around 0.25 million l.t. around 1250 (Kaeuper 1988:62, Henneman 1999:104). By the late thirteenth century the annual income of Philip IV had climbed to between 0.4 and 0.6 million l.t. (Kaeuper 1988). Thus, nominal income perhaps doubled, but prices also doubled. Philip's son Charles IV (1322–28) received average net ordinary revenues of 0.28 million l.t., which in real terms amounted to only 53 percent of what his father had enjoyed thirty years earlier (Henneman 1999:109). The accession of Philip VI (1328–50) brought the vast appanage of the Valois family into the royal domain, but his ordinary revenues (in real terms) amounted to only 80 percent of those available to Philip IV (Henneman 1999:109).

4.4 Crisis (1315–65)

Population Collapse

By the early fourteenth century, France, as well as most of Western Europe, was literally crammed with people. The "ecosystem" (to use Le Roy Ladurie's term) was strained to the breaking point and on the verge of collapse. The collapse experienced during the fourteenth century was the result of a typical concatenation of famine, pestilence, and war.

Famine struck first. By the early fourteenth century, agricultural production was barely enough to provide sustenance for the population, and the majority had just enough food to live. Famines had practically disappeared during the thirteenth century, but they returned again and again during the fourteenth. The first important famine hit France in 1302 (Carpentier and Le Mené 1996:353), but the sustained population decline most likely began after the multi-annual famine of 1315–17. In fact, during 1315–30 a series of terrible winters brought famine in, an alarming warning sign of the troubles to come during the following century (Braudel 1988:154–55).

The second blow was delivered by the Black Death. The first wave of bubonic plague swept France in 1348–49. Between a quarter and a half, and in some cases 80–90 percent, of the population perished, depending on the region (Braudel 1988:157). Recurrent plague epidemics were to hit France at intervals of roughly a decade during the rest of the century. For example, the second highest mortality peak in Lyon after 1348–49 was in 1361 (Lorcin 1974).

The plague imposed a disproportionate mortality on the poor. For example, at Albi between 1343 and 1357 the proportion of the very poor (owning possessions estimated at less than 50 livres) fell from 76 percent to 62 percent. At the same time, the middle stratum (50–200 livres) increased from 21 percent to 28.5 percent, and the proportion of the rich (over 200 livres) doubled from 4.2 percent to 8.1 percent (Dupâquier et al. 1988a:323). Thus, one consequence of the plague was a distortion of the social pyramid, making it even more top-heavy than it was before the plague (we saw the same pattern in the English data).

The effects of famine and disease, as well as war, on the population dynamics during the fourteenth century are well understood in a qualitative way, even if precise quantitative estimates are lacking (Dupâquier et al. 1988a). The French population, like that in other Western European polities, began declining after 1300 CE, then experienced a precipitous drop in the wake of the Black Death epidemic of 1348, followed by further losses as epidemics recurred (as in 1361) and fighting in the Hundred Years' War intensified. Overall population numbers declined by about one-half (Dupâquier et al. 1988b:149), from 20 million to 10 million. After that, for about a century population numbers fluctuated at a low level, starting to increase only during the second half of the fifteenth century.

Although the crisis of the fourteenth century brought much misery, the population collapse had also some positive effects, at least for the lower strata. A relaxation of Malthusian pressure brought economic relief to peasants and workers. Apart from periods of particularly intense warfare, real wages and the consumptions levels of ordinary people improved dramatically toward the end of the fourteenth century (table 4.3). In 1338 the Provençal drovers working on their lord's reserve ate a very crude kind of bread made mainly with barley. After the Black Death, barley bread was considered to be good enough only for the sheepdogs, while the laborers were entitled to wheat bread (Le Roy Ladurie 1987:70).

TABLE 4.3
Daily wages (s.t.), 1320–1500

Year	*Building worker at Rouen*	*Infantryman*
1320	1.5	1.0
1350	3.5	2.0
1380	4.0	5.2
1410	3.8	3.3
1440	4.5	2.7
1470	4.0	2.7
1500	4.5	3.4

Source: Bois (1984) and Contamine (1984).

Lords and Peasants

As we noted earlier, the beginning of the fourteenth century in France was characterized by elite overproduction. As the amount of surplus produced by peasants was shrinking, an example of the law of diminishing returns in action, the number of elites who were supported by the surplus was increasing. "To preserve caste, the lord was compelled to draw more, on peasant production, and by other means. On the other hand, any additional drain endangered the ability for self-subsistence of the peasant holding. The contradiction was insoluble and disruptive" (Bois 1984:260). The population decline of the years 1315–50 further exacerbated this basic contradiction. The post-1315 famines affected mainly the poorest strata of the society, and although many noblemen died in the plague, it had a disproportionate effect on the poor. As a result, the proportion of elites to the general population increased even beyond the already high levels of the early fourteenth century.

As their incomes declined, the elites had to look to "other means," in Guy Bois's words, to preserve their caste. The end result was intensification of the intraelite conflict for scarce resources. Particularly hard hit were the poorer nobles. Even in the thirteenth century a great number of the lesser gentry in Forez lived on 25 *livres viennois* (£5) or less (Perroy 1962:28). As the food prices doubled (or even tripled, as in the 1310s), these noble households slipped below the minimum level of consumption consistent with noble status. Indeed, some noble households must have starved during the famines of the early fourteenth century. By mid-century there were literally tens of thousands of destitute and desperate noblemen of fighting age. Philippe Contamine (1997:204) estimates that 25,000 if not 30,000 nobles flocked to the army of Philip VI in 1340 in the hope of military pay (there were 27,000 cavalrymen serving in the royal army in September

1340 [Sumption 1991]). It appears that the king and his lieutenants were surprised, even disconcerted by the huge numbers of men-at-arms responding to their call to arms (Contamine 1972:73). This disorganized and undisciplined crowd was one of the factors contributing to the subsequent French defeats at Crécy and Poitiers. The presence of huge numbers of men desperate and trained in the use of arms was a tremendous destabilizing factor.

Elite overproduction was not limited to the military class. "Between 1314 and 1343 the number of principal judicial officers of the various royal courts in Paris increased fourfold; the number of notaries by about the same; the 'sergeants' who enforced compliance with the orders of the King's ministers and judges increased sevenfold" (Sumption 1991:19).

State Collapse

At the same time that the intensity of intraelite competition and conflict was rising, the state was gradually losing its ability to keep internal peace and protect the country from external invasion. The main problem was financial. Before the reign of Philip IV (1270–1314), the Crown had no difficulty living off its ordinary revenues, and occasionally collecting extraordinary levies (needed, for example, to ransom Louis IX when he was captured while on crusade in Egypt). By the end of the thirteenth century, however, the ordinary revenues had stagnated in real terms, while expenses, especially for military operations, soared. To raise revenues, Philip IV exploited his feudal rights, demanded subsidies, imposed forced loans on the bourgeois, and manipulated the currency (Henneman 1999:105–6). These methods incurred much resentment, and the first half of the fourteenth century saw increasing resistance to taxation on behalf of various elites. The basic and essentially unresolvable problem was that the state competed with the elites for the shrinking surplus. Thus, we should modify the binary contradiction of Guy Bois, that between lord and peasant, to a trinary contradiction of the productive class–the elites–the state.

The lack of consensus on the need for national taxation had a direct effect on the ability of the state to wage war against the English. Philip VI (1328–50) and John II (1350–64) were unable to collect subsidies except in times of outright conflict, and were in a constant state of financial distress (Henneman 1999:110). As a result, France was always unprepared whenever military operations resumed after a truce. The military disasters of 1346 and 1347 (the defeat at Crécy, the loss of Calais) finally persuaded the Estates General in 1355–56 to authorize necessary taxation, but now their attempts to impose taxes ran into resistance at the local level. In the end, the Estates were unable to produce the money they had promised

TABLE 4.4
Dynamics of assaults in the Officiality of Cerisy (Normandy)

Period	*Number of assaults per year*	*Percent involving the use of weapons*
1314–1346	1.2	2
1370–1414	4.9	25
1451–1458	4.3	40
1471–1486	0.7	8

Source: Finch (1997).

(Henneman 1999:111). The collapse of royal finances was followed shortly by a general collapse of the French state, triggered by the defeat and capture of John II at Poitiers (1356).

The disintegrative phase of the Capetian cycle was dominated by a conflict known as the Hundred Years' War. The Hundred Years' War was not simply a dynastic conflict between the French and English kings but a period of great political instability primarily within France (Salmon 1976). As Braudel suggests (1988:159), it would be more appropriate to call it a "hundred years of hostilities rather than a hundred-year-war"—a period of recurrent state collapse and civil war. The conflict occurred at multiple levels. The highest-level factions were led by the great seigneurs of France—the king himself, the duke of Guyenne (who also was the king of England), the duke of Burgundy, and the count of Flanders. From there the level of conflict descended through the magnates (counts and barons) and various factions of nobility, down to knights and peasants. This multilevel nature of the conflict can be illustrated with the example of later medieval Gascony (Vale 1986). At the "national" level, Gascony was one of the military frontiers in the Anglo-French struggle. At the regional level, the period from 1290 to the middle of the fifteenth century was dominated by the feud between the houses of Armagnac and Foix over the succession of the viscounty of Béarn. At a more local level, private wars between lesser nobility proliferated in Gascony. Between 1290 and 1327, for example, at least twelve outbreaks of intraelite violence are recorded in surviving sources (Vale 1986:140). And then there were numerous bands of *routiers* and *écorcheurs* who robbed and killed indiscriminantly both lords and peasants or ran "protection rackets" from castles, fortified churches, and manor houses (Wright 1998).

Interpersonal violence—crime—increased in parallel with organized violence. Statistics on violent crimes in at least one locality indicate there was a crime wave during the fourteenth century that peaked around 1400 and subsided by the second half of the fifteenth century (table 4.4).

The Dynamics of Sociopolitical Instability (1290–1365)

The sociopolitical crisis of the fourteenth century developed in France by degrees. The first signs of growing instability appeared in the frontier regions toward 1300. We have already discussed the collapse of order in Gascony from 1290 on. At the opposite end of the kingdom, in urbanized Flanders, social conflicts first broke out between 1279 and 1281 and later around the year 1300. The origin of the troubles seems to have been tensions between the established urban patriciate and the newly enriched bourgeoisie, who used the proletariat as shock troops (Carpentier and Le Mené 1996:356). Eventually the struggle for power led to a full-blown rebellion and the battle of Courtrai ("the Battle of the Spurs") in 1302, when Flemish infantry crushed aristocratic French cavalry. In 1325–26 the urban communities of Flanders rose against their ruler, Count Louis of Nevers. The burghers were massacred by the French army at the field of Cassel (1328), and Flanders was temporarily pacified. However, in 1337 the Flemish revolted again and, under the leadership of van Arteveldt of Ghent, expelled Louis of Nevers (Perroy 1965). The Flemish rebellion opened the northern route for the English invasion under Edward III.

Meanwhile, other regions of France were also experiencing increasing instability. The north and east of France (Picardy, Burgundy) were sites of the baronial movement against royal taxation during the reign of Louis X (1314–16). In the county of Artois, the revolt against the central power became complicated by internecine fighting between the adherents of Robert of Artois and his aunt Mahaut, who both claimed the county (Hallam and Everard 2001:392–93). Robert of Artois lost the struggle and eventually ended up in exile in England, where he joined his voice to those urging Edward III to go to war against France. But the events in Brittany had a much more direct effect on the course of the Hundred Years' War. In 1341, Duke John III of Brittany died without direct heirs. The succession was disputed between two factions, Blois and Monfort. In the ensuing civil war the lesser nobles and the Celtic west supported the Monforts, while the great lords and the French-speaking bourgeois of the east rallied to the Blois faction. The English supported the Monfort faction by launching a *chevauchée* (a mounted raid whose purpose was to lay waste to the country) and besieging Rennes, Vannes, and Nantes (Seward 1978:49).

Another faction arose in the 1350s. It was led by Charles the Bad, the king of Navarre, who was son of Joan of France (and therefore a grandson of Louis X, giving him a reasonable claim on the French throne) and Philip of Évreux. This faction was sometimes referred to as the Évreux faction and sometimes as the Navarrese. Charles the Bad inherited substantial landholdings in Normandy and Ile-de-France, and he provided leadership to the dissident nobilities of these regions. Charles the Bad was a disruptive influence from 1354, when he murdered the French Constable (the chief military officer), to 1364, when the rising of his faction in Normandy and Ile-de-France was suppressed by Charles V.

These examples of internecine fighting (to which we should add the later factional conflict between the Armagnacs and the Burgundians) illustrate the thesis, generally supported by modern historians, that the Hundred Years' War was primarily an internal conflict. The international aspect of the war arose primarily (if not solely) because various rival factions appealed to the kings of England or France. Thus, the Monfort and Arteveldt factions invited Edward III to intervene in Brittany and Flanders, respectively. It was supposedly Jan van Arteveldt who suggested that Edward III should declare himself the king of France, in order to legitimize the Flemish support. Another example of the same trend is the resumption of war in 1369, which resulted from the appeal to Charles V by the count of Armagnac against the Black Prince. Finally, the darkest period of the war for the French, 1420–36, came about as a result of the alliance of the Burgundians and the English.

Intraelite conflicts brought a host of other rebellions and uprisings in their wake, of which we will mention only two, the Paris rebellion and the Jacquerie. In 1357 the dauphin (future Charles V), who was the head of state as a result of his father's capture at Poitiers, lost Paris to a coalition of urban elites led by the wealthy cloth-dealer Etienne Marcel. During the revolt the Paris mob murdered two royal marshals in front of the dauphin. Incidentally, the Marcel faction in Paris was allied with another troublemaker, Charles the Bad of Navarre. During the winter of 1357–58 the gangs of Anglo-Navarrese "were day by day conquering and laying waste the entire region between the Loire and Seine" (Froissart, cited in Fourquin 1978:136). The pillaging by men-at-arms, on top of the fiscal demands of the monarchy and the seigneurial reaction, pushed the peasants of Ile-de-France beyond the breaking point. The Jacquerie started in May 1358 and was suppressed by the nobles in June (Fourquin 1978:134–36).

The years 1356–60 were the nadir. Shocked by the state collapse, the nobility started to consolidate around the dauphin and achieved a general consensus on fiscal reform (Henneman 1999:112). The immediate stimulus for imposing taxes was the need to pay the huge ransom for John II, who had been captured at Poitiers. However, the ordinance of 5 December 1360 became a landmark in French fiscal history (Henneman 1999:113), establishing the basic framework of the ancien régime. It imposed the salt tax (*gabelle*) and indirect (sales) taxes on other types of consumption (*aides*). The Estates General agreed to another important new tax known as the *fouage* (the hearth tax). Direct taxes, such as the *fouage*, later renamed *taille*, became a long tradition in French royal taxation. Whereas indirect taxes primarily affected the urban population, direct taxes such as the *fouage* also bore on rural lordships. It was not popular with the nobility, but they did not raise much opposition because the primary purpose of this tax was to pay military salaries. In fact, it may appear surprising how little opposition there was to new taxes. The need to ransom the king was clearly one factor (in the end, the whole amount of ransom was never paid; instead, the government of Charles V wisely used the money to build a new army). Perhaps even more important was the collective realization that something had to be done or France would be lost. Another contributing factor was the massive "pruning" of the French nobility administered by the war. The worst disaster, that of Crécy, wiped out 10,000 of the "flower of the French nobility," and Poitiers accounted for another 2,500. Some thousands died at the naval battle of Sluys (1340). And unknown thousands died in the local civil wars and at the hands of the *jacques* of Ile-de-France. In short, by 1360 there were simply many fewer "noble thugs" to raise trouble—some had been killed off, others had inherited the property of their slain relatives. The swing in public opinion in favor of peace is evident in the new tone of the literature on warfare and chivalry. Whereas earlier the emphasis had been on the right to private war and the pursuit of honor and glory, now it addressed questions of discipline and public order (Henneman 1996:142). We should not, however, overestimate the strength of this consensus. It lasted for two decades, the 1360s and 1370s; when the new generation, which did not directly experience the collapse of 1356–60, came to power, it allowed things to fall apart again.

When Charles V became king in 1365, the national consolidation, even if temporary, resulted in a rapid recovery of the territory lost to the English. Unlike the huge and undisciplined throngs of the previous reign, the army of Charles V consisted of only 2,400 men-at-arms and 1,000 crossbowmen, of which 60 percent were mounted (Contamine 1972:138). These troops were permanently employed and regularly paid. The permanent forces were joined during periods of particularly intense activity by supplementary retinues of men-at-arms (bringing the total to the maximum of 5,200). The first military success of the new army was in crushing the forces of the Évreux faction in Normandy (led by Charles the Bad) in the spring of 1364 (Henneman 1999:115). In 1369 the war with the English resumed as a result of the appeal by the count of Armagnac, and before the death of Charles V in 1380 almost all French territory was regained. The English held only Bordeaux, Bayonne, Brest, Calais, Cherbourg, and Valais and their immediately surrounding territory.

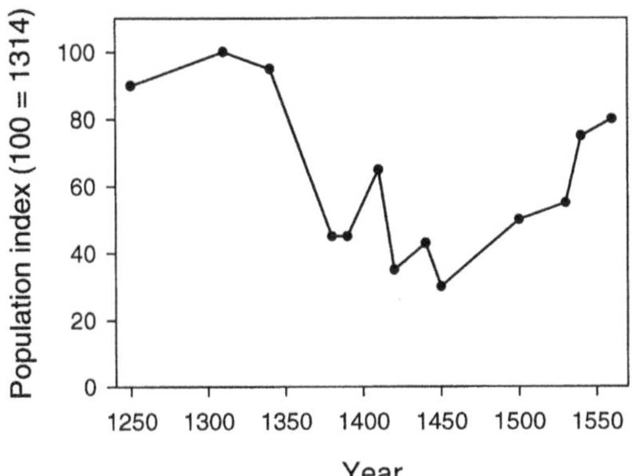

Figure 4.5 Population dynamics in Normandy, 1250–1560 (after Bois 1984).

4.5 Depression (1365–1450)

Population Stagnation

After the disasters of the mid-fourteenth century that reduced its population by a third and half, France entered a period of seeming stagnation until 1450. Stagnation, however, does not mean "steady state." Rather, this period was characterized by short periods of recovery followed by new collapses. The process can be illustrated with data from Normandy (Bois 1984:76). There were three periods of crisis, with population minima in 1380, 1420, and 1450, interspersed with two periods of partial recovery, and then by a sustained population growth after 1450 (figure 4.5).

The incidence of population decline is closely correlated with the intensification of internal war, not only because of war's direct effect on demographic rates but also because of its indirect consequences for the productive infrastructure. Similar dynamics of partial recovery followed by crashes were characteristic of other regions, although the timing of the fluctuations varied in accordance with regional variations in the fluxes of internal warfare and recurrent epidemics. Carpentier and Le Mené (1996:378–80) provide an overview of fluctuations in Hainault, Artois, Province, and Dauphiné. Altogether, they propose that the French population decreased between 1350 (that is, after the first shock of the Black Death) and 1450 (the lowest point) by a third. When this decline is added to the demographic catastrophe of the mid-fourteenth century (discussed in the previous section) the overall change between 1300 and 1450 is estimated to be around one-half (Le Roy Ladurie 1987, Dupâquier et al. 1988a). Some regions experienced declines that were even more catastrophic, such as the 70 percent fall in Normandy (Bois 1984). Furthermore, a reanalysis of some data suggests that earlier historians were sometimes too conservative in estimating the degree of population crash. For example, in a widely cited estimate, Fourquin (1964) calculated that the region of Paris lost one-half its population. However, a later reanalysis of the same data by Bois indicated a fall of 75 percent (Bois 2000).

The Effect of Persistent Warfare

The sociopolitical instability of the Hundred Years' War had an enormous impact on the productive capacity of French society (Braudel 1988: 160–61). Some areas were fought over repeatedly and suffered most. We have already quoted (in chapter 1) from the chronicle of Thomas Basin describing the devastation of Normandy. By 1450 the population of Normandy had fallen to 30 percent of its peak in the early fourteenth century (figure 4.5).

The Paris region was another area where fighting was prolonged, and its rural population may have decreased fourfold. The region suffered both because it was close to Flanders and Normandy, the sources of the English *chevauchées*, and because it was the national capital. Here is Petrarch on his visit to France in 1360: "I could scarcely recognise anything I saw. The most opulent of kingdoms is a heap of ashes; there was not a single house standing except those protected by the ramparts of towns and citadels. Where is now Paris that was once such a great city?" (quoted by Braudel 1988:161). Two generations later Paris was the battleground between Armagnacs and Burgundians, who "vied with each other to prove how far bloodthirstiness could go: murders and massacres never ceased. When the Burgundians entered the capital in May 1418, it was littered with Armagnac corpses 'piled up like pigs in the mud'" (Braudel 1988:160, the quote is from a contemporary *Journal d'un bourgeois de Paris*).

The south (especially southwest) was similarly devastated. Philippe de la Boissière wrote in the fifteenth century that "this land of Saintonge, except for the towns and fortresses, was deserted and uninhabited. . . . Where there had once been fine manors, domains, and heritages, towering bushes grew" (Braudel 1988:160). Some areas escaped devastation for a while. When the English under the Black Prince marched through the Massif Central in 1356, they found "the land of Auvergne which they had never before entered . . . so prosperous and so full of all manner of goods that it was a marvel to see" (Froissart, quoted in Braudel 1988:160). Needless to say, the prosperity of Auvergne did not survive the Black Prince and his troops.

Famine became endemic in France in the first half of the fifteenth century. There were crises in food supplies around Paris and Rouen in 1421, 1432, 1433, and particularly 1437–39. But these crises were not a fundamental cause of population stagnation; rather, they were an aggravating circumstance. The underlying cause was the war (Le Roy Ladurie 1987:35). This can be seen most graphically in the dynamics of the real wage (Allen 2001). The fourteenth-century population decline translated into excellent real wages for working people. Thus, in the first decade of the fifteenth century a building laborer in Paris could buy more than 20 kg of grain with his daily wage. Similarly high wages prevailed for several decades after the end of the Hundred Years' War. During the war decades of the 1420s and 1430s, by contrast, the laborer's wage collapsed to less than 8 kg of grain per day.

The problem was not lack of cultivable land or people to cultivate it. The fundamental problem was lack of security. Peasants abandoned villages for the relative safety of fortified towns. For example, around such Alsatian towns as Colmar, there were whole belts of dead villages. The land that was abandoned was allowed to turn fallow, or was lightly utilized for grazing cattle (Le Roy Ladurie 1987:37). Incessant warfare also destroyed infrastructure. For example, in the area of Langle (modern Pas-de-Calais), the drainage system was abandoned, and the land was first flooded and then deserted (Le Roy Ladurie 1987:38). The degree of village abandonment (similar to German *Wüstungen*) varied with region in France. The south was more strongly affected, with between 25 and 33 percent of villages abandoned in Provence. Many of these desertions were final, affecting one-quarter of localities in mountainous regions. In the north, by contrast, only 3–10 percent of villages were abandoned forever (Le Roy Ladurie 1987:38). Altogether, Le Roy Ladurie (1974:42) estimates that a minimum of 3–4 million ha of land was abandoned between 1350 and 1440.

Elite Dynamics

Incessant fighting affected aristocracy to an even greater degree than the commoner population. Enormous numbers of French nobles were dispossessed during this period (Wright 1998). The population collapse of the second half of the fourteenth century and the ensuing depression resulted in a divergent evolution of the economic well-being of nobility and peasants (Carpentier and Le Mené 1996:463). After some lag time, declining population pushed down grain prices and drove up real wages. Small people were the beneficiaries of the new economic conjuncture. It would be an exaggeration to call this period the "golden age" of peasants, because they continuously suffered from incessant warfare, periodic epidemics, and recurrent famines (themselves largely caused by warfare). Nevertheless, they usually had enough food to feed the family. And even during bad times, for example, between 1420 and 1440 in Paris, their wages were substantially above those during the peaceful period of 1520–60, when population densities again approached the ceiling of the carrying capacity.

The economic well-being of the nobility moved opposite to that of the peasants. They profited little from cheaper grain, because many grew food on their own estates, and in any case food did not loom as large in their consumption budget as it did for commoners. Because wages increased, nobles had to pay more for manufactures and services necessary for signaling their elite status (the alternative was a quiet slide into the ranks of commoners). In other words, nobles had to spend more just to maintain the level of living they had previously become accustomed to.

Unfortunately, noble incomes declined at the same time as their expenditures increased. Even before 1350, a good half of nobility enjoyed incomes of only 40 livres or less, less than a well-to-do farmer, who had an income of about 60 livres (Carpentier and Le Mené 1996:464). After his review of what is known about the noble incomes during the period between 1280 and 1340, Contamine (1997:107) concluded that the great majority of noble incomes were modest or even mediocre, and that it was quite problematic for them even to maintain their means of existence. The severe recession of the fourteenth century, coupled with the civil wars and peasant uprisings, resulted in nothing short of catastrophe. All sources of noble income declined: rents, revenues from justice, profits from seigneurial equipment such as mills and baking ovens, and tolls from fairs and markets (Carpentier and Le Mené 1996:465, Bois 2000:115). Most seigneurs lost one-half to three-quarters of their revenues between 1350 and 1450 (Bois 2000:115). Thus, in just thirty years (1335–64), the income of Jeanne de Navarre from her Champaign and Brie properties fell by 58 percent (from 23,000 to 10,000 livres). Between 1340 and 1400 the income of the abbey of Saint-Denis fell by 50 percent in nominal terms and by two-thirds in real terms (from 72,000 to 24,000 *setiers* of grain). The buying power in cereals of the seigneurial income of Jeanne de Chalon in 1420 was only 15–20 percent of that enjoyed by her grandparents in the 1340s (Le Roy Ladurie 1987:61–64).

The Dame de Chalon at least managed to survive modestly and pass on to her heirs some vestiges of her patrimony. Other less fortunate noble families disappeared as such: slaughtered in battle, succumbed to the plague, or ruined and plunged into the lower classes. In 1378 the average income of a knight in the *châtellenie* of Mello (in the *bailliage* of Senlis, the Paris region) was only 45 l.p, while squires had to do with only 25 l.p (B. Guenée, cited in Contamine 1997:89). The peaceful period of 1380–1410 saw some restoration of noble incomes. But with the resumption of civil war and English invasions, the revenues plunged to new lows. For example, the income of the castellanies of Laignes and Griselles in the county of Tonnerre fell from 500 to 238 l.p. between 1405 and 1425. In 1343, before the troubles, the *prévôté* of Tonnerre reported an annual revenue of 520 livres. The revenue then fell to 182 livres in 1405 and 114 livres in 1425 (Contamine 1997:110). The data from Normandy indicate income declined nearly 50 percent between 1400 and 1450 (Contamine 1997:111–12). An example of a more extreme collapse is provided by the seigneury of Sully (in the Orléans region), whose revenue fell from 700 l.p. in 1383–84 to 143 l.p. in 1455 (Contamine 1997:113).

The severe depression of landed incomes did not affect all noble families uniformly. Rather, it imposed a selection regime in which the weak and unlucky declined and eventually succumbed, while the strong and lucky held their own, or even got ahead. The impoverished nobles who attempted to maintain the levels of consumption necessary for preserving their status rapidly ran up debt, and eventually had to sell their lands. Thus, the majority of the *plèbe nobiliare*, those families that already were on the brink by 1350, were plunged beyond the point of no return. On the other hand, many magnate families during this period were buying up lands. It was easier for a *grand seigneur* to reduce consumption without crossing the line between nobility and commonality. Furthermore, magnates were better positioned to profit from the royal patronage (even though the volume of the flow of royal favors was greatly diminished during this era), and land was cheap. Another group that profited from the economic situation consisted of certain bourgeois, particularly those who provided administrators and legists for the state (essentially, these officeholders were the forerunners of the robe nobility that merged into the ruling class during the subsequent centuries). On the other hand, merchants apparently did not do particularly well (unless they had first become officeholders); at least this appears to be true for the Paris region (Fourquin 1964).

What were the consequences of these economic difficulties for noble numbers and replacement rates? There are a few regional studies that yield quantitative data documenting elite dynamics in medieval France. Lorcin's (1981) study of wills registered in the officialty of Lyon yielded some information on the number of living children at the time of death of a testator (table 4.5). These numbers incidentally give us information about the relative dynamics of the replacement rate (in order to calculate the absolute replacement rate, we would have to multiply it by the proportion of males among the children and also take into account the proportion of families that did not have any children; however, for our purposes, relative changes is what we need).

The data indicate that family sizes of both noble and non-noble families declined during the fourteenth century, then increased during the fifteenth century. The difference between the noble and non-noble families is instructive. During the fourteenth century, noble households tended to have substantially more children than non-noble families, but with time this differential declined, and even inverted its sign by the end of the fifteenth century. However, the "noble advantage" of greater family size was sub-

TABLE 4.5
Number of living children per testator having children

Period	*Nobles*	*Non-nobles*	*Differential*
1300–1340	4.3	3.2	+1.1
1340–1380	3.4	2.6	+1.2
1380–1420	3.8	2.8	+1.0
1420–1460	4.2	3.5	+0.7
1460–1500	3.7	5.3	−1.6

Source: Lorcin (1981), cited in Contamine (1997:59).

stantially reduced, if not nullified, by the tendency of a high proportion of noble daughters to become nuns. Two-thirds of noblewomen in Lyon entered a nunnery during the first half of the fourteenth century, but only 14 percent did so during the last half of the fifteenth century (table 4.6). These proportions should be compared to just 2.4 percent of non-nobles choosing a religious career during the whole period. It is clear that noble families shipped to religious houses their "surplus" female progeny, since the proportion of daughters becoming nuns increased from 15 percent for small families (three children or less) to 45 percent for the largest families (seven children or more). Also, a very substantial proportion of males chose a religious career.

The final interesting datum yielded by the study of Lorcin is the disparity between sex ratios of noble and non-noble families. In commoner families the ratio of males to females was 113:100, just as we would expect in a preindustrial society where a substantial proportion of women died in childbirth. The sex ratio of noble families was an astonishing 85 males per 100 females. In other words, there were one-fourth fewer noble males than expected. Partly this pattern must be due to a high proportion of women entering nunneries and thus being spared the dangers of childbirth, but most of the difference is probably due to the "hecatombs" of the English and civil wars. Taken together—falling family sizes, a high proportion of noblemen and noblewomen choosing a religious career, and a huge male deficit—these data suggest that the nobility of the Lyon region was under a substantial degree of pressure, to the point where this period can be appropriately characterized by a crisis of nobility. The pressure gradually relaxed during the fifteenth century; however, even by 1500 the replacement rates of noble households continued to lag that of commoners.

Some less detailed data from other regions appear to support the picture painted by the study of Lorcin. For example, the Breton family of Tournemine de la Hunaudaye produced an average of four children per marriage in the thirteenth century, 2.75 in the fourteenth, and 3.25 in the fifteenth (Contamine 1997:60). Urban elites were affected in a similar way,

TABLE 4.6
Proportion of children in noble families becoming priests or monks/nuns

Period	*Sons (%)*	*Daughters (%)*
1300–1350	45	64
1350–1400	22	40
1400–1450	22	29
1450–1500	16	14

Source: Lorcin (1981), cited in Contamine (1997:246).

as the data from Périgueux indicate: high family sizes in the second half of the thirteenth century, a decline to a minimum in the fifteenth century, and then an increase to 1500 (see table 4.1).

Economic difficulties, elevated mortality due to conflicts, and low replacement rates had a measurable effect on the rate of noble family and lineage extinction. Although the county of Forez (in south-central France) escaped the worst excesses of the Hundred Years' War, the rate of extinction of noble lineages in this region increased almost twofold, from 31 percent during the thirteenth century to 54 percent in the fourteenth century and 55 percent in the fifteenth century (Perroy 1962:31). In the region of Bar-sur-Seine the family extinction rate during the thirteenth century was 58 percent (thirty-five out of sixty), but this figure increased to 75 percent (fifteen out of twenty) during the following century (Contamine 1997:63). It should be noted that the Forez and Bar-sur-Seine data cannot be directly compared, because the former relate to lineages (potentially comprising several families) and the latter refer to individual families (thus, the rate of lineage extinction is expected to be less than that of families). In the Vésubie valley a third of all families faded away during the first quarter of the fifteenth century, implying an extinction rate of 80 percent per century. This was a much higher rate than during the fourteenth century, when the extinction rate was already a rather high 67 percent (Contamine 1997:63).

The Dynamics of Sociopolitical Instability (1365–1450)

France experienced a full-blown state collapse during 1356–60, followed by a period of temporary consolidation during which most of the territory was reconquered from the English. The consensus, however, proved to be temporary and began unraveling after the death of Charles V. The next reign, that of Charles VI (1380–1422), was to see the second state collapse of the Hundred Years' War. At the beginning of his reign, Charles VI was a minor, and the government was dominated by his uncles, the dukes of

Anjou, Berri, and Burgundy (also known as "the Princes of the Lilies"). The state policy was disrupted by factionalism. Some taxes were permanently annulled, such as the *fouage*; others were first annulled, then reimposed, such as the *aides*, and *gabelles*, although brief rebellions against them had to be crushed. The erosion of royal taxing power was accompanied by an erosion of royal revenues brought about by the diversion of large sums by the Princes of the Lilies, who pocketed virtually all taxes collected by the Crown in their appanages (Henneman 1999).

The social and political situation began to develop in a manner very similar to that of the 1340s and 1350s. Again, there were great crowds of impoverished nobles looking for military employment. Thus, in the fall of 1386 between 10,000 and 20,000 nobles flocked to L'Écluse, where preparations to invade England were under way (the invasion never took place) (Contamine 1997:205).

Elite factionalism gradually developed into an extremely bitter and sanguinary civil war. One of the main factions coalesced around Philip the Bold, Duke of Burgundy, who was the uncle of Charles VI. The opposing faction was led by the "Marmousets," a group that included the civil officials and military leaders close to the previous king, Charles V (Henneman 1996). The political program of the Duke of Burgundy was to use the resources of France to build an independent principality in Burgundy and the Low Countries. The Marmousets' objectives were to relieve the burden on the taxpayers while building up the resources in the royal coffers (Henneman 1996:141–42). The Marmousets were also supportive of the Italian project of another royal uncle, Louis of Anjou, and his son, Louis II, who had dynastic ambitions on the throne of Naples. Another important leader was the king's brother, Louis of Orléans, who gradually took over the Marmouset faction. As noble factionism grew, the central government was greatly weakened by the intermittent insanity of the king. To cut the long and confusing story short, eventually the French political scene became dominated by two great factions, one led by the dukes of Burgundy (the Burgundians) and the other first by Louis of Orléans (the Orleanists) and then by the Count of Armagnac, father-in-law of Charles, the new Duke of Orléans after his father was assassinated in 1407 (the Armagnacs).

After the assassination of Louis of Orléans, which was carried out under orders of John the Fearless of Burgundy (the son of Philip the Bold), France divided into two armed camps (Seward 1978:148). The Burgundians drew their strength from John's territories in the northeast and north, and from the Parisian bourgeoisie and academics. The Armagnacs were the party of the greater royal officials and high nobility, with a large following in the south and southwest. During 1407–14 the two factions battled for the capital, and both at different times appealed to the English for aid. By 1414 the Armagnacs had gained control of most of France, including the capital (Seward 1978:155), but John of Burgundy allied himself with the new English king, Henry V. In 1415 Henry V invaded France and won the great victory at Agincourt. The loss of 10,000 French knights was a terrible blow to the Armagnacs, because it reversed the balance of forces decisively in favor of the Burgundians. As the new Constable, the Count of Armagnac, was besieged in Paris by the Burgundian forces, the English conquest of Normandy proceeded completely unopposed (Seward 1978:172). In 1418 the Burgundian supporters rose up in Paris and killed thousands of Armagnacs. This was the occasion of the quotation from the bourgeois of Paris about the Armagnacs lying in the streets like slaughtered pigs. The dauphin (the future Charles VII) and the Armagnacs abandoned Paris to the Burgundians.

In 1419 Rouen surrendered to Henry V, and the English conquest of Normandy was complete. The English advance horrified John the Fearless, and he attempted to negotiate with the dauphin and the Armagnacs. But the Armagnacs revenged themselves on John of Burgundy by assassinating him at a conference with the dauphin at the bridge of Montereau. The new duke, Philip the Good, vowed vengeance and returned to the English alliance. Working with the Burgundians, the English overran northern France and installed themselves in Paris. By the Treaty of Troyes, Henry V married the daughter of Charles VI and was named the heir to the French throne, while the dauphin (future Charles VII) was disinherited. In 1422 both Charles VI and Henry V died. The infant Henry VI of England was recognized as king of France in the north, supported by the Burgundians, and crowned in Paris (1436).

The position of the Dauphinists (formerly Armagnacs) continued to deteriorate during the 1420s. In 1424 they lost the battle of Verneuil, and in 1428 the English began the siege of Orléans. Meanwhile, Lancastrian France had become a wilderness laid waste by its garrisons, by Dauphinist raiders, by deserters, and by *écorcheurs*. The *écorcheurs* or flayers were the heirs of the *routiers* of the previous century. They took their name from the custom of stripping their victims to the skin, or even flaying them alive (Seward 1978:194). It was during this period that the populations of Ile-de-France, Normandy, and doubtlessly many other regions declined to 25–30 percent of their 1300 peak.

The Disintegrative Trend Reverses Itself

The years 1428–29 were the nadir of the second French state collapse of the Hundred Years' War. The turning point came when Jeanne d'Arc lifted the siege of Orléans, followed by the coronation of Charles VII in Reims (1429). The conclusion of a treaty with the Duke of Burgundy (1435) brought the civil war to an end, and the French reconquest slowly gathered steam. Paris was recovered in 1436, Gascony (except Bordeaux and Bayonne) was reconquered in 1442, Normandy in 1450, and finally Bordeaux fell on 1453.

The decade after 1435 saw a permanent establishment of state finance in France (Henneman 1999:117). Indirect taxes (*aides*) were restored in 1435 (Languedoïl) and 1437 (Languedoc). In 1439 the Estates of Languedoïl granted direct taxes (*taille*) for one year to support regularly paid troops. The restoration of fiscal and political order was briefly interrupted by a revolt of princes in 1440 (the Praguerie), but the Crown continued collecting the *taille* without consulting the Estates. In 1445 Charles VII established a regular cavalry (*compagnies d'ordonnance*). By 1460 the restored fiscal system was producing 1.8 million l.t. a year, most of it coming from direct taxes, with only 50,000 l.t. from the royal domain (Henneman 1999:118). Thus, the basic fiscal system first introduced in the 1360s was finally implemented in the 1440s. A solid fiscal foundation was a factor of critical importance in ending the Hundred Years' War, but it itself was a consequence of the new-found feeling of national unity among the elites.

What was the basis of this new unity, and how did it replace the divisive atmosphere of the early fifteenth century? Two factors were at work. The first one was a shift in the social psychology: everybody was tired of incessant internal and external warfare. Around 1400 the yearning for peace was increasingly voiced. "*Veniat Pax*" (let there be peace) was the cry of an early fourteenth-century sermon by Jean Gerson (Tuchman 1978:537). Furthermore, although the conflict started as a civil war, it gradually transmuted into a national war of liberation against the English (Henneman 1996).

The second factor was that the nobility was numerically decimated, which removed the social pressure for elite factionalization that had fueled the civil conflict. The hecatombs inflicted on the French nobility during the second stage of the Hundred Years' War were comparable in magnitude to, if not greater (proportionately speaking) than, those of the first. The worst was undoubtedly Agincourt (1415), where 10,000 French nobles died (Contamine 1984). Among the fallen were more than ten dukes and counts, 120 barons, and 1,500 knights (Seward 1978:169). Earlier, many thousands of French nobles had participated in the crusade to free Hungary from the Turks, where they perished in the battle of Nicopolis (1396). The Dauphinist casualties at the battle of Verneuil (1424) were about 7,000, although many of them were Scots. But casualties in the large battles were probably only a minor part of the total drain on the French nobility. Untold thousands lost their lives in the civil wars and small-scale military operations (sieges, skirmishes) against the English. We have already referred to the massacre of Armagnacs in Paris (1418). King Henry V of England (as well as other military leaders of the time) was notorious for the atrocities he routinely committed. Best known is the killing of the prisoners he ordered on the field of Agincourt, but there were many others. For example, when he took the Armagnac castle of Rougemont (1421), he hanged the entire garrison. Those defenders who escaped and were later caught were drowned (Seward 1978:186). When dispossessed nobles in Normandy persisted in fighting a guerilla warfare, the English called them "brigands" and hanged them when they caught them (Seward 1978:178). Other atrocities include the butchering of 2,000 men, women, and children in Caen (1417), and Henry's refusal to allow 12,000 poor folk driven out of the besieged and starving Rouen to leave. He forced them to stay in a ditch, where most of them died of inclement climate (it was winter) and starvation (Seward 1978). The last two examples refer to commoners, but they illustrate how callous the fighting men were about taking life, and the nobility were often treated in the same way as commoners (except when there was the hope of a ransom). The result of this casual attitude to taking life was a population decline in general, but more specifically the decimation of nobility. Because the proportion of nobility among the general population declined between 1300 and 1450, the numbers of nobility decreased even more than the general population.

The crisis phases of secular cycles are typically characterized by increased social mobility, both upward and downward. The main factor driving the turnover of the social hierarchy is the growing economic inequality during the stagflation and crisis phases. As the conditions of overpopulation develop and large numbers of peasants are impoverished, some favored few nevertheless become richer. These families desire to translate their improved economic conditions into social status. Similarly, under the conditions of elite overproduction the majority of aristocrats lose ground and are faced with the prospect of downward mobility, but a few accumulate property and wish to move up into the magnate stratum. The pent-up demand for upward social mobility from elite and magnate aspirants during the crisis phase provides a cheap alternative for cash-strapped rulers to recompense their supporters. As a result, this is when we typically see evidence of upward social mobility. In medieval France, we can quantify this process by observing how the numbers of letters of ennoblement fluctuated between different reigns (Contamine 1997:67–68). According to this indicator, the movement of commoners into the ranks of the nobility greatly accelerated in the early fourteenth century and peaked during its second half (figure 4.6). During the rest of the fifteenth century, however, the rate of ennoblement declined to much lower levels, suggesting a greatly decreased upward social mobility. Because downward mobility continued unabated during this period, the net result was a substantial decline in elite numbers.

In the previous sections we have cited numerous data suggesting that the rate of extinction of noble families went up in the fourteenth and fifteenth

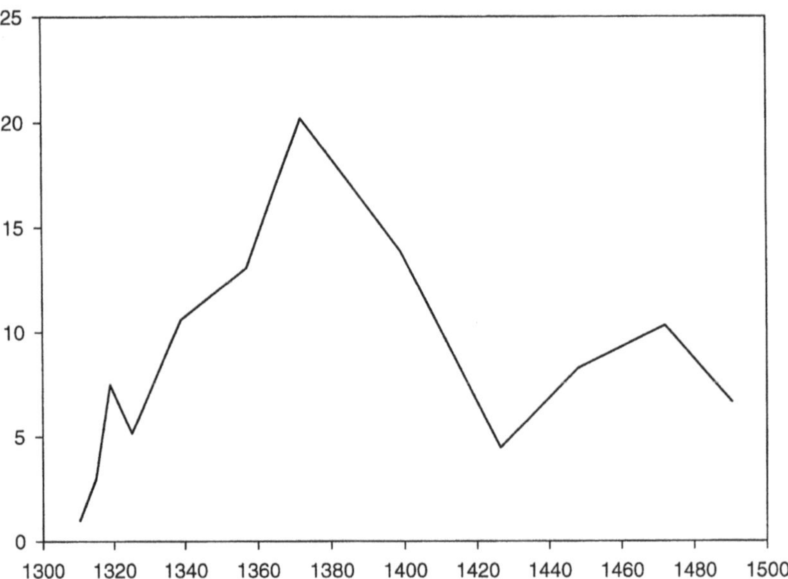

Figure 4.6 Upward social mobility in France, 1300–1500: royal letters of ennoblements (Contamine 1997).

centuries, compared to that of the preceding period. When upward mobility was also choked off (figure 4.6), it stopped compensating for the losses of old families, and the old nobility shrank in number. However, a conclusion that the old elites were replaced wholesale by new, recently ennobled elites would be too hasty. Many of the newly ennobled lineages did not manage to establish themselves and went extinct. Of the old lineages, some lost ground and disappeared, but others persisted and even managed to increase their lands. This process can be illustrated with the situation in the Sologne (in the county of Blois). The Sologne contained nine fiefs possessing the right of high justice. Five of these fiefs remained within the hands of the old nobility without interruption. Of the remaining four, one was seized by the Duke of Orléans for its debts, one was sold to another old noble family, and the last two were acquired by new nobility, the d'Ètamps family, originating in the late fourteenth century. Thus, the total number of old noble families shrank appreciably, but there was only one parvenue family to plug the resulting gap (Guérin 1960). A study by Maurice Berthe (1976) indicated similarly that in the county of Bigorre, there were forty fiefs in 1313 but only eighteen in 1429. Twelve fiefs disappeared, together with the villages on which their existence depended, while ten had been acquired by six of the surviving eighteen seigneurs (cited in Major 1981:23). Another example comes from the study of Edouard Baratier

(1971). In 1377 five villages in Provence were inhabited by thirty-eight nobles, of whom seventeen were not living as nobles (probably because they could not afford it). By 1427–31 the number of nobles had declined to twenty-two. In 1458 there were only six nobles left, but after that the number increased, and there were twelve nobles in 1474 (Major 1993:70). As the number of elite families was pruned, those that remained were strengthened.

4.6 Conclusion: "A Near Perfect Multi-secular Cycle"

The quotation in the heading is, of course, from Braudel (1988:131). Our starting date for the cycle differs from that of Braudel (there are reasons to believe that the period 950–1150 was a separate secular cycle in Western Europe), but if we focus on France between 1150 and 1450, then indeed, the data paint a nearly perfect example of a secular cycle.

All the major variables behaved during this period as postulated by the demographic-structural theory. Population, prices, and other economic variables for which we have data went through a high-amplitude oscillation. For example, the difference between population minima and the maximum was twofold (and in some regions, such as Normandy and Ile-de-France, the difference was three- and even fourfold).

Social structure also oscillated in a manner predicted by the theory, although the estimates of Contamine (1997), namely, that nobility accounted 1.8 percent of the total population around 1300 (decreasing thereafter to 1.5 percent in the fifteenth century,) are overly conservative. The average of the eleven regions for which he found data on noble-commoner proportions is 2.4 percent. Furthermore, after the famines and epidemics of the first half of the fourteenth century, the ratio of nobles to commoners should have increased even further, driven by variation in the mortality rate among classes. In other words, the decline in the elite-commoner ratio between 1350 and 1450 was probably more extreme than what is suggested by Contamine's estimates. The extreme nature of elite overproduction in fourteenth-century France is graphically illustrated by tens of thousands of "surplus nobility" seeking military employment but finding death or capture on the fields of Crécy, Poitiers, and others.

The strength of the state followed a grand cycle, from geopolitical successes during the twelfth and thirteenth centuries to persistent fiscal troubles and territorial losses of the Hundred Years' War, which were reversed only after 1450. The fall and then rise of political instability is graphically illustrated by the time distribution of coin hoards.

The main reasons for an excellent match between theoretical predictions and empirical patterns are probably two. The first is the slow advance of technology, especially agricultural technology, during the period. Thus, it appears that the carrying capacity of France hardly changed between 1150 and 1450, in contrast to the following early modern period. Second, during most of the period France was the hegemonic power in Western Europe (Tuchman 1978, Sumption 1991). Its dynamics were therefore primarily determined by endogenous rather than exogenous forces. The only major exception to this was the arrival of the Black Death from the steppes of Eurasia in 1348. But the plague epidemic arrived after the population had already started to decline, and thus it accelerated and deepened the ongoing decline rather than shifting the endogenously driven trajectory to an entirely different attractor.

Chapter 5

Early Modern France: The Valois Cycle (1450–1660)

5.1 Overview

During the early modern period France went through two secular waves, the Valois and the Bourbon cycles (we use the convention of naming the cycle after the dynasty that ruled during its integrative phase). In this chapter we dissect the demographic, economic, and social trends of the Valois cycle (we do not address the Bourbon cycle in this book because its dynamics, especially during the later phases, were greatly modified by the Industrial Revolution).

The end of the Hundred Years' War marked the beginning of a secular integrative trend in France. The expansion phase lasted until roughly 1520 and the stagflation phase from 1520 to 1570. The crisis of the Wars of Religion was followed by depression and another crisis of the Fronde. As a result, the disintegrative tendency prevailed during the period of 1570–1660. The cycle ended when Louis XIV, the "Sun King," assumed personal control of the government, marking the beginning of the expansionary phase of the next secular cycle.

Population and Economy

For reference, the population trend is depicted in figure 4.1a. As usual, the integrative phase was a period of sustained population growth. During the disintegrative phase population declines were interspersed with short-term periods of growth (these dynamics are discussed in more detail in section 5.6). Prices (see figure 4.1b and the discussion in the previous chapter) also behaved in a way generally consistent with the phases of the cycle: the great price inflation (the price revolution of the sixteenth century) was followed by deflation during the seventeenth. Real wages were the mirror image of prices (figure 5.1). During the sixteenth century real wages literally collapsed to one-fifth of their level in the "golden age" of the later fifteenth century. The seventeenth century saw some increase (with important fluctuations, to be discussed later), but the working classes never regained their economic ground: even at the peak of the later seventeenth century, real wages were less than half what they were two centuries earlier.

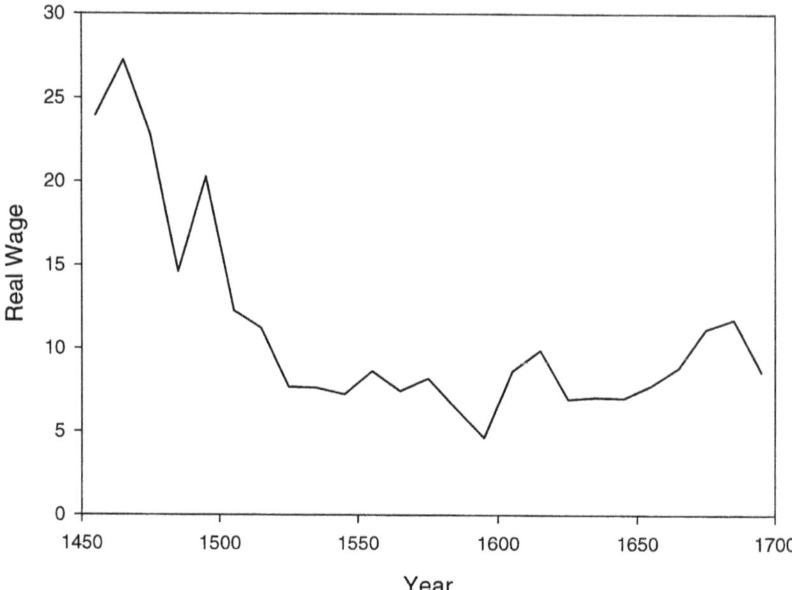

Figure 5.1 Real wage in France, 1450–1700, in kg of grain per day. The real wage is calculated by taking an average of the wages paid to laborers and craftsmen in Paris, as reported by Allen (2001), and deflating them by the price of wheat (Abel 1980).

Social Structure

The social structure of France around 1500 was not dramatically different from that of the medieval period. The rural population lived in 30,000 villages (parishes). At the top of the rural hierarchy was the seigneur, usually but not always a nobleman (Knecht 2001:8). According to the estimate of Contamine (1997:56), the proportion of nobles among the general population was 1.5 percent. There were about 200,000 persons in 40,000 noble families. Thus, many parishes had more than one noble family. The noble density was particularly high in Bretagne, where some parishes had more than ten nobles (Contamine 1997:54).

Below the seigneur in the social hierarchy came "farmers" (*fermier*). These were substantial peasants with 30 ha of land or more (Knecht 2001:9). Their abundant land, which they cultivated using their own and hired labor, permitted them to lead comfortable if not ostentatious lives (Le Roy Ladurie 1987:181), and left a surplus that could be used to buy more land or to set up as grain merchants or cattle-breeders. Farmers often acted as intermediaries between the seigneur and the rest of the peasants (Knecht 2001:9).

The first estate in the village was represented by the parish priest. The numbers of the secular clergy were in the region of 100,000, including 30,000 parish priests. There were about 100 bishops and several hundred abbots (Knecht 2001:9).

The urban society had its own hierarchy. The elites were divided between wealthy merchants and officeholders. Below them were artisans, smaller merchants, journeymen, and large numbers of manual workers.

The State

Time-series data on royal revenues during the sixteenth and seventeenth centuries are hard to come by, and the numbers given by various authorities often contradict each other. Figure 5.2 shows three views of royal taxation during the Valois cycle: (1) total taxes, calculated by Braudel and Labrousse (1977:979) for a set of years from 1453 to 1683 (original data from Chaunu), (2) a recent compilation of the total revenues between 1515 and 1788 (eighteenth-century numbers are not shown) by Kiser and Linton (2001), and (3) the *taille* (land tax) given in Bonney (1999). The latter two data sets are annual and were converted to decadal averages for presentation purposes. All data sets are expressed in the same units (millions of hectaliters of wheat). Although they disagree in detail, the overall picture is rather consistent. These data suggest that real revenues grew during the second half of the fifteenth century, owing to an increasing taxpayer base resulting from population growth and territorial conquest. During the sixteenth century state revenues stagnated and then declined in real terms, reaching their lowest point during the Wars of Religion. After the change of dynasty, the Bourbons were able to restore royal finances (apart from the fiscal collapse during the Fronde), and then, under Louis XIV, exceed the levels achieved by the Renaissance monarchs.

Because we do not currently have a good summary of French coin hoards for the period after 1385, we use the instability index developed by Sorokin (1937). In figure 5.3 we plot the index for the period of 1150–1700, giving us a synoptic view of both the medieval and early modern cycles. The first two periods of internal warfare, around 1200 and 1400, respectively, match well the peaks of coin hoard deposition (compare with figure 4.2). This increases our confidence that the two measures of sociopolitical instability reflect real historical processes. The third period of internal warfare is characterized by a double peak corresponding to the Wars of Religion and the Fronde. Territorial expansion generally occurred during the periods of internal stability and national consolidation (see figure 4.1c). The century

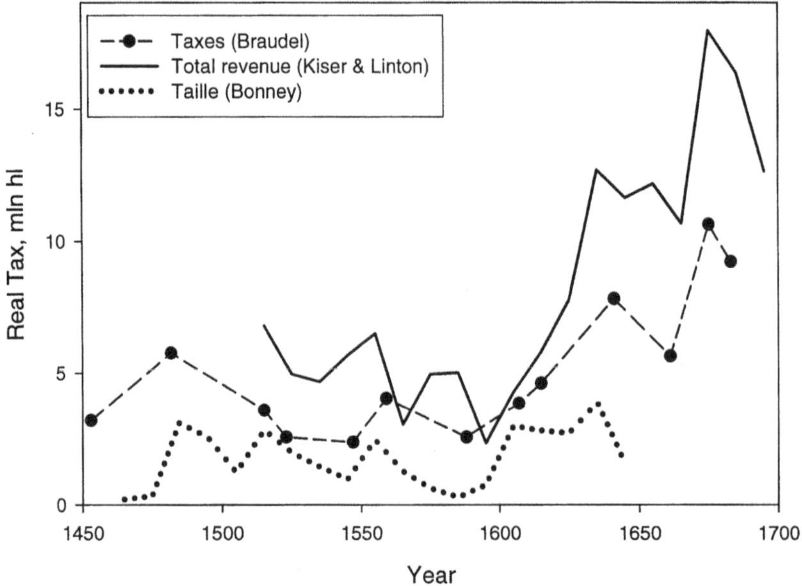

Figure 5.2 Royal revenues in France, 1450–1700. Data from Braudel and Labrousse (1977:979), Kiser and Linton (2001), and Bonney (1999).

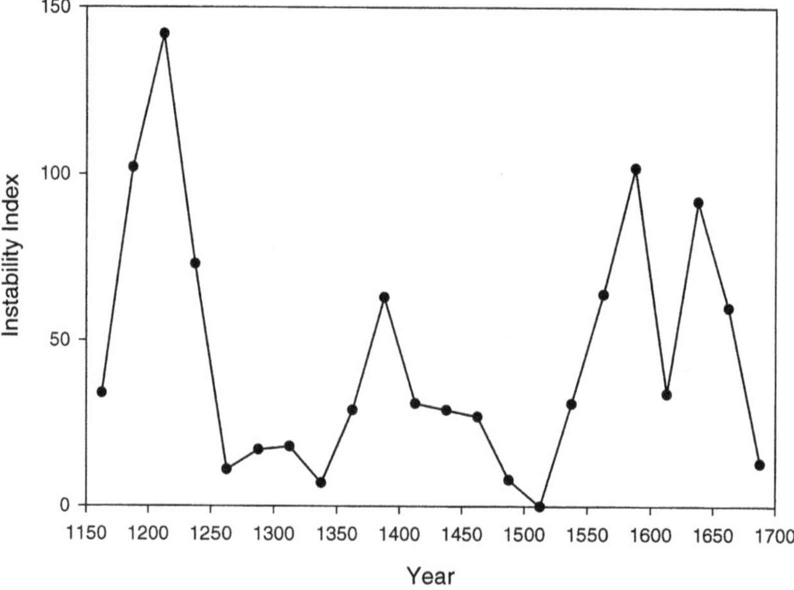

Figure 5.3 Sorokin's instability index for France, 1150–1700.

after 1450 resulted in an almost doubling of the French territory, followed by stagnation and even reverses until the beginning of the next cycle, when France enjoyed another period of territorial expansion under Louis XIV. We now turn to a more detailed discussion of phases in the Valois cycle.

5.2 Expansion (1450–1520)

General Population

The period between 1450 and 1520 was very favorable for demographic expansion. The first and foremost factor was the expulsion of the English from France and the end of the Hundred Years' War (usually dated to 1453). Another important threat to internal stability was removed when the Burgundian state collapsed in 1477 as a result of the defeat and death of Charles the Bold at the hands of the Swiss at Nancy. Epidemics continued to strike the population, but at a comparatively lower rate than during the fourteenth or seventeenth centuries.

Agricultural production increased (owing simply to the reclamation of previously abandoned land), and before 1520 famine was a rare event (Le Roy Ladurie 1987:11–12). A trend in the overall volume of agricultural production can be traced by examining the receipts of tithes (Le Roy Ladurie 1987:45–46). The lowest point of agricultural production in the Paris basin was achieved around 1440. Between 1450 and 1500, cereal production nearly doubled. In the south, the lowest point was earlier, between 1400 and 1430, and the overall supply of cereals doubled, or more than doubled by the end of the fifteenth century. It is likely, then, that food production in 1500 was double the minimum of the early fifteenth century. Population growth during this period was much more modest (it is difficult to give a quantitative estimate, but the increase was no more than 50 percent). In other words, the supply of food per capita, and by implication the standard of living, grew very substantially.

Another indicator of the high standard of living during the fifteenth century is provided by the real wages. The daily wage of a Parisian laborer could buy 16 kg of grain in the 1490s, compared to less than 4 kg one century later. Poitevin reapers had to work five days to earn the equivalent of 1 hl of wheat in 1467–72; in 1578 they had to work 14 days to earn the same. Generally speaking, during the sixteenth century wages lost more than two-thirds of their buying capacity (figure 5.3), and the high real wages of the fifteenth century were not to be matched until the late nineteenth century.

As a result of relative prosperity among the common people toward the end of the fifteenth century, the general mortality rate fell to a comparatively low level, and the obsession with death, so prevalent earlier in the century with its *danses macabre* and recumbent effigies of naked corpses, ceased to occupy cultural heights. The vigor of the demographic expansion was manifested in repopulation of the countryside and immigration after reconquest. For example, many villages in the Gironde that had been abandoned during the English wars were resettled with new colonists from the Occitan and French-speaking zones, starting with the reign of Louis XI (Le Roy Ladurie 1987:11).

The Elites

The noble fortunes began their recovery during this period (Carpentier and Le Mené 1996: Figure 29). The dynamics of the revenues of one noble family, the seigneurie du Plessis-Grammoire in Anjou, show that the worst period was the 1420s. The rising tendency becomes evident after 1460, and by 1500 the levels of 1300 are matched (in nominal terms). The restoration of noble incomes by 1500 appears to be a general pattern. For example, the seigneurie de Craon increased from less than 1,000 livres in 1396 to 1,700 livres toward 1500. The income of the lordship of Saint-Fargeau was about a hundred livres in mid-century; by 1484 it had increased to 500 livres (Carpentier and Le Mené 1996:468). A similar dynamic is demonstrated by several seigneuries in Normandy (Bois 1984:257, Dewald 1987) and by the House of La Trémoille (Weary 1977:D1007).

The State

The reconciliation of the Dauphinist and Burgundian factions in 1435 ended the civil war, except for two aftershocks. The first one was the Praguerie in 1440, a revolt by the great nobles against the king (Charles VII), with support from the dauphin (the future Louis XI). The second was the League of the Public Weal in 1465, a conspiracy against Louis XI by the dukes of Alençon, Burgundy, Berri, Bourbon, and Lorraine, again supported by the dauphin (future Charles VIII). After this last aftershock, France was not to see an elite rebellion for a century. The core regions of France were spared any serious fighting from 1453 to the start of the Wars of Religion in 1562 (Knecht 2001:3).

The increasing internal strength of France, both economic and sociopolitical, was rapidly translated by the ruling elites into territorial expansion. The state territory grew, first by a reconquest of the English-occupied lands, then by the reversal to the Crown of the appanages earlier granted to Valois princes. In 1477 Charles the Bold of Burgundy died in the battle of Nancy without male issue. Louis XI united the duchy of Burgundy with the Crown and occupied the county of Burgundy (Franche Comté). On the extinction of the house of Anjou in 1480, Anjou, Bar, Maine, and

Provence reverted to the French Crown. Other smaller incidents of territorial expansion were the acquisition of Cerdagne and Roussillon (1462) and the redemption of the Somme towns (1463). The last great duchy of medieval France that was still independent of the Crown, Brittany, was attached to France when Charles VIII married Anne of Brittany in 1491. In 1495 Charles VIII began a series of Italian campaigns that eventually mutated into the great Habsburg-Valois struggle for European hegemony in the sixteenth century. The territorial expansion of France during the fifteenth century was striking. From a low point in 1430 of 290,000 square kilometers, the territory controlled by the French kings reached 500,000 square kilometers in 1510. Increased territory and a growing population expanded the tax base of the kingdom. Between 1453 and 1515, state revenues tripled from 1.8 to 5.5 million *livres tournois* (l.t.) (Braudel and Labrousse 1977:979).

5.3 Stagflation (1520–70)

Population and Economy

By 1560 the population of France had doubled from its late medieval low (Dupâquier et al. 1988b), reaching 20 million, or roughly the same level as around 1300. In the late sixteenth century, however, population dynamics entered a different regime, one of short periods of growth interspersed with declines, leading overall to the stagnation of population numbers. The reason for the cessation of population growth is clear: population growth outpaced the ability of early modern agriculture to feed it. As we noted in the previous section, cereal production (as indexed by tithes) expanded rapidly in the post-1450 period. Between 1450 and 1505 production gains substantially outpaced population increases. After a brief transitional period (1505–20), the production of cereals continued to rise (until 1560) but at a slower pace, as the limit to the amount of available land was approached (Le Roy Ladurie 1987:121). Now it was population that outpaced production, and by 1560 the population was approaching the upper ceiling that could be supported in France, given the sixteenth-century level of technology.

This number makes sense (at least to the order of magnitude) in light of what we know about the productive capacity of medieval and early modern French agriculture. "At the rate of 210 to 240 kilograms of cereals per year per inhabitant (this figure takes into account children, who eat less than adults) and adding the quantities of grain necessary for sowing and for animal consumption, the 20 million inhabitants of France between 1550 and 1720 must have consumed 60 million quintals of cereals" (Le Roy Ladurie 1987:231). Since the annual cereal crop was produced on about 10 million ha (Le Roy Ladurie 1987:240), the average yield implied by these numbers is 600 kg/ha, or 8 hl/ha. The latter number is comfortably in the middle between average yields prevailing in the south (5 hl/ha) and those in the north (10 hl/ha), taking into account the rotation systems prevailing in each region (Le Roy Ladurie 1987:176).

The chronology of cereal production dynamics, with the ceiling approached around 1560 (and not exceeded until after 1700), is particularly relevant to the north of France. Elsewhere there were important regional variations. Thus, the south apparently reached a production peak during the 1540s. This maximum level was not to be bettered until a century later, between 1649 and 1678. In Alsace, by contrast, the best period was reached between 1600 and 1630, before the collapse of the Thirty Years' War (Le Roy Ladurie 1987:120). These regional variations are discussed below in the context of when population declines occurred in different parts of France.

Population growth had a direct effect on peasant to land ratios. In the depopulated fifteenth century, middle-sized landowners who owned about 10 ha accounted for about half of those listed in the cadastral surveys. Most of these fair-sized holdings had disappeared by 1550, some as a result of accelerating subdivision within families, others bought by nobles and urban bourgeois (Le Roy Ladurie 1987:56). In the Paris region land fragmentation achieved an incredible degree, with only 1.3 ha per tenant (Jacquart, cited in Le Roy Ladurie 1987:162)

Population growth also caused a general rise in ground-rents, although there were important geographic variations in the timing of rent increases. To start with, the ground-rents were very low in the fifteenth century. In the village of Vierzay (Soissonais) the rent was only 0.5 hl of grain per ha in 1448. By 1511 it had risen to 2 hl/ha (Le Roy Ladurie 1987:177). Between 1500 and 1560 rents stayed steady at about 1.5 hl/ha in the south of France and 2.5 hl/ha in the Paris region and Soisonnais. During the Wars of Religion rents slightly declined, but in the seventeenth century they again started to increase. About 1650–70 they rose to 3 hl/ha in Languedoc and to 5 hl/ha in the Paris region, which amounted to almost one-half the product, taking into account disparities in yields and rotation systems (Le Roy Ladurie 1987:177).

In other regions, such as the Hurepoix and Poitou, rent increases had already occurred by 1560. For example, the *métayers* in Poitou had to pay half their produce to the landlord in the sixteenth century (compared to a fourth to a third in the fifteenth century). These conditions of harsh *métayage* were relaxed only after 1650 (Le Roy Ladurie 1987:177–78).

Land prices increased. In the 1550s a hectare of plowland around Paris cost 63 livres. Two decades later land prices had increased to 150 livres per hectare (Le Roy Ladurie 1987:239–40).

The trend in real wages was typical of the stagflation phase. The average real wage of Parisian builders fell from 25 ± 2 kg of wheat per day, typical of peaceful periods of the fifteenth century, to 7–8 kg/day during the second half of the sixteenth century, and then to less than 5 kg/day during the disastrous decade of 1590–99 (figure 5.1). Agricultural wages also declined calamitously. The real wage of vineyard workers lost two-thirds to three-quarters of its value between 1495 and 1560. On the other hand, some categories of workers, such as hay-reapers, did somewhat better, losing only 30 percent in real terms during the same period (Le Roy Ladurie 1987:185–86). The fall in real wages affected not only the working poor. Whereas in 1480 the manager of a large farm near Narbonne received a salary equivalent to 31 hl of wheat, his successor's salary in 1590 was only 17.2 hl (Le Roy Ladurie 1987:69).

One stratum that did relatively well (or at least did not lose ground) during the stagflation phase was the farmers, who benefited from their situation as intermediaries between the lords and peasants. The economic conjuncture of rising grain prices, stagnating rents (whether decimal or fiscal), and rapidly falling wages worked to their advantage (Le Roy Ladurie 1987:181–84). As a result, during the sixteenth century (but unlike in the seventeenth century), farmers were able to hold their own and could even aspire to advance up the social hierarchy.

Elites

While the stagflation phase saw a progressive worsening of the economic situation of common people, for the elites the economic conjuncture was good, resulting in two related developments. First, growing inequality among commoners meant that although the majority of them were sinking into misery, a small minority did very well and acquired substantial wealth. These well-to-do commoners (the farmers discussed in the previous paragraph) and merchants naturally aspired to translate their wealth into status. Many such elite aspirants succeeded, generating a steady inflow into the ranks of nobility.

Second, given favorable economic conditions, many noble families provided substantial inheritances to their younger sons. This practice led to estate subdivision and the multiplication of nobles. For example, one of the richest French magnates, François de la Trémoille (1502–42), had to provide for five sons, and dowries for two daughters. This division of the estate and the subsequent Wars of Religion led to a drop in family revenues from 600 kg of silver in the 1530s to 430 kg in 1619 (Weary 1977, Major 1981). Another example is the Roncherolles family in Normandy, which divided its estates in 1570 among four sons. The barony of Pont-St-Pierre went to the eldest son, but the other three also got what amounted to substantial lordships (Dewald 1987:163). These two examples, of course, are no more than anecdotal evidence, but data on the noble families of the Bayeux region during 1463–1666 provide a firmer quantitative support (Wood 1980). During most of this period the numbers of ancient nobility (families who were ennobled prior to 1463) shrank, except during one time interval, 1540–98 (see table 5.2 and the discussion in section 5.5).

Driven by upward mobility and estate subdivision, the numbers of nobles increased dramatically during the sixteenth century. The numbers of *chevaliers* (knights), for example, doubled during the sixteenth century from 1,000 to more than 2,000 (Orlea 1980:59). But the top elite stratum (*pairs laïques*, or lay peers) expanded even faster, from only twelve in 1505 to thirty-six in 1588 (Labatut 1972). An inevitable result of this increase was intensifying intraelite competition for status and wealth. One way we can gage the increasing social pressure on the elites is by the incidence of intraelite violence, which during this period took the form of dueling (see also chapter 3). Dueling had almost disappeared in France during the fifteenth century and early sixteenth century (Harding 1978:77). Under François I and Henri II, a handful of judicial duels took place with royal sanction. After 1560, however, dueling for personal honor and without royal sanction became so common that La Noue believed more noblemen died from it than in combat. Estoile believed 7,000 to 8,000 were killed in the two decades after 1588 (Harding 1978:77,253). It was said that Henri IV granted more than 6,000 pardons for the killing of gentlemen in duels during the first ten years of the seventeenth century (Stone 1965:246). Dueling was effectively eliminated only a century later, during the rule of Louis XIV (Collins 1995:85).

Another sign of the ripening demographic-structural crisis was the increased competition for patronage among elite networks. The struggle between the Montmorency and Guise factions for control of court patronage is famous. After the death of Henri II, during the short reign of François II, the Guise faction managed to practically monopolize the royal patronage in their hands (Harding 1978:35). The death of François II and the alienation of the Guises from the court allowed Catherine de Medici to regain control of the royal patronage, but at the expense of alienating a large segment of the French elites.

Elites and the State

At the same time that the expanding elite numbers were putting increasing pressure on the state finances, the state's ability to collect revenue (in real terms) was declining (figure 5.2). The fiscal crisis of the state was a major precondition of the crisis of the Wars of Religion. In 1559 Henri II signed the Peace of Cateau-Cambrésis with the Spanish. The cessation of the Habsburg-Valois wars meant that "hundreds of noble sons were thrown back on the home estates, where the family resources were often insufficient to support them" (Bitton 1969). Moreover, the financial situation of the Crown made it impossible to continue the patronage system on the old footing (Briggs 1998:15). The Cardinal of Lorraine, beset by would-be clients, was reduced to threatening to hang the next man who asked for a pension (Briggs 1998:15). The contraction of the largesse of the state affected even the top magnates of the kingdom, the provincial governors (Harding 1978:47). The governors from southern and western provinces reported that they could not rely on the loyalty of their subordinates, who were attracted to the new religion. "As the era of the secret conventicles came to an end, service as 'protectors' for the Calvinist communities represented an available option to royal service for noblemen, and the pastors apparently resorted to straightforward bribery" (Harding 1978:49).

The Guises' monopoly of patronage bred much resentment on the part of those they excluded (Briggs 1998:15). The "Tumult of Amboise" (1560) was a conspiracy by some protestant nobles against the Guises. Most of the conspirators were petty seigneurs of ancient lineage (Salmon 1976:124).

As the financial crisis deepened, the wages of troops fell into arrears, and eventually the state lost control of the army. Contemporary letters (cited by Harding 1978:49–50) provide a wonderful illustration of this demographic-structural mechanism of state collapse (Goldstone 1991). One officer reported in 1561 that his unpaid troops in Brittany "have left to pillage. . . . In the end I expect to be all alone. There is so much due to the men of my company . . . that I am neither feared nor obeyed." A year later another officer described how his troops, who had not been paid in a year, "ate the horses in the garrison and then retired to their houses without a *sou*." The same year a third captain, lacking money to pay them, disbanded his Provençal levies, who dispersed in gangs that attacked Calvinists "all over the province," holding some for ransom and killing others.

With the onset of civil war in 1562, the royal finances completely collapsed. Desperate measures such as pawning royal jewels (Bonney 1999) and selling church property (which brought more than 13 million livres; Le Roy Ladurie 1994:240) were completely insufficient to keep up with military expenditures. The result was a spiraling state debt, which reached 296 million livres by 1595 (Bonney 1999). The debt was almost wiped out during the reign of Henri IV but ballooned again during the crisis of the Fronde, reaching 700 million livres in 1661 (Briggs 1998).

5.4 Crisis (1570–1600)

By the end of the stagflation phase the population of France had recovered to roughly the level that obtained before the fourteenth-century collapse. In the late sixteenth century and all of the seventeenth century, population growth ceased. The overall population of France (adding together rural and urban locations and northern and southern provinces) "stagnated," so that the French population of 1720 was essentially the same as that of 1560 (Le Roy Ladurie 1987:232). This does not mean that population numbers were in equilibrium: there were several temporal fluctuations, and different regions of the kingdom followed different trajectories. Here we focus on the temporal fluctuations, while deferring a discussion of regional variations to the next section.

Le Roy Ladurie distinguishes three classes of temporal fluctuations: (1) those occurring on the time scale of centuries (which we call secular cycles), (2) those occurring on the time scale of decades (which we call bigenerational cycles), and (3) those occurring on an annual time scale. During the period of 1560–1720 there were three fluctuations of the second type (Le Roy Ladurie 1987:233): (1) a population decline during the Wars of Religion, followed by some recovery during the reign of Henri IV and the early years of Louis XIII; (2) a decline during the Thirty Years' War and the Fronde, followed by a recovery under Fouquet and Colbert; and (3) the troubles of the second half of the reign of Louis XIV, followed by a sustained population take-off under his two successors that finally broke through the medieval ceiling of 20 million (see figure 4.1a).

The proximate mechanisms of population declines were the three scourges of plague, famine, and war. Measured by the number of communities hit by the plague (Biraben 1975), the incidence of epidemics increased from the minimum of 1,400 throughout the fifteenth and sixteenth centuries (figure 5.4). The plague reached pandemic levels first during the height of the Wars of Religion (in the 1580s) and then again at the peak of the Thirty Years' War (the 1620s and 1630s). In 1583 the plague may have killed one-third of the inhabitants of the city of Angers (Le Roy Ladurie 1987:270). Elsewhere in the Anjou many parishes lost one-quarter to one-third of their dwellers. In the seventeenth century the Anjou was hit repeatedly by comparable outbreaks in 1626–27, 1631–32, and 1639. The plague was carried by the movements of troops and spread throughout the kingdom, affecting in alternating waves the Massif Central, the Aquitain basin, the Armorican Massif, and the Paris basin (Le Roy Ladurie 1987:270)

Famine was widespread during this period, from the food shortages arising from the activities of the anti-Huguenot Catholic League in the 1590s, through the subsistence crises of 1630, 1649, 1652, 1661, and 1694, to the great grainless winter of 1709 (Le Roy Ladurie 1987:272). The immediate triggers of these crises were periods of very cold or very damp winters and unusually wet summers. For example, the famines of 1630 and 1661 occurred during peacetime and were entirely due to bad weather. However, such crises caused very short-term declines, what Le Roy Ladurie has called third-order fluctuations. "These fluctuations temporarily disturbed, with-

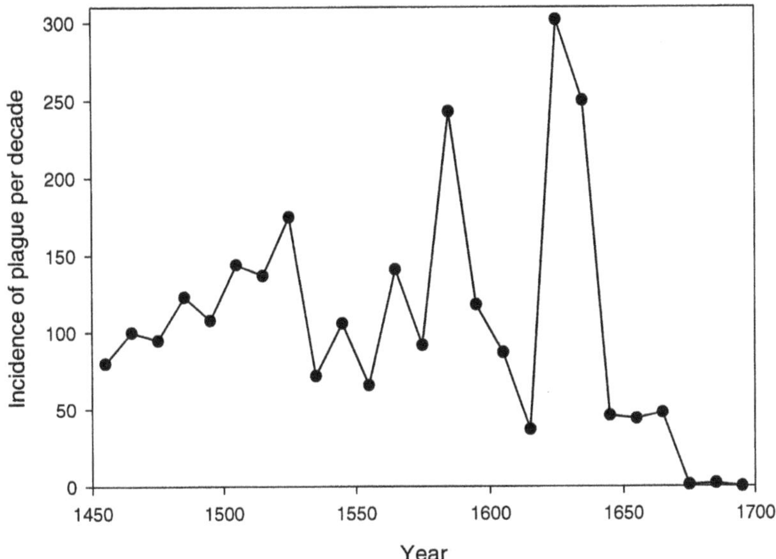

Figure 5.4 Incidence of plague in France, 1450–1700. Data from Biraben (1975).

out really altering them in a lasting way, the levels and ratios of population and food supplies" (Le Roy Ladurie 1987:276). During the famines of the 1590s and 1649–52, which had a much more lasting effect on population, the weather played a secondary role. It was civil war rather than the rain that killed the grain (Le Roy Ladurie 1987:273).

We should qualify this argument by noting that it applies most cogently to the first two population declines (occurring prior the 1660s). The third decline, in the two decades around 1700, occurred when the state was strong (although it coincided with a series of particularly intense external wars). In our opinion, therefore, it was not brought about by demographic-structural mechanisms. Historians have proposed various explanations for it, of which two appear most probable: a significant worsening of the climate and the great demands placed on the French peasantry by the aggressive external policy of Louis XIV. In any case, the issue of the third population decline falls outside the temporal framework of this chapter, and in the following we focus on the population dynamics up until 1660.

Although the proximate factors of population declines during this period (1570–1660) included epidemics and famine, it was often troop movements that spread epidemics, and the harvests were threatened or damaged by military operations and looting soldiers. Thus, the fundamental mechanism of population fluctuations was sociopolitical instability leading to civil war within the kingdom, and the weakening of the state, which made it susceptible to foreign invasions.

The period of heightened political instability in France lasted about a century, from 1562 to 1675 (table 5.1). There were two waves, the first marked by the Wars of Religion and culminating around 1590, the second a period of magnate rebellions, Huguenot insurrections, and peasant uprisings that culminated in the Fronde of 1648–53 (the double peak in figure 5.3 reflects these two waves).

The two peaks of internal warfare were separated by a relatively stable two decades under Henri IV and the early years of Louis XIII. The Wars of Religion may have resulted in a population loss of 20 percent or more (Benedict 1985:96). In Orléans, the population was reduced by one-third between 1561 and 1597 (Dupâquier et al. 1988b:197). The population of Rouen was reduced by more than a quarter between 1562 and 1594 (Benedict 1975:232). During the second period of sociopolitical instability, demographic losses in some regions were even greater. Thus, as a result of the combined effect of the Thirty Years' War and the Fronde, certain provinces in the north and east probably lost close to half their inhabitants (Dupâquier et al. 1988b:152). The south of France was much less affected (this is discussed in section 5.6).

5.5 A Case Study: The Norman Nobility

As a result of research by historians such as Guy Bois, James Wood, and Jonathan Dewald, we have excellent quantitative data on the nobility of one region of France, Normandy. The situation in Normandy is particularly interesting because this province appears to be reasonably representative of northern France. It is situated next to the core of the French state, but unlike Ile-de-France, its development was not heavily distorted by the influence of the capital with its royal court and the central administrative apparatus. Thus, what we learn about the Norman situation at the very least yields testable hypotheses about other French regions and France as a whole. Certainly, it appears that the insights of Guy Bois, developed from the Norman material, proved to be of general validity, especially for northern France, but also for the whole kingdom, as long as known variations in social structures between the north and the south are taken into account.

The Dynamics of Elite Numbers

The first issue is, what were the numerical dynamics of nobility, and in particular, how did the ratio of noble to commoner households evolve during the Valois cycle? Using a variety of data sources, Bois (1984:71–77) established that the peak of general population during the sixteenth century was achieved by 1560. In fact, the peak was essentially approached by 1540.

TABLE 5.1
Revolutionary situations in France, 1500–1900

1548	Pitaud insurrection in Guyenne
1562–63	First war of religion
1567–68	Second war of religion
1568–69	Third war of religion
1572–73	Fourth war of religion
1574–76	Fifth war of religion
1577	Sixth war of religion
1578–79	Seventh war of religion
1579–80	Eighth war of religion
1585–98	Ninth war of religion
1594–95	Croquant rebellions in southwest
1614–15	Civil war in Brittany
1617	War of Mother and Son
1619–20	War of Mother and Son
1621–22	Hueguenot wars
1625	Hueguenot wars
1627–30	Hueguenot wars (English intervention)
1629–30	Croquant uprising
1635–36	Croquant uprising
1637–41	Croquant uprising
1639	Norman rebellion
1643–44	Revolt of southwest
1648–53	The Fronde
1655–57	Tardanizat rebellion (Guyenne)
1658	Sabotiers rebellion (Sologne)
1661–62	Bénauge rebellion (Guyenne)
1662	Lustucru rebellion (Boulonnais)
1663	Audijos rebellion (Gascony)
1663–72	Angelets guerilla warfare (Rousillion)
1675	Papier Timbre, Bonnets Rouges rebellions (Brittany)
1702–06	Camisards rebellions (Cévenne, Languedoc)
1768–69	Corsican rebellion
1789–99	French revolutions and counterrevolutions
1815	Hundred Days
1830	July Revolution
1848	French revolution
1851	Louis Napoleon's coup d'état
1870	State collapse, occupation, republican revolutions
1870–71	Multiple communes

Source: Tilly (1993:151).

After 1540 baptism numbers in various communities stagnated (more precisely, they oscillated with periods of about a generation). Earlier we showed that the secular decline of the population in northern France took place between 1560 and 1660 (with shorter-term fluctuations around this trend), followed by population growth (interrupted by another decline around 1700). By 1720 the population numbers had probably regained the level of 1560.

The numerical dynamics of nobility exhibited a distinctly different pattern from the one characterizing the general (commoner) population. Based on a study of the periodic investigations of the nobility in the *élection* of Bayeux in Lower Normandy, Wood (1980) was able to reconstruct changes in their numbers during the period 1463–1666 (tables 5.2 and 5.3).

At first, the total number of noble households grew slowly. In the eighty years before 1540 the numbers of nobles expanded at a rate of less than 0.5 percent per year. During the same period, the general population of Normandy increased at an average rate of 1.1 percent per year (from 30 to 75 on the relative scale in Figure 2 of Bois 1984:76). As a result, the proportion of nobles to the total population declined. In fact, we can put an absolute estimate to this quantity as follows. In 1713 the *élection* of Bayeux contained 22,620 hearths (Wood 1980:22). The peak of 1560 must have been very close to this value, and by 1540 the population was perhaps 10 percent less. Thus, by 1540 there were at least 20,000 households in this region, of which 309 were noble, implying the proportion of nobility at 1.5 percent.

Between 1540 and 1600, while the general population stagnated (and in fact declined during 1570–1600), the numbers of nobility exploded. The growth rate during 1540–98 was more than 1 percent per year. During the first two-thirds of the seventeenth century the numbers of nobility stagnated (even declining between 1598 and 1624), but since the general population probably reached its minimum around 1660, the proportion of noble households among the total was at that time over 3 percent, double its value in 1540. To sum up, between 1460 and 1540 the numbers of nobles increased, but more slowly than the numbers of commoners, so that noble to commoner ratio decreased to 1.5 percent. Between 1540 and 1600 the commoner population stagnated while the numbers of nobles exploded; and between 1600 and 1660 both commoner and noble numbers stagnated, with the noble to commoner ratio at around 3 percent.

The nobility of the Bayeux region was primarily rural. One-third to one-half of them were sword nobles, and only between 3 and 6 percent served as officials or professionals (Wood 1980:75,86). To examine the dynamics of the robe nobility during the sixteenth century we turn to Dewald's (1980) study of the magistrates in the Parlement of Rouen. The numbers

TABLE 5.2
Numbers of nobility of the *élection* of Bayeux as revealed by the *recherches*, or periodic inspections of noble credentials by Crown officials.

	Noble families				
Year	*Total*	*Old*	*New*	*Anoblis*	*Condemned (%)*
1463	211	211	—	—	6.2
1523	273	177	96	41	—
1540	309	172	52	15	1.6
1598	559	229	179	77	1.4
1624	520	211	41	5	3.2
1666	592	183	109	28	6.0

Note: "Total" denotes the total number of noble households, "Old" denotes the number of noble families that were ennobled prior to 1463, "New" denotes the number of noble families appearing in the *élection* during the previous period, "*Anoblis*" denotes the number of new noble families that were ennobled during the previous period, "Condemned" denotes those family heads permanently condemned (refused noble status) by the *Recherche* Commissions.

TABLE 5.3
Rates of change in numbers of nobility of the *élection* of Bayeux

	Rate of change (% per year)		*Arrival rate (no. of families per year)*	
Period	*All*	*Old*	*New*	*Anoblis*
1463–1523	0.43	−0.29	1.6	0.7
1523–1540	0.73	−0.36	3.1	0.9
1540–1598	1.02	0.36	3.1	1.3
1598–1624	−0.28	−0.59	1.6	0.2
1624–1666	0.31	−0.18	2.6	0.7

Note: "Rate of change" is the proportional change (percent per year) in the number of noble families established at the beginning of the period and the end of the period. A negative sign indicates a decrease. "Old" denotes families whose nobility dated before the previous *recherche*, "Arrival rate" denotes the proportional increase (number of families per year) in the nobility as a result of the appearance of new families (both noble immigrants and recent *anoblis*), "*Anoblis*" denotes families known to have been ennobled during the period preceeding the *recherche*.

of high officials in Rouen experienced a tremendous growth during the sixteenth century (table 5.4).

Such a drastic expansion in the number of officials was not peculiar to Normandy. At the other end of France, in Montpellier, the number of officeholders almost quadrupled, from 112 in 1500 to 442 in 1600 (Greengrass 1985:122). It was estimated that in the whole of France, royal officials numbered slightly over 4,000 in 1515 (Salmon 1976:79). This number doubled during the next fifty years, then tripled again. By 1610

TABLE 5.4
The growth of the number of high officials in Rouen

Time period	*Cour des Aides*	*Parlement*	*Chambre des Comptes*	*Bureau des Finances*	*Total*
15th C	8	—	—	—	8
1499	8	35	—	—	43
1554	15	66	—	—	81
1600	15	83	64	12	174
Later 17th C	?	?	?	?	200

Source: Dewald (1980:69).

Note: In the late fifteenth century, before the establishment of parlement in 1499, there was only one sovereign court in Rouen (the *Cour des Aides*), which included eight members. Two hundred years later, the late seventeenth-century intendant Voysin de La Noiraye listed 200 members of Rouen's four sovereign courts. The lion's share of this growth occurred prior to 1600. Just the membership of parlement increased from thirty-five to eighty-three during the sixteenth century.

there were 25,000 officeholders in France (Le Roy Ladurie 1994:275). During the seventeenth century the numbers of officials oscillated wildly, increasing to perhaps 50,000 by the 1660s (a survey ordered by Colbert counted 46,047 venal officeholders). The administration of Colbert made a concerted effort to reduce this number, so that by 1670 Colbert was claiming to have suppressed 20,000 offices (Doyle 1996:23). Toward the end of the century the number of venal offices had again increased, as the government of Louis XIV used all expedients to raise money for a series of grueling foreign wars.

Causes Underlying the Growth of Elite Numbers

To sum up, the numbers of nobility greatly expanded between 1450 and 1660, with the bulk of the increase occurring during the second half of the sixteenth century. The numbers of robe nobility exhibited a particularly spectacular increase, but sword nobility numbers also increased substantially. In rural areas, such as the Bayeux region, the proportion of sword to robe nobles stayed roughly constant. How was this enormous expansion of nobility accomplished? The change in the number of nobles was determined by two processes: the natural increase in established noble families and the appearance of new nobles (*anoblis*) resulting from upward mobility. Table 5.3 (the column labeled "Growth Rate") gives the rate of change in the number of established noble families in the Bayeux region. For most time periods, the number of established families shrank, as a result of failure in the male line, emigration from the region, or loss of the noble status. In only one period, 1540–98, did the natural increase resulting from family splitting (when the family patrimony is split between two or more sons, each of whom establishes a separate nuclear family) overwhelm the forces reducing the number of old nobility. These dynamics are illustrated by the numbers of ancient nobility, those who were ennobled prior to 1463, which showed a decline from 1463 to 1540, an increase to 1598, and thereafter another decline (table 5.3).

The sixteenth century was the period of the greatest upward mobility. Because the majority of "new" nobles appearing in the Bayeux region were actually old nobles immigrating from elsewhere, to study upward mobility we need to focus on individuals who were elevated from commoner status to noble status, the *anoblis*. The social origins of the newly ennobled were quite diverse. But the main requirement for obtaining (and preserving) noble status was wealth, usually based on owning land, office, or both. Thus, families entering the nobility were already a part of the elite (or elite aspirants). Table 5.3 indicates that the dynamics of upward mobility largely paralleled those of already established nobility. The rate of appearance of *anoblis* grew throughout the sixteenth century, reaching a peak in 1540–98, then collapsed in the seventeenth century (table 5.3). Thus, the period 1540–98 was particularly favorable to the survival and multiplication not only of the old noble families but also of upwardly mobile commoners.

A more precise (in the sense of having better temporal resolution) look at the dynamics of upward mobility can be gained by examining the numbers of ennoblements that were registered with the Chambre des Comptes in Paris (figure 5.5). It is clear that the greatest influx of new nobles did not occur uniformly during the period 1540–98 but toward the end of the century, during the Wars of Religion. This correlation between civil war and the rate of ennoblements is not a spurious one, since all three peaks of ennoblement—1350–1410, 1570–1600, and 1640–60—occurred during periods of high sociopolitical instability.

Elite Incomes and Wealth

Why did the elites, both established and aspirants, do so well during the sixteenth century? The main requirement for upward mobility during this period was possession of sufficient wealth. Nobility was essentially open to any wealthy family, if it was willing to play by the rules and be patient. Strategies for achieving noble status included purchasing land (preferably a fief), acquiring offices, marrying well, and sending sons to the university or into military service.

The economic situation for elites and elite aspirants was also good during the middle part of the sixteenth century. The main engine of elite prosperity was the growth of income from agriculture. Landed revenues of a number of Norman seigneuries are known, and they show similar

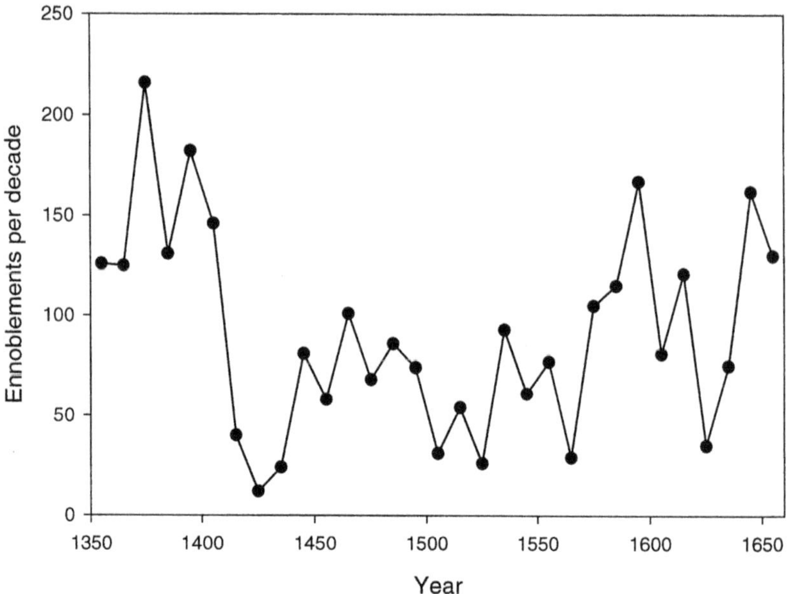

Figure 5.5 Ennoblements in France, 1350–1660 (Schalk 1982).

trajectories. For example, the receipts of the county of Tancarville collapsed during the first half of the fifteenth century, then enjoyed a mild recovery to 1510, followed by more rapid growth to the 1540s (Bois 1984:257). The total income of the Roncherolle family also collapsed during the fifteenth century. Between 1480 and 1520 the nominal revenue increased. Its real value when measured in grain stagnated (but grew when measured in "chicken-equivalents"). Between 1520 and 1570, however, revenues grew rapidly, in terms of both grain and poultry (Dewald 1987:234). In the seventeenth century, revenues stagnated. The estate of Saussey, belonging to the Maignart family of wealthy Rouen magistrates, provides another illustration of the same pattern (table 5.5). There was little movement between 1480 and 1520. The great jump in real revenues came between 1520 and 1560 (after 1575 revenues declined as a result of the economic troubles of tenants). A doubling of income in grain-equivalents, however, was an unusually good showing.

The responses of estates to the changing economic circumstances of the sixteenth century showed great diversity. Losses to inflation were serious on some estates held by the robe nobility of Rouen, especially on those whose "enfeoffed domains" were leased by money rents (Dewald 1980:208). Most typical were estates such as Bec Crespin, belonging to the Romé family. In the years 1517–29 all Bec Crespin revenues (including the demesnes and enfeoffed domain) were leased for 667 livres per year

TABLE 5.5
Total rent, Saussey

Date	*Rent in* mines *of wheat*
1483	92
1522	99
1566	174
1575	181
1583	168
1589	150
1594	72

Source: Dewald (1980:212).

(around 350 hl of grain at the Paris prices). The enfeoffed domain alone was leased for 2,075 livres (340 hl of grain) in 1604 and 3,150 livres (350 hl) in 1638. In other words, the total revenue in real terms increased between 1520 and 1600, since this number does not include the revenues from the demesne, and then stayed constant during the first half of the seventeenth century. Those Norman estates that could be followed were in much the same situation as Bec Crispin (Dewald 1980:208).

In sum, during the half-century after 1520 (that is, during the stagflation phase of the Valois cycle), average revenues from land at least kept pace with the price of grain, and on many estates grew in real terms. The most likely explanation for this pattern is the overpopulation during this period, which drove down real wages and pushed up real rents. Yearly income from office also increased at a rapid pace: between 1520 and 1610, fees charged by the magistrates of Rouen increased eightfold (Dewald 1980:158).

The growth in annual incomes and the total wealth of many Rouen magistrates can be followed by examining the probate records and account books. During the sixteenth century the typical income of a Rouen *parlementaire* grew tenfold, from 500 to 5,000 livres (table 5.6). In real terms, income more than doubled by the 1540s, then fell slightly as the 1580s approached. It is also interesting to follow the combined incomes of the magistrates as an estimate of what their cost was to the society as a whole. The combined income continued to expand throughout the whole period (table 5.6). This is an interesting and significant pattern: although the total income of all Rouen parlementaires increased substantially between the 1540s and the 1570s–1580s, the number of magistrates doubled, resulting in a decrease in per capita income.

We can check these results by looking at the salaries of officeholders in Montpellier (Greengrass 1985:122). The data are not strictly comparable, because for Rouen's magistrates we have estimates of total income (which is a better measure of their economic well-being), while for Montpellier

TABLE 5.6
Incomes of parlementaires of Rouen, 1500–1600

Period	*Numbers*	*Income (l.t.)*	*Price of wheat*	*Income (hl)*	*Combined income (hl)*
1500s	35	500	0.99	503	17,600
1520s	35	1,000	1.86	537	18,800
1540s	35	2,500	2.27	1,102	38,600
1570–80s	66	5,000	6.64	753	49,700

Source: Dewald (1980).
Note: Units: l.t., *livre tournois;* hl, hectoliter.

TABLE 5.7
Salaries of royal officers in Montpelier, 1500–1600

Period	*Numbers*	*Combined salaries (l.t.)*	*Adjusted for inflation*[a] *(l.t.)*	*Average real salary (l.t.)*
1500	112	14,885	59,540	532
1550	125	33,350	66,700	534
1575	253	67,520	67,520	267
1600	442	256,791	184,890	418

Source: Irvine (1979), cited in Greengrass (1985:table 6.1).
[a] Salaries are adjusted for inflation, taking the year 1575 as a base.

the data refer to salaries, with which the officials were (theoretically) remunerated. Furthermore, the Rouen data are for a particularly privileged stratum of the provincial robe nobility. Nevertheless, some patterns are shared by both data sets (table 5.7). In particular, there was a great expansion of official numbers as well as of their cost to society (in real terms). Second, the particularly rapid expansion of numbers of officials came during the third quarter of the sixteenth century, when their numbers doubled at both Rouen and Montpellier, and this numerical expansion was accompanied by a drop in the average income or salary.

It would be very interesting to examine the dynamics of the incomes of other segments of the nobility, but unfortunately, direct data for such an investigation are lacking. Dewald, however, was able to obtain a glimpse by examining marriage contracts, which provide an approximate idea of the relative wealth of different groups. Between the first half of the sixteenth century and around 1600 the median dowry in parlementaire marriages increased sixfold (table 5.8). Recollect that the annual income increased by about the same order of magnitude, from 1,000 to 5,000 livres (table 5.6). The dowries of lesser gentry (*écuyiers*), on the other hand, increased only twofold, while the growth of dowries in lawyer (*avocats*) marriages was intermediate between those of lesser gentry and parlementaires

TABLE 5.8
Dowries in Normandy, 1500–1614

	Median dowries (l.t.)	
Social stratum	*1500–1550*	*1568–1614*
Lesser gentry	1,320	2,625
Lawyers	1,375	5,368
Parlementarians	4,500	27,000

Source: Dewald (1980:128–29).

(table 5.8). During the same period wheat prices increased about fourfold. In other words, the lesser gentry were losing ground, the parlementaires were getting ahead, and the lawyers were just breaking even, or perhaps slightly slipping.

Compression of the Elites

The basic problem facing the nobility was the irreconcilable contradiction between two processes: total production stagnated after 1540 and even declined toward the end of the century, while the numbers of the elites grew inexorably. One result of this dynamic was increasing exploitation of peasants, but there were biological limits on how low the standard of living of the productive class could be driven. The second consequence, therefore, was the lower real income per elite capita. This does not mean that all elite families suffered equally. On the contrary, the basic dynamic, at least for a while, was for the rich to get richer while the poor got poorer (this is typical of the stagflation and crisis phases of secular cycles). Thus, the real income of the lesser gentry was declining by 1600, while the privileged segment of the robe nobility, the parlementaires, was growing more wealthy.

Within the parlementaire stratum, however, the same basic dynamic was also operating. Between 1499 and 1600 the numbers of parlementaires grew from thirty-five to eighty-three (table 5.4). The proximate reason for this growth was the Crown's fiscal difficulties, which were partially solved by a periodic sale of newly established venal offices. But it is also important to recognize that such offices were in great demand. In fact, as the number of venal offices was expanded, their price rose at a spectacular rate (Doyle 1996:11). A councillorship in the Parlement of Rouen sold for less than 5,000 livres in the 1570s, 10,000 l.t. in the 1580s, and 20,000 l.t. in the 1600s. It doubled again by 1615, yet again by 1634, and by the 1670s it had reached the highest point for office prices in the parlements, when it was evaluated at 88,000 l.t. (Dewald 1980:138–40). About half of the rise was due to inflation, but most (an almost tenfold increase in real terms) was driven by an intense intraelite competition. Economically, this increase

TABLE 5.9
Average dowries (l.t.) of major governors, 1493–1663

Social stratum	1493–1560	1560–1605	1605–1663
Major Governors	90,000	380,000	460,000

Source: Harding (1978:114).

in the cost of the office did not make sense; the offices were valued for their extraeconomic value—status. This interpretation is confirmed by the growing price of the seigneuries (fiefs), another kind of property sought primarily for its extraeconomic value. This inflation of fief values is indicated by the steadily decreasing returns on seigneurial property: from 10 percent in the early sixteenth century (1507) to 4–4.5 percent in 1563–97, 3.3 percent in 1601, and 2.2 percent in 1627 (Dewald 1980:203).

The rising costs of office, coupled with the rising costs of education (Dewald 1980:135–36), had dramatic effects on the economics of officeholding. Until about 1570 offices were sold for prices corresponding to the economic returns they offered. After the great office inflation of 1570–1630, offices were bought for prestige or the political importance they offered (Dewald 1980:143). By 1610 the chances of creating a new fortune from the profits of office had become very small (Dewald 1980:160). Whereas officeholding was one of the routes for upward mobility during the sixteenth century, the magistrate stratum became increasingly closed after 1600. The situation in Rouen mirrored more general developments in France as a whole. Prior to 1600, merchant families often moved directly into royal courts by buying an office in a chamber of accounts or even a parlement for their sons. After 1600, this mechanism for social mobility to the highest levels of the robe slowed down, and two or three generations of royal office, each one more exalted than the last, were generally required (Collins 1995:41). The seventeenth-century tendency of slower upward mobility is reflected in the social origin of the members of Parlement. In the mid-sixteenth century only 20 percent of them were sons of high officials; a century later 60 percent followed in their fathers' footsteps (table 5.10).

The seventeenth century thus was a period of retrenchment for the robe nobility of Rouen. Their numbers essentially ceased to grow (table 5.4), and upward mobility into their ranks was practically choked off. A similar pattern was observed for the rural nobility of Bayeux. The rate of appearance of *anoblis* families reached a peak of 1.3 families per year during 1540–98, then dropped off to 0.2–0.7 families per year during the first two-thirds of the seventeenth century (table 5.3). At the same time, resistance to accepting the nobility of upwardly mobile families intensified. Whereas dur-

TABLE 5.10
Social origins of parlementaires

	Proportion (%) who were sons of:			
Time period	*High officials*	*Lawyers and lesser officials*	*Noblemen*	*Bourgeois*
1539–58	23	18	8	9
1559–78	22	10	15	7
1579–88	28	11	6	4
1589–98	26	2	4	6
1599–1618	47	11	13	7
1619–38	60	5	11	4

Source: Dewald (1980).

ing the sixteenth century only 1.4–1.6 percent of families pretending to the noble status were condemned (denied the noble status), this proportion rose to 3.2 percent during the first half of the seventeenth century and to 6 percent during the second half (table 5.2). Note the cyclic return of the proportion condemned to the previous peak during the fifteenth century (6.2 percent in 1462), another period of nobility compression.

At the same time that upward mobility into the ranks of nobility was choked off, the size of the group of elite aspirants apparently shrank. As we mentioned earlier, one of the routes to noble status was the acquisition of a noble fief (seigneurie). Since the proportion of fiefs held by commoners is known, we can use it to obtain an idea of the size of the upwardly mobile stratum. The proportion of income from fiefs held by commoners increased from 8 percent in 1552 to 13 percent in 1587, and then declined to 2 percent in 1640 (Wood 1980:147). In other words, during the second half of the sixteenth century, the pool of elite aspirants grew, whereas during the first half of the seventeenth century it shrank to almost zero. During the same period the proportion of fiefs (by value) held by the old nobility increased from 52 percent to 72 percent, while the proportion held by new nobility declined from 17 percent to 12 percent. What apparently happened was that elite aspirants converted their holdings of fiefs into noble status during the sixteenth century and the early seventeenth century. As upward mobility dropped off after 1600, the descendants of the former elite aspirants became first new nobles and then old nobles.

While the proportion of old nobility among the landed elites increased, the total numbers of rural nobles in Normandy probably declined toward 1700. We do not have the data for the Bayeux region, but in another rural *élection*, that of Gisors, there were seventy-four noble households out of the total of 7,500 in 1703, or about 1 percent of the population

TABLE 5.11
Distribution (%) of annual revenues of noble families in the Bayeux region in 1639 and 1666

Income bracket (l.t.)	*1639*	*1666*
Less than 1,000	67.4	49.6
1,000–10,000	29.1	48.0
More than 10,000	3.5	2.4

Source: Wood (1980:128).

(Dewald 1987:91). In the *élection* of Rouen (excluding the city of Rouen), there were only 154 rural noble families out of population of 17,514, or less than 1 percent, in 1703. However, the regional capital was the home of additional 272 noble households and about 160 families of high royal officials (Dewald 1987:91).

Whereas the second half of the sixteenth century saw an erosion of incomes of the rural nobility (table 5.8), this decline was stopped, and even reversed sometime in the mid-seventeenth century. We are fortunate to have data on income distribution among the nobility of the Bayeux region at two points in time, 1639 and 1666 (Wood 1980:127–28). Mean family income rose from 1,400 to 1,900 l.t. between the two dates. Since the real value of a livre was approximately the same at these two dates, this 34 percent increase in nominal terms represents a real increase in noble incomes. But an even more striking change occurred in the median income: from less than 400 l.t. to 1,000 l.t. Whereas more than two-thirds of nobles disposed of an income of less than 1,000 l.t., by 1666 this proportion had declined to less than half (table 5.11). The category including the richest nobles also declined slightly; it was the "middle class" that increased, reflecting the declining degree of wealth inequality.

The purging of nobility of its poorest members continued during the first half of the eighteenth century. In the *élections* of Gisors and rural Rouen (excluding the city), the proportions of noble families with incomes of less than 1,000 l.t. declined to 46 and 41 percent in 1703 and to 11 and 16 percent in 1757, respectively (Dewald 1987:115). What was apparently happening was that poor nobles were dropping out of the ranks of nobility, while the number of better-off nobles (those with more than 1,000 l.t. of annual income) stabilized. Thus, in the rural Rouen region, there were ninety-one such nobles in 1703 and eighty-eight in 1757, while in Gisors there were forty such nobles in both 1702 and 1757 (calculated from Tables 32 and 33 in Dewald 1987). The proportion of impoverished nobles, however, began increasing again during the second half of the century, and on the Revolution's eve (1788) the proportions of poor nobles increased to 26 percent and 17 percent in the two *élections* (Dewald 1987:115).

Conclusions

Is there a general pattern underlying the material we have reviewed in this section? It appears so. The pattern is that the numbers (or, more precisely, the noble to commoner ratio) and per capita wealth of nobility existed in a state of dynamical interrelation. A decline in the noble-commoner ratio has a beneficial effect on noble incomes. Vice versa, increasing the number of nobles in relation to commoner numbers had a depressing effect on the mean incomes, and an even greater effect on the proportion of poor nobles. Incomes enjoyed by noble families also affected their numbers (this is a kind of feedback loop), because high incomes promoted family multiplication and upward mobility while low incomes compressed nobility by squeezing out the poorest stratum. The system was not dynamically closed, however, because it was affected by such factors (which themselves vary with the phase of the secular cycle) as commoner numbers (for example, high commoner numbers drive up rents and depress wages, benefiting the elites) and sociopolitical instability. On the one hand, civil wars sped up the ennoblement rate of elite aspirants, but on the other hand they elevated mortality, especially for young males. One overall effect of civil wars, thus, is a diminishing pool of elite aspirants—wealthy commoners and the younger sons of nobility—resulting in a (perhaps temporary) relief of the social pressure.

5.6 Depression (1600–1660)

Diverging Population Trends between North and South

Different regions of France exhibited significant variations in their demographic trajectories. France is a large and diverse country, and its many regions would not be expected to oscillate in synchrony. We can trace the divergent trajectories of regions using the data on tithes, demography, and the incidence of internal warfare. The main distinction we focus on here is that between the French-speaking north and the Occitan-speaking south. Secondary divisions of interest are the ethnic fringes of northern France, namely, Brittany, Flanders, and above all Alsace, which at that time was much more in the orbit of German rather than French politics.

The tithe records discussed by Le Roy Ladurie indicate that both the south and the north followed trajectories of the same shape, which, however, were shifted with respect to each other by twenty years. The fifteenth century's minimum in the south occurred between 1400 and 1430, and the expansion took off between 1430 and 1450. In the north, the minimum occurred during the 1440s, and the expansion started only after 1450, probably as a result of a lag in the incidence of war-caused disasters (Le Roy

Ladurie 1987:44–45). A century later the south was the first to achieve the maximum (around 1540), and thereafter production stayed flat to 1560. In the north the maximum was achieved twenty years later. The south was again the first to be affected by the devastation of the Wars of Religion. The documents on the sale of church property support the tithe records and indicate that by 1568 there was a "red zone" of maximum damage centered on Poitou, Aquitane, and Languedoc. This is where religious conflicts were the most intense and where the productive capacity was most seriously undermined by the conflict. By 1583 the worst affected zones were again in the Occitanian heartland: Aquitaine, Gascony, Languedoc, Rouergue, Auvergne, and Dauphiné. During the 1590s the war spread to the north. Normandy, Ile-de-France, Picardy, and Champaigne were all affected by the final convulsions of the Catholic League. However, the south was also subjected to continuing damage (Le Roy Ladurie 1987:251). Tithe records show three bad periods for Languedoc and the Mediterranean south. The first production fall (36 percent) occurred right after the outbreak of war in 1560. The second wave hit during the 1570s, when production was 43 percent less than the prewar level (1532–50). The third difficult period was between 1583 and 1596, when the average delivery of tithes was 36 percent below the prewar level (Le Roy Ladurie 1987:263). The adjacent regions were affected almost as badly. Auvergne lost 35–40 percent of its productive capacity, and Lyonnais lost 40 percent.

The French north also experienced a significant drop in production, but it did not occur until the 1590s, and generally there was less devastation than in the south. Overall, the regions in the north lost 33 percent, while the Paris region lost only 20–25 percent (25 percent in tithes and 16 percent in rents). Eastern France was similar to the south with respect to the depth of the fall, but the timing of the collapse was the same as in the north. Thus, in Burgundy, the net product of tithes (in kind) fell spectacularly between 1588 and 1600. Grain tithes during these twelve years fell 43 percent in relation to the prosperous period of 1550–68 (Le Roy Ladurie 1987:262–63). Finally, the least affected region in the sixteenth century was Alsace, where the net product of tithes fell only 7.3 percent (Le Roy Ladurie 1987:265).

During the seventeenth century the trajectories of different regions continued to diverge (and the parallelism was lost). The Mediterranean south seems to have escaped the economic and demographic catastrophes of the mid-seventeenth century (Le Roy Ladurie 1987:278). The tithes there expanded from the minimum of the 1580s until the 1670s, after which they again declined (figure 5.6). In fact, the south entered a period of long-term population decline that lasted from 1680 to 1740 or even 1750 (Le Roy Ladurie 1974:295, 317).

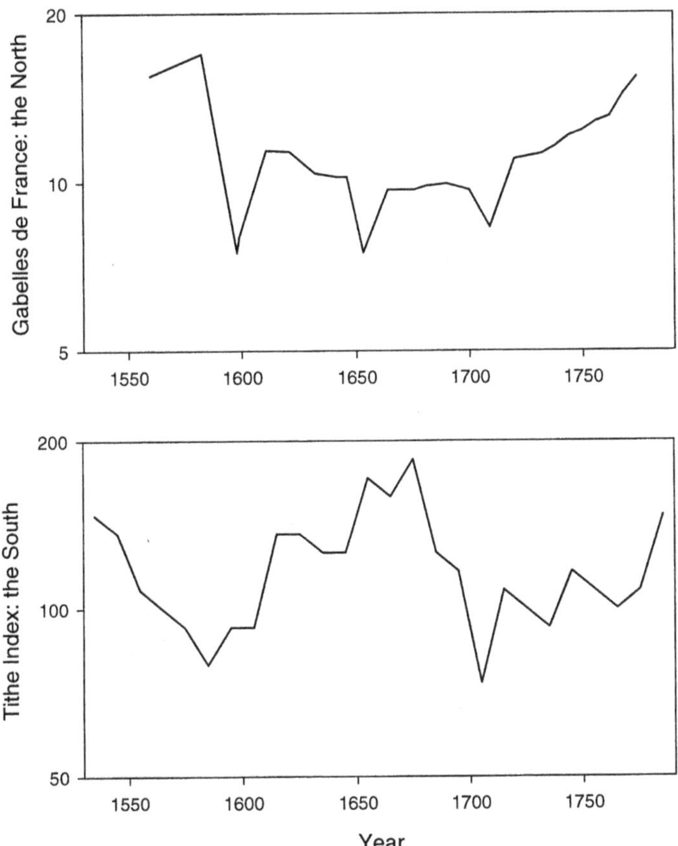

Figure 5.6 Diverging trajectories in northern and southern France, mid-1500s to mid-1700s. (a) Revenues from Gabelles de France (Le Roy Ladurie 1987:288), reflecting economic conditions in the north. (b) Tithes in the south (Le Roy Ladurie and Goy 1982).

In the north, there also was a recovery after the catastrophe of the 1590s, but in contrast to the south, the recovery was short-lived. The extreme northeast and north of the kingdom was affected by the fighting during the Thirty Years' War (1618–48). Thus, in Alsace (not a part of France at that time, but we have good data on production there), grain tithes collapsed to less than 10 percent of their peak value (Le Roy Ladurie and Goy 1982). Even after the peace, during the 1650s, production was only 30 percent of that in 1620. Northern regions such as Cambrésis were also devastated by military operations between the French and Spanish. Then came the Fronde, which was particularly devastating in the central regions of the kingdom. Thus, the curve of tithe yields around Beaune from 1500 to 1790 shows lows around 1590 and again from 1640 to 1660, followed by a rise from 1660 to 1720 (Benedict 1985:86)

In Languedoc and the Mediterranean south, tithes in kind recovered during the early seventeenth century, and the curve then flattens out around 1640. However, the tithes did not completely regain their level of the mid-sixteenth century (they were perhaps 5 percent below). In Auvergne, production remained 15 percent below the sixteenth-century peak, in Burgundy 13 percent below, and in the Lyonnais tithes also stagnated, except in the region around Lyons. Overall, the tithe records suggest that the productive capacity of the kingdom recovered during the early seventeenth century but did not exceed the previously achieved level of the mid-sixteenth century. The major exception to this pattern was the region around Paris, which apparently exceeded the sixteenth-century level. Thus, the net product in rents (in kind) from the estates of Notre-Dame-de-Paris increased to 44 percent above the previous peak in the 1580s (Le Roy Ladurie 1987:302). However, it is hard to decide how much of this increase was due to greater production and how much to greater exploitation of peasants.

Growth of Top Fortunes

The dynamics of the top fortunes often provide a useful indicator about fluctuations in the economic inequality. The largest private fortune of seventeenth-century France belonged, without a doubt, to Jules Mazarin, the notorious prime minister during the minority years of Louis XIV. Ministerial fortunes went on a dizzying roller-coaster ride during the seventeenth century. Henri IV's minister Sully, who was forced to resign his position in 1610, gained a fortune estimated at his death as 5.2 million livres (Barbiche 1978). On his death in 1642, Richelieu left his heirs a fortune of 22 million livres (Bonney 1999:127). This was a tremendous amount of wealth, but it was bettered by Mazarin, who left a fortune of 37 million livres to his heirs (Bonney 1999:127). This was a particularly striking achievement, because it was accomplished in eight years, between 1653 (Mazarin lost most of his previous wealth during the Fronde of 1648–53) and his death in 1661. Second-echelon ministers also did extremely well. Claude Bullion, Richelieu's finance minister (1632–40), gained a fortune of 7.8 million livres in just eight years of office. Nicolas Foucquet's assets were evaluated in excess of 15.4 million livres at the time of his arrest in 1661 (although his debts equaled his assets).

To place these numbers in perspective, we can compare them to what is known about the fortunes of the greatest noble houses. The fortune of one branch of the Bourbons, closely related to the king, the princes de Conti, was 12 million livres in 1655–65 and then declined to 7.6 million during the 1670s (Mougel 1971). Louis Gonzagues, Duc de Nevers, left an inheritance of 8 million, which was, however, encumbered by debts totaling 2.5 million (Harding 1978). The wealthiest noble house was probably that of the princes de Condé. Its total fortune in the early eighteenth century, shared among several branches, was estimated as 31 million livres (Roche 1967).

The scale of private gains by ministers from public office began to be brought under control during the reign of Louis XIV. Colbert's wealth was estimated at between 4.95 and 5.75 million, probably closer to the high end. Louvois gained a fortune of some 8 million in a career spanning two decades (1672–91). "After 1720, ministerial gains from office were small beer indeed compared to the situation before 1661" (Bonney 1999:127).

Reversal of the Disintegrative Trend

It is clear that the assumption of personal rule by Louis XIV in 1661 marked an important turning point in the history of France. The most dramatic development was the consolidation of the elites around the center, which ended the intraelite conflict that had plagued the preceding hundred years and channeled elite energies into wars of external conquest. The internal workings of how this consensus between the elites and the state was achieved has been admirably probed by William Beik (1985, 2005), using as an example the provincial aristocracy of Languedoc. Essentially, the last period of high sociopolitical instability, peaking with the Fronde of 1648–53, forced the elites to understand that they needed military, diplomatic, and economic protection of the center (Beik 1985:331). Between 1560 and 1660 various factions fighting in civil wars were either entirely composed of the elites or were elite-mobilized popular uprisings. After 1660 the elites withdrew their leadership, and uprisings dramatically declined (Beik 1985:12). Later popular uprisings, such as the rebellion of Cévennes peasants (1702–4), lacked support among the elites and were easily put down.

The new consensus allowed the government of Louis XIV to raise taxes to an unprecedented level in French history (see figure 5.2). The elites were, of course, the primary beneficiaries. First, the comparative distribution of tax flow between crown and regional elites in 1647 and 1677 (Beik 1985:267) shows that at least in Languedoc the regional elites were able to increase the share of taxes that remained in the province. Second, the lion's share of taxes went toward financing the wars of Louis XIV, which meant improved employment for the sword nobility. Furthermore, at least during the late seventeenth century, Louis's program of external conquest was highly successful.

The consolidation of the elites and reestablishment of law and order, however, did not immediately end the regime of population stagnation, since sustained demographic expansion began only after 1720. Real wages continued to increase until the 1680s (see figure 5.1) (although even at its peak, the real wage was less than half that of the "golden age" of the early fifteenth century). Agricultural wages "exhumed" by Jacquart and discussed by Le Roy Ladurie (1987:352) followed the same general pattern, at least around Paris. The two decades around 1700 saw another substantial population decline, although the determining (or at least a very important contributing) factor appears to be worsening of the climate. A sustained period of population growth began only after 1719 and lasted to 1790 (Dupâquier et al. 1988b:151). Thus, although the elite and state dynamics turned a corner around 1660, the demographic and economic trends indicated continuing stagnation to the end of the century. This appears to be an example of how real-life dynamics may not fit the neat division of the secular cycle into phases.

5.7 Conclusion

In many ways the Valois cycle (1450–1660) is another textbook example of demographic-structural mechanisms in action. We are lucky in that the historical record is good enough for us to test many mechanisms postulated by the theory with concrete and detailed historical data (and that this period attracted the attention of such giants as Emmanuel Le Roy Ladurie). These processes include the Malthusian effects of population growth, and how population growth and elite overproduction causes state breakdown. The case study of Norman nobility has thrown a lot of light on how elite overproduction develops and what consequences it has for the elites themselves as well as for other components of the social system.

In his pathbreaking work, Jack Goldstone (1991) did not discuss in any significant way the preconditions of the French Wars of Religion (although he devoted some space to a later conflict, the Fronde). Yet what happened in France from 1559 on matches very well the patterns he discerned in his study of other state collapses—the financial ruin of the state, its loss of control over the military, intensifying intraelite factionalism and competition, and finally full-blown civil war.

There were also some complexities of the interplay among different variables, mainly dealing with the demographic and economic dynamics of the commoner population during the late seventeenth century. Although we used 1660 as the end of the cycle, an argument can be made that the depression phase lasted to the end of the century. We think that the demographic-structural theory is an extremely useful tool for understanding historical dynamics, but history is complex, and we should not expect all of it to fit into a single neat scheme.

Chapter 6

Rome: The Republican Cycle (350–30 BCE)

6.1 Overview of the Cycle

A Secular Cycle during the Regal–Early Republic Period?

Although the fragmentary nature of sources allows us at most a hypothetical reconstruction of the economic and social dynamics of Rome during the regal and early Republic periods, we believe a case can be made that between 650 and 350 BCE, the Roman polity went through a complete secular cycle, with the integrative trend dominating before 500 BCE and the disintegrative trend holding until the early fourth century. Some evidence for this thesis comes from the cyclic dynamics of public building activity. The first peak came around 500 BCE, while the second occurred during the middle Republic (figure 6.1).

More important, during the fifth century BCE Rome went through a period of heightened sociopolitical instability (figure 6.2) typical of the disintegrative phases of secular cycles. The saw-toothed pattern in the curve probably arises as a result of the operation of "fathers-and-sons" cycles (Sorokin's time series is sampled at quarter-century intervals, and therefore cycles with average periods of fifty years show up as alternating high and low values).

The period of internal instability began in Rome in 509 BCE with the overthrow of the last king, Tarquinius Superbus, and the establishment of the Republic. Most of the fifth century and the early part of the fourth century were dominated by the Conflict of the Orders, a struggle between the elites and commoners as well as between different factions of elites (Raaflaub 1986, Cornell 1995, Ward, Heichelheim, and Yeo 2003:66). Two issues were at the center of the political controversy. One was the disposition of the public land. In the period from 486 to 367 there were twenty-five separate attempts made by the plebeians to have public land, especially newly conquered areas, redistributed in allotments to the citizens (Cornell 1995:270). The second issue was alleviation of debt burden. However, it is important to recognize that the "plebeians" were not a homogeneous social group. Whereas the majority of plebeians were motivated by these two issues, land and debt, the socially prominent and wealthy among them aimed at social and political equality with the patricians: they demanded that intermarriage between patricians and plebeians be officially permitted,

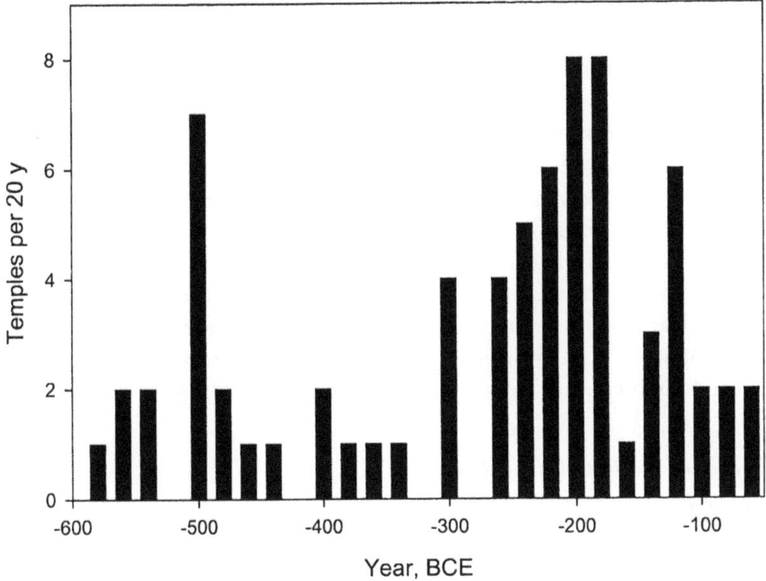

Figure 6.1 Temporal distribution of temple-building activity in Rome, ca. 600–50 BCE. Data from Richardson (1992).

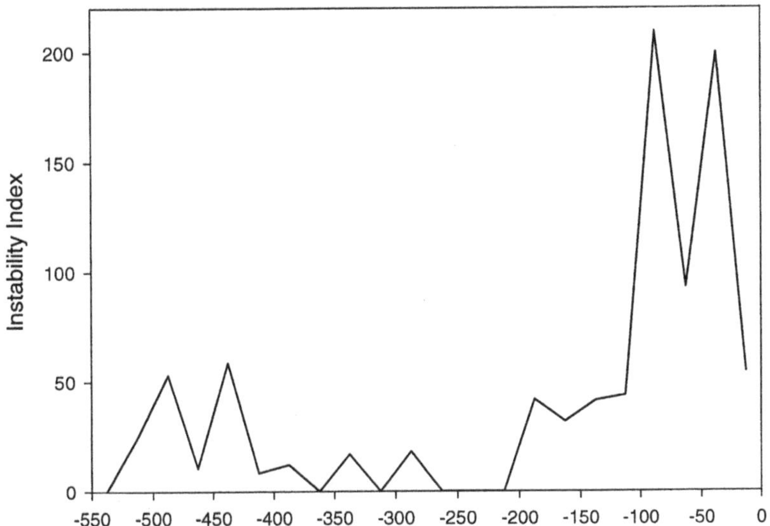

Figure 6.2 An index of sociopolitical instability in Republican Rome (Sorokin 1937).

and they wanted plebeians to be eligible for magistracies and priesthoods (Von Ungern-Sternberg 1986:354). The leaders of the plebeian movement were thus ambitious individuals from well-to-do families who wanted their share of the power (Cornell 1995:291) and who used the economic concerns of the commoners to mobilize political support for their political struggle against the patricians. The conflict between the patricians and the wealthy plebeians was ended by the enactment of the Licino-Sextian laws of 367, which transformed the political structure of the Roman state by ending all forms of discrimination against plebeians (Cornell 1995:340). The legislation created the conditions for merging the established and aspirant elites. "Without major difficulties, therefore, they [plebeians] melted into a new social and political elite, the 'nobility,' already in the second half of the fourth century" (Von Ungern-Sternberg 1986:355).

Phases of the Republican Cycle

The achievement of internal unity among the elites following the Licino-Sextian compromise of 367 marked the shift from the disintegrative to integrative trends and opened the long and highly successful period of Rome's territorial expansion. By the end of the fourth century BCE, Latium and Campania had merged together into a Roman-Campanian state, which involved agreement between the Roman and Capuan aristocracies to create a shared army. The great Capuan families were welcomed into the Roman senate (Le Glay et al. 1997:51). Internal unity created conditions for territorial expansion, which resulted in Rome first establishing control over peninsular Italy, and then acquiring a Mediterranean empire. During the third century BCE Rome had to fight a series of prolonged and bitter wars (the Second Punic War was particularly destructive) that delivered several shocks to population growth. Growth resumed after the end of the War with Hannibal (218–201), and Rome entered the stagflation phase around 180 BCE. There was no sharp transition between the stagflation and the crisis phase. Between 133 and 91 BCE Roman society slipped into crisis by stages. The first wave of severe instability was the series of civil wars between 90 and 71. It was followed by a relatively peaceful interlude in the 60s and 50s, and then the second series of civil wars from 50 to 31 BCE, which finally produced conditions for the reversal of the disintegrative trend. We use the end of the civil wars and the establishment of the Principate by Augustus as the end-point of the Roman Republican cycle. Therefore, the disintegrative trend (combining crisis and depression phases) is dated by us as the century between 130 and 30 BCE.

In the first century BCE, thus, the state and society of Rome were fundamentally transformed. The proximate factors leading to the collapse of the Republic and the establishment of the Principate were the series of civil

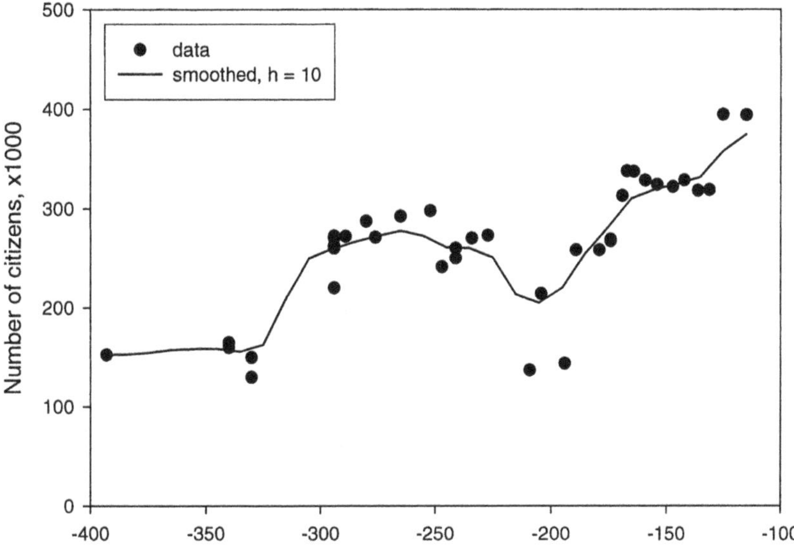

Figure 6.3 Numbers of Roman citizens, 400–100 BCE (Toynbee 1965:438–39).

wars that afflicted Italy during this century. Why Rome experienced this period of social and political instability, however, does not yet have a widely accepted answer. Probably the most influential model explaining this period is the one advanced by Keith Hopkins (1978). We offer an explanation, based on the demographic-structural theory, that in some parts coincides with Hopkins's model and in other parts diverges from it. Although we do not necessarily agree with all aspects of Hopkins's model, we are indebted to his pioneering effort.

Population Dynamics

We are lucky to have the census numbers for the Roman Republican period, transmitted by the annalists. The consensus among the Roman historians appears to be that these numbers can serve as a reasonably solid basis for reconstructing the dynamics of the Roman population (Scheidel 2001, 2004). The numbers refer not to the total population but only to adult free males.

The overall trend between 350 and 100 BCE was growth, which was interrupted by several sharp declines (figure 6.3). Population decreases correlate with periods of very intense warfare, the First and Second Punic Wars (264–241 and 218–201, respectively).

What we really wish to know, however, is not how the numbers of Roman citizens changed but what happened to the total population of peninsular Italy. The censuses cannot be taken as an index of total population, because they increased not only as a result of demographic growth but also when free inhabitants of certain annexed territories were admitted to Roman citizenship. There was a particularly massive enfranchisement of Italian allies following the Social War. Additionally, the Italian population was swelled by huge influxes of slaves from outside the peninsula, which became an increasingly significant factor as Rome's conquest of Mediterranean proceeded.

Population trends during the late Republic–early Principate period have been debated at length by demographers and economic historians. The main controversy has to do with the interpretation of the Augustan censuses. The proponents of the "high" count (Frank 1933, Lo Cascio 1994, Morley 2001) assume that the census numbers represent adult free males, while the proponents of the "low" count (Beloch 1886, Brunt 1971) believe that the numbers represent all free inhabitants of both sexes, with the possible exception of infants less than one year old. Here we follow Walter Scheidel (2001 [ed.], 2004, 2007), who accepts the Beloch-Brunt reconstruction, and refer the reader to his 2004 work for details of the argument.

Brunt (1971) concluded that the free population of peninsular Italy numbered around 3 million in both 225 and 28 BCE. These numbers are accepted by Scheidel with only minor variations. Hopkins (1978:68–69), also working with Brunt's numbers, argued that the population of the whole of Italy (including Cisapline Gaul) declined between 225 and 28 BCE from 4.5 million to 4 million. However, Hopkins assumed that in 225 there were 1.4 million inhabitants in northern Italy (Cisapline Gaul), and there are reasons to believe this figure is an overestimate (de Ligt 2004:733). Because very little is known about northern Italy, it seems safer to stick with the numbers for peninsular Italy alone.

The apparent stability suggested by roughly the same population size in 225 and 28 BCE, however, is deceptive—in fact, these estimates serve to anchor a secular population cycle that Italy experienced in the last two centuries BCE. The cycle occurred in three phases. To come up with quantitative estimates of change we follow Brunt's corrected census returns (his Table VII), and then use these Roman censuses as indicators of what was happening to the rest of the population in Italian peninsula. When we cite census statistics below, we round them to the nearest thousand.

In the first phase, between 225 and 200 BCE, the population declined as a result of prolonged and destructive Hannibalic war (Toynbee 1965). The magnitude of this decline is suggested by the census numbers during this period: from 273,000 in 225 to 214,000 in 203. (In 208 and 194 the numbers were 137,000 and 144,000, respectively, but Brunt convincingly argues that these very low counts represent either the stationing of large numbers of troops abroad or deficient census procedures, or both.) In proportionate terms, the decline is 22 percent, so let us say that the total free population declined from 3 to 2.35 million.

In the next phase, the second century BCE, the population increased. Brunt accepts the censuses of 168 (313,000) and 124 (395,000) as reliable. Estimating population growth between 203 and 168 is a bit involved because, according to Brunt, 26,000 Campanians (who switched sides in the Hannibalic war) were not counted in 203 but were included in 168. Taking this factor into account, he estimated the starting-point population as 214,000 + 26,000 = 240,000. The ending population is estimated as 313,000 + 33,000 (the estimated number of soldiers stationed abroad) = 346,000, or an increase of 44 percent. Thus, between 203 and 168 the free peninsular population increased from 2.35 to 3.39 million.

In 124 the census was 395,000, to which Brunt adds 38,500 soldiers, for a total of 433,500. The change between 168 and 124 in proportionate terms thus is 25 percent. In other words, the free population in 124 was 4.25 million.

In the last phase, the first century BCE, the population declined as a result of constant civil wars, a high urbanization index, and, during later stages, massive state-sponsored population transfers. Brunt's calculations based on the census of 69 suggest a population of 3.7 million (Brunt 1971:97, Scheidel 2004:9). Finally, by 28 BCE the population had declined further, to 3 million, returning to the level of 225. The reconstructed population dynamics are depicted in figure 6.4.

The graph in figure 6.4 is somewhat deceptive. For one thing, it is overly smooth. In reality, each estimate comes with at least a 10 percent error. Second, the start of population decline probably occurred in the early first century, rather than right after 124. The census of 114 reported essentially the same numbers as in 124, and the population probably stagnated until the beginning of the Social War in 91. In 85, reported census numbers rose to 463,000, but this increase probably reflects a partial enumeration of newly enfranchised Italian allies (Brunt 1971:93). Finally, all these numbers refer to the free population. The dynamics of the slave population are essentially inestimable (Scheidel 2005), but by the end of the cycle slave numbers probably reached 1–1.5 million. Thus, the total population (including both free and slave) decreased less during the first century than is shown by the graph (or even, conceivably, stayed flat).

Social Structure and Elite Dynamics

The top stratum (the magnates) of the Roman society during the Republican period was the senatorial order (*ordo senatorius*). Senators were the governing class: they served as government officials, monopolized the chief priesthoods, and provided officers for the army (Cornell 1995, Ward,

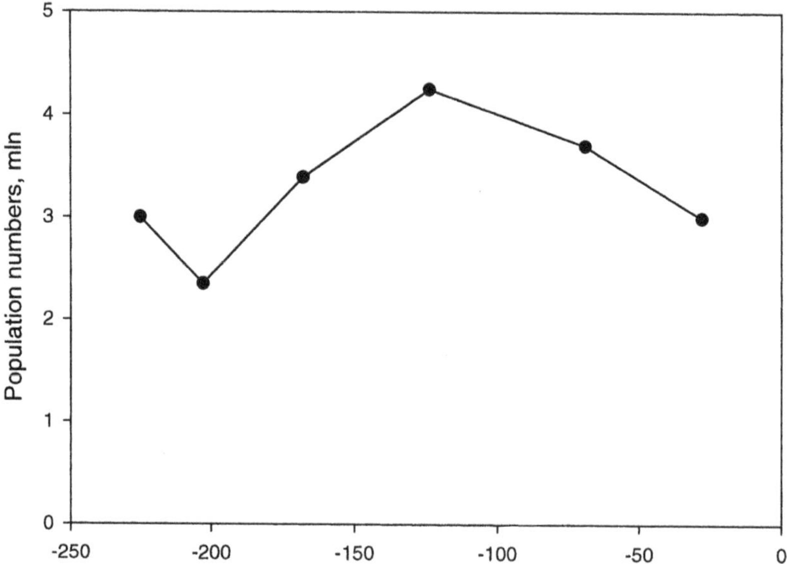

Figure 6.4 Estimated numbers of the free population in peninsular Italy from 225 to 28 BCE (based on data of Brunt 1971 and calculations in the text).

Heichelheim, and Yeo 2003). Senators came from both patrician and plebeian clans (*gentes*) and were wealthy landowners.

The equestrians (*equites*) were lesser aristocrats, called equestrians because originally they served as cavalry in the army. This stratum provided many businessmen—merchants who conducted overseas commerce and *publicani* who monopolized state contracts. In the late Republic, jury service was reserved for the equestrians.

At the beginning of the cycle (ca. 300 BCE), the majority of the commoner population consisted of small landowners—citizens and their families. Citizens served as infantry (hoplites) in the army and voted in the assembly of the arms-bearing males (*comitia centuriata*) and other popular assemblies that elected public officials. They were divided into five classes according to the value of their property (table 6.1). The wealthier citizens, those with property valued above 100,000 asses and the equestrians, had more than half the votes, and therefore dominated elections. On the other hand, they also paid the bulk of the property tax, the *tributum* (Cornell 1995:187).

The propertied citizens (*assidui*) were not poor. The third census class with property valued at 50,000 asses or more could not have been anything but "medium-sized" landholders (Rosenstein 2004:163). (An *as* around 200 BCE weighed two Roman ounces of bronze; its value was around 0.4 g silver.) On two occasions during the War with Hannibal the senate called for citizens in this census class to contribute one slave along with six

TABLE 6.1
Wealth (or annual income) of various strata in the Roman Republic in the late third century.

Stratum	*Income*	*Wealth*	*Notes*
Senator	60,000[a]	1,000,000	See note b
Equestrian	24,000[a]	400,000	Census qualification
Assiduus, 1 class	6,000[a]	100,000	Census qualification
Assiduus, 2 class	4,500[a]	75,000	Census qualification
Assiduus, 3 class	3,000[a]	50,000	Census qualification
Assiduus, 4 class	1,500[a]	25,000	Census qualification
Daily wage[c]	1,080	—	Crawford (1974:624) (3 asses per diem)
Assiduus, 5 class	750[a]	12,500	Census qualification
Slave	100	—	Minimal subsistence assuming 3 asses per modius

Source: Cornell (1995:179–81).

Note: Valuations are given in *asses*. The *as* around 200 BCE weighed 2 Roman ounces of bronze and was valued at 0.1 denarius or 0.4 g silver.

[a] Incomes estimated from wealth, assuming that annual income = 6% of wealth.

[b] The minimum wealth qualification was probably the same as for the equestrians, but senators were on average wealthier. In 214 BCE those with property worth more than 1 million asses were required to supply seven sailors for the fleet; senators supplied eight (Mitchell 1990:247–78), so average senatorial property must have been more than 1 million asses. The equestrian-senator proportion is also the same as in the Augustan census.

[c] Legionnaire pay, also probably the lowest daily salary paid by the state.

months of provisions as a rower in the fleet (wealthier citizens were expected to contribute more). This suggests a degree of wealth well above the subsistence level.

The lower strata of the Roman society included landless citizens (*proletarii*), foreigners, freedmen, and slaves.

The social structure during the Republic was very dynamic. Around 300 BCE the bulk of the population was most likely the smallholders (*assidui*), while landless *proletarii* were a minority. Brunt (1971:77) thought that in 218, *proletarii* amounted to half the citizen body. But as Rosenstein (2004:185) pointed out, this cannot be right. While *proletarii* did not serve in the army, they served as rowers in the fleet. In 214, at a time when there were no more than 20,000 *proletarii* serving in that capacity, the senate was forced to recruit slaves as galley rowers. Brunt calculates that in 214 about 100,000 citizens were under arms or had been killed. Assuming similar military participation ratios, these numbers suggest that in the late third century the ratio of *assidui* (who served in the army) to *proletarii* (who served as rowers) was roughly 10:2. Rosenstein (2002) estimates that, in fact, about 90 percent of the citizenry were *assidui*, because half of them (the older married men) were not drafted so that they could operate the farms.

In the third century the ratio of wealthy landowners (equestrians and senators) to nonelite landholders (*assidui*) was just under 1:10, as suggested by the numbers of Roman cavalry and infantry in 225 reported by

Polybius—23,000 and 250,000, respectively (the same proportion as in the regal period). Using this template together with the calculation in the previous paragraph, we arrive at the following breakdown of Roman social structure in mid-Republic: *equites* (including senators): *assidui* : *proletarii* 1:10:2 (or 1:10:1, if the Rosenstein estimate in the preceding paragraph is correct). To these categories we need to add unknown numbers of slaves and foreigners.

State Finances

The basic demographic-structural model was developed for states with approximately stationary territory. By contrast, the territory of Rome expanded from around 5,000 km^2 in the fourth century BCE to more than 3 Mm^2 (millions of square kilometers) by the end of the first century BCE (Taagepera 1979). Such a spectacular 600-fold territorial expansion is a factor of enormous significance and must be added to the basic model described in chapter 1. Territorial expansion helped solve the problem of landless citizens. It also affected how the Roman elites and the state secured their means of livelihood. Whereas in "typical" agrarian societies the elites and the state extract surplus from the commoner population in the form of rents and taxes, in Republican Rome the ruling class largely lived off the spoils of conquest. When the Third Macedonian War ended in 167 with a particularly large haul of booty, taxes levied on Italian land owned by Roman citizens were abolished (Hopkins 1978:38). The land tax was not reimposed until the end of the third century CE. The state took a cut of the booty resulting from the conquest and taxed conquered territories at the probable rate of 10 percent of the crop on average (Hopkins 1978:16). As a result of Rome's success at war, the state revenues more than quadrupled during the third century (table 6.2). However, during the succeeding century, while the population and the numbers of elites expanded, the state revenues stagnated at the level of 55–80 million sesterces (table 6.2). The main reason seems to be that after the Third Punic War (149–146 BCE), Rome had simply run out of wealthy states to conquer. The endemic war against the Spanish guerillas consumed men and treasure without yielding any significant booty. The next great leap of revenue expansion came only after the first round of civil wars.

Sociopolitical Instability

The two centuries between the last exit of the Plebeians in 342 and the First Servile War (135–132 BCE) were remarkably free of civil warfare (table 6.3). By contrast, the century following the murder of Tiberius Gracchus was one of almost continuous internecine war.

TABLE 6.2
State income

Date	*Millions of sesterces (HS) per year*	*Reference*
264–241 BCE	15	Frank (1933:66–67)
218–201 BCE	65	Frank (1933:95)
200–157 BCE	55	Frank (1933:145)
150–90 BCE	80	Frank (1933:228)
ca.65 BCE	200	Hopkins (1978:37)
ca.60 BCE	340	Hopkins (1978:37)
55–51 BCE	320	Frank (1933:332)
ca.50 BCE	380[a]	Harl (1996:54)

[a]This total probably includes the value of grain taxes of Sicily, Sardinia, and Africa.

Michael Crawford (1974) has argued that the deposition rate of coin hoards can serve as a faithful reflection of the conditions of internal instability affecting Italy during the middle and late Republic periods. Plotting Crawford data on coin hoards together with an index of internal warfare we observe a remarkable degree of parallelism (figure 6.5). The two curves do not coincide in all the details, as is only natural when we deal with real data. For example, the coin hoards trajectory has a minor peak in the 150s, and there were no significant internal disturbances during this decade. Crawford thought that these hoards could have been buried by legionnaires prior to leaving for, and dying in, external wars. Another possibility is that the peak in the 150s is simply a statistical fluctuation in the data (the period has only eight hoards).

The three major periods of internal war, on the other hand, are reflected in both curves: the Hannibalic wars of the late third century and the two civil wars of the first century. The second century was relatively peaceful. There were few hoards and no significant internecine infighting during the first half, while rising hoard deposits during the second half suggest growing sociopolitical tensions.

6.2 An Unusually Long Expansion (350–180 BCE)

After the wars with the Samnites and Italian Greeks, the Roman state ended up with indirect control of peninsular Italy, with about 20 percent of territory in the Ager Romanus. The territorial expansion was accompanied by growth of the citizen body (table 6.4).

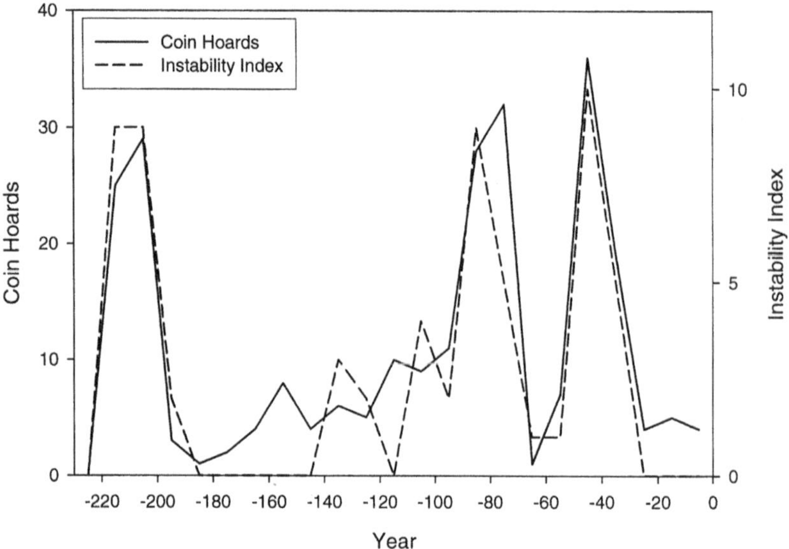

Figure 6.5 Instability in peninsular Italy (including Sicily), 220–0 BCE, as measured by two indices: (1) incidence of coin hoards per decade (solid line) and (2) proportion of years per decade in internal war (dashed line). Coin hoards from Crawford (1993:162). Internal war index is based on sociopolitical instability events listed in table 6.2 plus the War with Hannibal (218–201 BCE).

If we can trust the census data (and the consensus among historians seems to be that we can, at least from the late fourth century onward), then the Roman population almost doubled between the mid-fourth and mid-third centuries, while territory almost quintupled. As a result, the population density actually declined (table 6.4). This development explains to a large degree the alleviation of the land problem, which had plagued the Roman poor since the fifth century. The census numbers reflect not only (and perhaps even not primarily) demographic growth. Numbers of citizens were increased by the enfranchisement of the Latins and Campanians, while at the same time an estimated 70,000 Romans were lost to the citizen rolls as a result of colonization during the period 334–263 (Cornell 1995:381). Population growth was also undoubtedly slowed by the series of intense wars that the Romans fought during the late fourth century and all of the third century against first the Samnites, then the Italian Greeks and Pyrrhus, and last the Carthaginians. These wars were fought within central and southern Italy and resulted in much devastation. A particularly destructive war was the Second Punic War, 218–201 BCE (Toynbee 1965). Census numbers dropped from a high near 300,000 in 265 BCE to close to 200,000 or even less around 200 BCE (for the censuses of 209 and 194

TABLE 6.3
Sociopolitical instability in Rome, 350–0 BCE

Year	*Event*
342	The last exit of the Plebeians
287	Disturbances before "lex Hortensia"
198–6	Slave rebellions at Setia and Praeneste; Etruria
135–2	First Servile War
133	Murder of Tiberius Gracchus and his 300 followers
125	Insurrection at Fregellae
121	Murder of Gaius Gracchus and 3,000 followers
104–1	Second Servile War
100	Murder of Saturninus and his supporters
91–87	War of the Allies (Social War)
88–2	Civil War between Marius and Sulla
82–1	Sulla's Proscriptions
78–7	Insurrection of Marcus Lepidus
73–1	Third Servile War (Spartacus)
63	Insurrection of Catilina
52	Street rioting in Rome (Milo vs. Clodius)
49–45	Civil War (Caesar against Pompey and the Pompeians)
44	Assassination of Caesar
43	Proscriptions of the Second Triumvirate
43–2	Civil War (Brutus and Cassius vs. the Second Triumvirate)
41–40	Perusian War (Octavian vs. the Antonians)
37–6	War with Sextus Pompey
32–30	Civil War (Octavian vs. Antony)

Source: Sorokin (1937), supplemented by other sources.

TABLE 6.4
Roman census and territory for selected years, ca.330–225, and estimated population density

Year BCE	*Census (1,000 ind.)*	*Territory (1,000 km²)*	*Pop. density (ind./km²)*
330	150	5.3	85
294	262	14.0	56
280	287	17.4	50
265	292	24.0	37
234	271	24.0	34
225	273	25.6	32

Source: Census figures and territory from Brunt (1971: tables I and V).

Note: Assumes that adult males constituted one-third of the total free population.

Livy transmits the figure of around 140,000, and for 204, 214,000). Part of this drop was artifactual and reflected the absence of large numbers of Roman soldiers stationed away from Rome, and who were therefore not counted in the census (Brunt 1971), but there is also no question that the Roman citizenry suffered huge casualties (Ward, Heichelheim, and Yeo 2003:131). However, it is logical to assume that the numbers of females and children did not decline to the same extent as those of males of military age. As a result, the census numbers rapidly bounced back to the level of 250,000 in the early second century.

Falling population density due to war losses and territorial expansion meant that internal competition for resources ceased to be a factor in Roman politics (until the next stagflation phase, that is). Instead, all efforts of both aristocracy and commoners were directed at the struggle with external enemies. Aristocracy was also severely affected by war losses. For example, at the battle of Cannae (216 BCE) alone there were eighty senatorial casualties. Natural attrition and earlier battles also had taken a severe toll, resulting in ninety-seven additional vacancies between 219 and 217 (Raaflaub 1986:167). In other words, instead of the normal turnover of 10 percent over these three years, almost 60 percent of the senate was obliterated. The intense wars of the third century, in which the aristocracy was fighting on the front lines, thus helped to prevent elite overproduction.

Once the Second Punic War ended, in 201 BCE, all subsequent Roman wars were fought abroad (that is, outside peninsular Italy). Rome typically had the upper hand in those conflicts, and the casualties were lighter. As a result, the second century saw a period of sustained population growth. The census numbers increased from 258,000 in 189 to 394,000– 395,000 in 125 and 114 BCE. The estimated free population of peninsular Italy increased from 2.35 million to 4.25 million (section 6.1). Between 200 and 91 the Roman territory stayed unchanged (Crawford 1993:46), which implies that the population density increased by more than 50 percent. This increase refers only to free citizens, but the population of slaves grew even faster.

Archaeological data from southern Etruria also suggest that the population density increased during this period. The number of settlements in Ager Veientanus doubled between the fourth and first centuries BCE (Bintliff and Sbonias 1999). The period after 300 BCE also saw the decline of Etruscan towns and the dispersal of settlements into the countryside (Greene 1986:103). This is a typical pattern, often observed during the expansion phase of the secular cycle. It results from the increased security accompanying the disintegrative/integrative shift and is a sign of population growth (as the proportion of the population in urban environments with its negative population growth is reduced).

In summary, the expansion phase of the Republican cycle was characterized by two periods of population growth. The total number of Roman citizens first doubled between the mid-fourth and mid-third centuries. However, the territory controlled by the state increased even faster, with the result that the population density actually declined. During the second half of the third century population numbers declined as a result of a series of wars, culminating in the Second Punic war. Once the Second Punic War was over, in 201, population growth resumed. During the second century the number of citizens increased by more than 50 percent. Because the territory directly controlled by Rome was approximately constant during this period, population growth in the second century resulted in an increased population density.

6.3 Stagflation (180–130 BCE)

Demographic Trends in the Second Century BCE

The century between the tribuneship of Tiberius Gracchus (133 BCE) and the establishment of the Principate by Augustus in 29 BCE was dominated by persistent domestic strife that twice flared up into protracted and intense civil wars. This period of state collapse and chronic civil warfare (reviewed in section 6.4) has all the earmarks of a classic demographic-structural crisis, because its onset was preceded by popular immiseration, intense intra-elite competition, and the stagnation of state revenues. Here we review each of these trends in turn.

In the late Republic, the economic structure of the Roman polity underwent a deep transformation. Agriculture in the early and middle Republic was dominated by free landowners who worked small family farms and provided recruits for the legions (*assidui*). *Assidui* still outnumbered the landless citizens (*proletarii*) at the end of the third century by about 5:1 (or even 10:1), as estimated in section 7.1. By the late Republic the numbers of *assidui* had shrunk to an alarming degree, whereas the numbers of *proletarii* and slaves had experienced massive growth.

There is some question about precisely when the transformation took place. Until recently the consensus view (as put forth in the textbooks; see Ward, Heichelheim, and Yeo 2003) held that it began in the late third century. Historians such as Arnold Toynbee, Keith Hopkins, and Peter Brunt have argued that the wars of the third and second centuries, and especially the Second Punic War, undermined the relative agricultural stability established by the Licino-Sextian compromise of 367. Battle casualties inflicted by Hannibal's victories on the Romans were extraordinarily high—according to Polybius, 110,000 (although Brunt [1971] thinks such numbers are exaggerated). Moreover, the wars were fought in peninsular

Italy and caused widespread destruction of the productive infrastructure (Toynbee 1965, although Toynbee probably exaggerates the persistence of the effect). The Roman censuses reflect the demographic impact of the wars: 292,000 in 264 (just before the start of the First Punic War) and 214,000 in 203, near the end of the Second Punic War. Those soldiers who survived the wars "returned to find their farms run down and burdened by debts incurred to support their families. Not a few had been seized for debt or simply taken over by some larger neighbor" (Ward , Heichelheim, and Yeo 2003:131). Meanwhile, the elites, who got the biggest share of the profits from the overseas conquests, invested the bulk of their capital in land. Large-scale capital-intensive operations—*latifundia*—specialized in producing high-value products for the market:

> The transformation of a subsistence economy which had previously produced only a small surplus into a market economy which produced and consumed a large surplus was achieved by increasing the productivity of agricultural labour on larger farms. Fewer men produced more food. Under-employed small-holders were expelled from their plots and replaced by a smaller number of slaves. The rich bought up their land, or took possession of it by violence. They reorganized small-holdings into larger and more profitable farms in order to compete with other nobles, to increase return on their investment in land and slaves, and to exploit their slaves more effectively. . . . The mass eviction of the poor by the rich underlay the political conflicts and civil wars of the last century of the Roman Republic. (Hopkins 1978:2–5)

This conventional explanation for the late Republican transformation was summarized pithily if unsympathetically by Jongman (2003:105), as follows:

> When larger and larger Roman armies began to fight longer and longer wars in more and more distant lands, military service became increasingly burdensome to ordinary peasant citizens, the traditional backbone of the legions. As a result, many lost their land to ever more powerful rich, and left to increase the number of the urban poor. The rich, grown richer from the spoils of conquering the world, acquired the large estates through the purchase and occupation—legal or otherwise—of public and private land. To work the land they used the ever increasing numbers of slaves captured in Rome's wars of expansion.

Recently the consensus view was severely criticized by Jongman (2003), Rosenstein (2004), and de Ligt (2004, 2007). In a wide-ranging and closely reasoned book, Rosenstein argues that Rome's citizen soldiers were not victims of their city's imperial adventures but "willing and often enthusiastic participants" (Rosenstein 2004:60). Their enthusiasm waned only after the mid-second century: "Combat in Spain since 153 had been hard and unprofitable. Defeats were frequent, and the loss of life there often heavy. Conscripts were notoriously reluctant to go, just as Plutarch reports, and morale in the army was at rock bottom" (Rosenstein 2004:53).

Furthermore, new plantation agriculture appears in the literary and archaeological record in the mid-second century at the earliest, and it became widespread only during the age of Sulla (Rosenstein 2004:6). Thus, several generations elapsed between the period of heaviest war casualties and the rise of *latifundia*, throwing doubt on a direct causal link between the two processes.

Using demographic models and the calculus of agrarian economy, Rosenstein showed that most families of Roman smallholders could readily spare the labor of young males without going under. In fact, the main problem facing the Roman countryside during the second century (and many other agrarian societies during the appropriate phase of the secular cycle) must have been rural underemployment, rather than lack of labor to work the fields.

Rosenstein stands the consensus view on its head and argues that "an increasing number of smallholders and the prevalence of partible inheritance among them offer an attractive alternative to the conventional accounts of the origins of the agrarian crisis that Gracchus sought to solve" (Rosenstein 2004:155):

> The great many deaths of young Roman males between 218 and the last third or so of the second century are very likely to have made a significant contribution to the dramatic rise in population that took place following the defeat of Hannibal. . . . As the population multiplied and parents divided smaller and smaller inheritances among their children, the number of citizens whose wealth placed them among the *proletarii* may well have been increasing. . . . By 133 therefore Roman warfare in the years since Hannibal's invasion had not only contributed to a rapidly rising population but also produced a body of smallholders in the lowest census classes that was, overall, significantly poorer than their third-century counterparts and without much hope of improving their lot through their own efforts. And with the end of colonization of Italy after 181 the senate closed this safety valve for families unable to establish all their children on new farms. (Rosenstein 154–64 passim)

As we see it, Rosenstein advances an essentially demographic-structural argument. There is no question that the protracted series of wars had a great effect on Roman population dynamics, and must be taken into account. However, its effect is the opposite of the one postulated by the consensus view. It did not cause the civil wars of the first century but rather postponed the day of reckoning until then (thus the unusually long expansion phase of the Republican cycle).

The end of the Second Punic War introduced a century-long period of internal peace to peninsular Italy, since all succeeding conflicts were removed to the expanding frontier of the Roman Empire. Productive infrastructure damaged by the conflict was rapidly restored, creating conditions for rapid population growth. Growth was somewhat inhibited at first by high casualties in the external wars, and until 181 by colonization of the Po Valley.

Between 203 and 124 population numbers almost doubled, while the territory of Ager Romanus stayed constant between 188 and 85 BCE at 55,000 km^2 (Beloch 1964:101–2). Such a massive increase in population must have had the usual demographic-structural consequences for peasant economic conditions. In the Roman case, the effects of population growth were exacerbated by the universal pattern of equal division of property among the heirs. After two or three generations of rapid population growth, property fragmentation must have reached the point where each heir's share was grossly insufficient for feeding the family. Some (former) *assidui* undoubtedly sold their land to elites flush with the spoils of the Rome's conquests and eager to invest their fortune in land. Others tried to go on, ran up unsustainable debt levels, and also lost their land. The end result of this process was diminution of the class of small landowners, accompanied by the growth of landless *proletarii* and slaves (although the growth of slave numbers was not dominated by demographic processes internal to Italy but was a result of external conquests). Many of the landless citizens moved to Rome, while others probably rented land from the elite landowners. Jongman (2003), for example, argues that the degree of "latifundization" during the late Republic is overestimated.

Population growth brought about the usual Malthusian developments. After a period relatively free of epidemics during the later fourth and third centuries, the disease frequency increased again during the second century (Duncan-Jones 1996). Epidemics also became more severe. For example, Orosius claimed that the plague of 142 killed so many undertakers that the corpses were left to rot in their beds, eventually making Rome uninhabitable (Duncan-Jones 1996:113).

Economic Trends

We have extremely scanty information about the price and wage dynamics under the Republic, but what there is suggests that the century between 150 and 50 BCE saw a substantial inflation. Probably the best indicator is the military wages. In the late third century BCE a legionnaire received a daily pay of 3 asses per diem, or the cost of a modius of wheat (Harl

1996:212). This daily amount translates into an annual pay of 108 denarii (using a year of 360 days and 10 asses per denarius). The amount of 360 modii equals 2.34 tons of wheat, or about ten annual rations—quite a generous salary for a preindustrial society. In 141 the denarius was reevaluated at 16 asses, and the legionnaire's pay was set at 5 asses per diem, probably again reflecting the price of a modius of wheat (a quarter bushel) at that time. Thus, the annual pay increased to only 112.5 denarii (in nominal terms, staying constant in real terms), which suggest very mild inflation up to this point. The next time military pay was increased was a century later by Caesar in 46, to 225 denarii per annum (or 2.5 HS—sesterces—per diem). This doubling also probably reflects the price of wheat, since the "fair" price of wheat according to Cicero is 2.5 HS per modius (see the discussion in Duncan-Jones 1990:147–49). The Republic did not increase military wages between 141 and 46, instead compensating men with triumphal donatives and promises of land (Harl 1996:213). What probably happened, therefore, was that the price of wheat at least doubled between 141 and the onset of the civil wars in 91. We know that grain prices had already increased by the Gracchan times. The *lex frumentaria* of Gaius Gracchus, for example, provided for the state-supported sale of wheat to citizens at the price of 6.33 asses per modius (or 1.6 HS per modius), which was below the average market price (Ward, Heichelheim, and Yeo 2003:160). In fact, it is likely that the price of wheat increased even more than by a factor of two during the chaotic years of the civil wars, before it came down to the level of 2.5 HS per modius after political stability was established. Thus, the real pay of a legionnaire must have gone through the following dynamics: starting high at 2.34 tons of grain per annum in 141, collapsing by a factor of two (or more) in 90–71, and then regaining the 141 level by 10–9 BCE, profiting from the decline of wheat prices under the Principate.

The daily wage of an unskilled laborer apparently increased between the second and first century BC. According to Cato, it was 2 HS per day, while in Cicero's day a century later it was 3 HS per day (Wells 1992:186).

Another striking transformation of late-Republican Italy was the growth of industry, trade, and urbanization. Thus, the population of Rome tripled during the second century from roughly 150,000 to 450,000 (Chandler 1987). An alternative estimate has the population of Rome increasing from 150,000 in 200 BCE to 375,000 in 100 BCE and then to 600,000 in 50 BCE (Scheidel 2004:14). Two main factors drove this process. First, Rome's successful conquest transformed it into the capital of a Mediterranean empire. Wealth from the sale of booty, war indemnity, tribute, and state-owned mines poured into Rome, first enriching the elites and then "trickling down" to benefit the tradesmen and artisans who catered to the elites' needs. Expanded urban employment attracted rural immigrants. Second, increased numbers of peasants lacking land to feed themselves and their families migrated to the cities in search of economic opportunities. Thus, urbanization was driven by both pull and push forces (which parallels the English and French cases discussed in previous chapters). Toward the end of the second century, however, push apparently overwhelmed pull. There were not enough jobs for the immigrants to Rome, and housing was in high demand, driving rents up. Crime increased. The urban poor became increasingly discontented (Ward, Heichelheim, and Yeo 2003:135).

Elite Dynamics

The most striking development of the second century BCE was the increase in both the numbers and wealth of the Roman elites. As we saw in the previous section, archaeological data confirm the traditional view of simple lifestyles of early Republican elites. However, after around 300 BCE, we start seeing signs that elite consumption levels were beginning to increase. It is most clear in the curve of new temple building (figure 6.2). After a long spell with very few temples built in the later fifth and fourth centuries, temple-building activity began increasing around 300 and continued to increase throughout the third century BCE, reaching a peak in the second.

It may be argued that during the Republic, temple-building activity reflected success at war rather than elite consumption (new temples were often vowed by army commanders before a critical battle, and a significant portion of building expenses came from the booty). However, other indicators of aristocratic conspicuous consumption point in the same direction. Thus, beginning in the late fourth century, the number of monumental tombs in Etruria suddenly began increasing (Barker and Rasmussen 1998:286). On the basis of his analysis of economic data for more than 200 Roman senators, Shatzman (1975) concluded that their expenses rose steadily after the end of the Second Punic War (201 BCE) and reached a peak during the period after Sulla retired in 79 BCE:

> It is apparent that Rome's wars in the East caused a rise in the standard of living. Once the senators discovered the refined and sophisticated tastes of the Hellenic world, they were not slow to imitate what they found, and to increase their private outlay. This process, begun in the first half of the second century, reached extravagant heights in the first. Our information suggests it was consulars and *nobiles* who were chiefly responsible for this extravagance, but the entire senatorial class increased its cost of living. (Shatzman 1975:98)

The scale of private fortunes during the first century reached astronomical proportions. Of the senators for whom property values are known, five individuals possessed fortunes that were greater than 100 million HS:

L. Balbius, M. Crassus, L. Lucullus, Pompey, and L. Tarius Rufus (Shatzman 1975:35). To convert these numbers into silver equivalents, 1 HS is approximately equal to 1 g S. In other words, 100 million HS is roughly equivalent to 100 tons of silver.

"Ordinary" senators had fortunes of several million sesterces. For example, M. Cicero had 13 million. Cicero also wrote that a rich Roman needed an income of 100,000–600,000 HS per year. Since total fortunes and annual incomes in preindustrial societies usually relate in a ratio of 20–12 to 1, these income figures imply fortunes of 1.2–12 million HS. What is interesting is that there apparently was an increase in the scale of senatorial fortunes between the second and first centuries. Thus, L. Aemilius Paullus, who put an end to the kingdom of Macedon in 167, left a fortune of only 1.44 million HS at his death (Crawford 1993:75). This is an order of magnitude less than average fortunes a century later.

At the same time that the rich were getting richer, the poor were becoming progressively poorer. The capital wealth needed to qualify a man for the first *classis* was probably lowered from 120,000 to 100,000 asses (Crawford 1993:79) in order to counteract the effect of increasing impoverishment of the *assidui*. The lower boundary qualifying men as *assidui* (fifth class) was once 11,000 asses (Crawford 1993:97). It was lowered to 4,000 (during the first half of the second century), then to 1,500 (by 141), and eventually abolished altogether. In 107 Marius enrolled *capitate censi*, those without property who were simply listed in the census, *proletarii* (Crawford 1993:125). The numerical decline in the stratum of self-supporting freeholder (*assiduus*) is also manifested in the declining proportion of Roman citizens versus allies in Roman armies. By the end of the second century the ratio of allies to Romans was 2:1 (Crawford 1993:128).

Intraelite Competition

To gain an insight into the elite numerical dynamics during this period we turn to the study by Hopkins and Burton (Hopkins 1983: Chapter 2). This study focused on the top stratum of the Roman hierarchy, the consuls, the chief elected officials of the Roman Republic. Every year two consuls were elected, so that over the period of a typical generation of thirty years, there could be a maximum of sixty consuls (because the same individual was sometimes elected more than once, the actual number usually fluctuated between fifty and sixty). These fifty to sixty men at the top of the Roman hierarchy at any given time were relatively well documented and provide us with an excellent sample with which to investigate Roman elite dynamics.

The traditional view among historians holds that the Roman elites were dominated by a small circle of noble families. During the century preceding the year of Tiberius Gracchus's tribunate (133 BCE), ten clans (*gentes*) supplied 50 percent of all consuls, and another eleven clans supplied an additional 30 percent (De Sanctis, cited in Toynbee 1965). Among the patrician clans, Cornelii supplied twenty-three consuls, Aemilii eleven, and Fabii and Postumii seven each. Among the plebeians, Fulvii produced ten consuls, Marcelii nine, and Sempronii eight. Thus, a small proportion—5 percent—of more than 400 *gentes* that produced magistrates of any kind (consuls, praetors, curule aediles, etc.) dominated the top stratum of the Roman state.

Hopkins and Burton argued, on the basis of their analysis, that the degree of power concentration in the hands of a few families was exaggerated. They pointed out that one-third of all consuls elected in the period 250–50 BCE had no direct consular ancestor in the previous three generations. Only a third of all consuls had a consular son, and less than a quarter managed to transmit their consular status to a grandson. On the basis of their results, Hopkins and Burton argued that, contrary to the traditional view, "there was a continuous movement into and out of the Roman political elite during the last two centuries of the Republic" (Hopkins 1983:32).

There is no particular contradiction between the observation by Hopkins and Burton that 65 percent of consuls had a direct consular ancestor and that by De Sanctis that twenty-one clans produced 80 percent of the consuls. First, the two numbers are based on different time periods (250–50 vs. 233–133). Second, a clan usually consisted of several, sometimes many, families. Both sets of numbers thus indicate a strong but not absolute control of the political power by the established families. What is more puzzling is the low probability of transmitting consular status to descendants: 32 percent to a son, and 24 percent to a grandson. Such a strong anisotropy in consular ascendants versus descendants actually suggests that the consular stratum was undergoing some interesting dynamics during this period. Fortunately, Hopkins and Burton presented their data broken down by thirty-year periods (roughly, generations), which allows us to examine the temporal changes in the probability of status transmittal during 250–50.

In figure 6.6a we plot the inheritance of consular status between 250 and 50 BCE (data from Hopkins 1983: Tables 2.2 and 2.4). The solid line indicates the proportion of consuls that had either a consular father or a consular grandfather (it is important to add these two categories together because elite families often had to skip generations because their resources were depleted by vigorous and costly political activity necessary for achieving consulship). What we see is that the proportion of consuls with consular ascendants increased from 45 percent in 249–220 to 64 percent in 139–110. In other words, the nobles actually tightened their grip on consular power toward the Gracchan period. The same dynamic is observed

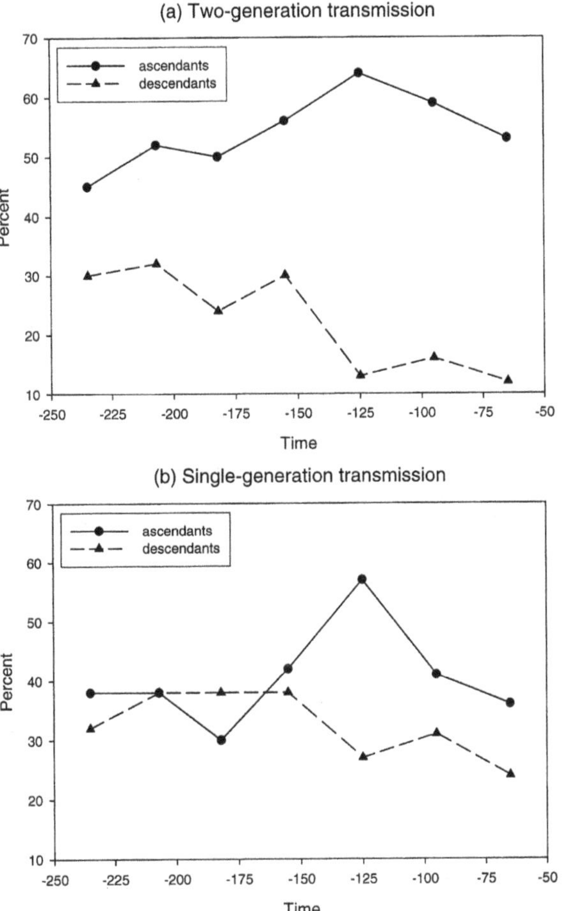

Figure 6.6 Inheritance of consular status, 250–50 BCE. (a) Two-generation transmission of consular status: consuls with a consular father and/or grandfather (solid line) and consular grandsons of consuls (dashed line). (b) Single-generation transmission: consuls with consular fathers (solid line) and consuls with consular sons (dashed line). Hopkins and Burton data from Hopkins 1983: Table 2.2, Table 2.4).

when looking at consuls with consular fathers: from 30–38 percent before 170 to 58 percent in 139–110 (figure 6.6b, solid line).

The second (dashed) line in figure 6.6a indicates the proportion of consuls that had a consular grandson. This curve, in contrast to the solid one, does not increase with time: it fluctuates around 30 percent until 169–140 BCE, then suddenly drops to 13 percent during 139–110 (figure 6.6a). Other measures of status transmittal experienced similar drops at the same time. The proportion of consuls with consular sons dropped from 38 percent to 27 percent (figure 6.6b, dashed line), while the proportion of consular great-grandsons dropped from 27 percent to 10 percent. Thus, paradoxically, at the same time that the nobles were tightening their grip on the consulate, their ability to transmit their status to their descendants decreased.

The only possible explanation of this dynamic is that the pool of aspirants for consular positions was steadily expanding during the second century. As increased numbers of nobles contended for the same maximum of sixty consular positions per generation, intraelite competition increased and the probability of losing grew. This trend led first to the choking off of upward mobility and the growing domination of the consulate by the nobles, followed by intensifying competition among their descendants.

Another set of numbers calculated by Hopkins and Burton (Hopkins 1983: table 2.7) supports this interpretation. They looked into the ability by the "inner elite" (that is, consuls with both consul fathers and grandfathers) to produce heirs that would become either consuls or praetors. During the second half of the third century, each member of the inner elite produced on average 1.25 consular or praetorian sons. Since this number is greater than one, the inner elite was actually expanding in numerical terms. Half a century later the average dropped below one to 0.83, and for the period of 139–80 is declined to half of its initial value, 0.63.

Yet another look at the same pattern is provided by comparing the asymmetry between the correlation of consular status among generations forward and backward in time. Hopkins and Burton noted that on average during the studied period, 40 percent of consuls had fathers that were also consuls, while only 32 percent had sons who were also consuls. In a stable situation in which elites replace themselves without either deficit or surplus, these two statistics should be the same. The data, however, suggest there was about a 25 percent surplus elite production in Rome per generation during this period. This conclusion follows from the observation that 32% of consuls were "consular fathers" (that is, consuls who had consular sons) and 40% were "consular sons" (that is, consuls who had consular fathers). Therefore, each consular father produced, on average, 1.25 consular sons. Since the total number of consular positions was limited, an extra 20 percent (0.25/1.25) of consular aspirants had to be frustrated in their ambitions to obtain a consulship than would be the case under stable conditions, and they and their descendants would have to suffer downward mobility into "mere" senators.

In actuality, the numbers averaged over the whole period hide fairly dramatic fluctuations in the consular father-son ratio. Plotting the proportions of consular fathers and consular sons by time period, we observe that until the middle of the second century, the two curves fluctuate at a roughly the same level (figure 6.6b). In fact, during the generation of 194–170 (the one following the severe pruning of the elites during the Hannibalic war), the proportion of consuls with consular fathers dipped to a mere 30 percent, while the proportion of consuls with consular sons stayed at 38 percent, suggesting that intraelite competition for consular status was greatly reduced during this period. By contrast, during the Gracchan period (139–110) the proportion of consuls with consular fathers shot up to 57 percent, while the proportion of consuls with consular sons dropped to less than half of it, 27 percent (figure 6.6b). As a result, the rate of elite overproduction peaked right before the century-long period of sociopolitical instability of the late Republic. The peak of intraelite competition fell within the next generation, roughly the period from the time of the Gracchi to the Social War.

State Finances

From 146 to 91 BCE Roman finances were relatively healthy. In 157 BCE the treasury reserve was built up to 72 million HS (Harl 1996:44), and on the eve of the Social War it was 80 million HS (Harl 1996:50). This equilibrium, however, turned out to be fragile, and the treasury reserve was rapidly consumed by the Social War. In fact, it looks like one long-term consequence of the Social War was that it destroyed the fiscal equilibrium of the late Republic. Increased financial difficulties after 91 are indicated by the debasement of the denarius to 95 percent silver content (Harl 1996:50). Furthermore, the state ceased to pay the soldiers. The treasury was empty in 89, for the first time since 213–12, during the darkest days of the Second Punic War (Crawford 1974:640). After the end of the war the financial situation was so desperate that the senate in 88 melted sacred treasures in order to finance Sulla's war in the East. This expedient yielded some 9,000 pounds of gold (Harl 1996:50), equivalent to 43.2 million HS (Crawford 1974:637). The looting of temple treasuries was also employed by Sulla and his allies during the civil war of 83–82. Once Sulla was in power and internal stability was reestablished, however, Sulla managed to get state finances in order. Thus, in 81 Sulla restored the denarius to purity (98 percent silver). A big factor in Sulla's fiscal success was his victories in the East—he gained from Mithridates an indemnity of 2,000 or 3,000 talents and fined the cities of Asia for five years of back taxes, amounting to 20,000 talents (Harl 1996:51), or 480 million HS. Amazingly, however, these huge treasures were immediately spent, and money shortages continued throughout the 70s. Sulla instituted new taxes and passed legislation authorizing the sale of *ager publicus* (Crawford 1974:638). During the 70s (at the peak of fighting in Spain against Sertorius), the denarius suffered another debasement to 96–97 percent silver (Harl 1996:54).

The basis for the solution of Rome's fiscal difficulties was laid by Pompey, who reorganized Spain and the eastern provinces so that taxation replaced predatory plundering (Harl 1996:54). As a result of Pompey's reorganization, Rome's revenues quadrupled (see table 6.2). The tribute from Gaul, conquered by Caesar, increased the total to 380 million HS. These revenues allowed the Republic to amass a great reserve that included 15,000 bars of gold, although we do not know how much a bar weighed (Crawford 1974:639). The reserve, however, was seized and immediately spent by Caesar in 49. A year later Caesar was short of bullion and was forced to lower the standard of his denarius to 95–96 percent fine (Harl 1996:55). What we see is recurring cycles of feast followed by famine. The cycle was repeated after the assassination of Caesar. In 44 there was a treasury reserve of 700 million HS, which was immediately squandered by Caesar's successors in their internecine wars (Harl 1996:56). During 44–42 the triumvirs again had to debase the denarius to 95–96 percent silver, and by 31 the denarius minted by Mark Antony had declined to 92 percent fineness (Harl 1996:59). Meanwhile, Octavian was able to increase the pureness of the denarius that he struck. In the Augustan period (after 27 BCE) the purity of the denarius was restored (to 98 percent), and it stayed that way for a century thereafter.

Increasing Social Pressures

Growing misery among the lower strata of the Roman society was matched by the increasing discontent among the elites (although, to be sure, for very different reasons). In the previous section we discussed the results of the analysis of the top elite stratum, the consular nobility. The data put together by Hopkins and Burton indicate that intraelite competition for consular positions greatly intensified toward the Gracchan period. An increasing numbers of aspirants for elite positions meant that even though the established nobility strengthened its grip on the consulships, a high proportion of its descendants were forced down the social ladder. Although we lack specific studies, the same dynamic must have affected the senatorial class, because the size of the senate stayed constant at 300 (until it was doubled by Sulla in the early first century, then doubled again by Caesar).

Working our way down the social hierarchy, we find that the nonsenatorial elites, the equestrian class (*ordo equestris*), found it increasingly difficult to achieve senatorial status and almost impossible to break into the ranks of the consular nobility (Ward, Heichelheim, and Yeo 2003:137). Social arrangements under the Roman Republic ensured that the "knights" (*equites*) would get their share of the profits resulting from Mediterranean conquests. Senators were excluded from state contracts to construct public works, operate state mines, collect taxes, and supply the military. These contracts were undertaken by companies of *publicani*, who came primarily from the equestrian class (Ward, Heichelheim, and Yeo 2003:134). During the first half of the second century, a large number of knights who had grown extremely wealthy from their activities as *publicani* invested their new wealth in more socially prestigious forms (mainly land) and developed aspirations to enter the senatorial class. Thus, the competition for the limited number of senatorial positions was aggravated both by the increasing numbers of aspirants from the established families (resulting from population growth) and by the pressure from the newly rich knights.

The elites of the allied Italian polities found themselves in a worse situation than the equestrians, because they were largely excluded from the profits of overseas conquests. As Rome became secure in Italy after the defeat of Hannibal, the Romans increasingly treated their Italian allies as subjects. The allies in turn began demanding citizenship, but the Roman elites obstinately refused to correct this palpable injustice (Ward, Heichelheim, and Yeo 2003:138). Actually, the Roman ruling class, faced with increasing competition from locally grown elite aspirants, was understandably not eager to add to it by admitting the Italian elites to citizenship.

At the same time that popular misery and intraelite competition were growing, state revenues stagnated (table 6.2). What was worse, by the middle of the second century the Romans had begun running out of wealthy civilized states to conquer. After the destruction of Carthage and Corinth in 146, there were no profitable wars until the conquests of Pompey and Caesar almost a century later. Instead, Rome had to deal with an exhausting and costly suppression of primitive tribesmen, as in Spain, pirates, slave rebellions, and a series of internal wars.

As all these trends intensified near the end of the second century, intraelite competition became increasingly violent. A combination of elite infighting and elite-mobilized popular movement and regional rebellions eventually led to a complete collapse of the state.

6.4 The Late Republican Crisis (130–30 BCE)

The first symptom of the onset of the disintegrative phase was slave revolts, which began breaking out all over the Roman world in 138 BCE:

> In Italy, a revolt was suppressed with the crucifixion of over 4500 slaves at Rome and surrounding towns. An uprising at the great slave market of Delos was put down by force of arms, as was another at the silver mines of Laurium, near Athens. In Pergamum, the war of Aristonicus (the bastard son of Eumenes II) and his Stoic "Sunstate" against Rome (132–129 B.C.) was simply a major revolt of slaves, proletarians, and

> soldiers. Worst of all was the slave revolt in Sicily, where normal slave thuggery and mugging had swelled into full-scale war about 136 B.C. under the leadership of a Syrian slave named Eunus. By vomiting fire and uttering oracles, he was able to persuade his 70,000 (some say 250,000) followers that he was Antiochus, the king of the Syrians. Only after several years of hard fighting, the murder of many landlords, and much damage to property were the Romans able to crush this revolt and extinguish its last sparks in 131 B.C. (Ward, Heichelheim, and Yeo 2003:136)

This First Servile War was followed by the Second (104–101), also in Sicily, and then the Third (73–71), led by Spartacus, as well as by lesser revolts in Campania and Apulia (Bradley 1989).

Peasant rebellions rarely succeeded in agrarian societies when they were confronted by unified elites, and slave revolts in late Republican Rome were not an exception to this rule. A much more dangerous threat to the state arises when the elites become splintered, and certain factions begin to mobilize popular support to be used in their quest for power. Tiberius Sempronius Gracchus was a politically ambitious young noble from a very prominent family. His father achieved the pinnacle of political success, having served as consul (twice) and censor (Ward, Heichelheim, and Yeo 2003:156). Owing to the processes discussed above, however, the nobles of the Tiberius Gracchus generation faced a much stiffer competition for the top offices than their fathers had. It was natural for one of them to use the swelling popular discontent as the engine of political advancement. Additionally, the great polarization of wealth, which resulted in a few superrich controlling immense fortunes while most of the citizens were landless, was patently unfair. Finally, the decline of the "middle class" of *assidui* who had traditionally provided the bulk of recruits to the Roman legions was endangering the very existence of Rome.

In 133 BCE Tiberius Gracchus was elected the tribune of the people and immediately introduced a law designed to break up the large private estates created out of public land and divide them among the landless citizens (Ward, Heichelheim, and Yeo 2003:154). After an increasingly bitter struggle over this bill, Tiberius and 300 of his supporters were murdered by a group of senators and their clients in the Forum. However, the land commission set up to administer the Gracchan land law continued to function after his death. During the next six years it allotted land to more than 75,000 men, achieving a partial alleviation of Rome's manpower crisis.

The death of Tiberius Gracchus formalized the split of the Roman elites into the factions of *populares* and *optimates*, and the struggle between the two groups eventually plunged Italy into bitter civil war. These elite factions, however, were not true political parties. Although the main conflict was between the *populares* and *optimates*, members of the same faction on occasion fought among themselves. The next leader of the *popularis* faction was Tiberius's brother Gaius Gracchus, who was elected the tribune of the people in 123 and again in 122 BCE. Gaius continued to support his brother's program of land distribution and introduced the famous *lex frumentaria*, which provided grain to the citizens of Rome at subsidized prices. He promoted other popular programs, such as colonization schemes and public works. Finally, he also attempted to procure citizenship for the Italian allies, but without success. During the two years of his tribunate Gaius dominated the political life of Rome, owing to his immense popularity among the plebs. This domination was short-lived, however. Gaius's political rivals united against him and engineered a defeat in his third attempt to run for the tribunate. Gaius died shortly thereafter during street fighting between his followers and enemies. Three thousand of his partisans were killed with him (Le Glay et al. 1997:103). The violent deaths of the Gracchus brothers were another sign that the Roman political framework was unraveling.

In summary, the two decades of the 130s and 120s BCE were a relatively violent period in Roman history (characterized by multiple slave revolts, the disturbances associated with the murders of the Gracchan brothers, and the insurrection of the allied town of Fregellae in 125), at least when compared with the previous and following decades, although the level of violence was nowhere near the peak it would reach two generations later (figure 6.5). As usually happens during the disintegrative phases of secular cycles, sociopolitical instability waxed and waned in a pattern of alternating generations. The violent Gracchan era was followed by two decades relatively free of conflict (at least of the internal kind). Important external conflicts during this period were the Jugurthine War in North Africa (111–106) and the war with the Cimbri and Teutones (105–101). One side effect of these wars was the rise of Gaius Marius, who became one of the most important *popularis* leaders during the later civil wars.

The relative sociopolitical stability did not last long, because the root cause of instability, competition for status resulting from elite overproduction, was in no way alleviated by the developments during the Gracchan period. It began unraveling shortly before 100 BCE, starting with the Second Servile War, which raged in Sicily from 104 to 101. Even more important, intraelite conflict flared up again in Rome. In 100 a *popularis* politician, Lucius Apuleius Saturninus, was elected tribune for the second time and embarked on a full program of social legislation. When ordinary methods for derailing legislation (vetoes, "omens," and violence) failed, the optimate-dominated senate passed the SCU against Saturninus and his followers. An angry mob of nobles and knights murdered Saturninus and his supporters (including the consul Gaius Servilius Glaucia). Marius, who in 100 was serving his sixth consulship, attempted to steer a middle course between the demands of the optimate and the *popularis* factions, but the elite polarization has gone so far that apparently no compromise was possible, even when espoused by such a hugely popular figure as Marius. In the end, Marius could not prevent the murders of the *popularis* leaders. He did not gain any support from the optimates but lost the confidence of the *populares*, and had to leave Rome in a kind of self-imposed exile without fulfilling his promise to obtain land for his soldiers.

During the decade that followed the murder of Saturninus and suppression of the *populares*, pressure continued to build up. The optimate leaders, who controlled the public affaires through their dominance at the senate, continued to deny land to Marius's veterans and answered the demand of Italian allies for citizenship by expelling any who resided in Rome (Ward, Heichelheim, and Yeo 2003:173). In 91 there was one last abortive attempt at reform by a moderate optimate faction led by Livius Drusus the Younger, but it again came to nothing as a result of Drusus's death at the hands of an unknown assassin. The following year the majority of Italian allies revolted against Rome (the Social War of 90–88).

The intensity of the warfare that affected Italy can be quite accurately measured by the frequency of dated coin hoards (figure 6.5). After a peaceful first half of the second century the curve begins to increase around 130 BCE. We do not see a peak during the Gracchan period, which was characterized by political infighting and urban crowd riots rather than full-scale warfare. The hoard indicator instead reaches a second peak after the Hannibalic war, during the 80s and 90s. This was the period of almost continuous civil war: the Social War, followed by civil war and the victory of the Marian faction (87), Marius's "Reign of Terror" (87–86), the civil war and victory of Sulla (83–82), Sulla's famous proscriptions (82–81), the rebellion of Lepidus (78–77), and the slave rebellion led by Spartacus (73–71). Outside Italy, the Marian leader Sertorius led a rebellion in Spain (82–72). A fragile (as it turned out) equilibrium was achieved in 70 under the consulship of Gnaeus Pompeius (Pompey the Great) and Marcus Licinius Crassus. Although Pompey and Crassus began their political careers as optimates (in particular, they both served as officers under Sulla), their legislative program was moderate (for example, they restored the powers of the tribunes, which had previously been taken away by Sulla). The consensus between the rival elite factions was sustained by the conflict fatigue, resulting from two decades of incessant fighting that left hundreds of thousands dead.

The 60s and 50s were characterized by the absence of widespread civil war (figure 6.5). This period of relative internal peace was disturbed only by the Conspiracy of Catiline (63), a rebellion that was easily suppressed by the consul Marcus Tullius Cicero, and by street fighting between the factions of the *popularis* Publius Clodius and the optimate Titus Annius

Milo (52). The military power of Rome was directed outward, and the two decades saw the first significant additions to the Roman territory since the middle of the second century. Pompey conquered Asia Minor and Levant (66–62), while Caesar conquered Gaul (58–51). Crassus, attempting to do the same in Parthia, lost his army and his life (53). Additionally, Pompey put an end to the Mediterranean piracy (68). However, despite relative internal peace, the fiscal health of the state remained fragile, and in 67 and 63 BCE political crises depleted the treasury (Harl 1996:49).

The final period of civil war began in 49, when Caesar crossed the Rubicon, and ended in 31, with the battle of Actium. Although Caesar began as a *popularis* politician, while Pompey was an optimate, the ideological differences became less and less important, and the nature of the conflict became a more or less naked power struggle between various elite factions. The first phase of the civil war (49–45) pitted Caesar against Pompey and Pompey's partisans after the Great One's death in Egypt (48). After the assassination of Caesar, the struggle was between, on the one hand, Caesar's assassins, Brutus and Cassius, and on the other Caesar's successors, Mark Antony, Lepidus, and Octavian (44–42). The period of 41–31 saw a confused struggle between Octavian, Mark Antony, and Sextus Pompey (the son of Pompey the Great) in various combinations. Eventually Sextus Pompey was defeated in Sicily and escaped to Greece, where he was executed (36), while Mark Antony was defeated in the battle of Actium (31) and committed suicide in Egypt (30). The establishment of the Principate by Octavian, or Augustus, as he was now styled, in 27 BCE marks the end of the Republican secular cycle.

6.5 The End of the Disintegrative Trend

In summary, the century following the tribunate of Tiberius Gracchus can be interpreted as the disintegrative phase of the secular cycle of the Roman Republic. There were three peaks of violence: a rather mild one during the Gracchan times (133–121), "Civil War I" (90–71) and "Civil War II" (50–31). The most important factor driving this century-long period of sociopolitical instability was elite overproduction. Other demographic-structural factors underlying the destabilization of the Roman Republic, popular misery and state insolvency, could be addressed only if the elites were able to develop a consensus. In fact, the basis for solving these two problems was laid by the conquests of the 60s and 50s but could not be utilized until consensus among the elites was restored under Augustus.

Such a consensus could only be achieved once the problem of elite overproduction was "solved" as a result of several processes that took place during the period of sociopolitical instability. Of particular importance were the two periods of civil war (90–71 and 50–31). The direct effect of sociopolitical instability was the physical liquidation of a portion of the elite. When the Marian faction won in 87, Marius's followers killed a number of their optimate enemies: "their mutilated bodies littered the streets and their heads, dripping blood, decorated the rostra" (Ward, Heichelheim, and Yeo 2003:178). Sulla's reign of terror five years later resulted in a much more thorough pruning of the elites. His victims included 15 men of consular rank, 90 senators, and 2,600 knights. Sulla's proscriptions thus had a significant impact on the elite numbers—90 senators accounted for 30 percent of the senate (300 members before Sulla's reforms). The proscriptions of the second triumvirate following Caesar's death in 43 BCE resulted in the execution of 300 senators and 2,000 equites (Stearns 2001). Untold numbers of elite aspirants perished in battle. For example, just during 91–82 as many as 200,000 men lost their lives, and perhaps 100,000 men during 49–42 (Crawford 1993:1). For example, just in 82 the struggle between Sulla and his opponents resulted in 50,000–70,000 dead in both armies. When Sulla gained Rome on November 1, he executed 3,000 of the 12,000 prisoners assembled on the Campus Martius (Le Glay et al. 1997:118). Some 40,000 Romans died at the battle of Philippi in 42 (Stearns 2001).

To these numbers we should add the 100,000 dead in the First Servile War (104–100) (Ward, Heichelheim, and Yeo 2003:170). Even if only 1 percent of these casualties were the elites or elite aspirants, this would add 3,000 to the total. We also have no idea how many people died in street fighting between various factions. After all, each time a leader like the Gracchi or Clodius was murdered, the same fate befell some dozens or hundreds of his followers. For example, in April 121, when Gaius was murdered, so were 3,000 of his followers (Le Glay et al. 1997:103). To give some perspective on the magnitude of elite losses during the civil wars, we note that by the end of the period, during the reign of Augustus, there were 600 senators and perhaps 5,000 equestrians (Jongman 1988:193). Adding together all the losses mentioned above we easily match these numbers, so the inescapable conclusion is that civil wars reduced the pool of elite aspirants by at least half, and this is likely an underestimate.

The second effect of sociopolitical instability was on reproductive rates (for a review, see Brunt 1971:131–55). The Romans employed a variety of family limitation practices, including abortion and infanticide. Dio noted a shortage of women in 18 BCE; he would be most familiar with the situation among the elite families (Brunt 1971:151). From this observation, the likely conclusion is that the Romans practiced female-biased infanticide.

The third effect of civil wars was the inflation of honors, which often occurs during the disintegrative phase because leaders of various elite factions find bestowing status a cheap way to reward followers. Thus, Sulla doubled the size of the Roman senate from 300 to 600 (81 BCE). Sulla expanded the number of quaestors to twenty and also increased the number of priests (Raaflaub 1986:167). The number of praetorships, which had been increased from two to four in 277 and then to six in 197 (Crawford 1993:71), was increased by Sulla further to ten (Crawford 1993:153). In 45, Caesar doubled the number of quaestors yet again, to forty, and also increased the number of praetors to sixteen. He immediately raised the membership of the senate from 600 to 900, filling the extra seats with his supporters (Ward, Heichelheim, and Yeo 2003:213). In fact, over the long run, the effect of Caesar's reforms would be to increase the number of senators to 1,200, since each quaestor automatically became a senator. By the time of Augustus's reforms, there were more than 1,000 senators (Ward, Heichelheim, and Yeo 2003:254). It is amazing that after a century of elite pruning by Marius, Sulla, and Caesar's successors, not counting the apalling losses in the civil war battles and street riots, there were enough elite aspirants left to fill more than three times the number of senate slots as were available in Gracchan times. The elite reproduction rate was probably below the replacement level during this period, which implies that the problem of elite overproduction a century before at the time of the Gracchus brothers was truly severe. The expansion of the senate was a means of "letting off steam"—it satisfied the demand for top status among the aspirant elites. But once they achieved the desired honor, they became dangerously exposed to the vicissitudes of civil wars, and served as fodder for mass purges every time the regime changed.

In addition to the elevated elite mortality and depressed reproduction rates there must have been another, difficult-to-detect process—acquiescence to downward mobility. There must have been many potential elite aspirants who saw that the likely consequence of their pursuit of higher status would be an untimely death on the battlefield or in a purge. They therefore could decide to be content with whatever modest status they already had, and choose to stay away from politics. An example of such a choice is Marcus Aemilius Lepidus, consul in 46 BCE and a member of the Second Triumvirate, along with Mark Anthony and Octavian. In 36, Lepidus and Octavian had a falling out. "Octavian boldly entered the camp of Lepidus and persuaded the legions to desert. Then he stripped Lepidus of any real power and committed him to comfortable retirement at the lovely seaside town of Circeii in Latium. Lepidus lived there peacefully for another twenty-four years" (Ward, Heichelheim, and Yeo 2003:225). It is hard to imagine a Pompey or a Caesar accepting such a comfortable retirement from the struggle, but people vary in how much they are driven by ambition. Another example is T. Pomponius Atticus, Cicero's confidant, publisher, and banker. This equestrian had more wealth than many senators but chose to stay away from politics. During the turbulent years of 88–65 he moved to Greece, where he was safe from Rome's political storms. After returning to Rome, he patronized the arts and literature and made so many important contacts that he was protected on all sides during the subsequent civil wars (Ward, Heichelheim, and Yeo 2003:234). At lower levels of the Roman social hierarchy there must have been many such Lepidi or Attici who, perhaps after a brush with death in the civil war, decided to return to their estates; and their numbers probably increased as the futility of internal war was demonstrated over and over again. The poet Tibullus exclaimed (probably in 32 BCE): "I don't want to die young and for nothing!" (Le Glay et al. 1997:171). Vergil's *Georgics* are filled with longing for peace: "so many wars throughout the world . . . the fields going to waste in the farmer's absence" (quoted from Wells 1992:15).

After the last period of civil war, the twenty years of "discordia, non mos, non ius" that began in 49, Italy was exhausted and ready to welcome a regime that offered peace (Brunt 1971:11). A century of sociopolitical instability had dealt with the problem of elite overproduction and also induced in Romans a powerful longing for peace. The rule of Augustus, as a result, rested on a broad popular consensus. For example, when Augustus in 23 BCE gave up the annual consulship he had held since 31, the people of Rome, fearing the diminution of his authority, rioted, trying to force him to accept the office (Wells 1992:15). The secular disintegrative trend reversed itself, and a new cycle of the Principate commensed.

6.6 Conclusion

In many ways the middle to late Republican period of Roman history differs from a "typical" secular cycle (if such a thing exists). One major complicating factor is the enormous territorial expansion of the Roman Empire between 350 and 150, and again during the interval between the two civil wars of the first century. The population decline of the third century, brought on by the struggle for supremacy in the western Mediterranean, is another, although related, complication.

Republican Rome was also a different kind of state from those we dealt with in chapters 2–5. There was very little separation between the elite and the state—for most intents and purposes, the senatorial class *was* the state. If the state is not an independent agent, distinct from the elites, then the standard demographic-structural model (chapter 1) needs to be modified. In particular, the fiscal difficulties of the state, culminating in its bankruptcy, cease to play the key role in bringing about the crisis. Indeed, although there are ample signs of financial difficulties during the civil wars of the first century (section 6.3), as far as we know, the finances were not in particularly bad shape before 91 BCE, when the Social War broke out.

The evidence we have reviewed in this chapter suggests that the main cause of state breakdown and recurrent civil wars during the first century BCE was elite overproduction. This interpretation is supported by our analysis of the Hopkins-Badian data on the inheritance of consular status. Additional indications of elite overproduction, which parallel patterns observed in other secular cycles, are the growth of economic inequality (especially the runaway expansion of top fortunes) and the inflation of honors (manifested in the doubling of the senate size by Sulla, followed by yet another doubling by Caesar).

As to the economic indicators of overpopulation, such as prices and rents, our knowledge of the economic history of Rome is too fragmentary to truly test these predictions of the theory. In fact, our reconstruction of demographic-structural dynamics, in general, is necessarily much more tentative for the Republican cycle than for better documented periods, dealt with in chapters 2–5. Yet we would argue that the empirical evidence that we reviewed in this chapter is broadly consistent with the theory of secular cycles.

Perhaps a better way to use the material in this chapter is not to test the demographic-structural theory but to ask instead how the theory could help us to throw new light on certain aspects of Roman history that have puzzled historians and caused controversy. A good example is the dispute between the proponents of the "low count" and the "high count" interpretation of Roman censuses.

According to Lo Cascio, the low count thesis of Beloch and Brunt has two unacceptable implications. First, it implies that the free population declined between 70 and 28 BCE. Actually, the low count also implies population decline between 125 and 70 BC (section 7.1). From the point of view of the demographic-structural theory, however, such a secular population decline is not only unsurprising but expected. Prolonged periods of intense internal warfare practically always result in population declines, sometimes very dramatic ones. There is nothing extraordinary about a population decline of 30 percent over a century, as we estimated in section 7.1. Both literary and coin hoard evidence amply attest to the intensity of late Republican civil wars. Although admittedly fragmentary, the various kinds of data that we reviewed above suggest that peninsular Italy was overpopulated in the late second century and not so at the time when Augustus established the Principate.

Second, Lo Cascio's critique points to the divergent trends between the declining rural population, implied by the low counters, and the growing numbers of urban dwellers (mainly in Rome). Again, far from being puzzling, this is a pattern that we see over and over again during the disintegrative secular phases. Rural population moves to cities in search of first employment, and later security. A high urbanization index is entirely consistent with a declining overall population, because premodern cities were population sinks.

Chapter 7

Rome: The Principate Cycle (30 BCE–285 CE)

7.1 Overview of the Cycle

The Principate cycle covers the three centuries between 27 BCE and 285 CE, from the establishment of the Augustan Principate to the accession of Diocletian. Because the bulk of territorial expansion was accomplished by the end of Augustus's reign, fluctuations in territorial size thereafter were relatively minor and had minor effects on social, economic, and demographic variables.

The expansion phase was the century under the Julio-Claudian and Flavian emperors. This was a period of population growth and economic expansion, somewhat marred by political instability at the very top, which, however, affected mostly the ruling class. Although six of the ten successors of Augustus—Caligula, Nero, Galba, Otho, Vitellius, and Domitian—were overthrown and met a violent end, this was accomplished by means of a palace coup rather than by a full-blown civil war. The most serious period of political instability was the one following Nero's death and lasted less than two years, from March 68 to December 69.

The stagflation phase began with the accession of Nerva (96) and ended with the arrival of the Antonine plague (165). This was a period of high political stability, when the empire was governed by the five "good" emperors (Nerva, Trajan, Hadrian, Antonius Pius, and Marcus Aurelius). As is usual during the stagflation phase, the elites did very well and their numbers grew. Thus, this period is usually considered the Golden Age of the Roman Empire. There was, however, increasing popular misery due to overpopulation and inflation (again, as is typical of the stagflation phases). The peak of state power, territorial extent, and economic prosperity (at least for the elites) was achieved during this phase. A number of social and economic indicators, such as the number of inscriptions and documents, building activity, and marble and brick production, peaked toward the end, around 130–50 (Greenberg 2003).

The crisis phase started with the first appearance of the Antonine plague (165). The consensus among the elites unraveled, and by the end of the period, when Commodus was overthrown, the situation developed into full-blown civil war (192–97). The period from 211 (when Septimus Severus was succeeded by Caracalla) to 285 is best thought of as the depression phase, characterized by incessant intraelite conflict, chronic civil war, and further population decline (resulting from the recurring epidemics of the 250s and 260s, among other causes). As usual, there were relatively peaceful interludes resulting from sheer exhaustion of the warring parties. The disintegrative trend reversed itself when Diocletian defeated his rivals and established the Dominate.

Population Dynamics

We are very fortunate to have three Augustan censuses and one Claudian census of the Roman citizen population (table 7.1). These numbers exclude slaves but include an unknown proportion of Roman citizens residing outside Italy. They suggest that the decline tendency characterizing Italian population during the first century BCE was reversed around 30 BCE, and that the population began growing at an accelerating rate (0.2 percent per year at the end of first century BCE versus 0.5–0.7 percent during the second). Brunt estimates that, given census undercounting and adding slaves, there were perhaps 7 million people total in Italy at the end of the Augustan period (14 CE), which would imply that the population in 28 BCE was somewhat below 6 million. We should note that Brunt believed that the increase in census numbers between 28 BCE and 14 CE was entirely due to enfranchisements of slaves and provincials, but we find his arguments unconvincing. The proportion of Roman citizens residing outside Italy did not become significant until the second half of the first century CE, so a substantial part of the increase in census numbers must be due to population growth in Italy. This only makes sense, since the establishment of the Principate marked the end of the destructive civil wars and the beginning of a long period of Pax Romana.

We do not have census data after 48 CE, but it is probable that population growth continued in Italy throughout the first century and then stagnated, or perhaps increased very slowly during the second (until the plagues). In general, it is thought that the greatest population growth occurred in the provinces of the Latin West other than Italy. Thus, Frier (2000), endorsing a previous estimate by McEvedy and Jones (1978), suggested that the total population of the Latin West increased from 25 to 42 million between 14 and 164 CE. This growth corresponds to a 40 percent increase in proportional terms. Thus, over the whole period, from 29 BCE to 164 CE, the population increase of the Latin West must have been at least 50 percent, and most likely more, because McEvedy and Jones tend to underestimate the degree of population fluctuations (as we saw, for example, in the English chapter). The initially more populous East increased less, from 20 to 23 million. At the peak, the total population of the Roman Empire is variously estimated as 60 million by Frier and close to

TABLE 7.1
Early imperial population censuses

Year	*Population (mln)*	*Implied growth rate*
28 BCE	4.063	—
8 BCE	4.233	0.2% p.a.
14 CE	4.937	0.7% p.a.
48 CE	5.894	0.5% p.a.

Source: Brunt (1971:113 and the 1987 postscript).

100 million by Beloch. The truth probably lies somewhere in between (Scheidel 2001b:64).

One piece of evidence that suggests the Italian population stagnated or even slightly declined during the second century is the institution of *alimenta*, public assistance for freeborn children instituted under Trajan (or perhaps Nerva) (Ward, Heichelheim, and Yeo 2003:337). This program was prompted by the perceived population decline of the impoverished small farmers, especially in central Italy, which resulted in a reduction in the number of Italian recruits to the legions. However, diminishing numbers of "middle classes" do not necessarily imply that the overall population was declining. Growing economic inequality, which is characteristic of stagflation phases, could reduce the numbers of smallholders at the same time that some small fraction of them move up into the elites, while the great majority slide down into poverty (see the previous chapter for a discussion of similar pressures during the second century BCE in Italy).

Archaeological data also support a population increase in the Roman Empire during the first two centuries CE but at the same time highlight geographic variation in population dynamics. A very useful contribution to this question is the survey of archaeological evidence by Lewit (1991). Lewit focused on a sample of 201 excavated farm and rural settlement sites in seven regions of the western Roman Empire. Dividing the overall time period into eight segments (100–0 BCE, 0–100 CE, 100–200, 200–250, 250–300, 300–350, 350–400, and after 400), she then determined the proportion of excavated sites occupied during each time segment (figure 7.1). We can see that in Italy, the occupation index curve begins at an already high level during the first century BCE, reaches a peak in the first century CE, and then declines during the second century. By contrast, the provinces tend to reach a maximum during the second century (figure 7.1). Minor exceptions are South Gaul, where the occupancy index is the same in both the first and second centuries, and South Spain, where the peak is achieved during the first half of the third century.

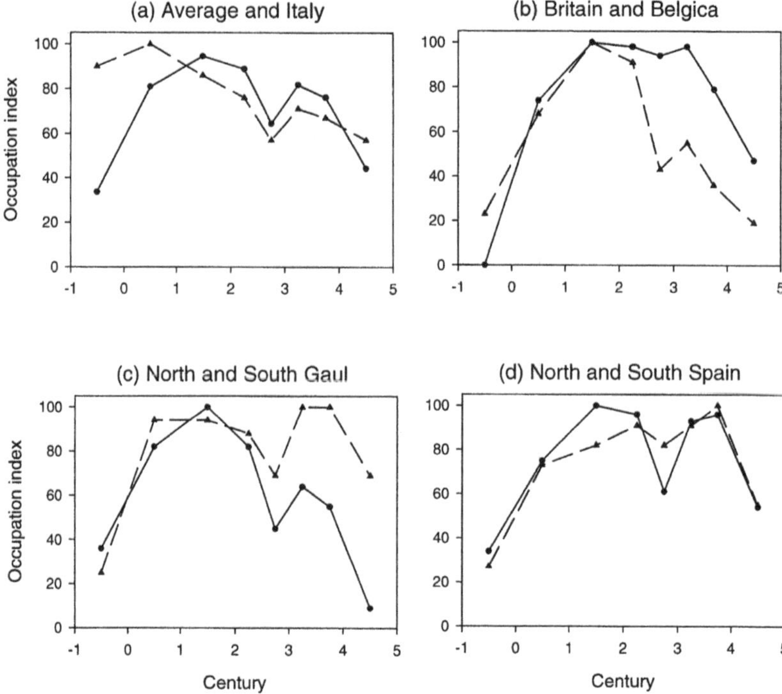

Figure 7.1 Occupation of rural sites in the western Roman Empire (Lewit 1991). In each panel, the first location is indicated by a solid line, the second by a dashed line. The data indicate two secular cycles, those of the Principate and the Dominate.

The second half of the third century was characterized by site abandonment in all seven regions. However, the degree of abandonment varied and was correlated with the severity of civil war or barbarian invasions (Lewit 1991). The contrast is most vivid between Britain, which escaped barbarian invasions in the third century, and Gallia Belgica, which was completely overrun by the Franks (see figure 7.1b).

Averaging regional curves, we see that the overall occupation index of the Latin West (assuming that North Africa followed suit) increased greatly during the first century CE, followed by a more gentle growth in the second century (figure 7.1a, solid line). After the peak in the second century, the occupation index began decreasing during the first half of the third century and hit a minimum in the second half. There was a recovery in the fourth century (during the next cycle of the Dominate), followed by a final collapse in the fifth, when the western Roman Empire was overrun by the Germanic invaders. Regional surveys support this picture. Thus, the Albegna Valley (Etruria) survey found twenty-three farms, villas, and villages in the first century. The number declined to fourteen in the second century and eight in the third. It then increased to eleven in the fourth century and declined again to six in the fifth century (data from Cambi and Fentress, cited in Bintliff and Sbonias 1999:5). This is the same pattern that Lewit found for Italy. Thus, it appears probable that the peak in the rural Italian population was achieved rather early, in the first century, while population in the rest of the empire continued to increase up to the mid-second century.

Still, we cannot connect the occupation index directly to population numbers, because site abandonment does not mean that all people inhabiting the abandoned sites died. In reality, we know that during stagflation and crisis phases, a substantial proportion of the rural population migrates to cities. On the other hand, the occupation index of *rural* sites (which is what Lewit focused on) is more directly related to another quantity of interest, the carrying capacity, defined as the number of annual food rations that are produced within the territory controlled by the state. It can be estimated by multiplying the cultivated area by average productivity of unit of land (for an example of the calculation, see the appendix to chapter 3). Between the second-century peak and the late third-century trough, the number of occupied rural sites in the Latin West decreased by 32 percent (figure 7.1a). Although it is theoretically possible that some of the land belonging to the abandoned farms was cultivated by peasants coming from elsewhere, in practice this does not happen during times of trouble because of security concerns. In fact, the cultivated area around sites that stay occupied tends to shrink as inhabitants abandon fields that are too far from the shelter provided by the walls or other fortifications (see chapter 5). Furthermore, during periods of high sociopolitical instability, people tend to move to settlements that have natural defensive features, such as hilltops, with the consequence that the best agricultural land, in the lowlands, falls out of cultivation. In sum, it is likely that the carrying capacity during the third century actually declined by at least a third from its peak. Once the carrying capacity declined, the population followed, but with a lag. Most peasants abandoning rural settlements may have moved to cities, including Rome. Under the high mortality–low fertility conditions of preindustrial cities, the populations of migrants gradually decreased until the overall population numbers approached sustainable levels, as determined by the reduced carrying capacity. This argument suggests that the relationship between the occupation index and population density was indirect and dynamic. Once the disintegrative secular trend sets in it is the carrying capacity that declines first, and population numbers follow with a lag time. It should take at least a generation, or even longer, for the system to come into some sort of equilibrium (and it may actually not do so

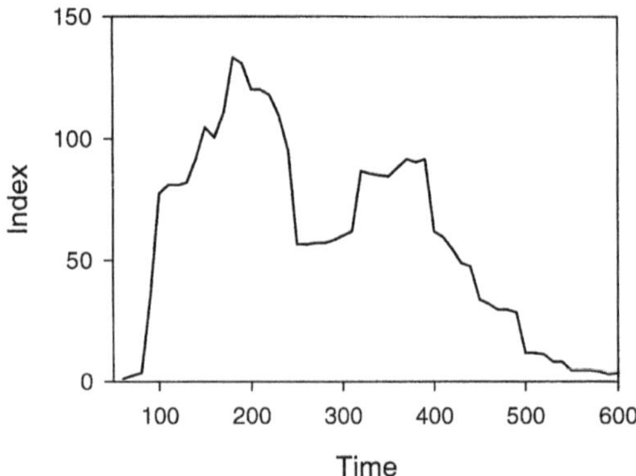

Figure 7.2 Importation of African red slip ware into the Albegna Valley (Etruria) (Bintliff and Sbonias 1999:5).

before the decentralization tendency is reversed and the carrying capacity begins increasing).

Certain economic trends during the empire can also be traced using archaeological data. For example, the rate of importation of African red slip ware into the Albegna Valley (Etruria) exhibits an increase during the second century and reaches a peak during the 180s and 190s (figure 7.2). After the third-century collapse, a second peak occurred during the last quarter of the fourth century, reflecting the secular cycle of the Dominate.

Social Structure and Elites

The social structure of the Roman Empire is sketched in table 7.2. The table presents a static view, but the social structure of the empire evolved substantially during the Principate. One development was a formal legal distinction that arose during the second century between *honestiores* and *humiliores*, resulting in the "dual penalty system" by the Severan age (Saller 2000:851). *Honestiores* included senators, equestrians, army veterans, and their families. They suffered less extreme and degrading penalties than *humiliores*, and the testimony of the upper-class members was recognized as more credible.

An even more important development was the increasing divergence, throughout the Principate, between the status and power hierarchies. Unlike in the Republic, the senatorial class did not monopolize the chief administrative posts in its hands. The Julio-Claudian emperors employed slaves or freedmen in a number of top administrative positions, such as heads of chancellery (Hopkins 1983). From the middle of the first century on, equestrians were increasingly employed in these positions. The equestrians, most of whom had a military background, became governors of all

TABLE 7.2
Social structure of the Roman Empire during the first century

Stratum	*Wealth*	*Income*	*Numbers*	*Notes*
Greatest fortunes	400,000	24,000[a]	2	Lentulus, Narcissus
Senator	1,000	60[a]	600	Minimum wealth qualifying one for senatorial status. A more realistic minimum is 8 mln HS (Wells 1992:187).
Equestrian	400	24[a]	5,000	Minimum wealth qualifying one for equestrian status
Decurion	100	6[a]	20,000	
Legionnaire	12[b]	1.2[c]	180,000[d]	
"Decent living"	—	1		Alston's estimate
Basic subsistence	—	0.1		Assuming 220 kg p.a. at 3 HS per modius

Source: Numbers and minimum wealth for senators, equestrians, and decurions are based on Jongman (1988:193); others are based on Alston (1998:217).

Note: "Wealth," total worth of property; "Income," annual income. All numbers in 1,000 of sesterces.

[a] Estimate using 6% of wealth (Jongman 1988:195).

[b] Retirement bonus.

[c] Annual pay.

[d] Harl (1996).

the important provinces. "By the end of the third century AD, the senate collectively and most senators individually were cut off from the exercise of political power on behalf of the state" (Hopkins 1983:183).

State Finances

Scattered indications of the empire's annual budgets and the state of its treasury are gathered in table 7.3. Basing his calculations on legionnaires' pay and the number of troops in the empire, Harl (1996:220) estimated the spiraling costs of the military during the Principate (figure 7.3a). Total annual expenditures on administration were probably of similar magnitude to military costs, and could have increased from 400 million HS to 1 billion HS between the reigns of Augustus and Septimus Severus (Harl 1996:227).

Duncan-Jones (1994:11–16) identified four phases the imperial finances went through under the Principate. Remarkably, his phases coincide almost exactly with the four phases of the cycle we delineated at the beginning of this chapter based on demographic and sociopolitical stability indices.

The expansion phase (27 BCE–CE 96) was characterized by intermittent financial difficulties, which were largely resolved by the end of the first century. Difficulties in funding army discharge bonuses under Augustus and Tiberius almost led to a mutiny (Duncan-Jones 1994:11). Tiberius was criticized as being stingy, but he managed to accumulate 2.7 billion HS in the treasury by his death. Tiberius's surplus was then spent by Gaius

TABLE 7.3
Annual budgets of the Roman Empire

Period	*Budget (HS billion)*	*Budget (tons silver)*	*Surplus/deficit (HS billion)*
Augustus (27 BCE–14)	0.4–0.45	400	
Tiberius (14–37)	0.5	460	
Surplus in 37			2.7–3.3
Deficit in 41			"Large"
Deficit in 70			–4
Vespasian (69–79)	1.2–1.5	1,100	
Surplus in 96			"Substantial"
A. Pius (ca.150)	0.8–1	670	
Surplus in 161			2–2.7
Funds in treasury in 193			0.001
Caracalla (ca.215)	1.4–1.6	610	

Source: Frank (1940), Duncan-Jones (1994), Ward et al. (2003).

(Caligula), who supposedly left a deficit on his death. The treasury recovered during Claudius's reign (41–54), likely helped by the funds that came from the goods of condemned senators and knights. Nero's reign (54–68), like Caligula's, saw huge expenditures that were offset to a certain degree by large seizures of property (condemnations, statues of precious metal, forced contributions). When Vespasian (69–79) became emperor, he had to deal with a huge deficit (4 billion HS). The supposed profligacy of Nero, however, may have been an exaggeration by the later tradition that tended to accuse the "bad" emperors of all kinds of sins (the same consideration should qualify the reports of the deficit left by Caligula).

Vespasian increased some taxes, renewed others that had fallen into disuse, and introduced new ones. Frank (1940:53) estimated the annual income under Vespasian as 1.2–1.5 billion HS. In other words, the revenues tripled during the first century of the Principate. As a result, Vespasian largely restored the health of the state finances, which allowed Domitian to raise the army pay. The small-scale debasement of the denarius under Nero was reversed by the Flavians.

The empire entered the stagflation phase (96–165) with very strong finances. The reigns of Trajan (98–117) and Hadrian (117–38) were characterized by large increases in spending that were apparently easily accommodated by the revenues (Duncan-Jones 1994:13). Imperially financed building activity reached a peak under Hadrian (Duncan-Jones 1990: Figure 10), and was also very intense under Trajan and Antoninus Pius (138–61). Antoninus Pius left a large surplus to his successors (2.7 billion HS). This was to be the last surplus reported until the fifth century (Harl 1996:94).

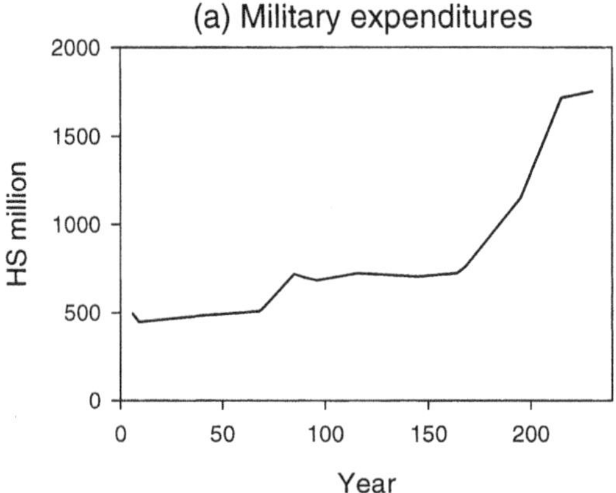

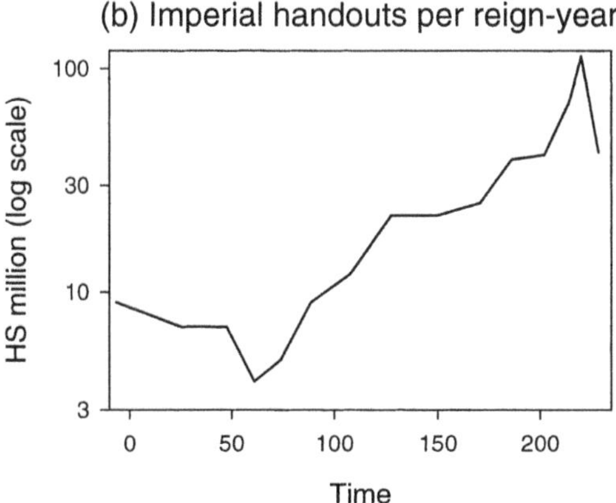

Figure 7.3 State expenditures during the Principate. (a) Estimated military costs (Harl 1996:220). (b) Imperial handouts (*congiaria*) (Duncan-Jones 1994:41).

The imperial finances unraveled during the crisis phase (165–192). Marcus Aurelius had to sell the gold vessels and artistic treasures of the imperial palace to finance his Danubian campaign of 169 (Ward et al. 2003:349). Commodus attempted to buy popularity by frequent and lavish cash handouts, *congiaria*. He spent around 40 million HS on *congiaria* per year, double the amount that was spent under Hadrian and Antoninus Pius (figure 7.3b). He also entertained the citizens with frequent chariot races, gladiatorial combats, and beast hunts in the arena (Ward, Heichelheim, and Yeo 2003:381). By itself, the spending on *congiaria* was not enough to break the treasury (it was perhaps 5 percent of the estimate revenues of the empire at the time). But the alarming growth of cash handouts to citizens was at least matched by the growth of handouts to the army (although we lack time-series data on this trend; see Duncan-Jones (1994)). Army costs constituted the bulk of the Imperial budget, and their growth was what caused the state bankruptcy. The financial difficulties of Commodus are reflected in the debasement of the denarius (which declined from 3 to 2 g of silver) and in the alarming increase in the executions of wealthy nobles and the confiscation of their property (Ward, Heichelheim, and Yeo 2003:382). The next emperor, Pertinax (193), again used the expedient of selling palace treasuries to raise cash.

After a brief period of relative stability under the Severi (193–235), state finances collapsed for good during the civil wars of 235–84. Probably the best indicator of the financial difficulties of the Roman state is given by the rate at which the main silver coin, the denarius, was debased by successive emperors (figure 7.4). The empire minted coins primarily for the purpose of paying the army, the bureaucracy, and making good on other state expenses. The Roman rulers recognized early on the value of debasement as a temporary solution to their fiscal difficulties. Thus, Nero reduced the silver content of the denarius (both by making it lighter and by increasing the percentage of base metal) to 3.14 g (compared to 3.72 g under Augustus). Vespasian further reduced it to 3.07 g, but once financial health was regained, Domitian increased the silver content of the denarius back to 3.28 g. While the state finances stayed healthy under the "good" emperors, the silver content of the denarius declined very slowly and was still just below 3 g under Antoninus Pius. However, by the end of the second century, the silver equivalent of the denarius had fallen precipitously to just 2 g, mainly as a result of increasing the proportion of base metal to one-third. Figure 7.4b shows the rate at which the denarius lost silver. The first peak occurred in the late second century, when Septimius Severus (193–211) became emperor and was faced with the task of stabilizing the state finances. The second peak occurred during the civil wars of 235–84. By the end of the reign of Gallienus in 272, the denarius had only 2.5 percent silver left in it.

Sociopolitical Instability

From the point of view of sociopolitical stability and public order, the period of the Principate can be divided into three distinct phases (see table 7.4 for the list of instability events affecting the political center). Political instability from Augustus to Domitian (30 BCE–96 CE) primarily affected the top elite strata, including the emperors, many of whom were deposed and murdered. In fact, the majority of Julio-Claudian emperors died violently. The senatorial stratum also suffered as a result of prosecution from reigning emperors or following unsuccessful plots. The nature of the insta-

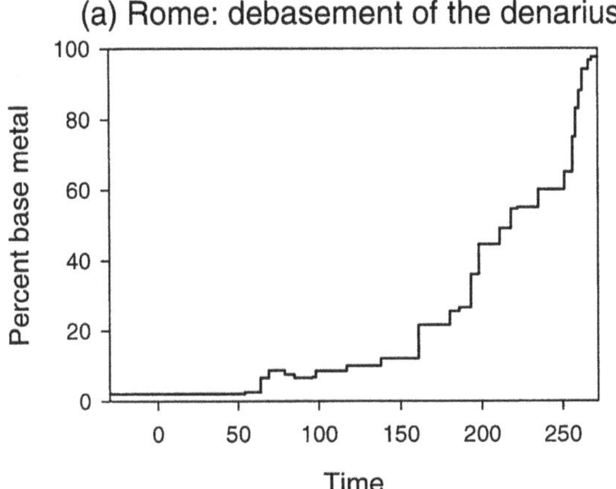

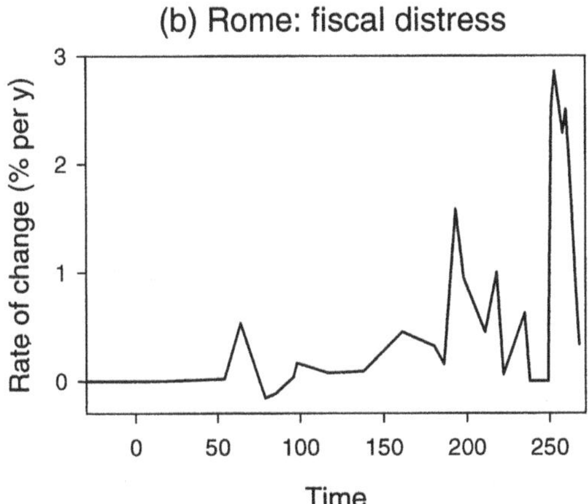

Figure 7.4 Financial difficulties of the state, illustrated by the debasement history of the denarius (Duncan-Jones 1994: Table 15.5). (a) Debasement of the denarius. (b) Fiscal distress measured as the rate of reduction in silver content per year.

bility, however, was largely confined to treasonous plots and coups d'état, with full-blown civil war flaring up only once, in 68–69.

The next period, from Nerva to Marcus Aurelius (96–180), was remarkable for its high stability—there were no major instability events at the imperial core, Italy. The third period, starting with the reign of Commodus, introduced a time of high instability, recurrent state collapse, and endemic civil war. There were periods of multisided civil war and multiple emperors in 192–97, and then almost continuously from 235 to 285.

The evidence of coin hoards (Christiansen 1985, Robertson 2000) paints a similar picture, but with variations due to localities where hoards were

TABLE 7.4
Sociopolitical instability in Italy, 30 BCE–285 CE

Year	*Event*
–22	Revolt at Rome
15	Disturbances at Rome
24	Rebellion of the slaves in southern Italy
41	Murder of Caligula; proclamation of Claudius
42	Conspiracy at Rome (Scribonianus)
59	Disturbances at Pompeii
64	Fire of Rome and disturbances
65	Conspiracy at Rome (Piso)
68	Uprising against Nero
69	Year of the three emperors; civil war
95	Conspiracy at Rome
96	Murder of Domitianus; Nerva
182	Conspiracy at Rome (Commodus's sister)
189	Famine revolution at Rome
192–97	Murder of Commodus, civil wars (multiple emperors)
211	Murder of Geta by Caracalla
217	Murder of Carcalla
218	Macrinus assassinated, civil war
221	Mutiny of army near Rome
222	Deposition of Elagabalus
228	Disturbances in armies in Rome (and Mesopotamia)
235–8	Deposition of Alexander Severus, civil war (multiple emperors)
244	Murder of Gordianus III
248–9	Revolts in Syria, Egypt, and at Rome; Philippus killed in battle
249–53	Civil war (multiple emperors), Gallus killed by his troops
258–68	Civil war (multiple emperors: "the Thirty Tyrants")
269	Revolt at Bologna and other cities
270	Civil war (Quintillus vs. Aurelianus)
274	Revolt at Rome (monetarii)
275	Disturbances at Rome after the assassination of Aurelianus
276	Deposition of Tacitus, Florianus
282–85	Civil war (multiple emperors); murder of Probus, Carinus

Source: Based on Sorokin (1937), supplemented by other sources.

buried (compare figure 7.5 to figures 7.6 and 7.7). The biggest peak in both provinces occurred during the second half of the third century. The secondary peaks show more variation. In both Alexandria and Britain a peak occurred during the 60s, probably associated with the civil wars of 68–69. This was followed by a trough around 100, and a gradual rise under the Antonine emperors. In Alexandria the second-century peak occurred earlier than in Britain, around 160. This spike is perhaps associated with the Egyptian uprising.

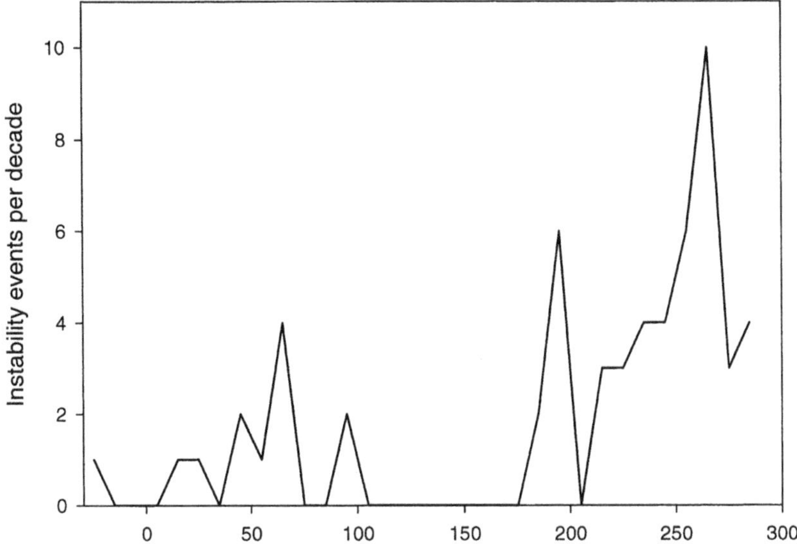

Figure 7.5 Roman Principate: sociopolitical instability index (based on data in table 7.4).

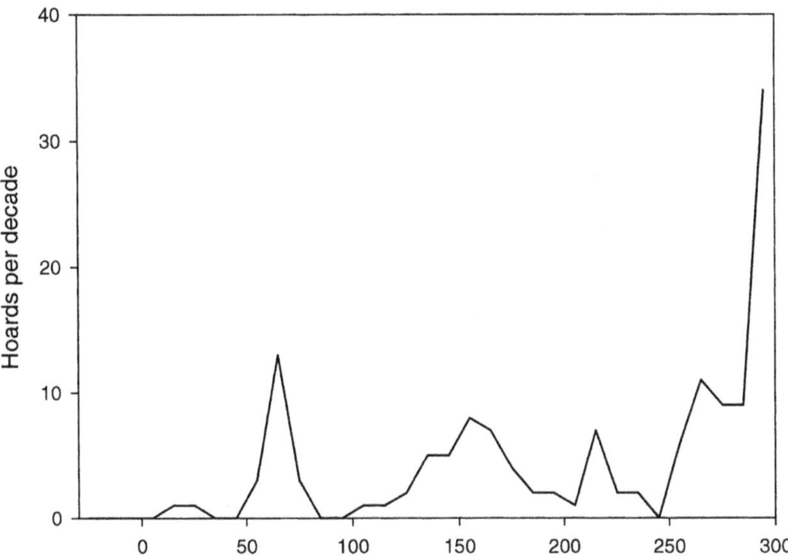

Figure 7.6 Time distribution of coin hoards in Alexandria, Egypt, during the Principate (Christiansen 1985).

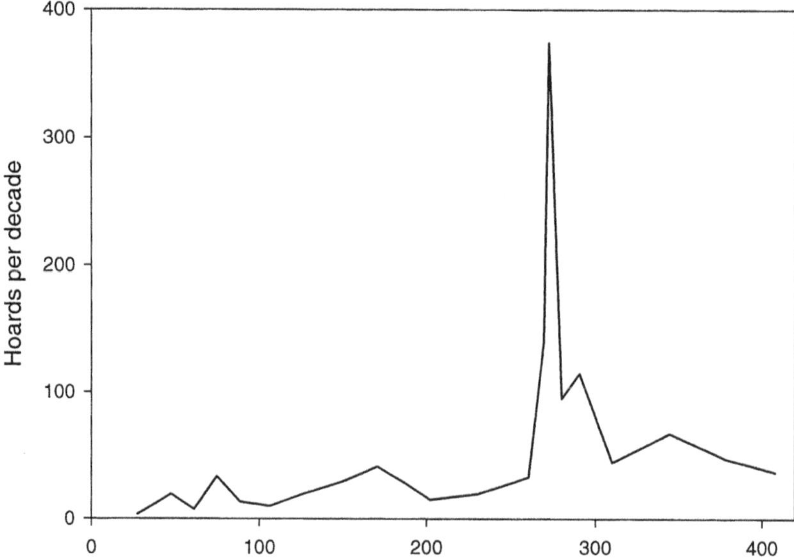

Figure 7.7 Time distribution of Romano-British coin hoards (Robertson 2000).

The time distribution of coin hoards published in *Corpus de Trésors Monétaires Antiques de la France* (Société Française de Numismatique, Paris, 1982) shows the same broad pattern, with a dominant third-century peak. However, hoards have been assigned by the experts to very broad temporal categories ("first century," "second century," or "the Julio-Claudians," "the Antonines"), which furthermore disagree between different volumes, so in the present form these data cannot be easily summarized.

7.2 Expansion (27 BCE–96 CE)

The Commoners

In the previous chapter we discussed the growth of economic inequality during the late Republic. One important consequence of the civil wars and the first years of the Principate was a significant reversal of this trend. The basic precondition of reduced inequality was the population decline that took place during the first century BCE, creating space where landless peasants (mainly veterans) could be settled. For example, in 36 BCE Capua gave up large tracts of deserted land for the settlement of Octavian's veterans, in return receiving lands in Crete and funds for the construction of a new aqueduct (Wells 1992:21–22). Not all land was obtained by purchase. After the battle of Philippi (42 BCE), Octavian simply stripped eighteen towns of their land, which was divided among the veterans. One of these towns was Cremona, where perhaps 3,000–4,000 veterans were given 35 iugera (9 ha) each, a very substantial land allotment. But such land seizures stopped with the end of the civil wars. In 30 and 14 BCE Augustus spent 860 million HS to purchase land to settle veterans (of which 600 million was spent in Italy and 260 million in the provinces). Large numbers of peasants emigrating to the provinces further decreased the population pressure on resources within Italy. Additionally, Walter Scheidel (2007) estimates that under the early Principate, as many as one in ten free Italian men left Italy for service in the legions. Most of them never returned, because the surviving veterans were resettled in the provinces. However, this outlet for "demographic steam" gradually became less important, as Italian military participation rates declined during the first century.

Thus, the Principate cycle began with greater numbers of relatively prosperous small landowners compared to the late Republic. However, it is likely that this relative prosperity rapidly eroded during the first century as a result of population growth. There was also a large number of slaves in Italy (Brunt estimates 2 million, but Scheidel revises this estimate down). The number of slaves probably diminished during the first two centuries CE (Saller 2000:851). First, there was a substantial diminution of territorial conquests after Augustus, and thus the supply of war captives declined. It is thought that the slave population could not reproduce itself biologically, as a result of manumission and lower birth rates. Second, as population growth resumed, the number of landless peasants began increasing. Thus, at the same time that the price of slaves increased owing to their scarcity, the real wages that could be paid to landless peasants declined owing to their abundance, and it became more profitable to lease land in return for rent, or to hire workers.

The Elites

At the opposite end of the social scale we have some scattered numbers indicating the wealth of the senatorial class. The richest men outside the imperial house who are known to us from the early empire were Gnaeus Cornelius Lentulus, consul in 14 BCE, and Claudius's freedman, Narcissus (Wells 1992:8). Each reputedly owned property worth 400 million HS. It is noteworthy that both these incomes belong to the early phase of the Principate. Apparently, the scale of the largest fortunes declined during the first century, partly as a result of persecution of the wealthiest aristocrats. Thus, Narcissus was poisoned by Agrippina, Nero's mother, after Claudius's death. Claudius (41–54) himself condemned to death thirty-five senators and many knights; a substantial part of their fortunes must have gone into the imperial treasury (Duncan-Jones 1994:11). Nero is said to have executed the six largest landowners in Africa Proconsularis and thus gained possession of the rich Bragadas Valley (Ward, Heichelheim, and Yeo 2003:322). When a number of plots against Nero proliferated, starting in 65, he forced a great number of senators and equestrians to commit suicide. These included such well-known personages as Seneca and the poet Lucan (Ward, Heichelheim, and Yeo 2003:322).

As a result of imperial persecution and the civil war of 68–69, the ranks of Roman senators had become depleted to about 200 (Ward, Heichelheim, and Yeo 2003:329–30). After the purges of Nero and Domitian, most of the old Republican noble families had disappeared (Ward et al. 2003:372). Under Trajan and Hadrian only some thirty senators are known who still bore the names of the old Republican nobility (Wells 1992:171). Of the twenty-six families that Augustus (27 BCE–14 CE) and Claudius (41–54 CE) elevated to patrician status, we know of only six still surviving under Trajan (98–117 CE) (Wells 1992:237). This is a very low rate of retaining elite status, 23 percent in less than a century, implying an extinction rate per twenty-five years of well over 30 percent, perhaps close to 40 percent. Here are some additional statistics (Hammond 1957:75): the proportion of patricians of Republican ancestry who can be identified in the senate within any given period declined from an average of about 16 percent under Augustus (27 BCE–14) to 4.5 percent under Nero (54–68), slightly over 2 percent in 69, only 1 percent in 96, and less than 1 percent in 117. These numbers imply a 50 percent extinction rate per twenty-five years. Similar factors affected the descendants of emperors. For example, Junia Calvina was the only descendant of Augustus alive in the 70s (Wells 1992:67).

The elite dynamics under the early Principate thus resemble very much the downfall of the "overmighty subject" under the Tudors (see chapter 3). Although some large senatorial fortunes were lost to the state as a result of imperial persecution, others joined it when wealthy senators became emperors (for example, Titus Aurelius Antoninus, who became the emperor Antoninus Pius). The end result was that during the first century, the relative power of the most powerful and wealthy private individuals declined substantially with respect to the state's fortunes.

Data on building dedications by private individuals support this conjecture. The curves of dedications per reign-year show an initial peak under the early Principate that declines during the first century. The low is reached under the Flavians and Hadrian, after which the curve increases and reaches the second peak under A. Pius in Italy (figure 7.8, solid line), M. Aurelius in Sabratha, Commodus in Thugga, and even S. Severus in Lepcis Magna (the last observation is mainly explained by the fact that Severus was a native of Lepcis Magna). However, funding whole buildings was possible only for the wealthiest members of the elite.

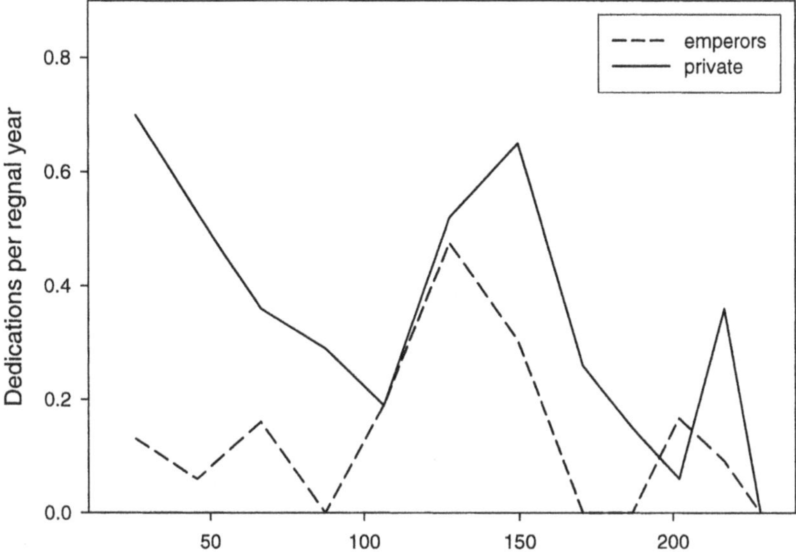

Figure 7.8 Time distribution of dated buildings in Italy. Solid line: private individuals, dashed line: emperors (Duncan-Jones 1990:213).

In summary, it appears that the fortunes of the top elite stratum, the magnates, first declined during the Principate, reaching a trough during the Flavian period, then increased under the five good emperors, reaching a peak during the second half of the second century. The nature of the magnate stratum, however, changed radically. Whereas the first century's aristocracy was still dominated by the senatorial order, during the second century senators lost power and persisted largely as a status group (Hopkins 1983:171–76). Power accumulated in the hands of provincial governors, military commanders of the legions, and the commanders of the Praetorian Guard, who typically were equestrians. Thus, one important trend that continued throughout the Principate was the senate's gradual loss of status as the repository of power elites. The center of gravity shifted from the senate to the imperial bureaucracy, and more precisely to the Imperial Council. This began as the *Consilium Principis*, an informal conclave of Augustus's friends and advisors, and was converted into a more permanent structure by Hadrian (Ward, Heichelheim, and Yeo 2003:344). During the second century the senate gradually lost any real influence on the imperial administration. The Imperial Council became the true successor of the old Republican senate after the reorganization by Septimius Severus (Ward, Heichelheim, and Yeo 2003:385).

(De)urbanization

Finally, let us consider the urbanization rate, or, more specifically, the population size of the capital. The authorities tend to agree that the population of the city of Rome doubled from the late second to the late first century BCE, reaching around 800,000–1,000,000 (Hopkins 1978:96ff., Morley 1996:36ff.). This estimate is based on the recorded numbers of recipients of the free wheat dole and occasional cash handouts (*congiaria*), which fluctuated between 150 and 320 thousand. The estimate of 0.8–1 million is derived by starting with 200,000–250,000 recipients, dividing it by the estimated proportion of males over ten years old (those who were eligible for the dole) to obtain the total free population, and adding guessed numbers of the elite and slave strata. However, the recorded fluctuations in the numbers of dole recipients make sense in light of demographic-structural theory, and we can use them to sharpen the dynamics of the numbers of Rome's inhabitants.

The fluctuations in the recorded numbers of corn dole recipients were as follows (Hopkins 1978:96ff, Morley 1996:36ff). Under the popularis tribune, P. Clodius (the 50s BCE), they swelled to 320,000. In 46 Caesar reduced them to 150,000 by organizing emigration to the provinces and tightening registration of those who qualified. Under Augustus the numbers increased again to more than 250,000, reaching another peak of 320,000 in 5 BCE. Three years later the numbers sank to just over 200,000, and on the death of Augustus corn dole recipients numbered 150,000 (at least, this was how many people benefited from his will). We see a definite pattern here: the urban population swells following protracted periods of civil war (with a time lag) and then is gradually reduced during periods of internal peace (see chapter 1 for the general discussion). This argument suggests that we can take the transmitted numbers at their face value. The peak number of 320,000, then, would imply some 1.2 million total inhabitants, while the trough number of 150,000 corresponds to 0.6 million (there is at least a 10 percent uncertainty associated with these estimates). We propose, therefore, that under the late Republic and during the early years of Augustus, the population of Rome swelled to 1.2 million, and by the end of his reign it had declined to 600,000. Naturally, during the peaks the city was horribly overpopulated, whereas when the population was halved, by 14 CE, the quality of life must have become much more bearable, even for the poorer citizen strata.

We do not know how population of the city of Rome changed during the first century, but it probably did not grow very much, if at all (that is the general rule during the population expansion phases, when typically the proportion of urban population to the total tends to decrease). During the stagflation phase (96–165), the urban population should have in-

TABLE 7.5
Legionnaires' wages

Time period	*Annual wage (HS)*	*Silver equivalent (g)*	*Wheat (quintals)*
Augustus (27 BCE–14 CE)	900	837	9.3
Domitian (81–96)	1,200	984	8.9
Severus (193–211)	1,600	816	6.6
Caracalla (211–217)	2,400	984	?

Source: Nominal wages from Greene (1986:59), silver equivalent of sesterces (HS) from Harl (1996), and wheat prices from Table 7.6.

creased. We know that the number of *vici* in the city increased between the reign of Hadrian (117–38) and the fourth century. Almost certainly this happened during the second century. Equally likely is that by the end of the third century, with the start of the next cycle of the Dominate, the population of Rome declined. The third-century wall marked a contraction from the regions occupied during the Augustan era (Morley 1996:38). In summary, the possible evolution of the urban population of Rome was an increase from 0.6 million in the first half of the first century to perhaps well over million at the end of the second, followed by a decline toward the end of the third.

7.3 Stagflation (96–165 CE)

Population Pressure and Economic Change

Price and wage data are very scarce for the Roman Empire outside Egypt. The only empire-wide wages we know about are those of the legionnaires (table 7.5). The nominal wage doubled during the first and second centuries, but when we express the wage in terms of grams of silver, we observe that it peaked at the end of the first century and declined during the second. Yet another look is afforded by translating the wage into wheat, using the Egyptian prices (see below). According to this measure, the soldier wages just barely compensated for inflation during the first century (the difference between 9.3 and 8.9 quintals is less than the uncertainty associated with estimating the real wage).

One area of the Roman Empire for which we have some documentation of economic trends is Egypt. Table 7.6 shows changes in the price of wheat during the first three centuries CE.

Both private transactions and official prices tell the same story. The nominal price of wheat doubled or more toward the second half of the second century. This trend was not due just to the debasement of Roman

TABLE 7.6
Wheat prices in Egypt (averages by period)

Time period	*Drachmas per artaba*	*Silver (g per quintal)*
Private transactions		
18 BCE – 47 CE	7.2	90
78–79 CE	10.6	116
112–135 CE	10.0	105
150–200 CE	15.3	124
250–300 CE	42.9	44
Official prices		
13 BCE – 65 CE	3.3	42
99–162 CE	9.0	94
246–294 CE	146	73

Source: Based on data in Duncan-Jones (1990:151–55).

coins during the second century (see below), because the price of wheat also increased when expressed in silver units. During the third century, the nominal price of wheat continued to rise, reaching 200–300 drachmas per artaba by the last quarter (Duncan-Jones 1990), but it appears that this increase was entirely due to debasement. When expressed in silver equivalents, we see that the price of wheat actually declined in the third century.

The best recent compilation of economic trends in Egypt during the second and third century is in Scheidel (2002). Scheidel reports on the means and medians of land prices, land rents, wheat and other commodity prices, and wages, in both nominal and real terms. The real (deflated) values are of particular interest, because rapid inflation due to debasement of the denarius during this period (see next section) makes nominal values uninformative. For example, there are some data on agricultural land prices in Egypt, but the interpretation of what these data tell us generated some controversy. Duncan-Jones (1974) gave the data in table 7.7. The median first increases and then decreases, which would make sense in demographic-structural terms. The third century decrease was probably even more profound, given the debasement of silver coinage. However, Duncan-Jones observed that both maximum and minimum prices kept increasing throughout the period. This trend throws doubt on the validity of the trend observed in the median price. Alston (1995) attempted to trace price trends separately in "low-quality," "average," and "high-quality" land. Scheidel (2002) instead used two categories (less or more than 600 drachmas per aroura). Both were roundly criticized by Bagnall (2005). For this reason, in the following we focus on real rents (there is also some information on the change in real wages from the second to the third century, which we review in section 7.4).

TABLE 7.7
Land prices in sesterces (HS) per iugerum

Period	*n*	*median*	*max*	*min*
First century	11	141	459	11
Second century	16	183	612	26
Third century	8	147	1,101	58

Source: Duncan-Jones (1974:366).

TABLE 7.8
Mean annual real land rents for wheat fields (artabas per aroura)

Period	*Arsinoite*	*Oxyrhynchite*	*Hermopolite*	*Herakleopolite*	*Average*
27 BCE–99 CE	7.37	5.41	—	—	6.39
100–165 CE	8.79	7.82	7.65	—	8.09
205–268 CE	3.23	5.89	6.27	4.91	5.08

Source: Scheidel (2002: table 1).
Note: Only means are shown; medians show the same trend. Based on 133 data points.

Changes in real rents are consistent among all regions and show an increase from the first century toward 165, the eve of the plague, followed by a decrease in the third century. The post-plague decline on average is 37 percent, suggesting a substantial population decrease resulting from epidemics and sociopolitical instability.

Elite Overproduction and Competition

In the previous chapter we used the statistics of Hopkins and Burton on consular ascendance and descendance rates to argue for an increasing intraelite competition toward the end of the Republican cycle. We are lucky in that these authors have also provided similar statistics for the Principate period. However, there are several caveats we need to take in consideration when considering these numbers. First, whereas the consuls of the Republican period were at the pinnacle of both the status and power pyramids, during the Principate they retained only status, while power passed into the hands of emperors and their top administrators, who by the end of the period were recruited almost entirely outside the senatorial order (mainly from the equestrians). Second, the data are much sparser than those for the Republic because Hopkins and Burton elected to investigate only every other generation of the consular aristocracy. Thus, instead of having eight data points to cover the period of the Principate, we have only four. Third, whereas under the Republic the number of men elected to consulship in any generation stayed roughly constant, because only two consuls could be

TABLE 7.9
Inheritance of consular status under the Principate

Period CE	*Consuls per year*	*Consular ascendants*		*Consular descendants*		*Competition index*[a]	
		3-gen.	*Fathers*	*Sons*	*3-gen.*	*1-gen.*	*3-gen.*
18–54	6	54	46	32	40	14	14
70–96	8	24	18	25	32	−7	−8
131–160	9	32	27	29	36	−2	−4
193–235	9	37	32	19	26	13	11

Source: Data of Hopkins and Barton, from Hopkins (1983).
Note: "3-gen." refers to three generations of ascendants (great-grandfather, grandfather, father) or descendants (son, grandson, great-grandson). "1-gen." is either a father or a son.
[a] Competition index is determined as the proportion with consular ascendants minus the proportion with consular descendants

elected in a year, during the Principate the number of consuls elected per year increased gradually to eight or ten under the last Antonines. This increase obviously affects the conclusions we draw from the difference between proportions of consuls with consular ascendants and descendants. As a result of these caveats, our conclusions below are much more tentative than in the previous chapter. The main problem is the sparsity of data; it would be extremely useful to complete the work of Hopkins and Barton by filling in the missing generations.

Hopkins and Burton's data (table 7.9) suggest that during the first century, the proportion of consuls with consular fathers dropped dramatically, from 46 percent to 18 percent. The proportion of consuls who had a consular ascendant extending three generations back exhibits the same qualitative dynamics. In other words, the grip of the hereditary nobility on consular status was substantially weakened. This trend makes sense in light of what we know about the elite dynamics. Old nobility was decimated during the Julio-Claudian periods. At the same time, the size of the consular stratum expanded substantially: under August, only 2.6 consuls, on average, were appointed per year. Hopkins and Burton estimate that by the end of the century, eight ordinary and suffect consuls were appointed every year. Assuming an average life expectancy of thirty years, the size of the consular stratum tripled during the first century, from 80 to 240 individuals.

In the second century the trend inverted, and the proportion of consuls with consular fathers climbed from 18 to 27 percent and then to 32 percent. The hereditary aristocracy thus was reasserting its grip on consular positions, although it never reached the same level of control it had in 18–54 (or during the second century BCE, as we discussed in the previous chapter).

The proportion of consuls with consular descendants fluctuated at a roughly constant level until the mid-second century, then plunged during the period of 193–235 (table 7.9). What is particularly interesting is the difference between the proportion of consuls with consular ascendants and those with consular descendants (the "competition index" in table 7.9). During both 70–96 and 131–60 this index is positive, suggesting a relaxation of intraelite competition. By the end of the second century we revert to the pattern typical of heightened competition and forced downward mobility, similar to that observed in the Gracchan period of the Republic.

Any conclusions based on these data must remain tentative until the gaps are filled in. But the data patterns, and especially the competition index, are consistent with our narrative in section 7.2 ("Elites"), where we argued that during the Principate, the fortunes of the top elite stratum first declined, reaching a trough during the Flavian period, then increased under the five good emperors, reaching a peak during the second half of the second century. Beginning with Marcus Aurelius and, especially, Commodus, we observe signs of elite overproduction and increased competition that eventually contributed to the state breakdown in the late second century.

One typical sign of elite overproduction is the growth of administrative posts. According to H. G. Pflaum (cited in Hopkins 1983:180), there were 64 equestrian posts in the provinces in the reign of Domitian (81–96) and 173 in the reign of Septimius Severus (193–211). Thus, although during the second century the territory of the empire expanded to a very insignificant degree (and in places even contracted), the number of administrative posts grew almost threefold, perhaps reflecting pressure from the surplus elites for government positions.

7.4 Crisis (165–97 CE)

Population

The population decline during the disintegrative phase of the Principate cycle resulted, as usual, from a complex combination of causes. It is probable that population numbers began declining in Italy during the second century (this is what occupation index data suggest; see figure 7.1a), but the first major, empire-wide shock was delivered by an epidemic that reached the Roman Empire in 165 and became known as the Antonine plague. The Antonine plague was probably smallpox, or a combination of measles and smallpox (Scheidel 2002). It was reputedly brought from the eastern Mediterranean by Roman troops returning from the Parthian War (Duncan-Jones 1996). In 165 it hit Nisibis and Smyrna. The following year it reached Rome. In 168 the plague raged in Rome and many provinces. By 169 it had caused annihilating losses in the number of taxpayers in Egypt as a result of death or flight. Reports of plague visitation, often causing catastrophic losses, crop up in 172, 174, 175, 179, 182, and 189 (Duncan-Jones 1996:115–17). Dio wrote that the plague of 189 in Rome was the worst he knew, sometimes killing 2,000 people per day (Duncan-Jones 1996:115). The Roman Empire was struck again by a catastrophic wave of epidemics in the 250s and 260s (Scheidel 2002).

The demographic impact of the Antonine plague is best documented in Egypt. In the Fayum area the tax base dropped between 33 and 47 percent (Duncan-Jones 1996:120). Smaller villages in the delta suffered even more: between 160 and 170 their populations declined by 70–93 percent (Duncan-Jones 1996:121). Some of this decline was due to flight rather than mortality, but most of the population did not have the means to escape the plague. Certainly, losses in the taxpayer base persisting for four years after the plague cannot be explained by emigration. Mortality continued to be severe during the later outbreaks. For example, one-third of the tax-paying population of the village of Socnopaiou Nesos in the Arsinoite died in January and February of 179. This Egyptian papyrus specifically recorded mortality, not flight (Duncan-Jones 1996:121). Outside Egypt no estimate of population losses from the epidemics of 165–89 seem possible. Literary sources report heavy mortality in a variety of places across the empire and among the soldiers (reviewed by Duncan-Jones 1996). Frier's (2000:815–16) estimate, namely, that up to 10 percent of the empire's total population may have perished in the plague, with the percentage perhaps twice that in cities and military camps, seems to us overly conservative. Many historians had similarly doubted that the Black Death of the fourteenth century could have caused a catastrophic mortality until modern research decisively demonstrated the scale of the catastrophe (see chapter 2). Our guess is that the mortality of the Antonine plague during the whole period of 165–89 was comparable to that of the Black Death in Western Europe during 1347–80, so Frier's estimate should be doubled or even tripled. A much more plausible estimate is that of Scheidel (2002), who points to a "massive mortality" of as much as 25 percent in the first ten to fifteen years of the Antonine plague (see also Zelener 2003).

At the same time, there is no need to overemphasize the importance of the plague for the subsequent course of the Roman history. The plague hit the empire when it was already under an enormous demographic-structural stress. In the absence of such stress, the population losses caused by the epidemics would have been made up in a generation, at most two. But by 165 the social system was already near a critical point, and the plagues pushed it beyond it. Arguing by analogy with the events of post-Black Death Western Europe (see chapter 2), we suggest that the Antonine plague imposed a higher mortality on the productive classes than on the elites. A serious elite overproduction problem had already developed by 165; the differential mortality due to the epidemic hastened and exacer-

TABLE 7.10
Real wages of agricultural laborers in Roman Egypt (index = 1 in the second century)

Period	*Daily wages*	*Monthly wages*
2nd C	1.00	1.00
250s–260s	1.25	1.17

Source: Scheidel (2002: table 10).

bated the developing political crisis. According to our theory, it was the ensuing century of sociopolitical instability that was responsible for preventing population recovery after the epidemics (and, in fact, probably caused further population decline).

The real wages (expressed in wheat equivalents) moved in the direction consistent with the idea of third-century population decline. By the 260s real wages had increased by about 20 percent compared to the preplague period. Other more anecdotal data support the general trends summarized above. For example, in the village of Theadelphia in the Fayyum, the 2,500 residents in the 130s cultivated 1,600–1,700 ha of arable land. In 216 an unknown but obviously diminished number cultivated 990 ha of arable land. What is of particular interest is that the arboricultural land (vineyards and orchards) increased from 140 ha in 158 to 415 ha in 216. "These documented changes indicate that, after the plague, fewer people had to be fed, and that these villagers enjoyed a higher living standard than in the 2nd c., either because they could afford to consume more wine and fruit or because they derived profit from selling these products to urban customers" (Scheidel 2002). The decreased importance of cereals in the commoner diet in post-plague Egypt parallels that in England after the Black Death.

Political Crisis

After the murder of Domitian and the installation of Nerva by the senate in 96, the Roman Empire entered a period remarkable for its internal stability. The "five good emperors" enjoyed the good will of the senatorial elite and other propertied classes and the loyalty of soldiers (Ward, Heichelheim, and Yeo 2003:335). Although social and economic pressures were rising, as described in the previous sections, the internal peace lasted until 165, when it was shattered by the arrival of the plague. The subsequent period has aptly been called the "Antonine military crisis" by Greenberg (2003:424): "the Germanic incursions into Pannonia in 167; the invasion of Italy itself by the Marcomanni, and Greece and the Balkans by the Costobocci in 170; devastating raids upon Spain and N. Africa by Mauri in 171; the Boukoloi revolt in 172; the rebellion of Avidius Cassius in 175; a subsequent wave of invasions of Spain and N. Africa in 177; protracted campaigning against the various German tribes until Marcus' death."

Despite these pressures, Marcus Aurelius was able to hold the ruling class of the empire together. The collapse occurred under his heir Commodus (180–92). It resulted from "divisions and jealousies among the members of the Imperial family, military officers, and powerful senators" (Ward, Heichelheim, and Yeo 2003:379). The first plot was hatched in 182, when a number of senators conspired with Commodus's sister Lucilla to assassinate him. It was followed by the execution of the conspirators and, later, a number of other senators who had been close to Marcus Aurelius. Disaffection also spread into the lower strata. Probably as a result of declining real wages, a series of mutinies occurred in the provincial armies, often called the Deserters' War, which seem to have spawned another attempt at assassination (Ward, Heichelheim, and Yeo 2003:380).

The reign of Commodus ended in what appears to be a classic secular state collapse brought on by fiscal bankruptcy. Commodus was poisoned during the end-of-the-year celebration, survived the attempt (probably vomiting most of the poison as a result of overdrinking), and was assassinated the next day when he was recovering in the bath, strangled by his wrestling partner, Narcissius, who joined the plot against Commodus (Ward, Heichelheim, and Yeo 2003:382). The next two emperors, Pertinax and Julianus, lasted only eighty-seven and sixty-six days, respectively. The senate called on Pescenius Niger, the governor of Syria, to seize the throne. Simultaneously, the armies of Britain and the Danube declared for their respective commanders, Clodius Albinus and Septimius Severus. The latter won the race to Rome and became the next emperor (193–211). The civil war continued from 193 to 197. Septimius first moved against Niger, defeating and killing him in 194. It then took a lengthy siege to reduce Niger's base of operations, Byzantium, which fell only in 195. Meanwhile, the Parthians meddled in the Roman civil war, and Septimius campaigned there in 194 and 195. Also in 195, Albinus, supported by a large following in the senate, crossed the channel into Gaul. After two more years Septimius's forces met and defeated the army of Albinus near Lugdunum (Lyons). Septimius allowed his troops to burn Lugdunum, then carried out a ruthless campaign of extermination against the adherents of Albinus in the provinces and in the senate (Ward, Heichelheim, and Yeo 2003:384).

7.5 Depression (197–285 CE)

The reigns of Septimius (from 197) and his son Caracalla (211–17) were relatively peaceful. These two decades appear to fit the pattern of generation alternation during the decentralization phase. But the equilibrium was fragile and slowly unraveled, beginning during Caracalla's reign. Up to 235 the sociopolitical instability took the form of palace coups. It began in 211, when Caracalla killed his brother and co-ruler Geta and carried out a purge against Geta's supporters. After that it was a monotonous litany of emperors assassinated and elevated: in 217 Caracalla was assassinated and Macrinus was installed, in 218 Macrinus was assassinated and Elagabalus was installed, and in 222 Elagabalus was assassinated and Severus Alexander was installed. Alexander lasted until 235, when he also was assassinated. With the death of Alexander, intraelite conflict took on the character of a general civil war, and the empire was simultaneously ruled by several emperors or pretenders (Stearns 2001): Maximinus "Thrax" was proclaimed emperor by the Rhine legions after the murder of Alexander. He beat back the thrusts of Sarmatians, Dacians, and Goths but was opposed by the senate. In Africa, the legions proclaimed as emperors the eighty-year-old proconsul M. Antonius Gordianus and his son, Gordianus II (238). Both perished in a war with the prefect of Mauretania, who supported Maximinus. In Rome the senate raised from their own numbers M. Clodius Pupienus and D. Caelius Calvinus Balbinus. Maximinus was slain by his own troops while besieging Aquileia (June 238). The Praetorian Guard murdered Pupienus and Balbinus and forced the senate to recognize the thirteen-year-old grandson of Gordianus, Gordianus III, as emperor (238–44). Gordianus was murdered by his praetorian prefect, Marcus Julius Philippus, known as "the Arab" (244–49). Philippus was killed at Verona (249) in battle against his commander in Dacia, Decius. Gaius Messius Quintus Traianus Decius (249–51) was slain by the Goths in 251. Gaius Vibius Trebonianus Gallus (251–53) was proclaimed emperor by the army of Moesia. During his reign a fifteen-year plague began. When he marched against his successor in Moesia, the Moor M. Aemilius Aemilianus, his own troops slew him (before October 253). Aemilianus (253) was proclaimed emperor, then murdered, by his own troops.

The Age of Gallienus (253–68, first co-ruler with his father Valerian, then sole ruler) saw the catastrophic external invasions and plague. Two-thirds of the population of Alexandira perished, and 5,000 people died in Rome every day (Ward, Heichelheim, and Yeo 2003:397). The internal warfare reached a peak, with the empire fragmenting and pretenders cropping up everywhere. This was the age of "thirty tyrants" (Stearns 2001). During the reign of Gallienus alone, eighteen usurpers attempted to seize the throne (Ward, Heichelheim, and Yeo 2003:397). Two-thirds of territory of the Roman Empire seceded (the Gallic Empire under Postumus and the Palmyrene Empire under Odenathus and Zenobia).

A watershed of sorts occurred in 268, when staff officers of Gallienus, all of them Illyrians, assassinated the emperor and assumed control of the empire. This cabal of frontier officers produced a series of emperors, known as the "Illyrian soldier emperors," whose rule was interrupted only by a short interlude in 275–76 when a senatorial candidate sat on the throne. The Illyrians began the task of restoring the empire. Their job was largely accomplished in 285 with Diocletian's victory over Carinus in the battle of Margus.

7.6 Conclusion

Although our database on the economic and social dynamics of the Roman Empire during the Principate is not as complete as one would wish, the empirical trends that it delineates are generally in agreement with the predictions of the demographic-structural theory. Thus, the population trend was up until the middle of the second century, followed by collapse and stagnation brought on by, first, the Antonine plagues, and then by endemic civil warfare of the third century. There were, however, important regional differences. In particular, it appears that the population of the imperial core (Italy) peaked earlier than in the provinces, and may have started declining even before the plagues.

The economic data are the sparsest part of the database. Quantitative series are available for only one province, Egypt, and even in Egypt the data are fragmentary and there are many gaps. What data exist, however, support the Malthusian dynamic of increasing popular immiseration toward the mid-second century and declining economic misery after the population decrease after 165.

The elite dynamics exhibited a typical phase shift with respect to the commoner population. While the general population grew during the expansion phase (27 BCE–96 CE), the elites (and especially the top stratum, the senatorial aristocracy) shrank and lost some of their wealth and power. The elite numbers and income expanded again during the stagflation phase (96–165 CE). As a result, one index of elite consumption, the expenditure on monumental buildings, had a curious two-humped shape, with one peak in the early first century and the second peak in the mid-second century (figure 7.8).

The state finances were healthy during the integrative phase. There were periods of fiscal strain during the first century, but they were fleeting. In any case, the large budget deficits reported for Caligula and Nero are suspect because of the hostility of the sources to these "bad" emperors. In contrast, the financial crisis during the disintegrative phase was very real, as indicated by the drastic debasement of the Roman coinage in the third century (see figure 7.4).

The integrative phase of the Principate cycle was also the period of external conquests, especially early on, and successful defense of the *limes* later. The state expenditures on public building reached a peak toward the end of the integrative phase (see figure 7.8). One feature that does not fit the model is the recurrent instability during the first century. However, most of it took the form of palace coups, and the only significant example of civil war during this period (following the overthrow of Nero in 68) lasted just eighteen months. The stagflation phase (96–165) had no significant instability events. By contrast, the disintegrative phase was characterized by recurrent civil war, barbarian invasions, and territory loss.

Overall, the fit between the theory and data is probably as good as it could be in historical applications. With the caveat that the data are somewhat scanty, the Principate period appears to be another nearly perfect secular cycle. Again, the probable reason for the good match between theory and data is that the Roman Empire was a gigantic state (the only other state that could even remotely threaten it was the Parthian Empire), and therefore its rise and fall dynamics were primarily governed by endogenous mechanisms.

Chapter 8

Russia: The Muscovy Cycle (1460–1620)

8.1 The Fifteenth-Century Crisis

The starting point of our investigation is the second half of the fifteenth century, because only from this date on do we have access to reasonably detailed sources on the agrarian history of Russia—the Novogorod scribe books. This does not mean that a demographic-structural analysis of earlier periods of Russian history is impossible. Such an attempt has been made in one of our earlier articles (Nefedov 2002). Although the fragmentary nature of sources allows us at most a hypothetical reconstruction of economic and social dynamics, we believe that a case can be made that prior to the middle of the fifteenth century, Russia experienced two secular cycles.

The first or Kievan cycle began with the East Slavonic colonization of territories that eventually became Russia and ended with the demographic-structural crisis of the 1220s to 1250s in the northwest (the Novgorod and Pskov lands). Other Russian principalities succumbed to the Mongol invasion during the 1240s. The demographic catastrophe of the mid-thirteenth century was followed by sustained population growth during the fourteenth century. By the end of the century we again observe numerous signs of overpopulation in the Novgorod Land. The severe climate and poor soils of the northwest could support only a relatively sparse population. As a result, it did not take much time for population growth there to reach the limits of subsistence. In central Russia, unlike in the northwest, there was still enough land to absorb the growing population. However, during the second quarter of the fifteenth century the rising principality of Moscow experienced a protracted period of civil war, exacerbated by the Tatar invasions. As a result, the causes of the crisis of the fifteenth century differed between major regions of Russia. In the northwest the crisis was caused by famines and epidemics, while in the Central Region the main cause was civil war and external invasions, with famine and disease as secondary consequences of sociopolitical instability (Nefedov 2002).

What was the scale of the catastrophe? How do we interpret the words of the chronicler, "few people remain in all Russian lands"? According to the archaeological evidence, the finds of leather shoe remnants and birch scrolls in Novgorod cultural layers declined by a factor of two during the first half of the fifteenth century (Izyumova 1959, Konovalov 1966). The implication is that the population declined by a similar factor. As we saw in earlier chapters that dealt with the economic effects of the Black Death, one of the indicators of a demographic catastrophe is a sharp decline in grain prices and the growth of real wages. After "the Great Pestilence" in the northwest, prices halved, and labor became very expensive. The daily wage increased to approximately 24 kg of rye (Nefedov 2002).

According to archaeological data, one-fifth of villages in the Moscow region were deserted (Yushko 1991:52–53). Population losses were undoubtedly even more severe, because the surviving villages must have also lost population to famines and epidemics. The rate at which stone buildings were constructed in Moscow and Tver declined abruptly by a factor of 2.5–3 (Miller 1989). As happened after the Mongol conquest, several chronicles were terminated, creating a gap in the chronicle coverage of Russian history extending to the mid-fifteenth century (Lurie 1994).

The sociopolitical crisis in the Moscow region was severe and lasted half a century, from the devastating Tatar invasion led by Yedigei in 1408 and the first plague epidemic of 1418 to the end of the internecine war in 1453. The cause of the crisis was the financial collapse of the Moscow Principality. The treasury was empty and the state was forced to devalue currency. During the first half of the fifteenth century the ruble lost 60 percent of its value. According to the demographic-structural theory, the severe financial crisis had to result in loss of control by the state. The situation had become so dire that in 1445, when the Great Prince Basil II had to repel a Tatar raid, he could gather together only one and half thousand warriors. As a result, at the Battle on the Nerli, Basil II was defeated and captured by the Tatars.

With the Great Prince in captivity, the civil war flared up anew. The Tatar raiding parties crossed the Oka river, meeting almost no opposition; plundered the core lands of the Muscovite state; and enslaved peasants "without count." The multiple causes of the crisis were interconnected and fed on each other. Economic collapse and reduced taxes lead to military weakness, which resulted in the civil war and external raids. High sociopolitical instability in turn deepened economic decline, causing famine and depopulation. "And they spent the remnants of the Russian land while quarreling among themselves," wrote the Novgorod chronicler, summarizing the end result of the princely feuds (Lurie 1994:56).

8.2 Expansion (1460–1530)

The crisis of the fifteenth century resulted in a significant decline in population numbers. As a result, during the second half of the century Muscovite Russia experienced economic conditions that were typical of the beginning of a secular cycle: low population density, high land-to-peasant ratios, high real wages, and relatively low land rents. Foreigners who visited Russia during this period marveled at large forests and an abundance of grain and livestock (Barbaro and Contarini 1873).

As we noted above, real wages were very high during the period following the end of troubles (the daily wage was more than 20 kg of rye). By the early sixteenth century real wages had declined somewhat but were still at a relatively high level. During the 1520s an unskilled worker in Moscow earned 1.5 dengas (0.6 g S) per day (1 denga = 0.395 grams of silver). We need to translate this nominal wage into the real one. The most common grains grown by Russian peasants were rye and oats. One quarter of rye (4 puds = 65.6 kg) plus one quarter of oats (2.7 puds = 44.3 kg) made up the unit known as *yuft'*. Using this grain unit, we can translate the nominal daily wage of 1.5 dengas into 11 kg of "grain" (rye and oats). Such a real wage is approximately the same as the one earned by unskilled workers in Germany in 1490–1510, during the expansion phase of the early modern cycle (Abel 1980, Nefedov 2003).

As to the land rents, we know that the typical size of land worked by peasants in central Russia during the beginning of the sixteenth century was 15 desyatins (16.4 ha). Peasants were required either to pay the quitrent or to perform corvée labor for the lord. For example, the corvée duties consisted of working an additional three desyatins for the lord (two of which were cultivated in any given year under the three-field system). Thus, under the corvée system a peasant family cultivated 18 desyatins (19.6 ha) and had to pay to the lord the crops from three of them (that is, one-sixth of the total). Eighteen desyatins was a large amount of land, and in the Novgorod Land it was typically cultivated by an extended family consisting of seven to eight members, including two adult men, and employing two to three horses. It is probable that large families were also typical of the Central Region. The typical yield ratio of land sown with rye was 1:3.3; for oats it was 1:3.1.

As the calculations in table 8.1 show, the estimated per capita consumption for a typical household of eight persons cultivating 15 desyatins was 425 kg. The minimum per capita consumption of grain in Russia is 250 kg per year (this is higher than what we assumed for Western Europe, because we need to take into account the higher energetic demands associated with the cold Russian climate). Thus, the consumption level characterizing Russian peasants in the early sixteenth century was quite good, especially when we take into account animal husbandry and forest products.

The reign of the Great Prince Ivan III (1462–1505) "was the most tranquil and happiest time" in the Muscovite land (Soloviev 1989:III:169). Famine, pestilence, and Tatar attacks abated for a time. Government docu-

TABLE 8.1
Estimated peasant budget, Central Russia

Assumptions	*Local units*	*Standard units*
Total area cultivated	15 desyatins	16.35 ha
Planted with rye	5 desyatins	5.45 ha
Seed input, rye	40 puds	656 kg
Yield ratio, rye	1:3.3	1:3.3
Net harvest, rye	92 puds	1,509 kg
Planted with oats	5 desyatins	5.45 ha
Seed input, oats	55 puds	902 kg
Yield ratio, oats	1:3.1	1:3.1
Net harvest, oats	115.5 puds	1,894.2 kg
Net harvest, rye + oats	208 puds	3,403 kg
Household size	8 persons	8 persons
Per capita net yield	26 puds	425 kg

ments of this period contain multiple mentions of new lands brought under plow and the resulting growth of cultivated area (Cherepnin 1960:166). Ivan III conducted two censuses in the Novgorod Land, one during the 1480s and another around 1500. During the period between the censuses the population increased by 14 percent. Thus, the population growth rate was on the order of 1 percent per year (AHNWR 1971:48–50). No comparable data exist for the central region, but fragmentary evidence suggests that the number of peasant households in various administrative regions (*volosti*) or manors (*imeniya*) increased by a factor of 1.5, two, or even three. Integrating these and other data, A. I. Kopanev (1959) concluded that the population of Russia grew by 50 percent during the first half of the sixteenth century, reaching the level of 9–10 million.

The most densely populated regions were located in northwestern Russia around Novgorod and Pskov. In the Novgorod Land population increased faster than the cultivated land. For example, the population of Derevskaya District (*pyatina*) grew by 16 percent between the two censuses (the 1480s and around 1500), while the amount of cultivated land increased by only 6 percent. The peasant-land ratio in this district was only 7 desyatins, half of what was typical of the neighboring Shelonskaya District. Archaeological studies indicate that the density of settlements in Derevskaya District during this period (1480–1500) was higher than at any time in the past (Konetskiy 1992:43). Heavy clay soils, never used before, were brought into cultivation. Agricultural intensification is also indicated by the increasing use of fertilizers, which became widespread during this period (Shapiro 1987:6,14).

8.3 Stagflation (1530–65)

Population and Economy

Chester Dunning (1997, 1998, 2001) was the first to use the demographic-structural theory in the analysis of Russian history during the sixteenth century. He noted that population growth beyond the means of subsistence in Russia during the sixteenth century led to price inflation (in this following the conclusions of earlier studies; see Blum 1956, Mironov 1985).

Before 1530 the price of grain remained relatively stable, with rye costing around 10 dengas per quarter (6 g of silver per quintal) (AHNWR 1971:21–22). During the 1530s, prices began to increase. For example, in 1532 the price of rye in the Iosifo-Volokolamsky Monastery (between Moscow and Tver) was 22 dengas per quarter. During 1543–44, as a result of crop failure, the price increased to 35–40 dengas (Man'kov 1951:104).

Tracing the connection between overpopulation and inflation, however, is complicated by an uneven regional development. Thus, the earliest signs of stagflation appeared in the northwest well before they turned up in the Central Region around Moscow. Before annexation by Moscow the Novgorod Land was dominated by large landowners, who exacted heavy rents from their dependent peasants (up to half the crop). After the annexation, in-kind rents were converted to money rents for the state peasants, significantly lightening the burden on them. On lands given to the military servicemen (*pomestie*), however, the press on peasants changed little, and sometimes even increased (AHNWR 1971:173, 373). Thus, peasants working the land belonging to the gentry had to pay heavy rents of 10–12 puds (180 kg) per person. According to the calculations of historians, grain production on gentry-owned lands in the first half of the sixteenth century in Vodskaya and Derevskaya districts, after deducting the rent, was unable to provide the minimal level of per capita consumption, 15 puds or 250 kg (AHNWR 1971:III:178). Low levels of personal consumption exposed the population to greater risk of mortality during periodic crop failures. Additionally, the chroniclers noted that in the northwest, epidemics were particularly severe (AHNWR 1971:II:33, Soloviev 1989:III:312). Finally, many peasants may have responded to the increasing exactions of the gentry by flight. As a result, between 1500 and 1540 the population of Vodskaya District declined by 17 percent, and in the Derevskaya Region by 13 percent (AHNWR 1971:II:290).

In the most populated regions, thus, stagflation had already begun in the early sixteenth century, and this process was speeded up by the high levels of extraction by the state and the gentry. At the same time, there was significant variation, even within the northwest. The conditions in

Bezhetskaya and Shelonskaya districts were more benign than in Derevskaya and Vodskaya districts. The first two districts increased in population between 1500 and 1540. In some locations the population grew by 27–45 percent (AHNWR 1971: II: 32–33, 42, 235, 290–91). Stagflation was spatially heterogeneous, and some districts suffered from it more than others.

Documentary sources are much sparser in the central regions, but here too population growth led to the diminution of peasant land allotments. By the middle of the sixteenth century there were instances where two or even three peasant households were sharing the standard allotment of 15 desyatins (Kolycheva 1987:64). At this time an average household in Borisovskaya District, near Vladimir, had 7.5 desyatins, less than in Derevskaya District (Kolycheva 1987:64). In Belozerskiy District the average peasant household had only 6 desyatins, an insufficient amount to produce enough grain to last until the next harvest (Prokop'eva 1967:102).

Overpopulation led to chronic peasant indebtedness. Peasants borrowed from the monasteries (the chief moneylending institution in Russia during this period), and when they could not repay their debts they lost their land. As a result, land held by the Russian Orthodox Church grew dramatically, and toward the mid-sixteenth century the Church owned an estimated one-third of all cultivated land in Russia (Zimin 1960:80).

In the mid-sixteenth century, after a long hiatus, famines and epidemics reappeared in Russia. In 1548–49 there was famine in the north (Mankov 1951:31). In 1552 Novgorod and Pskov experienced a terrible epidemic. In Pskov 30,000 people died. In 1556–57 there was another famine in the north (and also in the Trans-Volga Region). Peasants left the regions affected by famine and migrated south. By the end of the 1550s 40 percent of formerly cultivated land along the Dvina river was abandoned (Kolycheva 1987:172–74). Kolycheva (1987:172) characterizes the situation as "a highly unstable equilibrium," precisely what we would expect during the late stages of stagflation.

The first signs of the impending crisis are thus observable well before the start of the Livonian War (1557–82), which is often blamed by historians for the economic decline of northern Russia in the second half of the sixteenth century. Russia at that time was not a tightly unified economic system. At the same time as the north suffered from overpopulation and its attendant evils, central Russia was still in relatively good shape. In the Trans-Moscow Land, for example, population growth continued until 1560, although all cultivable lands had already been brought under the plow (Ivina 1985:233). In 1560–61, however, the Trans-Moscow Land experienced a famine. Grain prices rose from 10 dengas per quarter thirty years earlier to 50–60 dengas (from 6 to 26–31 g of silver per quintal). The monks of the Iosifo-Volokolamsky Monastery blamed the dearth of land and increased state exactions for this calamity (Ivina 1985:166).

Population growth in the central regions drove the real wages down. In 1520 a day laborer earned 11 kg of grain, in real equivalents, while in 1568 his pay was only 3.6 kg per day (Nefedov 2003). In other words, the real wage declined during this half-century by a factor of three, reflecting population growth beyond the available means of production. A daily wage of 3.6 kg may appear sufficient for subsistence, but we need to take into account that day laborers were hired for restricted periods of time, so that most of the time they were unemployed. Even if we assume a very generous 200 days of paid work per year (a standard assumption for Western Europe), the yearly income would work out to only 720 kg of grain, which was not even enough to support three persons in Russia. In reality, the period of employment in Russia, given its severe climate, was less. For example, in the late nineteenth century the summer pay of day laborers was three times the daily rate at which laborers hired on a yearly basis were paid (Nefedov 2003).

Monastery records provide us with information about real wages for workers hired year-around. The pay of agricultural laborers consisted of an in-kind portion, which equaled 16 puds or 262 kg of grain, and a cash portion (*obrok*), which in the 1550s was 80 dengas (=118 kg of grain). Thus, in real terms the yearly pay was 380 kg, not enough to support even two people. Later we observe such a low level of real wages during the severe famine of 1588–89. In other words, the level of consumption during the decade of the 1550s was as poor as during famine years (Nefedov 2003).

Other indicators of overpopulation and rural underemployment are the flowering of crafts, increased trade, and growing urbanization. Peasants of the densely populated Derevskaya and Vodskaya districts of the Novgorod Land could not grow enough grain to support their families, and many of them became small-scale traders and artisans. As a result, numerous settlements appeared in these districts that specialized in handicrafts and trade (Bernadsky 1961:108, AHNWR 1971:I:117–18). By the beginning of the sixteenth century Novgorod had become a substantial city with 5,500 households and about 30,000 inhabitants, 6,000 of whom were craftsmen. In other words, almost all of the male adult population were craftsmen (Tihomirov 1962:303–7). Pskov, similarly to Novgorod, had more than 6,000 households and a population of 30,000 (Zimin 1972:120). Seventeen churches were built in Pskov between 1516 and 1533, almost as many as in Moscow (Zimin 1972:123), which, according to the official census, had 41,500 households (Herberstein 1988). Ten percent of the population of the Novgorod Land lived in cities, which was probably the upper limit of urbanization, given the low agricultural productivity characterizing this region and period. Both Novgorod and Pskov were repeatedly hit by epidemics. During the reign of Basil III (1505–33) the chronicles mention at least four epidemics in the north, whereas there is no mention of disease in central Russia (AHNWR 1971:II:33, Soloviev 1989:III:312).

Elite Dynamics

The top level of the Russian social hierarchy was occupied by the appanage princes, who were close relatives of the Moscow rulers. Basil II, Ivan III, and Basil III devoted much energy to reducing the appanages belonging to their relatives, but then they bestowed new ones on their junior sons, which tended to perpetuate the appanage system. After a series of victories of Ivan III over Lithuania, a number of Lithuanian princes transferred their allegiance to Moscow. These noble houses (such as the Vorotynskys, Odoevskys, and Trubetskoys) were considered equal in status to the appanage princes.

The second level of the hierarchy was occupied by "service princes," who included many descendants of the great princes who ruled the Vladimir-Suzdal Land before the rise of Moscow. Their ancestors voluntarily subordinated themselves to Moscow and often continued as governors of their ancestral lands after these were annexed by Moscow.

The third level consisted of the "Old Muscovite" boyars, such as Morozovs, Zahar'ins, and Chelyadins. The ancestors of these boyars were the closest henchmen of the Moscow princes when Moscow was still one of the small principalities in the Vladimir-Suzdal Land. The Old Muscovite boyars traditionally occupied the most important positions in government (the equivalent of modern ministries).

The princes and boyars together made up the magnate stratum of Muscovite Russia. Below them were the "gentry" (*dvoryane i deti boyarskie*), who served as mounted warriors in the Russian armies. The gentry were further stratified into those who were based in Moscow (the middle-rank elites) and the rest, who were based in the provinces. Many of the provincial servicemen were quite poor—they had land with four or five peasant households (or even fewer), and their lifestyle differed little from that of the peasants among whom they lived. The overall size of the elite stratum is hard to estimate, but we know that the number of gentry cavalrymen who served on the Oka defensive line during the 1520s was 20,000 (table 8.2). Thus, there must have been at least that many military elite households.

During the first half of the sixteenth century the Moscow rulers encouraged the expansion of gentry cavalry, who provided the bulk of the army. As a result, the number of gentry servicemen grew very substantially, although we lack reliable data to quantify this growth. By the middle of the century the stocks of available land (with peasants) that could be granted

TABLE 8.2
Some numerical data indicating elite dynamics (from various sources)

Period		*Total*	*Source*
1520s	20,000	Southern frontier army	Herberstein (1988:113)
1560s	100,000–120,000	Total Muscovite army	Skrynnikov (1988)
1580s	65,000	Southern frontier army	Fletcher (2003:77–78)
1580s	80,000	Total Muscovite army	Fletcher (2003:77–78)
1630	15,000	Southern frontier army	Chernov (1954:125)
1630	27,000	All servitors	Chernov (1954:125)
1651	39,000	All servitors	Chernov (1954:125)
1700	23,000	Gentry owning peasants	Vodarski (1977:49, 64,73)
1737	46,000	Gentry owning peasants	Vodarski (1977)

TABLE 8.3
Percent of gentry servitors in the Novgorod Land with estates less than 150 desyatins, between 150 and 300 desyatins, or more than 300 desyatins, 1500–1540

Year	*< 150 des.*	*150–300 des.*	*> 300 des.*
1500	22	30	48
1540	39	39	22

to new servitors were exhausted. In 1500 land granted to the gentry on condition of military service (*pomestie*) constituted 58 percent of arable land in Shelonskaya District of the Novgorod Land, but in 1540 it was 98 percent of the total. Similarly, in Bezhetskaya District this proportion grew to 99 percent by 1544 (Chernov 1954:25). As the number of elite servicemen increased, the average size of their land allotments declined (table 8.3).

Sociopolitical Instability

We can follow the dynamics of sociopolitical instability in central Russia by looking at the temporal distribution of coin hoards found in the Moscow region (figure 8.1). After a small peak during the first half of the fifteenth century (probably reflecting the fifteenth-century crisis; however, the Russian economy at the time was poorly monetized, and the overall number of hoards is too low to make definite conclusions), the number of hoards per decade fluctuated between zero and three, reflecting generally orderly conditions in the heartland of the Muscovite state. The first jump in hoard numbers is observed during the 1540s and extends to the end of the century. Then came a huge jump during the Time of Troubles, fol-

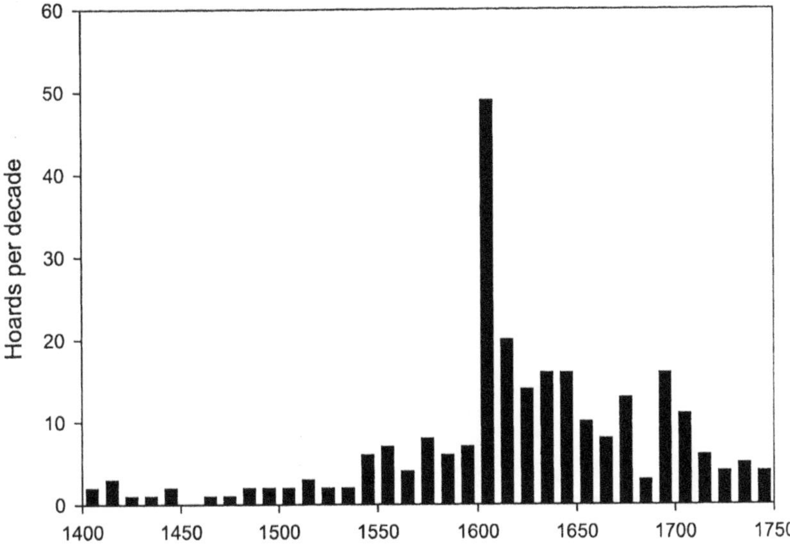

Figure 8.1 Time distribution of coin hoards found in the Moscow region, 1400–1750.

lowed by a gradual decline that was interrupted by another upsurge around 1700, followed by a low in the mid-eighteenth century.

The course of the narrative history is largely in agreement with the coin hoard dynamics. The reigns of Ivan III (1462–1505) and Basil III (1505–33) were characterized by internal unity and successful territorial expansion. When Basil III died in 1533, his son Ivan IV was only three years old. During Ivan IV's minority the state affairs were first directed by his mother, Helen Glinsky, and after her death in 1538 by the boyar duma (the supreme council of the state). The period of boyar rule (1538–47) was wracked by continuous strife between two noble clans, the Shuiskys and the Belskys. Power changed hands several times, and imprisonments, exiles, executions, and murders proliferated (Riazanovsky 2000:145).

The boyars divided the provincial governorships among themselves and sharply increased their demands (*kormlenie*) on the population (Soloviev 1989:III:436, 440). The magnates interfered in the process of distributing the service estates to the gentry. There is documentary evidence that the princes and the boyars seized large tracts of this land as their own (Kobrin 1980:172). The gentry felt themselves squeezed by large landowners, the lay magnates, and the monasteries. Litigation for land between the servitors and monasteries became common during the 1540s (Zimin 1960:76, 81).

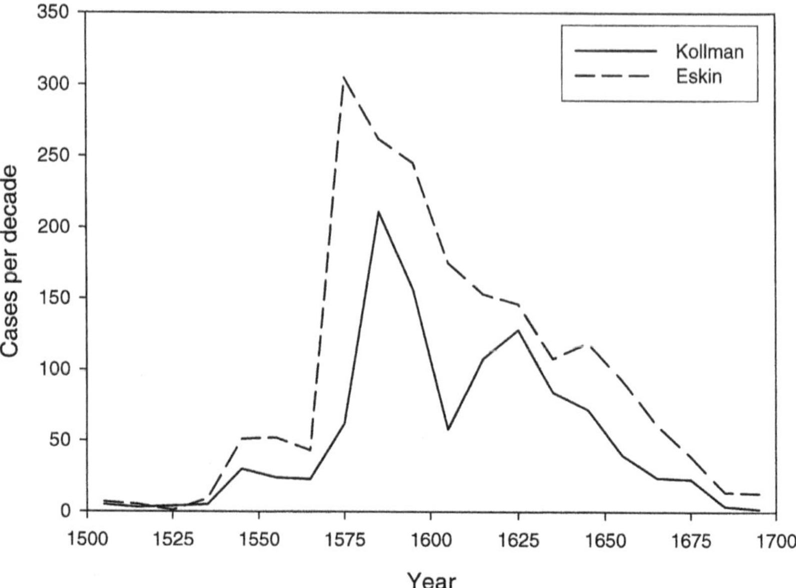

Figure 8.2 Precedence litigation in Russia, 1500–1700. The solid curve shows the dynamic pattern in the database collected by N. S. Kollmann; the broken line gives the dynamics in another databases, collected by Iu. M. Eskin (both sets of numbers are given in Kollmann 1999:138).

Another useful indication of intraelite competition and fractionation is provided by the dynamics of "precedence" litigation. Precedence (*mestnichestvo*) was a system of appointments for state positions, based on a hierarchical ranking of boyar families and prior service. Precedence litigations were disputes among the military leaders over service assignments (Kollmann 1999). Before 1540 there were only three to five litigation cases per decade, but during the 1540s it jumped to thirty (in the Kollmann database; see the solid curve in figure 8.2). Another huge jump, to over 200, occurred during the 1580s. Thus, the intensity of precedence litigation seems to provide a good leading indicator of intraelite struggles to come.

The failure of crops in 1546 led to a famine the following winter. When a great fire swept Moscow in June 1547 it triggered a popular uprising, the first one in the city since the foundation of Moscow Principality. The rioters wrecked the mansions of many boyars and killed one of the ruling magnates, Yuri Glinsky. The young tsar Ivan IV took matters into his hands. He repented publicly in Red Square and promised to rule in the interests of the people (Riazanovsky 2000:145). In 1549 he convened a zemskii sobor (Assembly of the Land, an institution similar to the Estates General), which

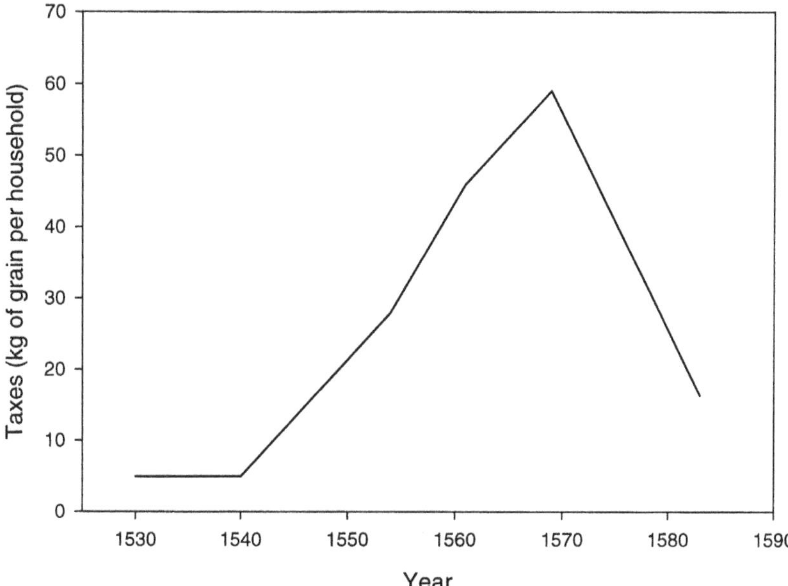

Figure 8.3 Dynamics of state taxes in Bezhetskaya District (in kg of grain per household) (Nefedov 2003).

further helped normalize the situation. The first two decades of Ivan IV's reign are known as the "good" half of the reign (Riazanovsky 2000:145). The government of Ivan IV undertook reforms of the military and local government and adopted a new law code.

Growth of Taxation

The good half of Ivan IV's reign also saw prolonged and intense external warfare. On the eastern front, Moscow was successful in defeating and annexing the lands of the Kazan and Aztrakhan Tatars (1552–56). On the western front, the Livonian War (1557–82) against the Poles and the Swedes resulted first in some gains, but it ultimately ended in defeat and loss of territory. Apart from the geopolitical goals of these wars, they also served the purpose of providing the elites, especially the impoverished ones, with employment and booty.

These wars were extremely expensive and resulted in a sharp increase of the state's press on peasants (figure 8.3). As we noted above, peasant consumption in parts of the Novgorod Land was already at the minimum sustainable level (15 puds or 250 kg per year) even before the Livonian

War. Extraction of an additional 3–4 puds (60 kg) of grain had to result in famine and epidemics. This is indeed what happened in, for example, Derevskaya District (AHNWR 1971: II:Table 36).

8.4 Crisis (1565–1615)

In 1565 Ivan IV created a separate institution, called the *oprichnina* (from *oprich*, apart or beside), that divided the state, the elites, and the whole society right down the middle (Riazanovsky 2000:150). Ivan established a separate administrative structure for the *oprichnina* and the rest of the country, the *zemschina*, which continued to be governed by the boyar duma. There were two sets of officials, one for the *oprichnina* and another for the *zemschina*. The countryside was also divided into two parts, and many landlords in the *oprichnina* territory were transferred out, while their lands were given to the new servitors of the tsar, called the *oprichniki*. Skrynnikov (1996) determined that more than 150 magnates, almost all of them of princely status, were removed to the Kazan Region.

In the beginning there were 1,000 *oprichniki*, but eventually their numbers grew to 6,000. Urged on by Ivan IV, the *oprichniki* instituted a reign of terror against the boyars, their relatives, and associates. A number of towns, the best known of which is Novgorod, were devastated by the tsar's henchmen. "It looked as if a civil war were raging in the Muscovite state, but a peculiar civil war, for the attackers met no resistance" (Riazanovsky 2000:151).

In essense, *oprichnina* was a coup d'état from above, in which Ivan IV used one segment of the elites (and elite aspirants) to wage civil war against the rest. Once the *oprichniki* played their role, they were in turn repressed. In 1572 Ivan declared the *oprichnina* abolished.

It was during this period of intense external and internal conflict (the Livonian War and *oprichnina*) that Russia experienced a demographic disaster of the first magnitude. The specific trigger was a poor harvest in 1567. By itself this was not an unusual occurrence—crops failed in medieval Russia on average every six to seven years. Normally such bad harvests did not result in a famine, because the peasants kept a year's worth of grain as a precaution. However, the increased press of taxation (figure 8.3), coming on top of an economic system stressed to the brink by overpopulation, meant that peasants could not afford to keep sufficient grain to tide them over a period of dearth. As a result, a major famine developed in the Central Region during the winter of 1567–68. Grain prices increased 8- to 10-fold. The crops failed again in the next year, the prices remained at the same high level, and the famine became worse (Skrynnikov 1975:162, Kolycheva

1987:177). In 1570 famine was followed by the plague. "It was one of those terrible epidemics of the Middle Ages that arrive roughly once a century and leave after themselves almost completely depopulated cities and villages," wrote E. I. Kolycheva (1987:178). The "Great Famine" continued on during the plague. There were numerous reports of cannibalism (Schtaden 1925:92).

Famine, plague, and intraelite conflicts weakened the ability of the state to repel external invasions. In 1571 the Crimean khan Devlet-Girey gathered together a huge host and invaded Muscovy. The Tatars attacked and burned Moscow, killing hundreds of thousands people. The territory around Moscow and south of it was devastated (Skrynnikov 1975:163, Kolycheva 1987:182). When the Tatars withdrew, they carried away with them 100,000 prisoners to be sold on the slave market of Caffa. In the late 1570s the Livonian War entered its final phase, the result of which was the loss of all territories conquered by Moscow earlier in the war, and even loss of some additional towns to the Swedes. The war finally ended with the peace treaties of 1582 with Poland and of 1583 with Sweden (Riazanovsky 2000:152).

We can assess the scale of the catastrophe of the 1570s by turning to the best-documented region, the northwest (Nefedov 2003). In Derevskaya District one-third of peasant allotments (*obezhi*) were deserted, owing to the mortality associated with famine and plague. Other allotments were abandoned by peasants unable to fulfill their tax obligations. In Derevskaya District three-fifths of allotments were deserted, although it is unknown what proportion was due to mortality and what to emigration. Parts of Bezhetskaya District lost 40 percent of population to famine and disease. Some idea of what happened in the Central Region can be gained from the conditions on the estates belonging to the Troitse-Sergiev and Iosifo-Volokolamsky monasteries. Around Moscow, where the impact of the Tatar invasion was the heaviest, 90 percent of previously cultivated land was deserted. In Suzdal District (*uezd*), the proportion of deserted lands was 60 percent, in Murom District 36 percent, and in Iuriev-Pol'sky District 18 percent. No doubt some of these lands were deserted as a result of peasants moving elsewhere. However, the magnitude of such emigration could not have been very great, because the Muscovite frontiers, where land was abundant, were particularly unsafe during the 1570s. The southern frontier saw three major invasions by the nomads, while the Volga Region was wracked by a rebellion. Thus, there was no region where peasants could move en masse, and it is likely that the numbers we have just cited bear witness to the huge scale of mortality affecting the Russian population during the 1570s (Nefedov 2003).

As usual, the population decline brought in its wake some amelioration of the economic conditions for the commoners. Thus, the daily wage increased sharply during the 1570s. The Vologda laborers in 1576 earned 3 dengas per day, while a quarter of grain cost 23 dengas. The real wage thus was 9.3 kg of grain per day, or 2.5 times greater than a decade before. In Iosifo-Volokolamsky Monastery the real wage of laborers also grew by a factor of 2.5. The pay of skilled workers, such as carpenters and tailors, grew twofold. Similar wage increases took place in other religious houses (Nefedov 2003).

Another sign of decreased population pressure was the fall of land rents (Nefedov 2003). The quitrent (*obrok*) on the gentry estates fell by a factor of three, from 10–12 to 3–4 puds per "soul." On the state-owned land the rents were approximately halved. Corvée obligations also declined by a factor of two or three (Nefedov 2003).

Thus, the demographic catastrophe of the 1570s led not to increased levels of peasant exploitation, as some historians have claimed, but, on the contrary, to a significant lightening of the burden. But this also meant that the ability of the state and the elites to extract resources from peasants using economic methods declined in a major way. In real terms, taxes paid by each household shrank three-, four-, or even fivefold, as in Shelonskaya District around Novgorod. The state revenues from the whole of Novgorod Land were halved by 1576, and in 1583 they were only *one-twelfth* the pre-catastrophe level (Vorob'ev and Degtyarev 1986:168).

The gentry servitors were also hard hit. Many estates completely lacked peasants to work the land. Only 7 percent of land was cultivated in Moscow District (*uezd*) and 25 percent in Kolomna District. In Derevskaya District more than a third of servitors had no peasants (AHNWR 1971:II:71, Kolycheva 1987:184). Lacking resources to support themselves, the gentry abandoned their estates. The Muscovite army, the bulk of which consisted of the mounted gentry servitors, lost half its number (Schtaden 1925:99, Skrynnikov 1988:13).

Ivan IV died in 1584. The reign of his son Fedor (1584–98) was a relatively peaceful period, even though Fedor was feeble-minded and the government was again in the hands of the boyars. This interlude between the periods of high political instability—between the *oprichnina* (1565–72) and the Time of Troubles (1604–13)—was probably due to the exhaustion of potential warring factions rather than any lasting solution to the basic contradiction between elite overproduction and declining commoner population.

The root cause of the continuing instability, which eventually led to the state collapse and civil war, known in Russian history as the Time of Troubles, was an acute shortage of labor, the economic distress of the elites, and the financial crisis of the state. The situation was similar to that of Western

Europe after the Black Death (see chapters 2 and 4), where the decrease in the supply of labor that drove wages up and rents down induced the nobility to employ extraeconomic, coercive methods in an attempt to maintain their revenues. In England and France these attempts failed, while in Poland and Prussia the elites were successful in enserfing the peasants (see discussion in section 1.1). Two centuries later in Russia under similar conditions the elites were also able to impose serfdom on the peasants.

However, enserfment could not resolve the economic problems of the elites. During the reign of Fedor (1584–98), the Russian army consisted of 80,000 cavalrymen, who received annual pay (in addition to service estates). Every year 65,000 cavalrymen served on the southern frontier guarding against the Tatar raids. Not all of these warriors were gentry, but, on the other hand, not all gentry received salary. Thus, by the end of the sixteenth century there were at least three times as many gentry servitors than in the reign of Basil III (1505–33), when 20,000 cavalrymen served on the steppe frontier. It is reasonable to assume that the overall numbers of the gentry increased by the same factor (three or more), whereas the commoner population was roughly the same as under Basil III, owing to the demographic catastrophe of the 1570s. In other words, the social pyramid became extremely top-heavy toward the end of the sixteenth century. It is clear that Russian peasants could not support such great numbers of the gentry, even if they were deprived of all of the agricultural surplus they produced. This contradiction could be solved only by abating the elite overproduction, which is what happened in the first half of the seventeenth century.

Enserfment was not a discrete event; rather, it was a process that occurred in stages spread out over many decades. A key period in the evolution of serfdom was the end of the reign of Fedor (1584–98) and the reign of Boris Godunov (1598–1605), when the government, under pressure from the gentry, issued a number of legislative acts that restricted the movement of peasants and extended the period during which a fugitive serf could be forcibly returned to his master.

Enserfment gave the landowners more power to extract surplus from the peasants. This is, for example, what happened at Iosifo-Voloklamsky Monastery, where the first attempt to increase corvée by 50 percent met with peasant resistance and had to be rescinded (Koretskii 1970:283–84, *Peasant History* 1990:257). Subsequent landlord initiatives were supported by the central authority. In 1601–3 corvée was doubled in many monasteries by the tsar's edicts.

Because of fragmentary data, no quantitative statements can be made about the conditions of peasants on the servitor estates. However, we know that petty gentry had very few peasants. For example, the average servitor in Tula Province was supported by only four peasant households (Koretskii 1975:86), but he had to equip himself for military service every year. As a result, the majority of servitors were compelled to deprive the peasants of all of their surplus, leaving them nothing with which to build up stores in case of recurrent crop failure.

The Time of Troubles

The socioeconomic situation in the first decade of the seventeenth century was in certain respects similar to that of forty years earlier, although during the 1560s it was the tax press of the state, not the elites, that pushed the peasants to the brink of survival. The trigger again was a very poor harvest resulting from cold and wet weather in 1601. Grain prices started climbing almost immediately. In the spring of 1601 a quarter of rye in the central region cost 30–32 dengas, but in the following fall it was already 60–70 dengas. In February 1602 the price of grain reached 1 ruble (200 dengas) per quarter (Koretskii 1975:11–19). In 1602 many peasants lacked viable seeds to sow the fields (because the early frosts in 1601 damaged the grain before it was harvested). In the fall, grain prices reached 3 rubles per quarter. The next year, 1603, the weather was good, but the fields were empty of crops, and the famine deepened (Skrynnikov 1988:38). Thus, the catastrophe was not due to "three years of incessant rains," as some authorities have proposed. In reality, bad weather was a major factor only during the first year of famine. Climate served as a trigger, but the explanation for the length and severity of the catastrophe must be sought in the top-heavy social structure that resulted in the relentless oppression of the productive class by the elites.

The great famine of 1601–3 had far reaching effects on the population, the state, and the elites. First, it resulted in vast suffering and an enormous mortality shock delivered to the general population. Avraamii Palitsin reported that 127,000 people were buried in Moscow alone (Palitsin 1955). Another witness wrote that "one third of the Muscovite Tsardom has perished from the famine" (Koretskii 1975:131). Starving peasants attacked the houses of wealthier peasants and servitor manors. Starting in the fall of 1602, banditry outbreaks became endemic in many regions (Koretskii 1975:208).

Second, it brought about the collapse of the state finances. The government of Boris Godunov went to extraordinary efforts to alleviate the suffering of the common people (Dunning 2004:69–70). It attempted to control the prices, but without success. The tsar then used the state's grain reserves, selling the stored surplus at half the market's price and distributing loaves of bread to the poor free of charge. Finally, the government was forced to spend huge amounts of money by giving away coins and bread to the poor in Moscow, Smolensk, Novgorod, and Pskov. In Moscow, for example, government agents distributed food and money to about 70,000 people every day (a large part of whom had migrated from the surrounding countryside). Eventually, these handouts had to be stopped because of depleted treasury (Dunning 2004:70).

Third, the famine created a huge pool of disaffected and desperate counterelites. Petty gentry were hit by the famine as badly as peasants. Many of them were forced to sell themselves into slavery in order to survive. In 1602 slave sales were nine times greater than in normal years (Dunning 2004:69). The trained cavalrymen, who sold themselves into slavery, were not employed in agricultural or domestic chores; instead, they joined the armed retinues of the magnates as elite military slaves. As the famine lengthened, the lords found themselves unable to support their large retinues, and many cut the military slaves adrift. These individuals were desperate, "armed and dangerous," and there were very many of them. According to a contemporary estimate, 20,000 former elite military slaves migrated to the southern steppe frontier, where they joined the ranks of disaffected cossacks and frontier servitors (Dunning 2004:72).

Unemployed military slaves, destitute servitors, runaway serfs, and cossacks from the southern frontier constituted a huge pool of manpower for the subsequent rebellions and civil wars. The first outbreak, the so-called Khlopko rebellion, was little more than a large band of bandits that operated in the Moscow region in the fall of 1603. Before they were finally suppressed they managed to defeat the government troops sent against them and kill their commander.

The next uprising (in 1604) was more serious and ultimately successful in toppling the state. It was led by an impostor who claimed to be Prince Dmitrii, the son of Ivan IV. False Dmitrii had started his invasion of Russia with the backing of the Polish magnates, but it is probable that the plot was initiated and secretly supported by certain boyar factions (Bussov 1961:100). The pretender had drawn most of his army from the southern frontier region, where a large number of frontier cossacks and servitors had recently been joined by massive influxes of former military slaves, destitute servitors, and runaway serfs. In April 1605 Tsar Boris died suddenly, and the magnate coalition, which he had until then managed to hold together, fell apart. Large segments of the elites went over to the False Dmitrii, and he entered Moscow in triumph in June 1605.

We do not need to describe the events of the ensuing civil war in detail. Suffice it to say that Dmitrii was overthrown and murdered by a faction of the boyars led by Vassili Shuisky in 1606. Shuisky became tsar but was deposed in 1610. Meanwhile a series of pretenders arose one after another, including another Prince Dmitrii who claimed to have miraculously escaped the death at the hands of the boyars. There was another popular rebellion led by Ivan Bolotnikov, and foreign interventions by the Poles and Swedes (at one point the Russian crown was offered to Wladyslaw, son of the king of Poland). In 1611 the continuing internal infighting and external invasions triggered a powerful unifying response by the Russian elites and people. In 1613 a zemskii sobor elected Mikhail Romanov, a scion of a prominent boyar clan, to the throne, thus bringing the Time of Troubles to an end.

The famine ended earlier: 1604 was a good year for the crops. The demographic catastrophe had its usual positive effect on the real wages. Servant wages in monasteries increased by 50 percent compared to the prefamine years (Nikolsky 1910). Rye cost 32 dengas per quarter, which was close to the prefamine level.

Thus, the years of famine and civil war resulted in another population decline, although its magnitude was probably not as great as that of the 1560s and 1570s. A shrinking population led to labor shortages and increased real wages. However, whereas after the first catastrophe the real wages increased by a factor of 2.5, after the Time of Troubles the increase was on the order of 1.5. The situation of the peasants improved, and the process of enserfment was de facto rolled back. Although all the laws tying peasants to land continued to exist, in practice they were unenforceable. It was very difficult to locate and bring back runaway peasants. This was a task beyond the resources of most gentry, and no government agencies existed to give them help. Furthermore, once the situation stabilized the government did everything to avoid further agitation among the peasants (Shapiro 1965:67). On the southern frontier, peasants were given a legal right to leave the estates of the gentry (Tihonov 1966:302).

The long and intense civil war shrank the elite numbers. If during the 1580s the numbers of cavalrymen who served every year on the southern frontier was 65,000, in 1630 only 15,000 of elite servitors were able to report for the frontier duty (table 8.2).

8.5 Conclusion

The end of the internecine warfare around 1450 created favorable conditions for sustained population growth. The second half of the fifteenth century was characterized by abundant land, relatively high consumption levels by the peasants, low grain prices, high real wages, and low levels of craft development and urbanization. Internal peace and order prevailed, while externally the state was involved in a series of successful wars of expansion.

The first signs of stagflation become visible in the Novgorod Land by the early sixteenth century, but in the Central Region they appear only toward the middle of the century. The stocks of free land for internal colonization had been depleted and land-peasant ratios became increasingly low, leading to high grain prices and low real wages and consumption standards. Reports of famines and epidemics became frequent in the chronicles. Peasants migrated toward cities in increasing numbers, towns and cities grew in population, and trade and crafts flowered.

Intraelite competition and fragmentation increased in the middle of the sixteenth century. The increase in the social tensions is manifested in the government's attempts at social reforms and in decreasing sociopolitical stability—for example, the Moscow revolt (1547) and the *oprichnina* of Ivan IV (1565–72). The stress of the Livonian War motivated the government to increase the tax burden beyond a sustainable level. Extraction not only of the surplus but of the resources needed for peasant reproduction brought the system to the point of collapse. The triggering event was two consecutive years of bad harvests (1567 and 1568). Since previous state exaction had left peasants no safety cushion, these natural calamities resulted in a terrible famine. Famine was followed by an epidemic and a disastrous external invasion by the Crimean Tatars. These factors together resulted in the population collapse of 1568–71.

The severe population decline resulted, as usual, in better standards of life for the commoners. However, the numbers of elites remained very high. Better wages and lower rents, combined with a smaller producing population, led to a drastic decrease in elite incomes. The elite landed servitors were the mainstay of the Russian army, but at this point the majority of them were unable to equip themselves and serve on the frontier. The government was thus forced to bind the peasants to land in order to give the servitors better ability to increase the rents. Enserfment resulted in a significant increase in the level of resource extraction from the peasants, especially by petty servitors who had only a few peasants to support themselves.

The sociopolitical instability of the 1560s and 1570s was followed by a relatively peaceful interlude in the 1580s and 1590s. During this period the population probably increased, but it was still far below the precrisis level. Thus, the basic contradiction between too many elite servitors and too few peasants was unresolved. The press of the landlords on the peasants resulted in the latter existing precariously on the verge of starvation, lacking any reserves in case of a poor harvest. The crop failure of 1601 triggered another massive famine. During the following three years, the general population experienced massive mortality, the state depleted the treasury while unsuccessfully trying to ameliorate the effects of the famine, and huge numbers of trained and equipped military personnel were left without any means of subsistence. The result was a bloody and prolonged civil war known as the Time of Troubles.

This internal struggle resulted in a reduction in elite numbers, but social equilibrium was not entirely attained. The second demographic catastrophe resulted in another population drop and an increase in the quality of life for the peasants, while elite incomes again declined. Thus, the economic position of the elites after the Time of Troubles remained difficult.

Chapter 9

Russia: The Romanov Cycle (1620–1922)

9.1 Expansion (1620–1800)

Population and Economy

The Time of Troubles delivered a terrible blow to Russia. Judging by census data, the population of the Novgorod Land in 1620 was half that in 1582 and one-tenth that in 1500.* On the estates of the Troitse-Sergiev Monastery, scattered over all central Russia, the cultivated area shrank by a factor of 10. Only one-eighth of the arable area in the Moscow Region was actually cultivated, according to the population census of 1626–29; of the rest, some was left fallow, but most sprouted forest (Got'e 1937:115–16, Degtyarev 1980:170, Vodarski 1988:54, AHNWR 1989:11). These regions, however, were the ones that experienced the worst devastation from the Livonian War and the Times of Troubles, and the total population of Russia declined to a lesser degree.

The Russian census of 1646 counted 551,000 peasant households and 31,000 urban households (Vodarski 1973:26). Assuming six persons per household and correcting for the undercount, which Vodarski estimated as 25 percent, we have an estimate of 4.5–5 million (Vodarski 1973). Kopanev (1959) estimated that in the 1550s the population of Russia was 9–10 million; thus, the intervening crisis reduced the population approximately by half.

Economic expansion gradually resumed during the 1620s. To a very large degree it was made possible by building the 800-km-long Belgorod defensive line that protected the southern frontier region from the Tatar raids. Farther south the fertile Black Earth Region started to be colonized in the mid-seventeenth century. The opening of the new fertile lands for peasant colonization from the central regions was a factor of huge importance for the subsequent history of Russia, because it removed the threat of overpopulation until the far future (and resulted in an abnormally long expansion phase).

Between 1646 and 1678 the size of the population (not counting the population in the annexed lands) increased from 4.5–5 million to 8.6 million. During this period the population of the Novgorod Land more than

* Following the practice of Russian historians, all dates in this chapter are given in the Old Style.

doubled, although still remaining a third lower than the level achieved in 1500 (Vodarski 1973:26–28, AHNWR 1989: Table 4). Population growth was particularly rapid in the south. By 1678 the population of the Black Earth Region had increased to 1.8 million people (compared to 3.5 million in the Central Region). The south became an important supplier of grain for the Central Region. By the end of the 1670s this region was exporting 1 million puds (16,400 tons) of grain, and government officials repeatedly and approvingly reported the growth of the grain supply that helped to reduce the prices (Vazhinski 1963:9).

Beginning with 1719 we dispose of detailed data on population dynamics, which were obtained by the so-called "revisions," regular censuses of the taxed population. When considering these numbers, it is important to take into account the substantial growth of the territory of the Russian state. To gain a better insight into the demographic dynamics, we will focus on the area that was encompassed by the revision of 1719, while excluding the territories that were gained later—Poland, Ukraine, and the Baltic regions.

The population of the Central Region (which includes the Moscow, Vladimir, Yaroslavl, Kostroma, Nizhny Novgorod, Tver, and Kaluga provinces) grew much slower than the population of the Black Earth Region (the Tula, Ryazan, Kursk, Orlov, Voronezh, Tambov, and Penza provinces) (figure 9.1).

Population growth rates fluctuated, and the general picture of rapid increase was punctuated by periods of much slower growth. As we discuss below, population growth slowdowns were a result not of overpopulation but of the occasional redistribution of resources in the state–elite–commoners system. For example, the crisis of the 1720s and 1730s was the result of a sharp increase in the tax pressure under Peter I that caused the famine of 1723–25. It has been estimated that around 300,000 people, or 3 percent of the total population, perished during this famine. The structural crisis of the 1780s was caused by an abrupt increase in the rent, which led to the famine of 1787–88 (Nefedov 2005:151, 182–83).

An abundance of free land suitable for cultivation meant that peasants were not stimulated to pursue crafts or migrate to towns. For this reason, the cities grew very slowly during the seventeenth century. Russian towns during this period served primarily defensive and administrative functions rather than being economic centers. Among town inhabitants, the various kinds of servitors—gentry, musketeers, or cossacks—heavily outnumbered craftsmen and traders. Vodarski (1966:279–89) estimated that the total urban population of 247,000 males in 1652 encompassed 139,000 servitors and 108,000 *posadskie lyudi* (people who pursued crafts and trade). The situation was much the same in 1678: 149,000 servitors and 134,000 craftsmen/tradesmen.

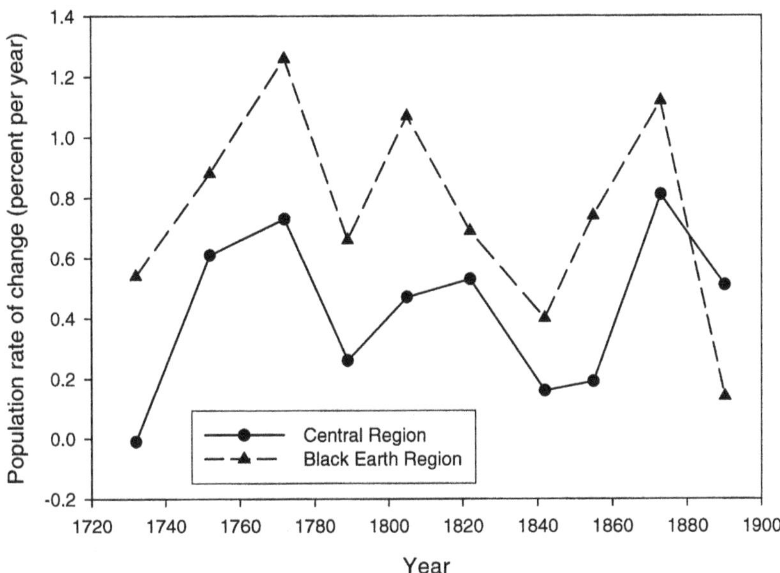

Figure 9.1 Rates of population growth in the Central and Black Earth regions, 1719–1897. Data from Rashin (1956:44–45, Table 19) and Kabuzan (1971a: Appendix I).

Slow urban growth persisted in the eighteenth century, and the military continued to be a substantial component of urban population. Between 1719 and 1796 the urban population (within the 1719 boundaries) grew by only 34 percent. In the more populated Central Region, urban growth was more substantial, 61 percent. According to the calculations of Mironov (1990:65, 71), the rate of population growth between 1743 and 1783 was 0.84 percent per year. The growth rate due to migration from the rural areas was only 0.04 percent, and the bulk of the growth, 0.8 percent per year, came from a natural increase in the urban population. The rural population grew much faster and, as a result, the share of the total population living in cities and towns shrank from 11.5 percent during the 1740s to 7.1 percent in the 1830s.

Contemporary sources indicate that during the seventeenth century, peasants were quite well off. Yury Krizhanich (1997:261, 286) noted that Russian peasants "lived much better than in the Greek, Spanish, and other similar lands, where either meat, or fish are very dear, while firewood is sold by weight." Adam Olearius (1980:329) testified that there was a great abundance of grain and pasture and large stocks of free cultivable land, and that in Russia one rarely heard about dearth.

Statistical data from several regions support the reports of Western travelers in Russia. Gorfunkel (1962:117), who studied the economy of Kirillo-

Belozersky Monastery, considered the period after the Time of Troubles the "golden age" of the monastery's peasants. According to the estimates of Kolesnikov (1976:301), the average amount of crops gathered per capita in Totem District (*uezd*) in northern Russia was 460–520 kg. In the 1680s–1690s an average household in certain monasteries in central Russia had between two and five horses. Peasant households on the gentry land owned on average of 2.2–2.6 horses and one or two cows (*Peasant History* 1990: 17). In Starorussky District during the 1660s an average household owned two to three horses and four to five cows (AHNWR 1989:126,134). An average household of the Pskovo-Pechorsky Monastery in 1639 consisted of five to six people, three to four horses, and four cows (*Peasant History* 1994:117). Even peasants who in the 1660s fled from the center to the south were not paupers; a typical household owned three horses and two cows (Novosel'sky 1945:60).

We are on even firmer ground when we consider the data on the real wages of rural workers. In the years 1640–47 the daily pay of an unskilled worker was 9 kg of grain. During the 1660s and 1670s, price inflation reduced it to 6 kg, but by the end of the century grain prices had fallen, and the real wage grew to 14 kg (Nefedov 2005:115). This was a very substantial level of consumption, similar to that of European peasants at the end of the fifteenth century (Abel 1973:189–92). This favorable consumption level was not exceeded in Europe until the nineteenth century.

During the eighteenth century consumption levels gradually declined. This trend is most starkly evidenced by the anthropometric data collected by Boris Mironov (2004), according to which the average height of army recruits declined by 4 cm during the century (figure 9.2). The decreasing tendency was not monotonic, however. For example, there was apparently a severe drop in the quality of life during the 1710s and 1720s, but during the next three decades the nutrition situation ameliorated, probably because of the increasing pace of colonization of the Black Earth Region. In the second half of the century the standard of living declined again. A particularly severe decrease occurred during the crisis of the 1780s.

Another important indicator of population growth is the price of grain (figure 9.3). During the reign of Peter I prices increased threefold. The end of the reign (1723–25) saw famine and structural crisis. After that, prices declined, and the general conditions became more favorable, although there was another famine in 1733–35. During the 1740s and 1750s prices stabilized at a low equilibrium as a result of the regular flow of grain from the Black Earth Region. A new period of inflation began in the 1760s, resulting in an abrupt jump in prices during the famine of 1766–68, which was made worse by rising rents. Finally, increasing demands on peasants by the gentry at the end of the eighteenth century did not permit the peas-

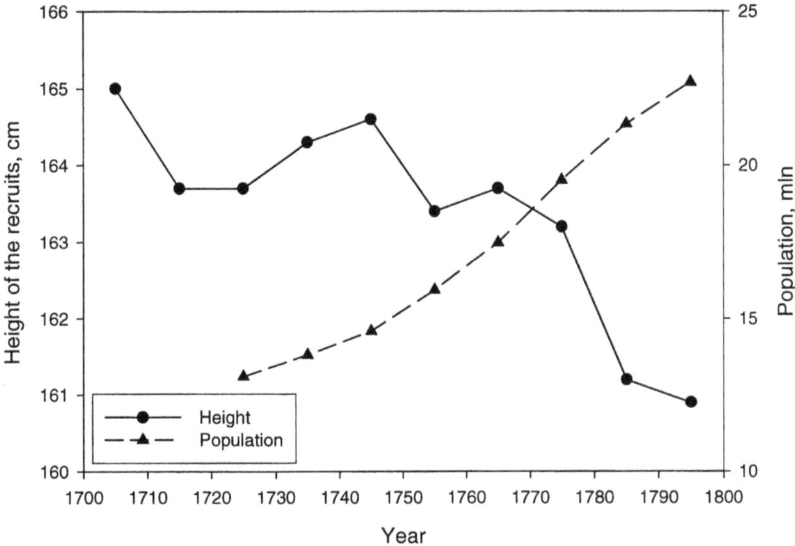

Figure 9.2 Average height of army recruits (plotted by year of birth) compared with population numbers (within the constant area of the first census). Data from Mironov (2004: Table 4) and Kabuzan (1971a).

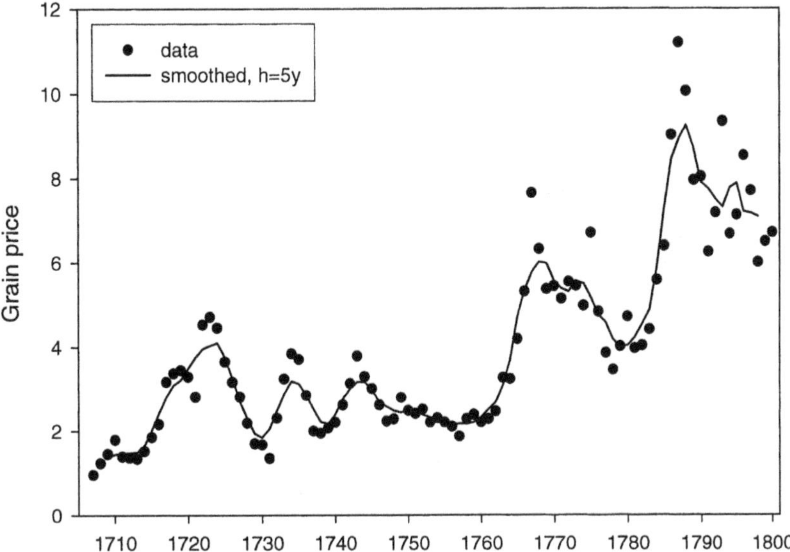

Figure 9.3 The price of one pud of rye in the Central Region in grams of silver (after Mironov 1985).

ants to build up stores of grain during the good years. The result was the structural crisis of the 1787–88.

The overall trend of price change during the eighteenth century thus fits the pattern predicted by the demographic-structural theory. However, prices grew not monotonically but in spurts, because they were affected not only by population increase but also by the colonization of the Black Earth Region and by the currency manipulations of the government, which introduced copper and paper money. The influence of the money supply was very substantial, because the amount of money circulating per capita of population increased during the eighteenth century severalfold. We can take this monetary inflation into account by dividing the nominal price index by the index of currency circulation per capita (figure 9.4).

The normalized price index (figure 9.4) suggests that the real fall in prices during the 1750s was much greater than suggested by figure 9.3. In other words, the organization of grain transportation from the Black Earth Region had a very real effect on grain prices in the Central Region. This effect, nevertheless, was a temporary one, and by the end of the eighteenth century continuing population growth had pushed the grain prices to a new peak.

The Elites

The confiscations of Ivan IV and the Time of Troubles delivered a heavy blow to the *votchina* (allodial) possessions of the boyars and the gentry. In Tver District, for example, in 1548 there were 318 *votchinas*, averaging 370 desyatins of arable land. In the 1620s, by contrast, there remained 197 *votchinas*, with an average size of 137 desyatins. Thus, the overall area of allodial lands shrank by a factor of 4.3. In the Central Region an average *votchina* had only 4.2 peasant households (Shvatenko 1990:29, 189).

The *pomestie* landowning system (estates held in return for service) also was in crisis, not because of a lack of land but because there were not enough peasants to work it. The estates of the wealthiest gentry, those based in Moscow, had on average twenty-four male peasants (including unmarried ones). In the provinces the conditions were much less favorable. In Shelonskaya District in 1626–27 an average gentry servitor possessed 3.8 households with 6.2 male "souls," and 35 percent of estates had no peasants at all (Vorob'ev and Degtyarev 1986:47, 48, 138). The combined effect of having fewer peasants and a two- to threefold decline in the quitrents meant that the gentry incomes were only one-tenth the level of a century before. The Swedish diplomat Peter Petreus reported that right after the Time of Troubles, the gentrymen could not afford leather shoes and had to wear *lapti* (peasant shoes woven from straw) (Kliuchevskii 1991:86). The gentry numbers declined. As we noted in the previous chap-

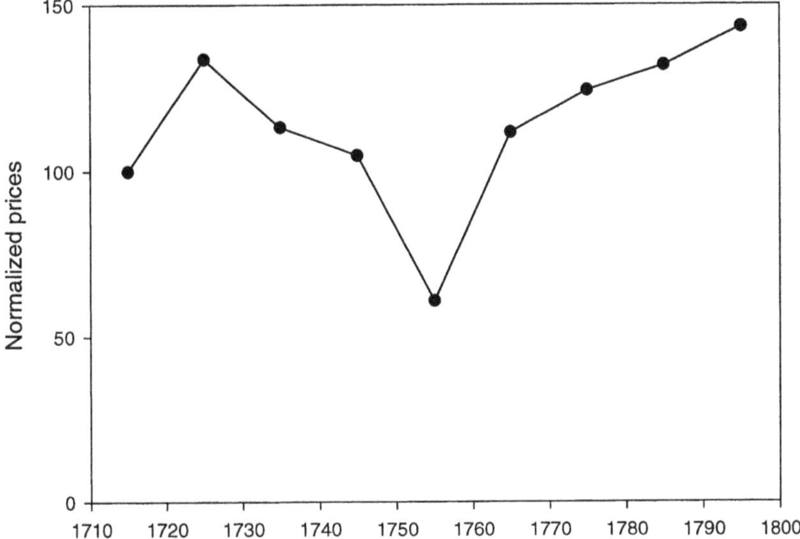

Figure 9.4 Normalized index of grain prices for the Central Region, obtained by dividing the nominal price index by the index of currency in circulation per capita.

ter, the nominal size of the gentry cavalry during the 1580s was 80,000, of which 65,000 actually served every year on the frontier. The comparable numbers for 1630 were 27,000 and 15,000 (Chernov 1954:125).

Although the gentry numbers experienced a dramatic decline, the socioeconomic balance between the strata was not yet regained. The gentry incomes remained very low, and the gentry servitors insisted on more effective control over peasants, which meant establishing serfdom. During the 1640s the gentry obtained what they wanted. Serfdom was fully instituted in Russia with the *Ulozhenie* (Law Code) of 1649.

Tihonov (1974:202) argued that the imposition of serfdom immediately led to the growth of *barschina* (corvée), which was one of the chief causes of the rebellion headed by Stepan Razin (1670–71). The uprising, in turn, forced the gentry to decrease *barschina*. Here we note the interesting parallelism between the events that followed the imposition of serfdom in the 1590s and 1650s. In both cases, increased pressure by the gentry on peasants triggered popular uprisings. However, the outcome of the peasant rebellions was very difficult. Unlike during the Time of Troubles, the elites were not divided during the 1670s, and the state was relatively strong. As a result, the uprising of the cossacks and peasants was speedily suppressed by the government forces. Nevertheless, in both cases the peasant resistance resulted in at least a temporary setback in the ability of the landowning elites to extract surplus from the peasants.

Economic conditions were also an important factor in determining the dynamics of surplus extraction. During the long and difficult war with Poland (1654–67), the government attempted to solve its financial problems by minting large quantities of copper money, which resulted in inflation and a rapid growth in grain prices. Trade disruption, a fall in the real value of quitrents (because of inflation), and increased expenditures forced the gentry to increase *barschina*. The postwar normalization of economic conditions, however, allowed the elites to decrease *barschina* and replace it with the quitrent (Nefedov 2005).

In the final analysis, the imposition of serfdom did not lead to heavier corvée demands on peasant labor. The quitrent also did not increase in nominal terms, although declining grain prices led to an increase in real terms to 3.5–4 puds per soul. The real gain of the landowning elites was not from any increases in the rent but from their ability to increase the number of peasants on their estates, as a result of new legal barriers preventing peasant escape. In the Novgorod Land, for example, the average number of male peasants per gentry estate increased from fifteen in 1646 to twenty-six in 1678.

As we discussed above, in the mid-seventeenth century a substantial proportion of gentry did not have peasants (*odnodvortsy*, or "single-holders"). The proportion of single-holders among gentry was particularly high in the southern frontier regions, where the government, beginning in the late sixteenth century, aggressively recruited servitors among peasants and cossacks. During the 1670s and 1680s the southern servitors were censused by government agents, and in the process of this revision single-holders were demoted from the gentry to the soldier rank. Later, under Peter I, single-holders were given the status of government peasants, that is, free peasants who were not assigned to any gentry (Vodarski 1977:62, Vazhinski 1983:44).

As a result of these changes in status, the gentry stratum was restructured and its size shrank. In 1651 the gentry servitors numbered 39,000, while in 1700 there were 22,000–23,000 gentry landowners (and serf-owners). An average gentry landowner had nineteen peasant households and sixty male serfs. The averages, however, do not reflect the great degree of inequality in land holdings. Forty-seven percent of gentry were smallholders who owned between one and five peasant households. On average they had 2.4 households and 8.8 male souls. By contrast, the wealthiest 464 nobles (2 percent of the total) owned 43 percent of all serfs, with each owning, on average, 355 households and around 1,300 male souls (Vodarski 1977: 49, 64, 73).

Between 1700 and 1737 the number of gentry estate-owners increased from 22,000–23,000 to 46,000, while the number of estates (some gentry owned more than one estate) grew from 29,000 to 63,000. At the same time, population growth was slow during this period, owing to the increased press of state taxes and declining levels of consumption. Thus, the number of elites increased faster than the general population did, and the average size of gentry holdings decreased from sixty to forty male souls (Vodarski 1977:77, Table 8). As a result, gentry incomes also decreased (Faizova 1999:50).

The size of the nobility relative to the general population continued to grow during the last half of the eighteenth century. Within the constant territory of the first revision (census) the proportion of gentry increased from 0.5 percent in 1744 to 0.59 percent in 1762, and then to 0.68 percent in 1795 (Kabuzan 1963:154). The number of peasants per noble landowner declined, while the proportion of impoverished gentrymen increased.

At the same time that the numbers of elites grew, so did their consumption levels. Many historians attribute this trend toward more luxurious living to the spread of European influence, or "Europeanization" (Danilova 1970:138, Kamenski 1999:290). The total consumption by the elite stratum, therefore, had to increase, either at the expense of peasants or at the expense of the state. The struggle for resources between the elites and the state went on during the reigns of Anne (1730–40) and Elizabeth (1741–62). In 1762 the nobility won a signal victory when Peter III abolished the gentry's service obligations to the state.

The "gentry revolution" of 1762 resulted in a significant redirection of resources from the state in favor of the elites. This process took the form of declining real taxes. The minting of huge amounts of copper money during the Seven Years' War (1756–63) resulted in a doubling of grain prices. Because the government was unable to increase the tax rate, which remained the same in nominal terms, real taxes were halved. The lightening of the tax load on the peasants gave the landlords an opportunity to increase quitrents (figure 9.5).

By 1794 inflation had eroded the state's exactions on the peasants to one-fourth the level of the first half of the eighteenth century (figure 9.5). The slack was apparently taken up by increased quitrents. Data on the growth of quitrent and corvée are available for only a few estates, one of which is fortunately the huge Yuhotskaya estate of the Sheremetevs. Another, although indirect, indication of the growth of quitrents on private estates is provided by the increasing quitrents imposed on the state peasants. The government-imposed quitrent probably increased in parallel with the quitrent of gentry-owned peasants, although at a lower level (Chechulin 1906:121). Thus, it is likely that the Yuhotskaya estate data reflect a typical pattern of quitrent increase for other gentry estates. The same trend was also identified by Mironov (1992: Table 6).

The data plotted in figure 9.5 thus suggest that until the 1750s, the curves of per capita taxes due to the state and rents due to the landowners

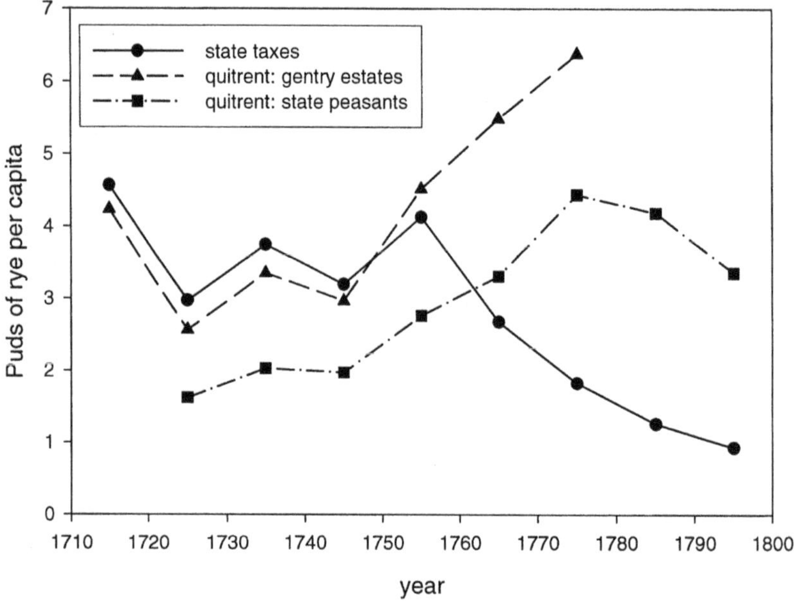

Figure 9.5 Dynamics of per capita state taxes and quitrents in the Central Region (Nefedov 2005). The data on quitrents in the gentry estates come from the Yuhotskaya estate.

moved in parallel. During the second half of the century the curves diverged. As the proportion of the peasant surplus going to the state decreased, it was not the peasant who profited but the lord.

In fact, the economic and legal conditions of peasants worsened during this period. The manifest of 1762 was the final step that turned the peasant into the property of the gentry (Beliaev 1903:283). The end result of this process was the famine of 1787–88, which forced the landlords to reduce the quitrent in real terms (figure 9.5). Paul I (1796–1801) reacted to the worsening peasant conditions by limiting *barschina* to three days a week. He also attempted to reimpose on the nobility the obligation to military service. These initiatives triggered another conflict between the state and the elites, which ended with a coup d'état in which Paul was assassinated.

The State

The crisis of the early seventeenth century weakened the state power and led to the collapse of the tax system. The reestablishment of government control was one of the most important tasks for the new dynasty. However, an attempt to increase taxes during the 1620s ran into resistance from both peasants and gentry, because higher state taxes had to come

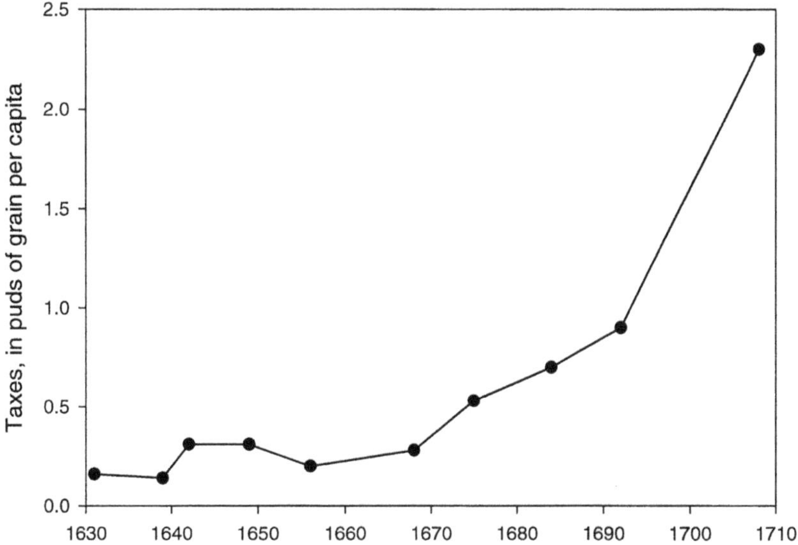

Figure 9.6 State taxes on serfs in puds of grain per capita (Nefedov 2005).

at the expense of the rent. The gentry bombarded the government with collective petitions (*chelobitnye*), and the government had to retreat (Veselovski 1916:488–93).

Higher taxes were rescinded not only on the lands that were worked by the state peasants, which were located mainly in the north and on the Vyatka river. The overall taxation level was mainly determined by the tax rate borne by privately owned serfs. In the 1670s this level was quite low (figure 9.6). During the second half of the century the taxation rate grew, reaching 0.8 puds per soul, but it was still far below the burden that the peasants bore during the time of Ivan IV (1.7 puds per capita). In other words, during the seventeenth century the state was unable to recover the taxation ability it had before the 1570s.

A dramatic redistribution of resources from the peasants and elites to the state was achieved only as a result of the reforms of Peter I (1682–1725). The capitation tax (*podushnaya podat'*), introduced by Peter I, replaced all previous direct levies. After the stabilization of prices in the 1730s, the capitation and salt taxes added up to 3.9 puds per soul. Compared to the pre-petrine period, taxes increased five- to sixfold (figure 9.6), while the military expenditures increased 2.5-fold (Nefedov 2005).

The high level of state taxes continued during the reigns of Anne (1730–40) and Elizabeth (1741–62). The "gentry revolution" of 1762, however, redistributed the resources in favor of the elites (as we discussed in the previous section). Being unable to compensate for the losses due to infla-

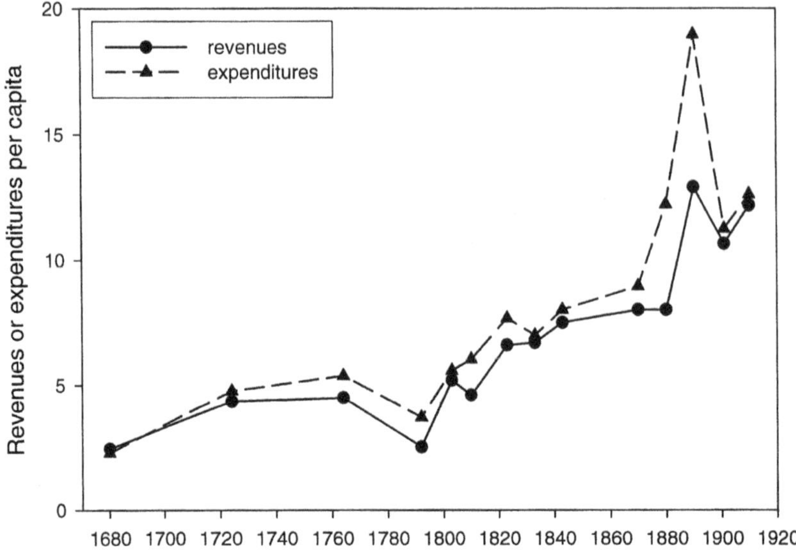

Figure 9.7 Real revenues and expenditures of the state budget per capita of population (in puds of grain). The revenues include direct and indirect taxes, but not state borrowing. Thus, the amount borrowed by the state can be seen on the graph as the difference between expenditures and revenues (the expenditures, however, include interest payments on loans). Data from Pogrebinski (1953: 93, 95), Belousov (2000:40, 42), and Nefedov (2005:169).

tion, Catherine II (1762–96) kept the state finances afloat by printing large amounts of paper money (*assignatsii*). The result was runaway inflation, and during the reign of Catherine prices increased threefold (compared to the price stability under Anne and Elizabeth). Inflation cut into the real revenues of the state budget, which forced the government to print more money, and so on. This vicious cycle persisted until the reign of Nicholas I (1825–55).

The real per capita taxes were halved during the reign of Catherine (figure 9.7). This was compensated somewhat by the population growth, which increased by 70 percent during this period. Still, the real state revenues at the beginning of the reign were less than at its end.

The financial measures undertaken under Paul I (1796–1801) attempted to compensate for the devaluation of the capitation tax. The tax rate was increased by 26 percent, from 0.9 to 1.2 puds per soul, but this was still only one-third the taxation rate under Elizabeth. The emperor, however, increased the quitrents of the state peasants by 33–66 percent, depending on the economic development of the province. Thus, peasants in the Central Region paid to the Crown 4.2 puds per soul, while in the Black Earth

Region the rate was higher, 6.7 puds. Overall, the state peasants paid the Crown about five times as much as privately held serfs (Nefedov 2005). As a result, under Paul the real state revenues increased from 2.6 to 5 puds of grain per capita.

Regional Variations

Different parts of the huge Russian Empire inevitably developed at dissimilar rates. The Central Region was the first one to enter the stagflation phase, which happened in the 1730s–1740s. The minimal amount of land necessary to support a peasant family during this period was 1–1.2 desyatins per capita (Koval'chenko 1967:264). Data from the Crown estates within Moscow Province (*guberniya*) suggest that in many districts, such as Khatunskaya, Selinskaya, and Gzelskaya *volosti*, the stocks of land fell to 0.5–0.9 desyatins per capita (Volkov 1959:22). The superintendent of Crown properties Baron Rosen wrote that peasants of Moscow Province were short of bread due to insufficient land and poor soils (Volkov 1959:22). The crop failure of 1733 caused famine and the flight of peasants. Between 1732 and 1735, one-tenth of the peasants fled from the Crown villages of Moscow Province. There was another famine in 1742–43. The Administration of Crown Estates took steps to solve the problem of overpopulation by moving peasants to Voronezh Province (14,000 were resettled in 1745). Despite these efforts, there was not enough land for all peasants, and one-seventh of households had neither horses nor cows (Alefirenko 1958:38, Volkov 1959:23, 40, Indova 1964:100–101).

Recurrent famines and peasant flight from the Central Region kept its population at a constant level of 4.5 million between 1719 and 1744, while the population of the provinces of Vladimir, Yaroslavl, and Nizhny Novgorod actually declined. Scarcity of land, recurrent famines, and population stagnation all suggest that the Central Region was in the stagflation phase at this point. The arrival of stagflation was hastened by the tax increases under Peter I. Whereas previously a peasant household could subsist on 1 desyatin per capita, higher taxes tipped it below a sustainable level.

The conditions of stagflation compelled an economic restructuring of the Central Region. First, the paucity of land resulted in a massive substitution of labor obligations (*barschina*, or corvée) with money obligations (*obrok*, or quitrent). By the 1780s the great majority of peasants in the Central Region (62 percent) were switched from corvée to quitrent (Rubinshteyn 1957:101). The transition to cash quitrents gave the peasants an incentive to practice crafts and trades. Up to two-thirds of peasants in Moscow District (*uezd*) supplemented agriculture with such pursuits.

Because serfs were bound to land and could not migrate to towns, crafts and trades developed in "industrial villages." These rural craftsmen had to buy imported grain to feed their families. Thus, the economic system that evolved in the Central Region during the eighteenth century was dependent on interregional grain trade. In other words, the continuing existence of population in the Central Region would have been impossible without the rise of grain plantations in the recently colonized Black Earth Region. The Black Earth Region became the granary of Russia, while the Central Region specialized as an industrial region. While population in the Central Region stagnated, in the Black Earth Region it continued to grow and, by the end of the century, exceeded that of the Central Region (Kabuzan 1971: Appendix II).

The southern landowners encouraged peasant immigration by offering reduced quitrents. Prince A. D. Menshikov required quitrents of only 2–3 puds per capita (Troitski 1968:125). This low level of quitrents persisted in the southern parts of the Black Earth Region (the provinces of Voronezh and Kursk) until the 1760s. The peasants there cultivated large plots of land, around 2.5 desyatins per capita, and even hired seasonal labor migrants from the central provinces (Rubinshteyn 1957:252, Milov 1998:205, 213)

During the 1720s, before the industrial specialization of the central provinces, the overall volume of trade in grains was 2.5 million puds per year (Rubinshteyn 1957:407). In the 1780s, the grain traded on the markets in only two Black Earth provinces, Orlov and Kursk, was 24 million puds (Rubinshteyn 1957:258, 404, Koval'chenko and Milov 1974:211–13). The interregional grain market encompassing the Central and Black Earth provinces formed in the 1740s and 1750s. The main transport arteries were rivers flowing north (Koval'chenko and Milov 1974:211–13). Evidently, it was the grain import form the south that caused the decline of rye prices in the Central Region: between the 1740s and 1750s prices fell by 20 percent (Mironov 1985).

9.2 Stagflation (1800–1905)

Population and Economy

Stagflation began in the central provinces of Russia in the mid-eighteenth century, while in the Black Earth Region overpopulation developed much later. Thus, the temporal breakpoint proposed here, 1800, is even more approximate than usual.

The economic dynamics of Russia during the first half of the nineteenth century were reconstructed from the reports of provincial governors (Koval'chenko 1959). Complete data are available for thirty-eight of the fifty provinces of European Russia (table 9.1a). These data allow us to estimate the average consumption level of the Russian population simply by

TABLE 9.1
Dynamics of population numbers, yield ratios, total crop harvested, and per capita consumption during the stagflation phase

Years	*Population (mln)*	*Yield ratio*	*Net yield (mln puds)*	*Net yield per capita (puds)*	*Export per capita (puds)*	*Per capita consumption (puds)*
(a) Data for 36 of 50 provinces of European Russia						
1802–11	28.8	3.5	696	24.2		
1841–50	38.9	3.5	818	21.0		
1851–60	42.7	3.4	806	18.9		
(b) Data for the 50 provinces of European Russia						
1851–60	58.4	3.4	1107	19.0	1.0	18.0
1861–70	62.1	3.5	1190	19.2	1.6	17.6
1871–80	69.6	3.9	1399	20.1	3.4	16.7
1881–90	79.8	4.3	1690	21.2	4.8	16.4
1891–1900	91.8	5.0	2084	22.7	4.8	17.9
1900–10	108.1	5.4	2612	24.2	5.6	18.6

Source: Data for 36 of 50 provinces (a) from Kovalchenko (1959). Data for the 50 provinces of European Russia (b) from Nefedov (2005).

Note: For the period before 1850, data are available only on 36 of the 50 European provinces of Russia. Per capita consumption (last column) for the period after 1850 is calculated by subtracting grain exports from the net crops.

dividing the net production of crops per year by the number of people. This approach works until 1850, because grain export up until that date was negligible in comparison to the total production (2.7 million puds per year in 1841–45, or about 2 percent of the total).

As population increased during the first half of the nineteenth century (table 9.1a) personal consumption declined from a high level near 24 puds to a level below 19 puds per capita. In other words, we see here the classic Malthusian mechanism in action—population growth overtaking increases in production, resulting in falling rates of consumption per capita. The population growth rate also declined, from 0.91 percent per annum in 1795–1833 to 0.58 percent in 1834–50 and 0.49 percent in 1851–57 (calculated from data in Kabuzan 1963: Table 17).

During the first two decades after the emancipation of the serfs in 1861, the economy of Russia entered a period of deep restructuring. One of the important drivers of the change was the building of railroads that connected interior provinces with seaports and international trade. The average export of grain in early 1840s was 27 million puds per annum, but by the late 1880s it had become 257 million, or 23 percent of the net grain production in the whole of Russia (Pokrovski 1947: 251, 317–18).

The second important trend was the growing agricultural productivity–yield ratios increased from 3.4 to 5.4 between 1850 and 1910 (table 9.1b).

The third trend was the continuing population growth (table 9.1b). From the point of view of personal consumption levels, the three trends essentially canceled each other. As we see in table 9.1b, the level of personal consumption slightly declined toward the 1880s and then increased. By the early twentieth century it was at about the same level as in the mid-nineteenth century. In other words, the gains of increased agricultural productivity were eaten up by the combined effects of population growth and grain exports. This informal argument is supported by the quantitative model, based on empirically determined parameters, for the dynamics of carrying capacity in the fifty provinces of European Russia between 1850 and 1910 (Nifontov 1973: Tables 23, 28, 40, 47; Nefedov 2005:253–54).

The Statistical-Economic Department of the Food Supplies Ministry calculated in 1918 that the minimal level of grain consumption needed to support a household (including food for people and supplementary forage for the domestic animals) was 18.7 puds per year (Losinsky 1918:23, 28). Although domestic animals required less grain during the second half of the nineteenth century than in 1918 (more land was available for pasture and haying), it still seems reasonable to conclude that during the second half of the nineteenth century, personal consumption fell to or below the minimal sustainable level (table 9.1b). Furthermore, the numbers in table 9.1b represent averages that hide important heterogeneities in the peasant condition resulting from both growing economic inequality and temporal variation in yields due to climate fluctuations. Even B. N. Mironov, who argued for a more optimistic view of peasant conditions around 1900 than most Russian historians, estimated that 30 percent of the peasantry was chronically malnourished (Mironov 2002:37). This proportion must have increased during the periods of crop failure.

The Effect of the Great Reforms on the Peasants

The emancipation of the serfs in 1861 dramatically reduced the demands of landowners on the peasants, because the quitrent was substituted with much smaller redemption payments (payments that peasants owed their former owners as compensation for the land). On the negative side, however, former serfs lost part of the land they worked prior to the reforms. In the Black Earth Region the average amount of land held by peasants was reduced from 1.54 to 1.28 desiatins per capita. This plot included non-arable land (used for pasture, haymaking, etc.). The arable part was about 1 desyatin per capita, which yielded at the time 14 puds of grain, not enough to support even one person, and peasants had to pay redemption payments and taxes.

The economic position of the state peasants, however, was much better than that of the former serfs. In the Black Earth Region the former state peasants owned an average of 2.4 desyatins of land per capita. However,

TABLE 9.2
Social structure of the Russian peasantry, 1600–1900

Years	*Wealthy*	*Middle*	*Poor*
1600–1750	15	53	32
1751–1800	10	48	42
1801–1860	16	56	30
1896–1900	18	23	59

Source: Mironov (1985: table 6).

Note: Wealth is estimated by the number of houses, with the poorest having zero to one, the middle category two, and the wealthy more than two. The table shows the percentage in each class at each date.

the continuing population growth during the post-reform period eroded land possessions of even the state peasants: between 1877 and 1905 the average amount of land per household decreased from 15.1 to 12.5 desyatins. Former serfs fared even worse: their average landholdings decreased from 8.9 to 6.7 desyatins.

Thus, the post-reform Russian peasantry stratified into two groups that were comparable in size. The former state peasants were relatively well off, while the former serfs started at a serious disadvantage, and most were destined for poverty. In addition, rapid population growth during the second half of the nineteenth century under the conditions of stagflation was a potent force driving increased economic inequality (table 9.2). Thus, although the average level of consumption may have stayed at approximately the same level, a growing proportion of peasants were poor and led a precarious existence.

An even more dangerous factor was the temporal variability in yields, especially when several poor years came one after another (Wheatcroft 1991). Between 1870 and 1914 there were two such periods in Russia—in 1889–92 and 1905–8 (figure 9.8). The famine of 1891, following a sequence of poor harvest years that exhausted grain stores, caused 400,000 fatalities (Robbins 1975:171). The poor harvests during 1905–7 were one of the triggers of the revolution.

Urbanization

Between 1863 and 1914 the proportion of the population living in towns increased from 9.9 percent to 14.4 percent (table 9.3). The "industrial" provinces, located in the Central and Northwestern regions, however, urbanized at a much more rapid rate than the agrarian provinces (located mostly in the Black Earth Region).

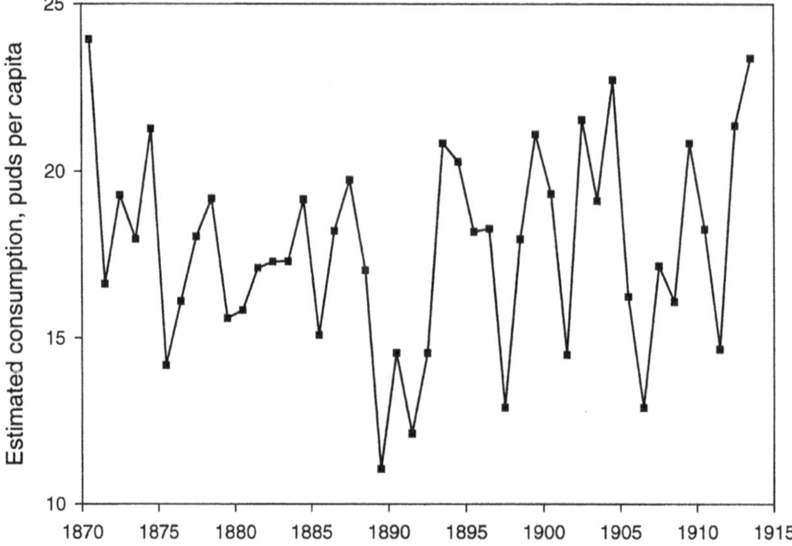

Figure 9.8 Per capita consumption of grain in European Russia, estimated by subtracting grain exports from net yields (Nefedov 2005).

TABLE 9.3
Urbanization in Russia between 1863 and 1914

Region	*1863*	*1897*	*1914*
Industrial provinces	14.1	21.5	25.0
Agrarian provinces	8.3	10.0	10.3
All European Russia	9.9	12.9	14.4

Elites

As we discussed earlier, the proportion of nobles in the total population increased during the eighteenth century. This process continued during the next century (tables 9.4 and 9.5). The majority of the nobility were petty gentry who had few or even no peasants. The government was concerned about this "noble proletariat" and took steps to reduce their number. Nicholas I (1825–55) issued an edict in accordance with which impoverished gentry were reclassified as single-holders or state peasants. As a result, the numbers of petty gentry declined substantially in the two decades following 1838.

The social structure of territories formerly with Poland-Lithuania, which was annexed in the late eighteenth century, was quite different. Within Russia proper in 1795 there were 112,000 male nobles, while in the annexed territories the *szlachta* numbered 251,000. There were only

TABLE 9.4
Numbers of nobility (males only) in European Russia (in the constant territory within the borders of 1772), 1782–1858

Year	*Nobles (thousands)*	*Personal nobles (thousands)*	*Nobles per total population (%)*	*Serfs per noble*
1782	84		0.64	76
1795	112		0.77	64
1816	156	66	0.92	48
1834	166		0.80	52
1850	190		0.82	45
1858	218	94	0.84	39

Source: Kabuzan (1971b: tables 1–3).

TABLE 9.5
Numbers of hereditary nobles in Russia, 1858–1897

Year	*Nobles (thousands)*	*Average estate size (desyatins) (Black Earth Region)*
1858	234	
1870	305	176
1897	478	104

Source: Korelin (1979:40, 292–93).
Note: The numbers given are for the forty-one provinces of European Russia, excluding the nine western provinces that were part of Poland-Lithuania, because in these provinces the *szlachta* was a very high proportion of the population.

fourteen peasants per noble in Poland-Lithuania, while in Russia the ratio was 64:1. The petty Polish nobility took the land away from peasants on a massive scale, "compensating" them with monthly payments of grain that were barely enough to survive on. One government report noted that "the misery of the serfs is extraordinary . . . peasants, especially those belonging to petty landlords, find themselves in calamitous and oppressed conditions" (cited in Shepukova 1959: 132).

The numerical growth of the noble estate was not the only reason for the increased demands on the peasants. Exposure of the Russian nobles to European fashions after the Napoleonic Wars fueled the rise of conspicuous consumption. The content analysis of several dozen memoirs suggests that the lifestyle of four-fifths of the large landowners could be described as one of "conspicuous luxury," "aggressive, unrestrained luxury," "ostentatious splendour," or "extravagance." Poorer gentry attempted to follow the luxury standards set by their betters, with disastrous consequences for their finances (Smahtina 2003:58, 60–61).

The emancipation of the serfs in 1861 resulted in a sharp redistribution of resources from the nobility to the peasants. The quitrent and corvée were replaced with redemption payments and state taxes. Although the freed serfs were compelled to rent land from the gentry, because most did not have enough of their own, on balance, the revenues of the former serfholders suffered.

The emancipation of the serfs caused serious dislocations for the landowners who specialized in producing grain for the market, especially those who relied on corvée labor. Many were unable to adapt to the new conditions and failed. Between 1862 and 1877, the number of gentry-owned estates contracted by 11,000, or 8.4 percent of the total. Twelve percent of the land held by nobility was lost to other social estates (*sosloviya*). The nobles sold 21 percent of their lands in the Central Region and 12 percent in the Black Earth Region. The estates belonging to ruined gentry were bought by the merchants and the petty bourgeois (Korelin 1979:56–57)

The nobility understood that it could not reverse the reforms, so it demanded other kinds of reparations from the state. One such compensation could be an aristocratic constitution that would transfer part of the power of the monarchy to the nobility (Sladkevich 1962:76, Hristoforov 2002:47). An 1862 report to the emperor by the minister of internal affairs P. A. Valuev stated that the nobility "aims at a certain degree of participation in the administration. Until their objectives are to a certain extent satisfied, there will be neither peace nor truce" (Valuev 1958:143). Eventually the government was forced to make concessions and created a system of self-government (*zemstvo*) in the provinces (*gubernii*) and the districts (*uezdy*). P. A. Valuyev wrote in his diary that the court used the establishment of the *zemstvo* as a means to avoid having a constitution foisted upon them (Valuev 1961:241). *Zemstvo* councils were elective organs whose members were selected separately from three classes: the landowners, the townspeople, and the peasants. The nobles, however, played the dominant role. Eighty-five percent of members of the provincial assemblies in 1865–67 came from the nobles and merchants. *Zemstvo* assemblies assigned and gathered local taxes; however, *zemstvo* self-government was limited to economic issues, while matters of law and order remained within the purview of the provincial governors.

Another way in which impoverished nobles could compensate for the falling revenues from the land was through government service. Education provided credentials that gave an advantage in the competition for the jobs, so the gentry youth entered the colleges and universities en masse (Leikina-Svirskaya 1971:56–57, Korelin 1979:96). About half of the students in the middle schools and the universities were the children of nobles and government officials. Most students were very poor. A combination of abject poverty and exposure to new social ideologies from Western Europe, such as Marxism, radicalized the students (Leikina-Svirskaya 1971, Brower 1975:230).

Between 1860 and 1880 the number of students in the middle schools increased from 17,800 to 69,200, while the number of university students grew from 4,100 to 14,100 (Leikina-Svirskaya 1971:51–57). This period saw the formation of a new social stratum, the *intelligentsia*, which grew together with the expansion of education. The elite overproduction was the most important process underlying the formation of the intelligentsia, half of which had personal roots in the noble estate.

The state was unable to find employment for all gymnasium and university graduates. Whereas the number of students increased fourfold, the size of the government bureaucracy increased by only 8 percent from 119,000 to 129,000. Even if we add to this number the 52,000 new *zemstvo* positions, it is still evident that only a minority of elite aspirants could be employed. Faced with poor employment prospects, many students found the alternative pursuits, such as revolutionary activity, an attractive option (Bergman 1983:11). Sixty-one percent of the revolutionaries of the 1860s, the "nihilists," were students or recent graduates, and an even larger proportion (70 percent) were children of nobles or officials (Leikina-Svirskaya 1971:298, 302).

A decade later, the revolutionaries were still heavily recruited from the elite strata. Out of 1,665 radicals who were arrested in 1873–79, 28.2 percent were nobles, 16.5 percent were clergy, and 13.4 percent were military. Only a minority were of peasant origin (13.5 percent), and the same proportion were petty bourgeois. Thirty-eight percent of the leadership of the radical "Popular Will" organization had noble origins, 10 percent came from the clergy, and 7 percent from the merchant estate. Two-thirds of these professional revolutionaries studied in the university, but half of those failed to graduate because of lack of money or antigovernment activity (Itenberg 1965:374).

During the post-reform period the process of noble impoverishment continued apace. The government attempted to slow down this process by offering subsidized credits to the gentry. Despite this aid, the amount of land owned by the nobility continued to shrink (table 9.6). At the same time, the numbers of personal nobles doubled (table 9.5).

Between 1877 and 1905 the proportion of petty gentry increased from 50 to 59 percent of the total. These petty noblemen owned tiny parcels of land, on average 30 desyatins, or not much larger than the land owned by well-off peasants. The Special Commission of 1892 noted that these estates could hardly serve as sufficient means of supporting the level of consumption that was expected by this social stratum (*soslovie*) (Solov'ev 1979:205).

TABLE 9.6
Total amount of land owned by the nobility in Russia, 1861–1905

Year	*Desyatins (mln)*
1861	77.8
1877	73.1
1892	57.7
1905	53.2

Source: Solov'ev (1979:200).

The State

An important trend during the first half of the nineteenth century was the weakening of the influence of the nobility on the state (Mironov 2000). Nicholas I (1825–55) resuscitated the policies of Paul I (1796–1801) and attempted to reestablish a centralized bureaucratic apparatus. One reflection of the increasing power of the state was the growth of the Crown revenues (figure 9.7). In real terms the revenues per capita of population increased from 5.2 to 7.6 puds. The government was unwilling or unable to increase direct taxes on the serfs and instead relied on indirect taxes and increased rents on the state peasants.

The growth of revenues permitted the state to maintain the high level of military expenditures that was reached during the Napoleonic Wars. In 1833 Russia was the most powerful European state, with an army of 860,000, or 1.43 percent of the total population (compared to 0.83 percent under Catherine II). However, the Industrial Revolution, which gathered steam in northwestern Europe after 1800, transformed the balance of forces within Europe. The result was a defeat in the Crimean War (1853–56), which forced Russia into social reforms.

The most important task was the emancipation of the serfs, because the war resurrected the elite fears of a peasant uprising at a time when the state's attention was concentrated on prosecuting the war. Grand Duke Constantine, after reading De Toqueville's book on the French Revolution, remarked, "if we do not carry out a peaceful and complete revolution with our own hands, it will inevitably happen without us and against us" (Druzhinin 1946:536). His brother Alexander II (1855–81) expressed the same sentiment in his address to the Moscow nobility: "We live in such an age that it will happen sooner or later. I think you are of the same mind as me: it would be better to begin to abolish the serfdom from above than to wait until it abolishes itself from below" (*Golos* 1916:393). In the end, the Great Reform of 1861 was successful in reducing the social tensions while redistributing resources from the nobility to the peasantry and the state.

Emancipation of the serfs allowed the state to increase taxes, including the capitation tax on the former serfs, something the government was unable to do previously because of resistance from the nobility. In 1861–67 the capitation tax increased almost twofold. In 1863 the government introduced the real estate tax on urban properties. In 1872 it started taxing the land of the nobility. Although this land tax was not initially very large, its introduction marked the end of an important noble privilege, freedom from direct taxation. Despite these and other tax increases, the state revenues stayed practically flat in real terms because of rapid inflation (figure 9.7).

The changing geopolitical environment required from Russia a rearmament of the army and huge investments in new industries and railroads. The conditions of stagflation meant, however, that the state was chronically short of financial resources and was forced to borrow heavily. Between 1861 and 1880 the government borrowed more than 1.6 billion rubles. As a result, in 1885–95 the interest on the loans exceeded 40 percent of the government budget, that is, twice the amount spent on the military.

Intensifying geopolitical competition forced the government to take further steps to increase its revenues. Between 1887 and 1890 the new minister of finances, I. A. Vyshnegradsky, increased customs tolls and indirect taxes, which allowed him to raise the tax burden on the population to a new level (figure 9.7). In 1897 the state monopoly on alcohol production was imposed, which yielded a quarter of revenues during 1900–1903. After 1890, real taxes exceeded and stayed above the level of 10 puds per capita (figure 9.7), which allowed the government to more than double the military expenditures, from 210 million rubles in the 1880s to 490 million rubles in 1900–1903.

Sociopolitical Instability

The growing demands on the serfs during the first half of the nineteenth century met with increasing peasant resistance (figure 9.9). The great majority of disturbances occurred on the gentry-owned estates, reflecting the growing difference in the social and economic conditions between serfs and state peasants. According to the data examined by V. A. Fedorov, 59 percent of disturbances in the Central Region were caused by the new impositions on the peasants, such as increased quitrent or corvée, dispossession of land, and harsh punishments. A change in owner caused 20 percent of disturbances, because it was often associated with worsening peasant conditions, or it raised hopes of emancipation (some landlords made such provisions in their wills). Another 15 percent resulted from rumors of emancipation by the tsar's decree.

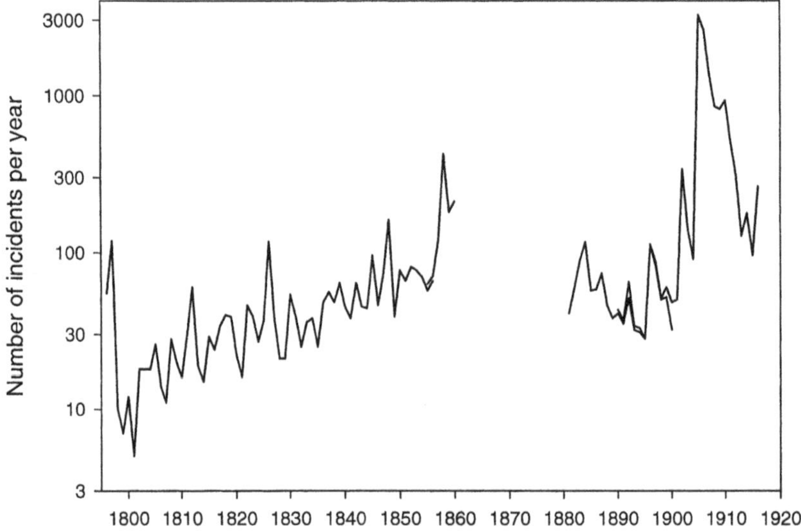

Figure 9.9 Dynamics of peasant disturbances. Data for 1796–1856 and 1881–1900 are from Litvak (1967: Table 1), for 1855–60 from Zayonchkovski (1963), and for 1890–1916 from Dubrovsky (1956). Note the logarithmic scale of the *y*-axis.

In an average year only 0.3 percent of peasants in the Central Region took part in such actions (Litvak 1967:46). However, the massive eruptions that occurred in 1797, 1812, 1826, and 1848 (figure 9.9) caused much concern among government officials, who were afraid that the accumulated social pressure could find an outlet in a general peasant uprising. The main cause of the unrest in 1796–97 was the peasant expectations of serfdom abolition that had been raised by the reforms of Paul I. In 1826 similarly the peasants hoped for changes following the beginning of the new reign of Nicholas I. When instead the peasants were confronted with rising rents, rioting affected some of the largest noble estates with thousands of serfs. For a while the noble landlords were afraid the disturbances would grow into a "Second Pugachev Rising" (Litvak 1967:46, Rahmatullin 1990:169–70). Another high point of peasant rioting occurred in 1848. Several factors played a role, including famine and a cholera pandemic. There were also emancipation rumors triggered by the 1847 decree that allowed peasants to buy their freedom when an estate was sold because of debt. The final factor was the European revolutions of 1848; when all these factors combined, the result was the disturbance peak of 1848 (Rahmatullin 1990:58, 19, 198).

The increasing pressure from continuing peasant rioting and agitation was an important factor in the decision of Alexander II (1855–81) to free the serfs. An 1857 report of the Third Department of His Majesty's Own

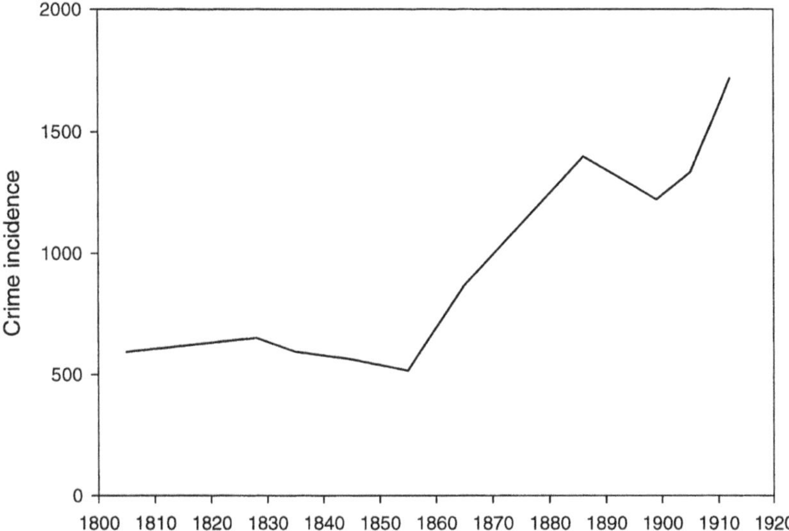

Figure 9.10 Dynamics of criminality in Russia as the number of total crimes per 100,000 persons (Mironov 2000:II: Table 5.6).

Chancery (the political police) pointed out that the peasantry was in an "agitated state" as a result of the rumors of imminent emancipation and that massive unrest was likely. This is precisely what happened next year (figure 9.9). In the post-reform period the number of peasant disturbances declined, although there were unrest peaks toward the end of the century, usually associated with the ascent of a new emperor that raised peasant hopes for a land reform.

The "Fathers-and-Sons" Cycles

Although the demographic-structural pressures grew steadily during the nineteenth century, sociopolitical instability increased not monotonically but in waves, with a period of roughly two generations (forty to sixty years). Instability grew during the "liberal" reigns of Alexander I (1801–25) and Alexander II (1855–81) and declined during the "conservative" reigns of Nicholas I (1825–55) and Alexander III (1881–94), as can be seen in, for example, the crime statistics (figure 9.10).

We lack direct estimates of revolutionary activity during the nineteenth century. However, capital punishment in tsarist Russia was reserved for the most serious political crimes. Thus, the number of executions per year provides a useful indication of revolutionary activity (to be more precise, the number of executions should be proportional to the product of revolu-

TABLE 9.7
Number of "named executions" (see text) per time period, 1811–1917

Period	*Executions*
(a) Executions per decade, 1811–1904	
1811–20	0
1821–30	11
1831–40	1
1841–50	3
1851–60	0
1861–70	17
1871–80	22
1881–90	30
1891–1900	0
1901–4[a]	0
(b) Executions per year, 1905–1917	
1905	175
1906	1116
1907	631
1908	712
1909	243
1910	72
1911–17	8.1[b]

Sources: (a) Gernet (1907); (b) Usherovich (1933).
[a] The four years before the revolution of 1905–7.
[b] Annual average for the period.

tionary activity and the intensity of the government efforts to suppress it). Table 9.7 shows the temporal distribution of "named executions," that is, executions of persons whose names were known to the compilers of executions lists. This statistic is an underestimate of the total number of executions, but this is not a problem for our purposes, because we are interested in the relative dynamics of this index.

The intensity of revolutionary struggle, as indicated by the number of executions, shows two peaks during the nineteenth century, followed by another one in the early twentieth (tables 9.6a and 9.6b). The first and rather mild upheaval of the nineteenth century occurred during the 1820s. The Decembrist Rising in 1825, an elite-led military revolt that was suppressed within a single day, accounted for five executions. Six other incidences of capital punishment reflected a peasant insurrection in Kiev Province and a coup attempt in Siberia in 1826.

The next and much more serious period of instability occurred during the 1860s–1880s with an outbreak of the anarchist campaign of bombings and assassinations that culminated in the successful assassination of the tsar in 1881. In 1878–79 Russia also experienced its first significant industrial strikes in St. Petersburg.

The 1890s were a relatively calm period, but in the early twentieth century instability began increasing again. Crime rates, which had declined during the late nineteenth century, started rising again (figure 9.10). Student protests and disturbances became almost continuous from 1898 on. The Socialist Revolutionaries resumed the terror campaign, assassinating a number of officials in 1902–5, including two ministers of the interior and a grand duke (Riazanovsky 2000:406). In 1905 Russia experienced its first revolution.

9.3 Crisis (1905–22)

Elite Fragmentation in the Decades before the Revolution

The elite fragmentation became apparent during the 1870s, when part of the impoverished nobility became involved in the populist (*narodniki*) movement. The populists' program was called "going among the people." Some 2,000 activists went to the villages to become teachers and doctors and to foment a peasant revolution that they hoped would overturn the old order and establish the new and socially just future. The "going among the people" campaign met with very little success among the peasant masses and was suppressed by the police in 1877. Sixteen hundred populists were arrested. After two mass trials, 200 activists were convicted and received various kinds of punishments (Ginev 1986:33–34).

Following this failure the populists turned to revolutionary conspiracy, assassination, and terrorism. In 1878 Vera Zasulich, a daughter of an impoverished noble family, shot and wounded the military governor of St. Petersburg in retaliation for his ordering a political prisoner to be flogged. Her trial evoked a great resonance among the educated classes (intelligentsia), and a sympathetic jury acquitted her of any wrongdoing. The trial of Zasulich showed that a huge legitimacy gap had opened up between the government and broad segments of the elite. Beginning in 1879 the members of the terrorist organization "The People's Will" made seven attempts to assassinate Alexander II, the last of which, in 1881, was successful. The People's Will consisted of some eighty local organizations in sixty-seven cities with a total membership of around 500. It was directed by the Executive Council, the majority of whom were very young, most 25–27 years old. Nearly half of the Executive Council (thirteen members) came from the noble estate (Ginev 1989:25–26).

Another part of nobility expressed its discontent in less radical ways. These elites coalesced into the Zemstvo-Constitutionalist movement, which drew support from the local self-government (*zemstvo*). The

Zemstvo-Constitutionalists aimed to replace the autocracy of the tsar (*samoderzhavie*) with a constitutional monarchy that would govern the country with the help of elected representatives of the "public," by which the constitutionalists understood only the upper strata. In 1904 the constitutionalists together with representatives of the liberal intelligentsia founded the Union of Liberation. The program of the Liberals did not propose any measures for resolving the agrarian question or for improving the lot of the workers. It focused entirely on the struggle against the autocracy and for the constitution and political freedoms (Shatsillo 1976:75, Miliukov 1990:274). Clearly, the liberal political movement, at least during its early period, had no intention of seeking popular support.

The successors of the populists, on the other hand, based their strategy of antigovernment struggle on mobilization of popular masses. In 1901 several smaller opposition groups were merged into the Socialist Revolutionary Party. The social composition of the party was as follows: 45 percent of the members were peasants, 43 percent were workers, and 11.2 percent were intelligentsia. In the upper echelons of the party, however, 78 percent were intelligentsia, and most of them were of noble origin, just as was the case for the populist organizations of the 1870s (Leonov 1987:52, 64, 57).

Another opposition group was the Social Democratic Party, which was formed in 1903. Its program mirrored in many ways the Liberal program, but it added the demand to limit the working day to eight hours in order to attract worker support. The Social Democrats originally were also dominated by the intelligentsia, but they were able to grow rapidly by attracting workers. In 1905 the ranks of the party numbered 9,000 members, of which 62 percent were workers, 5 percent peasants, and 33 percent intelligentsia (Utkin 1987:12, 17, 22).

The Revolution of 1905

The triggering event was the Russian defeat in the war with Japan (1904–5), which undermined the legitimacy of the government and consolidated the forces of opposition. In September 1904 the key Liberal and Socialist Revolutionary leaders met in Paris and agreed to coordinate their actions aiming to overthrow the government (Shatsillo 1982:55–57). In November the Union of Liberation organized a *zemstvo* congress in St. Petersburg, which demanded an elected representative assembly. "It was an idyll of the liberal nobility leaders—they wanted representation of the propertied classes," P. N. Miliukov (1990) later wrote in his memoirs.

The *zemstvo* congress was followed by 120 local assemblies in thirty-four cities that brought together representatives of the nobility and intelligentsia, who supported the congress's demands. The opposition also attempted to organize popular demonstrations. In January 1905 in St. Petersburg they instigated a massive procession of workers who were supposed to hand the tsar a petition that demanded a constitutive assembly (Nefedov 2006). During the demonstration the police fired at the crowd and killed more than a hundred people, causing the incident that became known as "Bloody Sunday." The massacre further undermined the authority of the state and led to a wave of strikes (although mainly in the Polish provinces of the empire). In Moscow the strike lasted about a week and involved 20,000 people, but violent altercations were avoided. In the industrial Vladimir Province only 8,000 (out of 140,000) factory workers went on strike (Nachalo 1955:668–83).

While admitting the extent of disturbances, Prime Minister S. Yu. Witte nevertheless remained optimistic about the situation, saying that 80 percent of the populace had not yet been affected by the revolutionary propaganda. However, Minister A. S. Ermolov warned the tsar that the government could not count on the nobility for support (Ganelin 1991:80). There was also outside pressure—the French bankers recommended to the tsar to make concessions to the liberal opposition, warning that otherwise it would be difficult to secure further loans (Kokovtsov 1992:69–71). As a result, Nicholas II agreed to create an elected representative assembly in March 1905.

The right wing of the liberal movement welcomed these concessions, and the pressure from the opposition temporarily relented. The worker protests also declined. In March only one-tenth as many people participated in political strikes as did in January (Rabochii 1981). P. N. Miliukov wrote that at that time, "the revolutionary movement had not been able to penetrate the masses, instead there was a 'simulation of revolution' by the intelligentsia" (Miliukov 1990:95). The liberals on the left wing, however, wanted to keep the pressure on the tsar. During the congress of the Union of Liberation that took place on March 25–28, they added to their program a new demand to distribute the state land to landless peasants. Where there was not enough state land, they proposed that private land would be divided among the peasants, while former owners were to be compensated with cash. Another demand was to limit the working day to eight hours. As to the representative assembly that was promised by the tsar, the left-wing liberals insisted that it would be elected on the basis of universal and equal suffrage (Shahovski 2001:589).

An imperial manifesto on the state duma published in August 1905, however, specified an advisory organ that was to be elected through a multistep indirect process. The liberal opposition, therefore, directed all of its efforts to mobilize the masses on their side. The chief player in the organization of the general strike in October 1905 was the All-Russian Railroad Union (ARU)—a trade union of engineers, technicians, and managers that was created by the liberals. The union represented the middle rank employees recruited from the intelligentsia. There were practically no workers among its 6,000 membership (the total number of workers employed by the railroads was 700,000). Although the ARU members were less than one percent of all railroad employees, they were able to bring to a complete stop practically all railroads in Russia, by disrupting technical services, for example, dispatcher or telegraph services (Pushkareva 1975: 44, 119, 127, 148, 152, 154).

The grinding stop of all railroads gave a powerful impetus to the strike movement. At some factories the workers took advantage of the situation to present their demands to the owners. Other factories stopped simply as a result of the lack of raw materials. Mobs of striking workers stormed the still-operating factories and forced work stoppage there. According to the data of the Inspection of the Factories, 519,000 workers were on strike in October—about a third of all workers in Russia. Thus, although the strike was initiated by the liberal intelligentsia, its further development took a life of its own (Keep 1963:219, 222, Bovykin 1981:156, 161). The workers of St. Petersburg created a new organ for coordinating striking activity, the Soviet (council) of Worker Deputies, which was imitated in other cities and later became one of the most important forms of organizing and directing revolutionary action.

Nicholas II and his government were forced to capitulate. The tsar signed the October Manifesto that essentially transformed the *samoderzhavie* (autocracy) into a constitutional monarchy. The manifesto guaranteed civil liberties and provided for an elected legislation, the state duma. The manifesto thus addressed the aspirations of the liberal elites but did nothing for workers, who demanded an eight-hour working day and increased pay. It also did nothing to stop the growing peasant rebellion.

The railroad strike triggered not only the general workers strike, but also mobilized the peasants. V. M. Gohlener, on the basis of his studies of the peasant movement in Saratov Province, concluded that peasant agitation began in villages that were located near railroads and then spread into the hinterland (Gohlener 1955:200). An additional factor that caused peasant discontent was the crop failure of 1905. In the seven provinces of the Black Earth Region, the net harvest was only half what it was during the previous quinquennium. The Volga Region was similarly affected (Obuhov 1927:78–79, 103–7). The grain slated for export, which was stored on the noble estates, presented an irresistible temptation to the millions of peasants who did not have enough food to last them through the winter.

The long-term factor of peasant landlessness, thus, combined with the temporary weakening of the state power and crop failure to cause the peasant uprising. According to the data of the Ministry of Internal Affairs, between October and December 1905 peasants plundered around 2,000

TABLE 9.8
Revolutionary actions of the peasant masses in 1905–6

Month	*Number of actions*
October 1905	219
November 1905	796
December 1905	575
January 1906	179
February 1906	27

Source: Dubrovsky (1956:42).

noble estates (one-fifteenth of the total). In some localities, such as Balashovski District of Saratov Province, practically all estates were destroyed (Prokopovich 1907:26, Gohlener 1955:233).

Unrest and disorder increased in the cities in parallel with rural areas and culminated in an insurrection of the workers in Moscow in December 1905. The ARU participated in a railroad strike that impeded the operations of the troops, which remained loyal to the government. After several days, however, the military was able to get the trains going and move reinforcements to Moscow. Ten days after it began the Moscow insurrection was suppressed. In rural areas mass disturbances also began declining after a peak in November (table 9.8).

The peasant and worker uprisings served as a graphic lesson of the dangers associated with revolution, and the majority of the nobility abandoned the liberal movement. Liberals were expelled from the *zemstvo* assemblies and the nobility consolidated on the platform of property preservation and against the land reform that would redistribute land from nobles to peasants.

By January 1906 the worker and peasant uprisings had been suppressed and the active phase of the revolution was over. Subsequent political conflicts played out within the framework of the legislature (the duma). The attempts by the liberals to initiate the agrarian reform were resisted by the government, which took the side of the landlords and refused to consider alienation of private land, even with compensation. The conflict between the duma and the government led to the dissolution of the first two dumas. In 1907, finally, the government was able to obtain a cooperative legislature by adopting the election law that gave a disproportionate representation to the nobility. During the same year public order was largely restored.

The revolution of 1905–7 thus largely proceeded along the lines postulated by the demographic-structural theory. During the period of stagflation the elites fragment, resulting in the rise of opposition groups. Popular

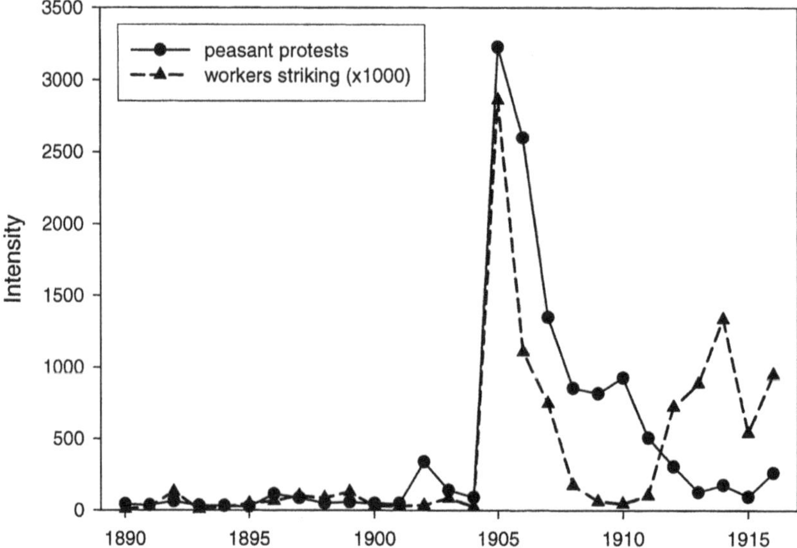

Figure 9.11 Dynamics of peasant and worker protests, 1890–1916 (Dubrovsky 1956:42).

immiseration enables these counterelites to mobilize the masses in the struggle against the state. However, the interests of the counterelites and the common people are not the same. When the elite leaders achieve their goals, they abandon the revolution, or even join with the government in suppressing popular uprisings, as it happened in 1905. Furthermore, the revolutionary experience of 1905–7 showed the opposition the dangers of uncontrolled popular explosion. Although the radicals continued to hope for a social revolution, most were killed or driven into exile. The liberal opposition, on the other hand, which represented the largest segments of the elites, repudiated revolutionary methods in their struggle with the government after 1905–7.

Sociopolitical Instability between the Revolutions

The revolution of 1905–7 forced the government to begin reforms whose goal was to regain the peasant support. These belated efforts were largely ineffective (Danilov 1992:60). The suppression of revolution did not mean returning to prerevolutionary conditions. Peasant disturbances subsided gradually, and their level during 1908–10 was still an order of magnitude greater than before the revolution (figure 9.11). While the rural disorder declined in 1912–13, the locus of instability shifted to the cities, which experienced a renewed wave of strikes that lasted until the outbreak of

TABLE 9.9
Dynamics of serious crimes (annual averages, in thousands)

Type of crime	*1874–83*	*1884–93*	*1899–1905*	*1906–8*	*1909–13*
Against the public order	13.2	16.6	23.3	56.2	55.4
Against religion	1.0	1.6	1.4	1.5	5.2
Against the state	—	—	2.0	2.9	2.3
Against the government	3.3	3.8	9.9	13.1	22.1
Against the person[a]	22.4	32.3	153.8	134.3	149.2
Against the private property	57.5	40.8	136.0	208.7	245.5

Source: Mironov (2000:II: table 8.9).
[a] Includes murders, rapes, and assaults.

World War I. Significantly, the crime wave did not recede after the end of the revolution (table 9.9).

The period of 1906–8 includes two revolutionary years, and the average criminality level was correspondingly high (especially notable was the great jump in crimes against private persons and private property after 1900). After the revolution, however, criminality did not decline and for certain types of crimes actually increased. For example, the number of crimes "against the government" (*protiv poryadka upravleniya*) in 1909–13 was greater than during the revolutionary level of the preceding period. This increase suggests that the revolution did not end in 1907 but continued in the form of chronic and numerous (if small in scale) protest actions. The populace, whose aspirations were frustrated during the revolution, was not resigned to the continuing state of affairs. The crimes against private property include arsons of landlord estates committed by peasants. In 1910–11 the number of arsons and small protest actions was actually greater than in 1907, the last year of the revolution.

The government was aware of the tense social climate, and how it could affect the ability of Russia to fight the war that most considered imminent. In the end, however, Nicholas II decided to enter the war, although many of his contemporaries felt this decision doomed tsarism. The most pessimistic forecast was made by the Member of the State Council P. N. Durnovo, who, because of his position, had an intimate knowledge of the internal state of the country. If the war turns to be victorious, then fine and well, wrote Durnovo.

> But if there is defeat, then a social revolution, with all its excesses, is unavoidable. All reverses will be blamed on the government. A furious campaign against the government will be launched in the legislature, triggering revolutionary actions across the land. The latter will advance socialist slogans that will mobilize broad segments of the population, demands of the black repartition (of land from landlords to peasants)

followed by a general division of all valuables and property. The defeated army, having lost by that time the most reliable cadres and swayed in its large part by the peasant yearning for the land, will be too demoralized to maintain law and order. The legislative organs and oppositionary intelligentsia parties, who lack any authority among the people, will not be able to control the popular waves that they raised, and Russia will be cast into hopeless anarchy, the outcome of which cannot be predicted. (Durnovo 1922)

The logic of Durnovo's forecast was that a defeat in the war against Germany would lead to the same consequences that followed defeat in the war with Japan, the revolution of 1905–7, but in a more extreme form. Durnovo predicted that discontented elite factions would again begin revolutionary agitation and mobilize the peasant masses by promising them land. In reality, this prediction was not quite right. What occurred in February 1917 was a "revolution without revolutionaries."

Most historians believe that Russia could have avoided revolution if not for World War I (Hobsbawm 1962). In an influential analysis of social revolutions in France, Russia, and China the historical sociologist Theda Skocpol (1979) advanced a similar argument. Jack Goldstone, however, pointed out that early modern states were almost constantly at war: "From 1550 to 1815 there were few decades in which Europe was free from major wars. Moreover, the scale and cost of warfare was constantly growing. Yet in these centuries state breakdown was sharply cycling, including a peak during the relatively peaceful (in terms of interstate conflict) mid-nineteenth century" (Goldstone 1991:20).

War was a test of robustness that social systems had to endure almost constantly. During the stagflation phases, when their social structures were particularly fragile, most states failed the test of war. The string of defeats experienced by Russia in the Crimean War (1853–56), the Russo-Japanese War (1904–5) and World War I were symptomatic of this internal fragility.

An analysis of Russian wars during the nineteenth century identified three mechanisms that translated war conditions into crisis (Nefedov 2005:232–33). The first problem confronting the country was an insufficiency of armaments that led to military reverses, which undermined the state's legitimacy. The second problem was that during the stagflation phase the government could finance the war only by printing more paper money, which caused hyperinflation, market failure, disruption of the flow of provisions to the cities, and hunger strikes. The third and most important problem was that the social pressures brought on by stagflation fragmented the society. Peasant landlessness and general popular immiseration made peasant uprisings or an insurrection of peasant conscripts in the army particularly likely, while broad segments of the elites were alienated from the state.

The crisis brought on by World War I unfolded very much according to this scenario. The Russian army was vastly inferior to the German and Austrian armies in artillery and other weapons. The supply of weapons and ammunition quickly ran out, and in the beginning of 1915 up to a quarter of new recruits arrived at the front without rifles. In the summer of 1915 the Russian army suffered a grave defeat when the Germans advanced into Galicia (Utkin 1976:258–59, Riazanovsky 2000:418).

The military reverses of 1915 sharply undermined the authority and legitimacy of the government and, in accordance with Durnovo's prediction, brought on a storm of antigovernment accusations in the duma. However, having learned their lesson in 1905, the opposition did not attempt to involve the popular masses in their conflict with the government. Thus, contrary to Durnovo's prediction, the antigovernment campaign did not result in a popular revolution.

The effect of the military defeats on the army were much more serious (Nefedov 2005:391–94). The losses in 1915 amounted to 2.4 million soldiers, of which 1 million were POWs. The casualties (killed and wounded) during the summer campaign of 1916 were not much less than in 1915, while the number of troops captured increased to 1.5 million. Statistics show that the ratio of troops killed to those that surrendered in the Russian army was 1:3, while in the German, French, and English armies this statistic varied between 1:0.2 and 1:0.26. The readiness with which Russian soldiers surrendered to the enemy was one indication of their low morale and unwillingness to be fed into the bloody meat grinder of the war. Another form of protest, in addition to voluntary surrender, was the high rate of desertion. By the beginning of 1917 there were perhaps 1–1.5 million deserters. On several occasions military units refused to advance against the enemy ("soldier strikes"). In the fall of 1916 there were mutinies at Gomel and Kremenchug logistics centers behind the front lines that involved thousands of soldiers. A general soldier uprising was becoming increasingly more likely. Thus, by the beginning of 1917, the state had lost much of its ability to control the army (Nefedov 2005:391–94).

The third factor, in addition to the loss of legitimacy and increasing army unreliability, was the worsening economic conditions. At the start of the war nobody anticipated shortages of bread (Kondrat'ev 1991). The export of grain was forbidden; also banned was the use of grain for alcohol production. Thus, the agricultural production within Russia should have been more than ample for both the army and civilian population needs. The problem, however, lay not with the production of food but with its distribution, the failure of which was an indirect effect of the government's fiscal policy.

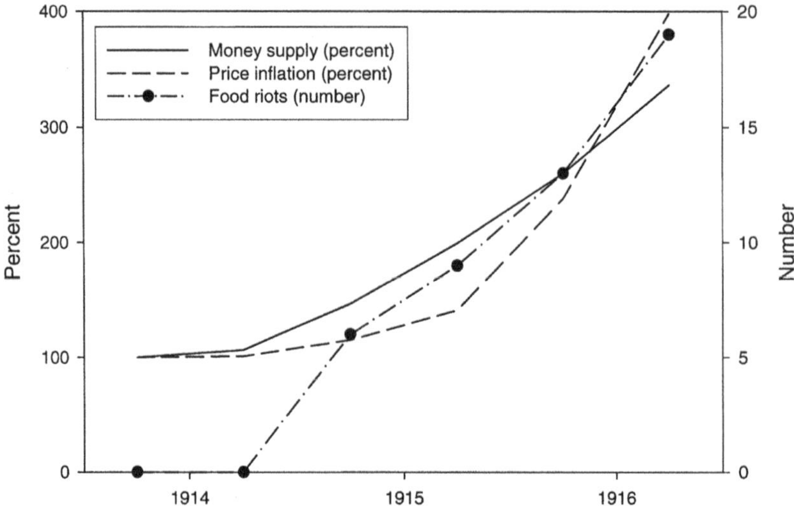

Figure 9.12 The money supply, price index, and number of major food riots in Russian cities (without Siberia, the Caucasus, and Don Province). Data are plotted by half-year periods. (Sources: Kondratev 1991, Kiryanov 1993.)

In 1914–15 the tax revenues were 2.9 billion rubles, and during the war years they could not be increased. Military expenditures, on the other hand, grew from 2.5 billion rubles in 1914 to 9.4 billion in 1915 and 15.3 billion in 1916. Over the course of the war the military expenditures added up to 30.5 billion rubles. The tsarist government was able to raise 7.5 billion in internal loans, and another 6.3 billion came as loans from the allies (Sidorov 1960). But these loans covered less than half the expenditures. The huge military expenses could not be financed using the normal budgetary mechanisms, and the government was forced to print paper money to cover the deficit. This inevitably led to runaway price inflation (figure 9.12).

At first prices grew slower than the money supply, but in 1916 they accelerated and overtook the supply. This suggests a reduction in the supply of goods, of which food was the chief one. The mechanism underlying this dynamic is simple. When the suppliers of a good (in this case, rural grain producers) observe a rapid increase in the price of the good, they have an incentive to withhold the supplies from the markets so they can get a better price later. The primary sufferers from the resulting deficit are urban dwellers. A deficit of bread and its high price cause mass discontent. The queues that form in front of bakeries or food stores concentrate the discontented, and any small event can trigger an outbreak of rioting, which has the potential to grow into full-blown uprising. A well-known example of this dynamic is the Parisian food riots during the French Revolution.

Figure 9.12 shows that the number of major food riots (when thousands of people clashed with the police or army troops) increased together with rising prices. What was worse, from the government point of view, is that government troops began to sympathize with rioters. The first incidence of the cossacks refusing to disperse the crowds occurred during the food riots in Orenburg in May 1916. Later that year there were nine more such cases (Kir'yanov 1993).

Another sign of the impending catastrophe was the shrinking supply of grain stored in elevators and railroad and port warehouses (Kondrat'ev 1991:187). In November 1915 the grain stores amounted to 65 million puds, and during the spring and summer of the following year they shrank, as usual. But in the fall of 1916 they were not replenished and continued to decline until they dropped below 10 million puds by December. The harvest in 1916 was worse than in 1915, and the producers withheld the grain from the markets in expectation of better prices (Kir'yanov 1993).

The government was forced to employ coercive methods and threats of confiscation to find enough grain to supply the army, but this left almost nothing for the civilian population (Nefedov 2005:394–402). In January and February 1917, urban centers received only 20 and 30 percent of the planned grain deliveries, respectively. In the winter of 1916–17 the provisioning crisis reached catastrophic proportions. Numerous memoirs of those years describe the dearth of bread and huge lines at food stores (Nefedov 2005:39–402).

The February Revolution

The economic problems described in the previous section gradually intensified as the war went on, and toward the end of 1916 the fiscal crisis resulted in the disintegration of the distribution system. The economic collapse was soon followed by political collapse.

In the fall of 1916, rising bread prices caused a new wave of food riots and worker strikes in the industrial regions. The first major hunger protest in St. Petersburg took place in October 1916. Many soldiers joined the protesters, and rioters could be dispersed only thanks to resolute measures by the guard units. During the following winter the provisioning crisis deepened. In the beginning of 1917 the mayor of Moscow, M. V. Chelnokov, sent four telegraphs to the prime minister warning that the scarcity of food was about to cause starvation, which would be followed by protests and agitation among the inhabitants of the capital (Sidorov 1960:497).

The army also was at the brink of starvation. At a meeting of the General Staff in December 1916 it emerged that the provisioning of the troops was about to deteriorate in the near future. "It was not explained to us why the economy was in disarray, but we were told that nothing could be done about this calamitous state of affairs," wrote A. A. Brusilov (2001:199). It became necessary to decrease the food rations of frontline troops from three to two pounds per day, while the troops behind the lines received only 1.5 pounds. Because of lack of oats, horses were starving, and as a result, the artillery lost its mobility. The army could no longer advance, and in case of retreat, loss of the artillery and the supply train was assured (Brusilov 2001:204).

December 1916 was notable for unprecedented mass protests among the soldiers. During the Mitava operation, the Seventeenth Infantry Regiment refused to advance against the enemy. It was then joined by several other regiments, and disturbances spread through three army corps, involving tens of thousands of soldiers. The authorities were able to regain control only with difficulty. A hundred of the most active protesters were executed, and a few more hundreds were condemned to forced labor (Zayonchkovski 1938:108). The most dangerous tendency, however, was that the army was rapidly running out of provisions. In early February the northern front had food stores sufficient for only two days. On the western front the flour stores were completely exhausted and soldiers were fed on canned food and hard biscuits. The army was on the brink of mutiny; in fact, two infantry regiments on the Caucasian front rebelled on February 22–23 (Gavrilov 1991:60)

The provisioning situation was worse in the cities. During the first two months of 1917, Moscow and St. Petersburg received only 25 percent of food they needed. From mid-February the press reported that the introduction of a food rationing system was imminent and that an adult would be entitled only to one pound of bread per day (children were to get half that). The news caused people to attempt to stock up on food before the system was implemented, and this rapidly turned into a panic. On February 14 one newspaper reported that thousands of inhabitants were lining up at grocers and bakers, despite the freezing weather, in the hope of buying a loaf of bread (Leyberov 1990:60). Spontaneous hunger strikes and demonstrations began on February 23. By evening, 60,000 workers were on strike, and there were several clashes between protesters and the police (Leyberov 1990:71–77).

On February 24 the number of striking workers increased to 200,000. The police dispersed the demonstrators, but they soon coalesced in other places. On February 25 the demonstrations had become quasi-legal. The military stood by irresolutely, while many cossacks were fraternizing with the protesting mobs (Startsev 1984:10, 117, Leyberov 1990:87). In the evening the military commander of St. Petersburg, General Khabalov, received a telegram for the tsar with a demand to bring an end to the turmoil. Although the authorities were reluctant to use force to suppress the protests, they were compelled to issue the fateful order.

As is clear in retrospect, giving such an order to unreliable troops would provoke them to an almost inevitable uprising of their own. The great mass of the soldiers in St. Petersburg were peasants who had been called up in early 1917 and were waiting to be sent to the front. These former peasants had their own grievances against the ruling order and were unwilling to die for it. Furthermore, the few veterans among them, who had been sent back to the front after recovering from battlefield injuries, told the new recruits about the firestorm of bullets and shells and the terrible losses among the frontline troops. "The soldier masses were inspired by only one passionate desire—a miracle that would save them from the necessity to go to the slaughter" (Oldenburg 1992:618).

On February 26 the troops were ordered to fire at the demonstrating crowds, and on the same day the Pavlovsky Regiment mutinied. This mutiny was suppressed, but next morning the Volynsky Regiment mutinied, and the uprising spread to other regiments through a chain reaction process. The column of mutineers marched across St. Petersburg from one barracks to the next, and the regiments, one after another, joined the uprising, with much rejoicing and shooting in the air. On the morning of February 27 there were 10,000 mutineers. By midday their numbers had increased to 26,000, and in the evening to 66,000. On the next day, 127,000 troops joined the uprising, and on March 1 there were 170,000, that is, practically the entire St. Petersburg garrison (Oldenburg 1992:618).

The subsequent events are well-known: the abdication of Nicholas II, the rule of the Provisional Government established by the duma, and the violent overthrow of the Provisional Government by the Bolsheviks (the October Revolution). The Bolshevik coup triggered a general civil war that lasted until 1921, but eventually the Communist Party was able to reestablish central control and reconquer most of the territories of the Russian Empire. The civil war was generally over by 1922, when the Union of Soviet Socialist Republics was organized, with the exception of the Central Asian region, where the Soviet authorities suppressed the native partisan movement (the "basmachi") only in 1926.

9.4 Conclusion

The demographic-structural theory was formulated for agrarian societies, and the question arises as to whether it is applicable to industrializing states, such as Russia around 1900. We think that the theory is generally applicable, because during this period the great majority of the Russian population—80 percent in 1913 (Mironov 2000: Table 2.18)—were still peasants. Nevertheless, industrialization affected the economic and social dynamics of Russia and has to be taken into account. During the second half of the nineteenth century Russia experienced a substantial growth of agricultural productivity, one of the most important preconditions of the industrial take-off (Rostow 1990). The increasing productivity of Russian agriculture after 1870 (see table 9.1) substantially expanded the carrying capacity and ameliorated the negative effects of rapid population growth.

Another modifying factor that had even more influence on the Romanov cycle was the territorial expansion and peasant colonization of the conquered lands. As we noted in section 9.1, the Central Region was showing all indications of stagflation by the 1730s–1740s. The stagflation in the Central Region was made worse by the high tax levels that were imposed during Peter I's reign, but even after the tax rates were lowered by Catherine II, the position of peasants did not improve, because the increased demands of the gentry immediately took up the slack. If there were no Black Earth Region to colonize, it is quite likely that Russia would have experienced its next state collapse during the Age of Revolutions, probably at the same time as France, with which it was closely synchronized between 1400 and 1750 (Turchin 2003b). In Russia, however, the crisis was postponed by a century. The formation of the interregional grain market between the Black Earth Region and the Central Region allowed the former to specialize in food production and the latter to develop a protoindustrial orientation.

Thus, the period between 1620 and 1800 that we have classified as expansion does not fit well the typical dynamics of expansion phases that are predicted by the demographic-structural theory. Instead, it would probably be better to consider the period between 1620 and 1905 as two integrative trends following one another. First comes Expansion I to 1730, followed by Stagflation I in the Central Region. Meanwhile Expansion II continues on in the Black Earth Region until the 1840s, after which general stagflation (Stagflation II) sets in. Such doubled-up integrative trends are not uncommon, especially in large countries. For example, in China the carrying capacity doubled during the Sung era from 50–60 million, which was the typical population ceiling during the first millennium, to 110–120 million as a result of the introduction of high-yielding varieties of rice and the colonization of southern China (Korotayev 2005:186–88).

The crisis phase of the Romanov cycle also had several idiosyncratic features, although at the beginning it followed a classic demographic-structural scenario. At the end of the stagflation phase in 1905, the majority of peasants did not have sufficient land to feed their families, while elite overproduction deeply divided the ruling class. With the majority of elites profoundly alienated from the state, all it took to trigger the revolution was a relatively trivial reverse in the Russo-Japanese war. When the demands of the opposition for a greater say in the governmental policy were frustrated by the tsar's refusal to implement liberal reforms, it turned to the popular masses for support and succeeded beyond its wildest imaginations. The railroad strike initiated by the small liberal-dominated union led to the general workers' strike and then to a peasant uprising. The peasants, whose main motivation was to acquire land, primarily attacked not the state but the land-owning elites. Partly satisfied by the concessions wrung out of the tsar and, more important, frightened by the extent and intensity of the popular uprising, the majority of the elites abandoned the struggle against the state, and many even joined the state in its efforts to suppress the revolution.

In the period between the revolutions, the level of sociopolitical instability continued to be high—not much lower than during the revolution, and much higher than before 1905 (figure 9.11). We think, thus, that the whole period between 1905 and 1922 should be considered a continuous crisis period. The revolution of 1905 did not resolve either of the two main problems that brought it on, peasant landlessness and elite overproduction. The state was able to suppress the active phase of the revolution with the help of the troops brought from the Far East after the end of the Russo-Japanese War, and of the liberal segment of the elites. But the calm was more apparent than real, as the continuing high level of peasant disturbance and worker strikes indicates. Any temporary weakening of the state authority and power could have sparked another social crisis. The stress of World War I provided the spark.

The mechanism leading to the next crisis involved three intertwined processes: the collapse of the state legitimacy as a result of military defeats, runaway inflation and the market collapse leading to food riots, and the increasing unreliability of the troops. The fact that the revolution was triggered by the food riots in St. Petersburg on February 23 was to a certain degree a happenstance. But it had to happen sooner or later, because food riots started during the previous fall and continued to erupt under the Provisional Government, which was able to solve the provisioning problem no better than the tsar's government.

The February food riots in St. Petersburg should have been suppressed had the government retained control over the troops. Unlike in 1905, however, this was no longer the case. The army was decimated by military defeats, and the government could no longer even feed it. The soldiers who mutinied in February 1917 were peasants, many drafted just a few months earlier. These were the peasants who had demanded land in 1905 and did not get it; many of them hated their landlords and the state that took the landlord's side in the conflict over land. Now they were confronted with a choice: either go into the meat grinder of the war and die, or join the rebelling workers. It is not surprising that they chose the latter. It is also symptomatic that whereas the workers demonstrated with the slogans demanding bread, the peasants' slogans were "Land and Liberty."

In 1917 the elites continued to be fragmented; however, the main opposition party, the liberals, did not desire the revolution (see Nefedov 2005: Sections 5.2 and especially 5.4). The radicals, the Socialist Revolutionaries and the Social Democrats, were decimated after the revolution of 1905–7, and those that remained were driven into exile. In 1917 the radicals completely misread the revolutionary situation that was developing in Russia. In a January 1917 lecture that he gave in Zurich, V. I. Lenin stated that he would never see a revolution in Russia (Katkov 1997:18). At the beginning of the February Revolution, the social revolutionaries and the Mensheviks referred to it derisively as the "spontaneous stomach movement." Apparently they were unaware of how close this characterization was to Malthusianism.

Chapter 10

General Conclusions

The main goal of this book has been to determine how well the predictions of the demographic-structural theory map onto empirically observed patterns in the historical societies we studied. We focused on four fundamental variables: population numbers (in relation to carrying capacity), social structure (specifically, the numbers and consumption levels of the elites), the strength of the state (typically measured by its fiscal health), and sociopolitical instability. In our empirical investigation we attempted to measure as best as we could the dynamics of these variables. Where possible we looked at data that directly demonstrated the dynamics of the key variable, and where this approach was impossible we searched for proxies. Secular cycles also affect many other aspects of historical societies, and where such data were available, we included them in the analysis. Our empirical investigation looked at eight secular cycles in four countries. In this concluding chapter we summarize our results and delineate promising future avenues of research.

10.1 Population Numbers

The match between theoretical predictions about population dynamics and empirical patterns was quite good. Generally speaking, integrative phases were characterized by sustained long-term population growth, although this ascending trend could be interrupted and even temporarily reversed when factors not taken into account by the theory intruded. The most conspicuous example is the population declines in Republican Rome during the First and Second Punic Wars. Where our data are particularly good, as in the case of early modern England, we observe much smaller fluctuations, for example, during the 1560s in England (see figure 3.1a). The general rule is, nevertheless, that the effect of such setbacks during the expansion phase is temporary, and any losses are made up quickly.

Disintegrative phases were generally periods of population decline or stagnation. Dramatic population declines took place during the crisis phases of the Plantagenet, Capetian, Principate, and Muscovy cycles. We argue that the Republican cycle also ended with a population decline in Italy, but this remains controversial. In two cycles, the Tudor and Valois, absolute population numbers declined less dramatically, and the general trend was stagnation rather than collapse. However, in the Tudor case, population pressure on resources (population relative to the carrying capacity) exhibited a very substantial decline (by 35 percent between 1650 and 1750). We would not be surprised to learn that a comparable decline affected the population pressure in the Valois cycle. Finally, our examination of the Romanov cycle stopped at the crisis stage, and therefore we do not offer estimates of how population pressure declined over the course of the complete disintegrative phase (we will pursue this question in future work).

Among the various economic trends that could serve as proxies for population dynamics, the most useful, without any doubt, is the real wage. Where our data are good, the inverse relationship between the population pressure on resources and the real wage is very tight (see, for example, figure 3.10). However, this relationship holds only before the Industrial Revolution. After 1800 in England the relationship between population and real wages was completely transformed.

There are some early indications that a most useful noneconomic proxy for population pressure may be the average height of populations (Komlos 1990, Steckel 2004, Koepke and Baten 2005). The basic idea of the approach is that population pressure on resources results in reduced levels of nutrition. Inadequate nutrition of growing human beings (infants and juveniles) results in stunted adult stature. Thus, it should be possible to observe population fluctuations indirectly by measuring how average heights of individuals changed with time (figure 10.1).

In our earlier work (Nefedov 1999, Turchin 2003b) we proposed a tentative chronology for secular cycles in Western Europe (table 10.1). There is a remarkable degree of congruence between this chronology and the fluctuations of average heights in Europe (the data in figure 10.1 were not used in any way to construct the chronology of the secular cycles). Interestingly, the relative height of peaks in the graph corresponds well with what we know about the relative height of population peaks achieved during various secular cycles. Thus, the population peaks during the Roman period were much higher than during the Middle Ages. The drastic population collapse of the sixth century in particular is very well reflected in the remarkable increase in average stature. On the other hand, population peaks of the last medieval (Capetian) and the first early modern (Valois) cycles matched and even exceeded those of the Roman times.

10.2 Elite Dynamics

Data on elite dynamics were harder to obtain than general population data, and we were often forced to rely on informed judgments by specialists. Nevertheless, quantitative estimates of elite-commoner ratios were available in the Plantagenet, Tudor, Capetian, and Muscovite cases. Less quan-

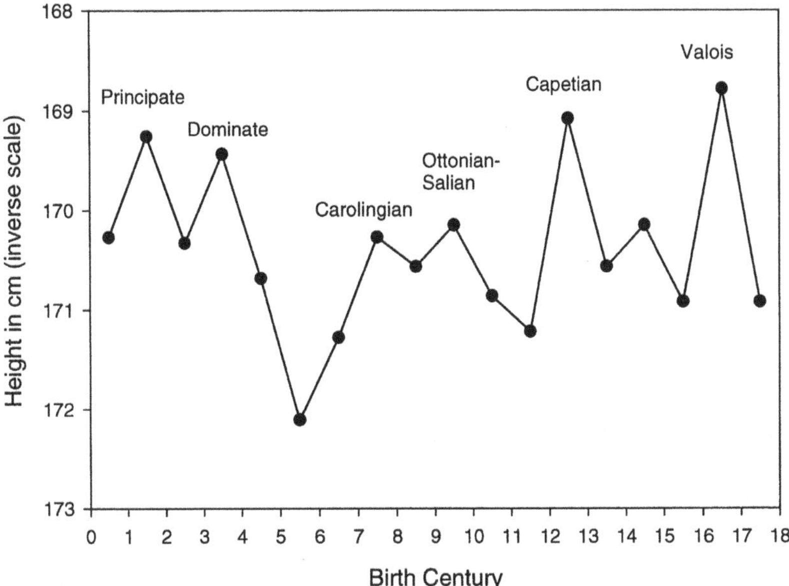

Figure 10.1 Average height of Europeans during the two millennia CE. Data are from skeletal material (Koepke and Baten 2005). Heights are plotted on an inverse scale, so that the peaks in the graph correspond to population peaks (because periods of high population density should correlate with low average heights).

titative estimates in other cases were in agreement with the predictions of the theory regarding the development of elite overproduction (peaking during the crisis phase) and its abatement (with the trough occurring during the expansion phase of the next cycle). We found that various measures of conspicuous consumption provided useful proxies for the expansion and contraction of elite numbers and appetites. One proxy variable that should be available in many cases is the rate of construction of temples or churches (for example, figures 2.5 and 6.1). Consumption rates of such luxury goods as wine in England (where commoners drank beer) can sometimes give us an excellent insight into how the "footprint" of the elites changed with time (between 1300 and 1460 the amount of wine drunk by the English elites declined fourfold; see section 2.5).

One apparently ubiquitous feature of elite overproduction is growing economic inequality. We were able to obtain time-series measures of inequality (by looking at the ratio of top fortunes to contemporaneous mean or median incomes) for the Plantagenet, Valois, and Roman Republic cycles. Certain indicators of intraelite competition that have been proposed in the context of the Tudor-Stuart cycle turned out to be useful in other case studies: litigation (the Muscovy cycle), education (the Romanov cycle), and the dueling rate (the Valois cycle).

TABLE 10.1
Summary of the chronological sequence of secular cycles in Western Europe

Secular cycle	*Integrative phase*	*Disintegrative phase*
Republican Rome	350–130 BCE	130–30 BCE
Principate	30 BCE–165 CE	165–285
Dominate/Merovingian	285–540	540–700
Carolingian	700–820	820–920
Ottonian-Salian	920–1050	1050–1150
Capetian	1150–1315	1315–1450
Valois	1450–1560	1560–1660
Bourbon	1660–1780	1780–1870

Note: This chronology focuses on the dominant state in Western Europe: first the Roman Empire, then the medieval German empires, and finally France.

10.3 The State

Data on the fiscal health of states were available for every studied cycle, although their quality varied from case to case. Nevertheless, the data were good enough to yield several surprises. It is true there was at least some evidence of fiscal difficulties associated with the crisis stage in all case studies. However, this is not a very strong result, because preindustrial states constantly overextended themselves under the pressure of war, and state fiscal difficulties, even bankruptcy, did not necessarily result in state breakdown. In one case study, that of Republican Rome, there is no evidence of serious fiscal difficulties until after the civil war broke out. Republican Rome was also one case in which the state had the least degree of autonomy from the elites, the senatorial class. As we noted in section 6.6, the theory needs to be modified to take such cases into account.

Furthermore, although in some cases we observed declining real revenues during the stagflation phase (the Plantagenet and Tudor cycles), in others (the Romanov and, probably, the Musocovite cycles) the state was actually able to continue raising per capita real taxes until the moment of the crisis (and in the Muscovite case, such exactions were an important factor contributing to triggering the crisis). However, what is important is not whether the revenues declined in absolute terms but whether they declined relative to expenses. For example, Goldstone's (1991, 2008) study of what we have called the Bourbon cycle showed that both real revenue and per capita taxation grew until the eve of the French Revolution. However, the fiscal collapse of the state was one of the clearest elements of the late eighteenth-century crisis in France. The problem was that the state expenses grew much faster than revenues, owing to a vastly expanded cadre of elite officeholders and rising military expenses.

The fiscal dynamics during the disintegrative secular phases, however, yielded some surprises. Our initial expectation was that during these periods, states should be uniformly incapable of acquiring enough revenue to function. Instead, we found that the typical dynamics of state revenues went on a veritable roller-coaster ride. Periodically, rulers succeeded in persuading the populace and elites to accept high taxes, but such episodes of internal accord did not last very long. As a result, we observed wild swings in revenues during the disintegrative parts of the Plantagenet (figure 2.6), Tudor (figure 3.3), Valois (figure 5.2), Muscovite (figure 8.3), and Romanov (figure 7.7) cycles. These revenue swings are apparently associated with the father-and-son dynamics. Civil wars not only induce, after a lag, a powerful desire for social peace, they also make the elites more amenable to compromising with the state over the need for taxation. The next generation (which did not directly experience civil war) is much less willing to yield to the state's demand for revenue. The growing antagonism between the state and the elites is one of the factors that may bring about another round of civil wars.

10.4 Sociopolitical Instability

Sociopolitical instability is a key variable of the demographic-structural theory, and it is gratifying that we were able to obtain quantitative estimates of its dynamics for all the studied cycles. The simplest method for quantifying sociopolitical instability is to plot the number (per unit of time) of "instability events," such as peasant uprisings, regional rebellions, coups d'état, and civil wars. In making these estimates we were greatly aided by the previous work of authors such as Pitirim Sorokin (1937) and Charles Tilly (1993). We present such graphs for the Plantagenet (figure 2.7), Capetian and Valois (figure 5.3), Republic (figure 6.5), and Principate (figure 7.5) cycles.

Indices of instability based on the analysis of the written sources have the advantage that they can be developed for any period for which we have a sufficient density of sources. The drawback of this approach, however, is that it is inherently subjective. Actual instability occurrences are first filtered through the perceptions of contemporaries and later affected by the various biases of compilers of historical chronicles; finally, the modern investigator has to decide whether any particular disturbance qualifies as "major" to be included in the list of instability events. We need a better, more objective method for quantifying instability, and it is fortunate that an excellent proxy variable is available in the frequency of coin hoards. We have been able to use compilations of coin hoards to estimate instability dynamics in the Plantagenet (figure 2.7), Tudor (figure 3.4), Capetian (figure 4.2), Republic (figure 6.5), Principate (figures 7.6 and 7.7), and Muscovite (figure 8.1) cases. It is gratifying that the instability indices based on written sources and the coin hoard proxy are largely in agreement. When two sets of numbers, obtained in a completely independent manner, show similar patterns, our confidence that both methods generate reasonable results is boosted.

In one case, the Romanov cycle, we decomposed generic instability into three component processes: peasant disturbances (figure 9.9), worker strikes (figure 9.11), and revolutionary activity as indicated by the number of "named executions" (table 9.7). For a number of case-studies (see figures 2.9, 2.10, 3.6, and 9.10 and table 4.4) we were also able to locate data on violent crime. We should note, however, that the crime rate, being usually an expression of violence between individuals, is a variable distinct from sociopolitical instability (intergroup violence), and these two variables do not have to fluctuate in synchrony.

In summary, we have a rich database on the dynamics of sociopolitical instability. These data show that the dynamics of instability are complex and evolve on at least two distinct temporal scales. At the scale of centuries, there was a marked tendency of instability events to be bunched in some periods but not others. These instability waves recurred with a period of roughly two (sometimes three) centuries, so that a century of high instability would be followed by a century of lower instability. The pattern is most clear where we have long-term data. For example, between 1150 and 1700, there were three instability waves in France, arriving roughly every two hundred years (figure 5.3; see also coin hoard trends in figure 4.2). Additionally, there are multicentury hoard compilations for two European regions that exhibit a very similar pattern (figures 10.2 and 10.3). The graphs show clear instability waves during the late medieval period and the seventeenth century.

As we show in chapters dealing with specific cases, the instability waves were dynamically associated with demographic dynamics, but there was a phase shift between the two variables. Stagflation phases, when population numbers peaked, were relatively peaceful and orderly, and instability reached a peak during the following phases of crisis and depression. This empirical pattern is precisely what the demographic-structural theory predicts.

Can we make the above statement more precise and quantitative? Given the limitations of historical data and the complexity of the dynamical pattern (variability in oscillation periods and phase shifts, as well as such complicating factors as the fathers-and-sons cycles), we need to employ an appropriately coarse-grained procedure. This question, then, can be approached as follows. First, we identify the population growth and decline phases. Although quantitative details of population dynamics for historic

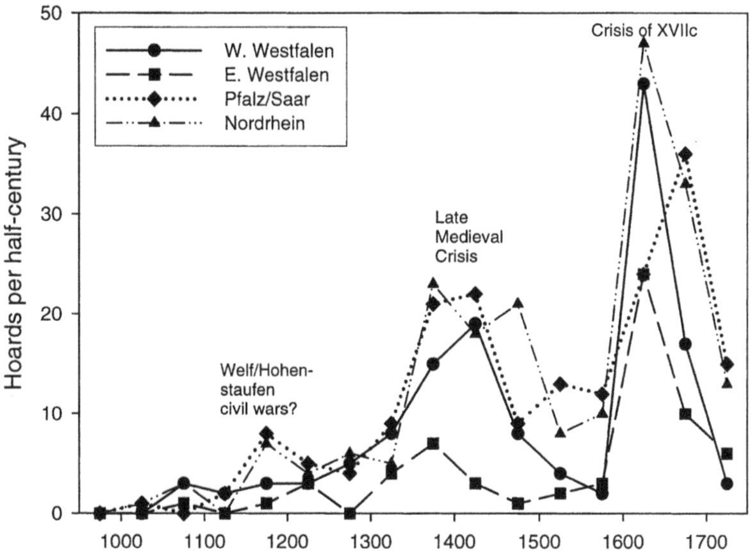

Figure 10.2 Temporal distribution of coin hoards found in northwestern Germany (Ilisch 1980: Table 6). The four curves show the number of hoards per half-century found in four regions: East Westphalia, West Westphalia, Pfalz/Saar, and Nordrhein.

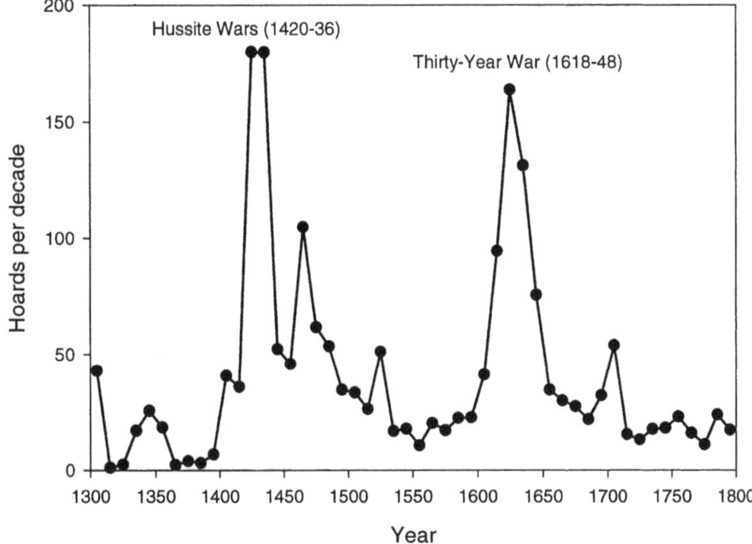

Figure 10.3 Temporal distribution of coin hoards found in the Czech Republic (Bohemia, Moravia, and Silesia) (Nohejlova-Pratova 1955).

TABLE 10.2
Instability events per decade during the population growth and decline secular phases: The seven complete secular cycles studied in this book

	Growth phase		*Decline phase*	
Secular cycle	*Years*	*Instability*	*Years*	*Instability*
Plantagenet	1151–1315	0.78	1316–1485	2.53
Tudor	1486–1640	0.47	1641–1730	2.44
Capetian	1216–1315	0.80	1316–1450	3.26
Valois	1451–1570	0.75	1571–1660	6.67
Republican	350–130 BCE	0.41	130–30 BCE	4.40
Principate	30 BCE–165 CE	0.61	165–285	3.83
Muscovite	1465–1565	0.60	1565–1615	3.80
Average (±SE)		**0.6 (±0.06)**		**3.8 (±0.5)**

societies are rarely known with any precision, as we saw in the preceding chapters, there is usually a consensus among demographic historians as to when the qualitative pattern of long-term growth changed. Second, we count instability events, using the indices of instability based on the written sources (we do not do it here, but the same approach can be also applied to instability proxy data, such as incidence of unrecovered coin hoards). Finally, we compare the incidence of instability events per decade between the population increase and population decrease phases. The results of applying this procedure to all seven complete case-studies (omitting the Romanov cycle) are shown in table 10.2. The empirical regularity is very strong: in all cases, instability is greater during the declining phases than during the growth phases (*t*-test; $P << .001$).

This is a striking result, and apparently one not limited to the secular cycles studied in this book. For example, we can apply the same procedure to the more than two millennia of Chinese imperial history. We used the population data from Zhao and Xie (1988) and the instability data from Lee (1931) (for a more detailed discussion of these data series, see Turchin 2003b: Section 8.4). Focusing on the periods when China was unified under one dynasty, we obtained the results shown in table 10.3. Again, the pattern is consistent and striking.

Thus, when instability is examined on an appropriately coarse temporal scale (essentially centuries), there is an excellent match between theoretical predictions and observed empirical patterns. However, the complicating factor is that instability also fluctuates on a finer time scale, that of human generations. This pattern is especially clear during the disintegrative phases of secular cycles, when peaks of particularly intense internal warfare recur at an interval of fifty years, give or take ten, with periods of fragile peace between them. Such "fathers-and-sons" dynamics, to a greater or

TABLE 10.3
Instability events per decade during growth and decline secular phases: The Chinese dynastic cycles.

	Growth phase		*Decline phase*	
Secular cycle	*Years*	*Instability*	*Years*	*Instability*
Western Han	200 BCE–10	1.5	10–40	10.8
Eastern Han	40–180	1.6	180–220	13.4
Sui	550–610	5.1	610–630	10.5
Tang	630–750	1.1	750–770	7.6
Northern Sung	960–1120	3.7	1120–1160	10.6
Yuan	1250–1350	6.7	1350–1410	13.5
Ming	1410–1620	2.8	1620–1650	13.1
Qing	1650–1850	5.0	1850–1880	10.8
Average (±SE)		**3.4**		**11.3**

lesser degree, occurred during the disintegrative phases of all eight cases that we examined in this book. In addition, fathers-and-sons cycles were discernible during integrative phases in medieval England, where baronial rebellions tended to occur every sixty years between 1100 and 1500 (figure 2.7), and in nineteenth-century Russia (figures 9.9 and 9.10 and table 9.7).

Finally, there was a class of instability events that did not fit either secular or fathers-and-sons rhythms. The examples include the mid-first-century crises in the Principate (most notably the "year of three emperors," 68–69 CE), the mid-Tudor crisis (between 1539 and 1563), and the Pugachev rebellion in Russia (1773–75). These crises were not predicted by the demographic-structural theory, and their occurrence underscores the point we have made repeatedly: the theory does not describe historical dynamics in all of their complexity. Clearly, mechanisms other than overpopulation and elite overproduction can bring about political crises, rebellions, and outbreaks of civil war. On the other hand, these "nondemographic-structural crises" were milder both in intensity and, especially, duration than the demographic-structural ones. Thus, although the theory does not explain all instances of instability, its prediction of alternating secular trends of stability versus instability is supported in all eight empirical case studies.

10.5 Are There General Laws of Historical Dynamics?

We end the overview of empirical results on a more speculative, even provocative note (in the sense that we wish to provoke controversy). There is a longstanding debate among scientists and philosophers as to whether history has general laws. In the nineteenth century some thinkers, emboldened by spectacular successes in physics and biology, argued that the scientific study of history, which means searching for general laws, is possible. For example, in the epilogue to his novel *War and Peace*, Leo Tolstoy proposed that the laws of history could be discovered by employing methods similar to those used in statistical physics or evolutionary biology, and this view was shared by many nineteenth-century historians (Beard 2002). During the twentieth century the opinion among the philosophers and historians swung in the opposite direction. For example, the philosopher Karl Popper (1957) thought that historical processes were too complex and history was too different from natural sciences to have general laws such as those discovered in physics or biology.

The general thrust of our research program goes very much against this consensus. A basic premise of our study is that historical societies can be studied with the same methods physicists and biologists used to study natural systems. We started with a general theory, which has been formalized in our previous work by translating it into mathematical models (e.g., Turchin 2003b: Chapter 7). As a result of this formalization, we have a set of specific and quantitative predictions about a suite of demographic, economic, social, and political variables (detailed in chapter 1; see table 1.1). As discussed earlier in this chapter, not all predictions of the theory have been borne out by the data. Such an outcome should be expected, since theories in natural sciences are also not expected to be right all the time. For most variables, the match between model predictions and empirical time series was quite impressive. Furthermore, where the theory failed (as in its prediction of revenue dynamics during the disintegrative phases), it did so in an interesting way. Instead of the theoretically predicted pattern we saw another one, and where there are recurring patterns, there may be general processes underlying them. In other words, the observed regularities suggest how the theory could be improved. Such an iterative approach—in which theoretical predictions are compared with the data, the theory is modified in light of the obtained results, and then new data are brought in to test the predictions of the modified theory—is at the heart of making scientific progress in both natural and social sciences, and, we believe, in historical applications as well.

The general implications of our results, then, are that some sort of general regularities of the historical process appear to exist. At the present time we cannot state them in the same precise form as formulations of many physical laws, with defined mathematical forms and universal constants. Perhaps "laws of history" will never attain the same level of precision as that achieved in some areas of physics; the future will show. But it is possible to formulate some of the general principles of the theory that have received broad empirical support, if in a more qualitative fashion. Here is our preliminary attempt at doing so, with the understanding that the proposed generalizations are tentative and likely to be improved with subsequent empirical and theoretical research.

One generalization can be called the neo-Malthusian principle: during periods of sustained population growth, if the output of the agrarian economy does not keep pace with the population, a number of relative price trends will be observed. One trend is rising prices for basic foodstuffs, energy, and land. Another one is falling real wages for labor. These trends are simply a consequence of the law of supply and demand. Thus, as the supply of labor increases, and if the demand for it is limited (which it is in agrarian economies), the price of labor inevitably decreases. We saw this pattern in all empirical studies with a greater or lesser degree of clarity, depending on the quality of the data. The most striking illustration of this principle is figure 3.10b, which shows a very close relationship between the population pressure on resources and real wages in England, 1150–1800.

Another generalization, dealing with the elite dynamics, is also a consequence of the law of supply and demand. The principal kind of wealth in agrarian societies is land. The elite landowners profit from overpopulation in two ways. First, they are consumers of labor: they need peasants to work their land, servants to carry out domestic chores, and craftsmen and artisans for producing items for status consumption. Second, their property, land, produces food and other commodities, such as fuel and raw materials, the demand for which increases together with the growing population. Because the items they consume become cheaper while the items they produce increase in value, the elites greatly profit from overpopulation. The process, however, is dynamic, and a favorable economic conjuncture for the elites means that, first, their numbers increase from both biological reproduction and upward social mobility, and second, they become accustomed to ever greater levels of consumption. In the end, elite numbers and appetites outgrow their "carrying capacity" (based on the labor of commoners). Just as overpopulation results in large segments of commoner population becoming immiserated, elite overproduction similarly results in large segments of elites becoming impoverished (not in absolute terms, as with common populace, but relatively to the standards of consumption needed to maintain the elite status). This generalization thus may be called the principle of elite overproduction. One consequence of this dynamic is that the rate of elite overproduction should be shifted in phase (should lag behind) the rate of general population growth. The case studies in this book provide ample empirical support for this model prediction: whereas population growth rate peaks during the expansion phase, elite overproduction develops during the stagflation phase.

A third possible generalization deals with the causes of sociopolitical instability. The demographic-structural theory proposes three principal causes of the onset of a disintegrative trend (that is, a lengthy period of heightened instability): overpopulation, elite overproduction, and a fiscal crisis of the state. As we discussed in section 10.4, however, some causal factors are relatively more important than others. In particular, a factor that appears to be always associated with high instability (at least in the eight cases we examined) is elite overproduction. Overpopulation, by contrast, results in popular immiseration and discontent, but as long as the elites remain unified, peasant insurrections, slave rebellions, and worker uprisings have little chance of success and are speedily suppressed. Furthermore, when the population declines during the disintegrative periods, there is often a substantial lag time between population density reaching a low level and the restoration of internal peace and order. The third component, the fiscal crisis of the state, is usually present but sometimes is missing as triggering factor leading to civil war (see section 10.4). Thus, overpopulation and fiscal crisis are important contributing factors, but the dominant role in internal warfare appears to be played by elite overproduction leading to intraelite competition, fragmentation, and conflict, and the rise of counterelites who mobilize popular masses in their struggle against the existing order.

The three generalizations we have just discussed are only a sample from many more potential generalizations arising from recurrent patterns that we noted in the historical cases we studied. For example, there may be a general principle underlying the shifts in social mood from a desire for change to a yearning for peace and stability, which appears to play an important role in creating relatively peaceful interludes during the disintegrative trends (what we termed the fathers-and-sons cycles) and in ending the disintegrative trend, a reversal that starts the new secular cycle. It is possible that this pattern can be quantified, perhaps by analyzing the content of speeches, political writings, and newspaper editorials, but this remains a task for the future.

Our concluding thoughts are these. We believe it is possible to obtain quantitative empirical estimates for many variables that are needed to test theories of historical dynamics. Furthermore, our models, and the demographic-structural theory in particular, have matured to the point where they can be used to make quantitative and testable predictions. Many of these predictions are supported by the data. Others failed, but often in interesting ways that suggest further development of the theory. The historical process is very complex, and we have to live with severe data limitations; nevertheless, it is possible to apply the standard scientific approach to the study of history. We are optimistic about the future prospects of history as science.

Acknowledgments

The authors wish to thank Adam Burke for editorial comments on chapter 1. Walter Scheidel and Nathan Rosenstein offered many useful comments on the Roman chapters. Our greatest debt of gratitude, however, is to Jack Goldstone. Not only was he responsible for setting forth the theoretical framework on which our book builds, he read the whole manuscript and provided a lengthy and extremely useful critique that made the resulting work much better.

References Cited

Abel, W. 1966. *Agrarkrisen und Agrarkonjunktur*, 2nd ed. Verlag Paul Parey, Hamburg.

Abel, W. 1973. *Crises agraires en Europe (XIIe–XXe siecle)*. Flammarion, Paris.

Abel, W. 1980. *Agricultural fluctuations in Europe: From the thirteenth to the twentieth centuries*. St. Martin's Press, New York.

AHNWR. 1971. *Agrarian history of northwest Russia from the second half of the fifteenth to the beginning of the sixteenth century (Agrarnaya istoriya Severo-Zapada Rossii. Vtoraya polovina XV–nachalo XVI veka)*. Nauka, Leningrad.

AHNWR. 1989. *Agrarian history of northwest Russia of the seventeenth century (Agrarnaya istoriya Severo-Zapada Rossii XVII veka)*. Nauka, Leningrad.

Alefirenko, P. K. 1958. *Peasant movements and the peasant question in Russia in the 30s–50s of the seventeenth century (Krestyanskoe dvizhenie i krestyanskiy vopros v Rossii 30–50-x godah XVIII veka)*. Publishing House of the Academy of Sciences of the USSR, Moscow.

Alexander, M. A. 2002. *The Kondratiev cycle: A generational interpretation*. Writers Club Press, San Jose, CA.

Allen, R. C. 1992. *Enclosure and the yeoman*. Clarendon Press, Oxford.

Allen, R. C. 2001. The great divergence in European wages and prices from the Middle Ages to the First World War. *Explorations in Economic History* 38:411–47.

Alston, R. 1995. *Soldier and society in Roman Egypt: A social history*. Routledge, London.

Alston, R. 1998. *Aspects of Roman history: AD 14–117*. Routledge, London.

Armstrong, S. 1998. Carolingian coin hoards and the impact of the Viking raids in the ninth century. *Numismatic Chronicle* 158:131–64.

Aston, T. H., and C.H.E. Philpin, editors. 1985. *The Brenner debate: Agrarian class structure and economic development in pre-industrial Europe*. Cambridge University Press, Cambridge.

Bagnall, R. 2005. Evidence and models for the economy of Roman Egypt. Pages 187–204 in I. Morris and J. G. Manning, editors, *The ancient economy: Evidence and models*. Stanford University Press, Stanford.

Baratier, E. 1971. *La démographie provençale du XIIe et XIVe siècle*. S.E.V.P.E.N., Paris.

Barbaro, I., and A. Contarini. 1873. *Travels to Tana and Persia by Iosafa Barbaro and Ambrogio Contarini*. Translated from the Italian by William Thomas and S. A. Roy, edited, with an introduction, by Lord Stanley of Alderley. London.

Barbiche, B. 1978. *Sully*. A. Michel, Paris.

Barker, G., and T. Rasmussen. 1998. *The Etruscans*. Blackwell, Oxford.

Bartlett, R. 2000. *England under the Norman and Angevin kings: 1075–1225*. Clarendon Press, Oxford.

Bean, J.M.W. 1991. Landlords. Pages 526–86 in E. Miller, editor, *The agrarian history of England and Wales. Vol. III: 1348–1500*. Cambridge University Press, Cambridge.

Beard, C. A. 2002. *The economic basis of politics*. Transaction Publishers, New Brunswick, NJ.

Beckett, J. V. 1986. *The aristocracy in England: 1660–1914*. Blackwell, Oxford.

Beik, W. 1985. *Absolutism and society in seventeenth-century France: State power and provincial aristocracy in Languedoc*. Cambridge University Press, Cambridge.

Beik, W. 2005. The absolutism of Louis XIV as social collaboration. *Past and Present* 188:195–224.

Beliaev, I. D. 1903. *The peasants of Russia* (*Krestiane na Rusi*). Publishing House GPEB, Moscow.

Beloch, J. 1886. *Die Bevölkerung der griechisch-römischen Welt*. Dunkel and Humbolt, Leipzig.

Beloch, J. 1964. *Der Italische Bund unter Roms Hegemonie*. Bretschneider, Rome.

Belousov, R. A. 2000. The state budget of pre-revolutionary Russia (Gosudarstvenniy byudzhet dorevolyucionnoy Rossii). Pages 357–99 in A. Vinogradov, editor, *Economic history of Russia in the nineteenth and twentieth centuries: The modern view (Ekonomichskaya istoriya Rossii XIX–XX vv.: Sovremenniy vzglyad)*. ROSSPAN, Moscow.

Benedict, P. 1975. Catholics and Huguenots in sixteenth-century Rouen: The demographic effects of the religious wars. *French Historical Studies* 9:209–34.

Benedict, P. 1985. Civil war and natural disaster in northern France. Pages 84–105 in P. Clark, editor, *The European crisis of the 1590s*. George Allen and Unwin, London.

Beresford, M. 1967. *New towns of the Middle Ages: Town plantation in England, Wales, and Gascony*. Praeger, New York.

Berger, R. M. 1993. *The most necessary luxuries: The mercers' company of Coventry, 1550–1680*. Pennsylvania State University Press, University Park.

Bergman, J. 1983. *Vera Zasulich: A biography*. Stanford University Press, Stanford.

Bernadsky, V. N. 1961. *Novgorod and the Novgorod Land in the fifteenth century* (*Novgorod i Novgorodskaya zemlya v XV veke*). Publishing House of the Academy of Sciences of the USSR, Moscow and Leningrad.

Berry, B.J.L. 1991. *Long-wave rhythms in economic development and political behavior*. Johns Hopkins University Press, Baltimore.

Berthe, M. 1976. *Le Comté de Bigorre: Un milieu rural au bas Moyen Âge*. S.E.V.P.E.N., Paris.

Betzig, L. L. 1986. *Despotism and differential reproduction: A Darwinian view of history*. Aldine, Chicago.

Bintliff, J., and K. Sbonias, editors. 1999. *Reconstructing past population trends in Mediterranean Europe (3000 BC–AD 1800)*. Oxbow, Oxford.

Biraben, J.-N. 1975. *Les hommes et la peste en France et dans les pays européens et méditerranéens. Tome I*. Mouton, Paris.

Bitton, D. 1969. *The French nobility in crisis: 1560–1640*. Stanford University Press, Stanford.

Blum, J. 1956. Prices in Russia in the sixteenth century. *Journal of Economic History* 16:182–199.

Bohna, M. L. 2000. Political and criminal violence in fifteenth-century England. Pages 91–104 in R. W. Kaeuper, editor, *Violence in medieval society.* Boydell Press, Woodbridge, Suffolk, UK.

Bois, G. 1984. *The crisis of feudalism.* Cambridge University Press, Cambridge.

Bois, G. 2000. *La grande dépression médiévale: XIVe–XVe siècles.* Presses Universitaires de France, Paris.

Bolton, J. L. 1980. *The medieval English economy: 1150–1500.* Rowman and Littlefield, Totowa, NJ.

Bonney, R. 1999. France, 1494–1815. Pages 123–76 in R. Bonney, editor, *The rise of the fiscal state in Europe, c. 1200–1815.* Oxford University Press, Oxford.

Borsch, S. J. 2005. *The Black Death in Egypt and England: A comparative study.* University of Texas Press, Austin.

Boserup, E. 1966. *The conditions of agricultural growth: The economics of agrarian change under population pressure.* Aldine, Chicago.

Boserup, E. 1981. *Population and technological change: A study of long-term trends.* University of Chicago Press, Chicago.

Bovykin, V. I., editor. 1981. *The working class in the first Russian revolution of 1905–1907 (Rabochiy klass v pervoy rossiyskoy revolyucii 1905–1907 gg.).* Nauka, Moscow.

Bowden, P. 1967. Statistical appendix. Pages 814–70 in J. Thirsk, editor, *The agrarian history of England and Wales. Vol. IV.* Cambridge University Press, Cambridge.

Bradley, K. R. 1989. *Slavery and rebellion in the Roman world, 140 B.C.–70 B.C.* Indiana University Press, Bloomington.

Braudel, F. 1988. *The identity of France. Vol. II: People and production.* HarperCollins, New York.

Braudel, F., and E. Labrousse. 1977. *Histoire économique et sociale de la France.* Presses Universitaires de France, Paris.

Brenner, R. 1985a. Agrarian class structure and economic development in pre-industrial Europe. Pages 10–63 in T. H. Aston and C.H.E. Philpin, editors, *The Brenner debate: Agrarian class structure and economic development in pre-industrial Europe.* Cambridge University Press, Cambridge.

Brenner, R. 1985b. The agrarian roots of European capitalism. Pages 213–327 in T. H. Aston and C.H.E. Philpin, editors, *The Brenner debate: Agrarian class structure and economic development in pre-industrial Europe.* Cambridge University Press, Cambridge.

Briggs, R. 1998. *Early modern France: 1560–1715,* 2nd ed. Oxford University Press, Oxford.

Britnell, R. 1997. *The closing of the Middle Ages? England, 1471–1529.* Blackwell, Oxford.

Britnell, R. H. 1995. Commercialization and economic development in England: 1000–1300. Pages 7–26 in R. H. Britnell and B.M.S. Campbell, editors, *A commercialising economy: England 1086 to c. 1300.* Manchester University Press, Manchester, UK.

Brooks, C. W. 1989. Interpersonal conflict and social tensions: Civil litigation in England, 1640–1830. Pages 357–99 in A. L. Beier, D. Cannadine, and J. M. Rosenheim, editors, *The first modern society.* Cambridge University Press, Cambridge.

Brower, D. R. 1975. *Training the nihilists: Education and radicalism in tsarist Russia.* Cornell University Press, Ithaca, NY.

Brown, I. D. 1971. *A bibliography of coin hoards of Great Britain and Ireland, 1500–1967*. Special publication no. 6. Royal Numismatic Society, London.

Brunt, P. A. 1971. *Italian manpower: 225 BC–AD 14*. Clarendon Press, Oxford.

Brusilov, A. 2001. *Memoirs (Moi vospominaniya)*. ROSSPAN, Moscow.

Bussov, K. 1961. *The Moscow Chronicle (Moskovskaya khronika)*, 1584–1615. Publishing House of the Academy of Sciences of the USSR, Moscow and Leningrad.

Cameron, R. 1989. *A concise economic history of the world: From Paleolithic times to the present*. Oxford University Press, New York.

Campbell, B.M.S. 1981. The population of early Tudor England: A re-evaluation of the 1522 Muster Returns and 1524 and 1525 Lay Subsidies. *Journal of Historical Geography* 7:145–54.

Campbell, B.M.S. 2005. The agrarian problem in the early fourteenth century. *Past and Present* 188:3–70.

Carpentier, È., and M. Le Mené. 1996. *La France du XIe au XVe siècle: Population, société, économie*. Presses Universitaires de France, Paris.

Chandler, T. 1987. *Four thousand years of urban growth: An historical census*. St. Gavid's, Lewiston.

Chechulin, N. D. 1906. *Essays on the history of Russian finances in the reign of Catherine II (Ocherki po istorii russkix finansov v tsarstvovanie Ekateriny II)*. Senatorial Printing House, St. Petersburg.

Cherepnin, L. V. 1960. *The formation of the Russian centralized state in XIV–XV centuries (Obrazovanie russkogo tsentralizovannogo gosudarstva v XIV–XV vekah)*. Socegis, Moscow.

Chernov, A. V. 1954. *Armed forces of the Russian state in the fifteenth–seventeenth centuries (Vooruzhennye sily Russkogo gosudarstva v XV–XVII vv.)*. Voenizdat, Moscow.

Christiansen, E. 1985. The Roman coins of Alexandria (30 B.C. to A.D. 296). *Coin Hoards* 7:77–140.

Chu, C. Y. C., and R. D. Lee. 1994. Famine, revolt, and dynastic cycle: Population dynamics in historic China. *Journal of Population Economics* 7:351–78.

CIA. 2002. *The world factbook*. CIA, Washington, DC (http://www.cia.gov/cia/publications/factbook/docs/history.html).

Clark, G. 2007a. *A farewell to alms: A brief economic history of the world*. Princeton University Press, Princeton, NJ.

Clark, G. 2007b. The long march of history: Farm wages, population, and economic growth, England 1209–1869. *Economic History Review* 60:97–135.

Clay, C. G. A. 1984a. *Economic expansion and social change: England 1500–1700. Vol. I: People, land and towns*. Cambridge University Press, Cambridge.

Clay, C. G. A. 1984b. *Economic expansion and social change: England 1500–1700. Vol. II: Industry, trade and government*. Cambridge University Press, Cambridge.

Cohen, J. E. 1995. *How many people can the Earth support?* W. W. Norton, New York.

Collins, J. B. 1995. *The state in early modern France*. Cambridge University Press, Cambridge.

Collins, R. 1979. *The credential society: An historical sociology of education and stratification*. Academic Press, New York.

Collins, R. 1993. Maturation of the state-centered theory of revolution and ideology. *Sociological Theory* 11:117–28.

Contamine, P. 1972. *Guerre, état et société à la fin du Moyen Age: Études sur les armées des rois de France 1337–1494.* Mouton, Paris.

Contamine, P. 1984. *War in the Middle Ages.* Blackwell, Oxford.

Contamine, P. 1997. *La noblesse au royame de France de Philippe le Bel à Louis XII.* Presses Universitaires de France, Paris.

Cornell, T. J. 1995. *The beginnings of Rome: Italy and Rome from the Bronze Age to the Punic Wars (c. 1000–264 BC).* Routledge, London.

Cornwall, J. 1970. English population in the early sixteenth century. *Economic History Review* 23:32–44.

Coulton, G. G. 1907. *Priests and people before the Reformation.* A. Strahan, London.

Crawford, M. 1993. *The Roman Republic,* 2nd ed. Harvard University Press, Cambridge, MA.

Crawford, M. H. 1974. *Roman Republican coinage. Vol. II.* Cambridge University Press, Cambridge.

Danilov, V. P. 1992. On the nature of agrarian evolution in Russia after 1861 (O kharaktere agrarnoj revoljucii v Rossi posle 1861 goda). Pages 53–63 in M. A. Beznin, editor, *Peasant economy: History and modernity* (*Krestianskoe hozyaystvo: Istoriya i sovremennost'*). *Part I.* Publishing House of the Vologodski Pedinstitut, Vologda.

Danilova, L. V. 1970. On the question of the causes of the rise of serfdom in Russia (K voprosu o prichinax utverzhdeniya krepostnichestva v Rossii). Pages 130–40 in *The 1965 Almanac of Agrarian History of Eastern Europe* (*Ezhegodnik po agrarnoy istorii vostochnoy Evropy za 1965 g.*). Publishing House of Moscow University, Moscow.

de Ligt, L. 2004. Poverty and demography: The case of the Gracchan land reforms. *Mnemosyne* 57:725–57.

de Ligt, L. 2007. Roman manpower and recruitment during the Middle Republic. Pages 114–31 in P. Erdkamp, editor, *A Companion to the Roman Army.* Blackwell, Malden, MA.

Dean, T. 2001. *Crime in Medieval Europe: 1200–1550.* Longman, Harlow, UK.

Degtyarev, A. Ya. 1980. *The Russian village in the fifteenth–seventeenth centuries: Essays on the history of rural population* (*Russkaya derevnya v XV–XVII vekax: Ocherki istorii selskogo rasseleniya*). Publishing House of Leningrad University, Leningrad, 1980.

Denholm-Young, N. 1969. *The country gentry in the fourteenth century.* Clarendon, Oxford.

Dewald, J. 1980. *The formation of provincial nobility: The magistrates of the Parlement of Rouen, 1499–1610.* Princeton University Press, Princeton, NJ.

Dewald, J. 1987. *Pont-St-Pierre, 1398–1789: Lordship, community, and capitalism in early modern France.* University of California Press, Berkeley and Los Angeles.

Dobb, M. 1963. *Studies in the development of capitalism.* International Publishers, New York.

Dobson, B. 2001. General survey: 1300–1540. Pages 273–90 in D. M. Pallister, editor, *The Cambridge urban history of Britain. Vol. I: 600–1540.* Cambridge University Press, Cambridge.

Doyle, W. 1996. *Venality: The sale of offices in eighteenth-century France.* Clarendon, Oxford.

Druzhinin, N. M. 1946. *The state peasants and the reform of P.D. Kiselev. Vol. I (Gosudarstvennie krestiane i reforma P. D. Kiseleva. Tom 1)*. Publishing House of the Academy of Sciences of the USSR, Moscow.

Dubrovsky, S. M. 1956. *Peasant movements in the revolution of 1905–07* (*Krestianskie dvizheniya v revolyucii 1905–1907 gg.*). Publishing House of the Academy of Sciences of the USSR, Moscow.

Dubrovsky, S. M. 1963. *The Stolypin agrarian reforms* (*Stolypinskaya agrarnya reforma*). Publishing House of the Academy of Sciences of the USSR, Moscow.

Duncan-Jones, R. 1974. *The economy of the Roman Empire*. Cambridge University Press, Cambridge.

Duncan-Jones, R. 1990. *Structure and scale in the Roman economy*. Cambridge University Press, Cambridge.

Duncan-Jones, R. 1994. *Money and government in the Roman Empire*. Cambridge University Press, Cambridge.

Duncan-Jones, R. P. 1996. The impact of the Antonine plague. *Journal of Roman Archaeology* 9:108–36.

Dunning, C. 1997. Does Jack Goldstone's model of early modern state crises apply to Russia? *Comparative Studies in Society and History* 39:572–92.

Dunning, C. 1998. The preconditions of modern Russia's first civil war. *Russian History* 25:119–31.

Dunning, C. S. L. 2001. *Russia's first civil war: The time of troubles and the founding of the Roman dynasty*. Pennsylvania State University Press, University Park.

Dunning, C. S. L. 2004. *A short history of Russia's first civil war*. Pennsylvania State University Press, University Park.

Dupâquier, J., J.-N. Biraben, R. Ètenne, C. Pietri, P. Luce, H. Bautier, H. Dubois, A. Higounet-Nadal, C. Klapisch-Zuber, A. Sauvy, and E. Le Roy Ladurie. 1988a. *Histoire de la population française. Vol. I: Des origines à la Renaissance*. Presses Universitaires de France, Paris.

Dupâquier, J., J.-N. Biraben, R. Ètenne, C. Pietri, P. Luce, H. Bautier, H. Dubois, A. Higounet-Nadal, C. Klapisch-Zuber, A. Sauvy, and E. Le Roy Ladurie. 1988b. *Histoire de la population française. Vol. II*. Presses Universitaires de France, Paris.

Duplessy, J. 1985. *Les Trésors Monétaires Médiévaux et Modernes Découverts en France. Vols. I and II*. Bibliothèque Nationale, Paris.

Durnovo, P. N. 1922. Memoir (Zapiska). *Krasnaya Nov* 6:195–97.

Dyer, C. 1980. *Lords and peasants in a changing society: The estates of the bishopric of Worcester, 680–1540*. Cambridge University Press, Cambridge.

Dyer, C. 1989. *Standards of living in the later Middle Ages*. Cambridge University Press, Cambridge.

Dyer, C. 2000. *Everyday life in Medieval England*. Hambledon and London, London

Dyer, C. 2002. *Making a living in the Middle Ages: The people of Britain 850–1520*. Yale University Press, New Haven, CT.

Earle, T. 1997. *How chiefs came to power: The political economy of prehistory*. Stanford University Press, Stanford, CA.

Easterlin, R. 1980. *Birth and fortune*. Basic Books, New York.

Easterlin, R. A. 1996. *Growth triumphant: The twenty-first century in historical perspective*. University of Michigan Press, Ann Arbor.

Eisner, M. 2003. Secular trends of violent crime: Evidence and theoretical interpretations. *Crime and Justice: An Annual Review* 31.

ESFDB. 1995. European state finance database. Compiled by Richard Bonney (http://www.le.ac.uk/hi/bon/ESFDB/).

Everitt, A. 1967. Farm labourers. Pages 396–465 in J. Thirsk, editor, *The agrarian history of England and Wales. Vol. 4: 1500–1640.* Cambridge University Press, Cambridge.

Faizova, I. V. 1999. *The "Liberty Manifesto" and gentry's service in the eighteenth century ("Manifest o vol'nosti" i sluzhba dvoryanstva v XVIII stoletii).* Nauka, Moscow.

Farmer, D. L. 1988. Prices and wages. Pages 716–817 in H. E. Hallam, editor, *The agrarian history of England and Wales.* Volume II: 1042–1350. Cambridge University Press, Cambridge.

Farmer, D. L. 1991. Prices and wages, 1350–1500. Pages 431–525 in E. Miller, editor, *The agrarian history of England and Wales.* Volume III: 1348–1500. Cambridge University Press, Cambridge.

Fedorov, V. A. 1990. *The peasant movements in Central Russia, 1800–1860 (Krestianskoe dvizhenie v tsentral'noy Rossii 1800–1860).* Publishing House of Moscow University, Moscow.

Finch, A. J. 1997. The nature of violence in the Middle Ages: An alternative perspective. *Historical Research* 70:249–68.

Fischer, D. H. 1996. *The great wave: Price revolutions and the rhythm of history.* Oxford University Press, New York.

Fletcher, J. 2003. *On the Russian State: Russia of the sixteenth century in the memoirs of foreigners (O gosudarstve russkom: Rossiya XVI veka v vospominaniyah inostrantsev).* Rusich, Smolensk.

Fossier, R. 1968. *La terre et les hommes en Picardie jusqu'a la fin du XIIIe siècle.* Béatrice-Nauwelaerts, Paris.

Fourquin, G. 1964. *Les campaignes de la région parisienne a la fin du Moyen Age.* Presses Universitaires de France, Paris.

Fourquin, G. 1978. *The anatomy of popular rebellion in the Middle Ages.* North Holland Publishing Co., Amsterdam.

Frank, T. 1933. *An economic survey of ancient Rome. Vol. I: Rome and Italy of the Republic.* Johns Hopkins University Press, Baltimore.

Frank, T. 1940. *An economic survey of ancient Rome. Vol. V: Rome and Italy of the empire.* Johns Hopkins University Press, Baltimore.

Frier, B. W. 2000. Demography. Pages 787–816 in A. K. Bowman, P. Garnsey, and D. Rathbone, editors, *The Cambridge ancient history,* 2nd ed. *Vol. XI: The high Empire, A.D. 70–192.* Cambridge University Press, Cambridge.

Fryde, E. B. 1991. Peasant rebellion and peasant discontents. Pages 744–819 in E. Miller, editor, *The agrarian history of England and Wales. Vol. III: 1348–1500.* Cambridge University Press, Cambridge.

Fryde, E. B. 1996. *Peasants and landlords in later medieval England.* St. Martin's Press, New York.

Ganelin, R. Sh. 1991. *The Russian autocracy in 1905: Reforms and the Revolution (Rossiyskoe samoderzhavie v 1905 g: Reformy i revolyutsiya).* Nauka, St. Petersburg.

Gavrilov, L. M. 1991. The Russian army on the eve of the February Revolution (Russkaya armiya nakanune Fevral'skoy revolyutsii). *Istoricheskie Zapiski* 114:48–72.

Gernet, M. N., O.B. Goldovsky, and I. N. Saharov, editors. 1907. *Against capital punishment (Protiv smertnoy kazni).* E. D. Sitin Printing House, Moscow.

Ginev, V. M. 1986. The splendid generation (Blestyaschaya pleyada). Pages 5–53 in S. S. Volk, editor, *The revolutionaries of the 1870s* (*Revolyutsionery 1870-h godov*). Lenizdat, Leningrad.

Ginev, V. N., and A. H. Tsamutaly. 1989. The struggle for freedom (V bor'be za svobodu). Pages 4–43 in S. S. Volk, editor, *"The Popular Will" and "the Black Repartition"* (*"Narodnaya Volya" and "Cherniy Peredel"*). Lenizdat, Leningrad.

Given-Wilson, C. 1987. *The English nobility in the late Middle Ages: The fourteenth-century political community.* Routledge and Kegan Paul, London.

Gohlener, V. M. 1955. Peasant movements in Saratov Province during the First Russian revolution (Krestianskoe dvizhenie v Saratovskoy gubernii v gody pervoy russkoy revolyutsii). *Istoricheskie Zapiski* 52:186–233.

Goldstein, J. 1988. *Long cycles.* Yale University Press, New Haven, CT.

Goldstone, J. A. 1991. *Revolution and rebellion in the early modern world.* University of California Press, Berkeley and Los Angeles.

Goldstone, J. A., editor. 1998. The encyclopedia of political revolutions. *Congressional Quarterly,* Washington, DC.

Goldstone, J. A. 2002a. Population and security: How demographic change can lead to violent conflict. *Journal of International Affairs* 56:3–21.

Goldstone, J. A. 2002b. *Revolution: Theoretical, comparative, and historical studies*, 3rd ed. Wadsworth, Fort Worth.

Goldstone, J. A. 2008. The social origins of the French Revolution revisited. Paper presented at the 2008 meetings of the Society for French Historical Studies, Rutgers, NJ.

Golos. 1916. *Golos minuvshego* 5–6: 5.

Gorfunkel, A. H. 1962. The historical meaning of the Peasant War of the beginning of the seventeenth century (K voprosu ob istoricheskom znachenii Krestianskoy voyny nachala XVII veka). *Istoriya SSSR* 4: 112–18.

Got'e, Yu. A. 1937. *The Trans-Moscow Land in the sixteenth century* (*Zamoskovniy kray v XVI veke*), Socegiz, Moscow.

Gray, H. L. 1934. Incomes from land in England in 1436. *English History Review* 49:607–31.

Greenberg, J. 2003. Plagued by doubt: Reconsidering the impact of a mortality crisis in the 2nd c. A.D. *Journal of Roman Archaeology* 16:413–425.

Greene, K. 1986. *The archaeology of the Roman economy.* University of California Press, Berkeley and Los Angeles.

Greengrass, M. 1985. The later wars of religion in the French Midi. Pages 106–34 in P. Clark, editor, *The European crisis of the 1590s.* George Allen and Unwin, London.

Grigg, D. 1980. *Population growth and agrarian change.* Cambridge University Press, Cambridge.

Grigg, D. 1989. *English agriculture: An historical perspective.* Blackwell, Oxford.

Griziotti-Kretschmann, J. 1935. *Il problema del trend secolare nelle fluttuazioni dei prezzi.* Università di Pavia, Pavia.

Guérin, I. 1960. *La vie rurale en Sologne aux XIVe et XVe siècles.* Editions de l'Ecole des Hautes Etudes en Sciences Sociales, Paris.

Gurr, T. R. 1980. *Handbook of political conflict.* Free Press, New York.

Hallam, E. M., and J. Everard. 2001. *Capetian France: 987–1328*, 2nd ed. Longman, Harlow, UK.

Hallam, H. E. 1988a. The life of people. Pages 818–53 in J. Thirsk, editor, *The agrarian history of England and Wales. Vol. II: 1042–1350*. Cambridge University Press, Cambridge.

Hallam, H. E. 1988b. Population movements in England, 1086–1350. Pages 508–93 in J. Thirsk, editor, *The agrarian history of England and Wales. Vol. II: 1042–1350*. Cambridge University Press, Cambridge.

Hammond, M. 1957. Composition of the senate, A.D. 68–235. *Journal of Roman Studies* 47:75–81.

Hanawalt, B. A. 1976. Violent death in fourteenth and early fifteenth century England. *Journal of Comparative Studies in Society and History* 18:297–320.

Hanawalt, B. A. 1979. *Crime and conflict in English communities: 1300–1348*. Harvard University Press, Cambridge, MA.

Harding, R. R. 1978. *Anatomy of a power elite: The provincial governors of early modern France*. Yale University Press, New Haven, CT.

Harl, K. W. 1996. *Coinage in the Roman economy, 300 B.C. to A.D. 700*. Johns Hopkins University Press, Baltimore.

Harvey, P.D.A. 1973. The English inflation of 1180–1220. *Past and Present* 61:3–30.

Harvey, S. 1976. The knight and knight's fee in England. Pages 133–73 in R. H. Hilton, editor. *Peasants, knights, and heretics: Studies in medieval English social history*. Cambridge University Press, Cambridge.

Harvey, S. 1988. Domesday England. Pages 45–136 in J. Thirsk, editor, *The agrarian history of England and Wales. Vol. II: 1042–1350*. Cambridge University Press, Cambridge.

Hatcher, J. 1977. *Plague, population and the English economy: 1348–1530*. Macmillan, London.

Hatcher, J. 1996. The great slump of the mid-fifteenth century. Pages 237–72 in R. Britnell and J. Hatcher, editors, *Progress and problems in medieval England: Essays in honour of Edward Miller*. Cambridge University Press, Cambridge.

Hatcher, J., and M. Bailey. 2001. *Modelling the Middle Ages: The history and theory of England's economic development*. Oxford University Press, Oxford.

Heal, F., and C. Holmes. 1994. *The gentry of England and Wales*. Stanford University Press, Stanford, CA.

Henneman, J. B. 1996. *Olivier de Clisson and political society of France under Charles V and Charles VI*. University of Pennsylvania Press, Philadelphia.

Henneman, J. B. 1999. France in the Middle Ages. Pages 101–22 in R. Bonney, editor, *The rise of the fiscal state in Europe, c. 1200–1815*. Oxford University Press, Oxford.

Herberstein, S. 1988. *Notes on Muscovy* (*Zapiski o Moskovii*). Publishing House of Moscow University, Moscow.

Hill, C. 1982. *The century of revolution: 1603–1714*. W. W. Norton, New York.

Hilton, R. H. 1966. *A medieval society: The West Midlands at the end of the thirteenth century*. Weidenfeld and Nicolson, London.

Hilton, R. H. 1985. Introduction. Pages 1–9 in T. H. Aston and C.H.E. Philpin, editors, *The Brenner debate: Agrarian class structure and economic development in pre-industrial Europe*. Cambridge University Press, Cambridge.

Hobsbawm, E. J. 1962. *The Age of Revolution, 1789–1848*. New American Library, New York.

Hollingsworth, T. H. 1964. The demography of the British peerage. *Population Studies*, suppl. 2:18.

Hollingsworth, T. H. 1969. *Historical demography*. Cornell University Press, Ithaca, NY.

Hopkins, K. 1978. *Conquerors and slaves: Sociological studies in Roman history*. Cambridge University Press, Cambridge.

Hopkins, K. 1983. *Death and renewal: Sociological studies in Roman history*. Cambridge University Press, Cambridge.

Hoskins, W. G. 1976. *The age of plunder: King Henry's England: 1500–1547*. Longman, London.

Hristoforov, I. A. 2002. *The "aristocratic" opposition to the Great Reforms: The end of 1859s–mid-1870s ("Aristokraticheskaya" oppozitsiya Velikim reformam: Konets 1850–seredina 1870-h gg.)*. Russkoe Slovo, Moscow.

Hughes, A. 1991. *The causes of the English civil war*. St. Martin's Press, New York.

Ibn Khaldun. 1958. *The Muqaddimah: An introduction to history*. Translated from the Arabic by Franz Rosenthal. Pantheon Books, New York.

Ilisch, P. 1980. *Münzfunde und Geldumlauf in Westfalen in Mittelalter und Neuzeit*. Aschendorff, Münster.

Inayatullah, S. 1997. Ibn Khaldun: The strengthening and weakening of Asabiya. Pages 25–32 in J. Galtung and S. Inayatullah, editors, *Macrohistory and macrohistorians*. Praeger, Westport, CT.

Indova, E. I. 1964. *The Palace Economy in Russia: The first half of the eighteenth century* (*Dvortsovoe hozyaystvo v Rossii: Pervaya polovina XVIII veka*). Nauka, Moscow.

Irvine, F. 1979. Social structure, social mobility and social change in sixteenth-century Montpellier. Ph.D. thesis, University of Toronto.

Itenberg, B. S. 1965. *Revolutionary populist movement* (*Dvizhenie revolyutsionnogo narodnichetsva*). Nauka, Moscow.

Ivina, L. I. 1985. *Internal colonization in Russia of the sixteenth century* (*Vnutrennee osvoenie zemel' v Rossii v XVI v*). Nauka, Leningrad.

Izyumova, S. A. 1959. On the history of leather and shoe manufacture in Novgorod the Great (K istorii kozhevennogo i sapozhnogo masterstva Novgoroda Velikogo). *Materialy i Issledovaniya po Arkheologii SSSR* 65:192–223.

Jessopp, A. 1892. *The coming of the friars*. Putnam, New York.

Johnson, A. W., and T. Earle. 2000. *The evolution of human societies: From foraging group to agrarian state*, 2nd ed. Stanford University Press, Stanford, CA.

Jones, W.R.D. 1973. *The mid-Tudor crisis (1539–1563)*. Barnes and Noble, New York.

Jongman, W. 1988. *The economy and society of Pompeii*. Gieben, Amsterdam.

Jongman, W. 2003. Slavery and the growth of Rome: The transformation of Italy in the second and first centuries BCE. Pages 100–122 in C. Edwards and G. Woolf, editors, *Rome the cosmopolis*. Cambridge University Press, Cambridge.

Kabuzan, V. M. 1963. *Population of Russia in the eighteenth–first half of the nineteenth centuries* (*Narodonaselenie Rossii v XVIII–pervoy polovine XIX v.*). Publishing House of the Academy of Sciences of the USSR, Moscow.

Kabuzan, V. M. 1971. *The dynamics of population distribution in Russia in the eighteenth–first half of the nineteenth centuries* (*Izmeneniya v razmeschenii naseleniya Rossii v XVIII–pervoy polovine XIX v.*). Nauka, Moscow.

Kabuzan, V. M., and S. M. Troitskii. 1971. *Dynamics of numbers, relative weight, and distribution of the gentry in Russia in 1782–1851* (*Izmeneniya v chislennpsti, udel'nom vese i razmeschenii dvoryanstva v Rossii v 1782–1851 gg*). *Istoriya SSSR* 4:153–59.

Kaeuper, R. W. 1988. *War, justice, and public order: England and France in the later Middle Ages*. Clarendon Press, Oxford.

Kamen, H. 1971. *The iron century: Social change in Europe in 1550–1660*. Weidenfeld and Nicholson, London.

Kamenski, A. B. 1999. *From Peter I to Paul I: Reforms in Russia in the eighteenth century* (*Ot Petra I do Pavla I: Reformy v Rossii XVIII veka*). Russian State University for the Humanities, Moscow.

Kanzaka, J. 2002. Villein rents in thirteenth-century England: An analysis of the Hundred Rolls of 1279–1280. *Economic History Review* 55:593–618.

Katkov, G. M. 1997. *The February Revolution* (*Fevral'skaya revolyutsiya*). Russki Put', Moscow.

Keene, D. 2001. London from the post-Roman period to 1300. Pages 187–216 in D. M. Pallister, editor, *The Cambridge urban history of Britain. Vol. I: 600–1540*. Cambridge University Press, Cambridge.

Keep, J. L. H. 1963. *The rise of social democracy in Russia*. Clarendon Press, Oxford.

Kerridge, E. 1953. The movement of rent: 1540–1640. *Economic History Review* 6:16–34.

King, E. 1979. *England: 1175–1425*. Charles Scribner's Sons, New York.

King, P. 1971. *The development of the English economy to 1750*. MacDonald and Evans, London.

Kir'yanov, Yu. V. 1993. Mass demonstrations caused by high prices in Russia: 1914–February 1917 (Massovye vystupleniya na pochve dorogovizny v Rossii: 1914–fevral 1917 g.). *Otechestvennaya Istoriya* 3:3–18.

Kiser, E., and A. Linton. 2001. Determinants of the growth of the state: War and taxation in early modern France and England. *Social Forces* 80:411–48.

Kishlansky, M. 1997. *A monarchy transformed: Britain, 1603–1714*. Penguin, New York.

Kliuchevskii, V. O. 1991. *Relations by foreigners on the Musovite State* (*Skazaniya inostrantsev o Moskovskom gosudarstve*). Prometei, Moscow.

Knecht, R. J. 2001. *The rise and fall of Renaissance France: 1483–1610*, 2nd ed. Blackwell, Oxford.

Kobrin, V. B. 1980. The establishment of the pomestie system. *Istoricheskie Zapiski* 105:150–195.

Koepke, N., and J. Baten. 2005. The biological standard of living in Europe during the last two millennia. *European Review of Economic History* 9:61–95.

Kokovtsov, V. N. 1992. *From my past: Memoirs. Vol. I: 1903–1919* (*Iz moego proshlogo: Memuary. Tom 1: 1903–1919* gg.). Nauka, Moscow.

Kolesnikov, S. P. 1976. *The northern village in the fifteeenth century* (*Severnaya derevnya v XV–vtoroy polovineXIX veka*). Severo-Zapadnoe Isdatel'stvo, Vologda.

Kollmann, N. S. 1999. *By honor bound: State and society in early modern Russia*. Cornell University Press, Ithaca, NY.

Kolycheva, E. I. 1987. *Agrarian formation of Russia in the sixteenth century* (*Agrarniy story Rossii XVI veka*). Moscow.

Komlos, J. 1990. Nutrition, population growth, and the Industrial Revolution in England. *Social Science History* 14:69–91.

Kondrat'ev, N. D. 1991. *The grain market and its regulation during the war and revolution* (*Rynok hlebov i ego regulirovanie vo vremya voyny i revolyutsii*). Nauka, Moscow.

Kondratieff, N. 1984. *The long wave cycle*. Richardson and Snyder, New York.

Konetskiy, V. Y. 1992. *K istorii sel'skogo rasseleliniya v doline reki Lovat' v epohu sredenvekov'ya in Novgorod and novgorodskaya zemlya*. Novgorod.

Konovalov, A. A. 1966. Periodization of Novgorod birch scrolls and the evolution of their content (in Russian). *Soviet Archaeology* 2:62.

Kopanev, A. I. 1959. The population of the Russian state in the XVI century (Naselenie Russkogo gosudarstva v XVI v). *Istoricheskie Zapiski* 64:237–44.

Korelin, A. P. 1979. *The nobility in post-reform Russia, 1861–1914* (*Dvoryanstvo v poreformennoy Rossii, 1861–1904 gg.*). Nauka, Moscow.

Koretskii, V. I. 1970. *Peasant enserfment and class struggle in Russia* (*Zakreposchenie krestian i klassovaya borba v Rossii*). Nauka, Moscow.

Koretskii, V. I. 1975. *Formation of serfdom and the First Peasant War in Russia* (*Formirovanie krepostnogo prava i pervaya krestianskaya voyna v Rossii*). Nauka, Moscow.

Korotayev, A., A. S. Malkov, and D. A. Khalturina. 2005. *The laws of history: Mathematical modeling of historical macroprocesses. Demography, economics, and wars* (*Zakony istorii: Matematicheskoe modelirovanie istoricheskikh makroportsessov. Demografiya, ekonomika, voyny*). KomKniga, Moscow.

Kosminsky, E. A. 1956. *Studies in the agrarian history of England in the thirteenth century*. Oxford University Press, Oxford.

Koval'chenko, I. D. 1959.The dynamics of agrarian production in Russia during the first half of the nineteenth century (Dinamika urovnya zemledelcheskogo proizvodstva v Rossii v pervouy polovine XIX veka). *Istoriya SSSR* 1:53–86.

Koval'chenko, I. D. 1967. *Russian enserfed peasantry in the first half of the nineteenth century* (*Russkoe krepostnoe krestianstvo v pervoy polovine XIX v.*). Publishing House of Moscow University, Moscow.

Koval'chenko, I. D., and L. V. Milov. 1974. *The all-Russian agrarian market: The eighteenth–beginning of the nineteenth centuries* (*Vserossiyskiy agrarniy rynok XVIII–nachalo XX veka*). Nauka, Moscow.

Krizhanich, Yu. 1997. *Politics* (*Politika*). Novii Svet, Moscow.

Labatut, J.-P. 1972. *Les ducs et paires de France au XVIIe siècle*. Presses Universitaires de France, Paris.

Lander, J. R. 1976. *Crown and nobility: 1450–1509*. McGill–Queen's University Press, Montreal.

Langdon, J., and J. Masschaele. 2006. Commercial activity and population growth in medieval England. *Past and Present* 190:35–81.

Le Glay, M., J.-L. Voisin, Y. Le Bohec, and D. Cherry. 1997. *A history of Rome*. Blackwell, Oxford.

Le Roy Ladurie, E. 1974. *The peasants of Languedoc*. University of Illinois Press, Urbana.

Le Roy Ladurie, E. 1987. *The French peasantry: 1450–1660*. University of California Press, Berkeley and Los Angeles.

Le Roy Ladurie, E. 1994. *The royal French state: 1460–1610*. Blackwell, Oxford.

Le Roy Ladurie, E., and J. Goy. 1982. *Tithe and agrarian history from the fourteenth to the nineteenth centuries: An essay in comparative history*. Cambridge University Press, Cambridge.

Lee, J. S. 1931. The periodic recurrence of internecine wars in China. *The China Journal*, March–April, 111–63.

Lee, R. D. 1986. Malthus and Boserup: A dynamic synthesis. In D. Coleman and R. S. Schofield, editors, *The state of population theory: Forward from Malthus*. Blackwell, Oxford.

Leikina-Svirskaya, V. R. 1971. *The intelligentsia in Russia during the second half of the nineteenth century* (*Intelligentsiya v Rossii vo vtoroy polovine XIX veka*). Mysl, Moscow.

Leonov, M. I. 1987. The numbers and composition of the Socialist Revolutionary Party in 1905 and 1917 (Chislennost i sostav partii eserov v 1905 i 1907 gg.). Pages 49–95 in P. P. Korelin, editor, *Political parties of Russia in the revolutionary period, 1905–1917: A quantitative analysis* (*Politicheskie partii Rossii v period revolyutsii 1905–1907 gg. Kolichestvenniy analiz*). Publishing House of the Academy of Sciences of the USSR, Moscow.

Lewit, T. 1991. *Agricultural productivity in the Roman economy A.D. 200–400*. Tempus Reparatum, Oxford, UK.

Leyberov, I. P., and S. D.Rudachenko. 1990. *Revolution and bread* (*Revolyutsiya i khleb*). Mysl, Moscow.

Li, R. S. K. 2002. Alternative routes to state breakdown: Towards an integrated model of territorial disintegration. *Sociological Theory* 20:1–23.

Lindert, P. H., and J. G. Williamson. 1982. Revising England's social tables 1688–1812. *Explorations in Economic History* 19:385–408.

Litvak, B. G. 1967. *A statistical investigation of the peasant movement in Russia of the nineteenth century* (*Opyt statisticheskogo izucheniya krestianskogo dvizheniya v Rossii XIX v.)*. Nauka, Moscow.

Lo Cascio, E. 1994. The size of the Roman population: Beloch and the meaning of Augustan census figures. *Journal of Roman Studies* 84:23–40.

Loades, D. M. 1999. *Politics and the nation: England 1450–1660*. Blackwell, Oxford.

Lorcin, M.-T. 1974. *Les Campagnes de la région lyonnaise aux XIVe et XVe siècles.* Imprimerie BOSC, Lyon.

Lorcin, M.-T. 1981. *Vivre et mourir en Lyonnais à la fin du Moyen Age*. Editions du CNRS, Paris.

Losinsky, A. E., editor. 1918. *The 1917 grain harvest in Russia* (*Urozhay khlebov v Rossii v 1917 g.*). Izdatelstvo Moskovskogo Oblastnogo Prodovolstvennogo Komiteta, Moscow.

Lurie, Y. S. 1994. *Two histories of Rus' in the fifteenth century: Early and late, independent and official chronicles on the formation of the Muscovite state* (*Dve istorii Rusi 15 veka: Rannie i pozdnie, nezavisimye i oficial'nye letopisi of obrazovanii Moskovskogo gosudarstva*). Dmitri Bulanin, St. Petersburg

Macunovich, D. J. 2002. *Birth quake: The baby boom and its aftershocks.* University of Chicago Press, Chicago.

Madge, S. J. 1938. *The Domesday of Crown lands: A study of the legislation, surveys, and sales of royal estates under the Commonwealth.* Routledge, London.

Major, J. R. 1981. Noble income, inflation, and the Wars of Religion in France. *American Historical Review* 86:21–48.

Major, J. R. 1993. *From Renaissance monarchy to absolute monarchy.* Johns Hopkins University Press, Baltimore.

Malthus, T. R. 1798. *An essay on the principle of population.* J. Johnson, London.

Man'kov, A. G. 1951. *Prices and their movements in the Russian state during the XVI century* (*Tseny i ikh dvizhenie v Russkom gosudarstve XVI veka*). Publishing House of the Academy of Sciences of the USSR, Moscow and Leningrad.

Matusiak, J. 2005. Mid-Tudor England: Years of trauma and survival. *History Review* 52:31–36.

McEvedy, C., and R. Jones. 1978. *Atlas of world population history.* Facts on File, New York.

McFarlane, K. B. 1973. *The nobility of later medieval England.* Clarendon Press, Oxford.

Mertes, K. 1988. *The English noble household: 1250–1600.* Blackwell, Oxford.

Merton, R. K. 1968. The Matthew Effect in science. *Science* 159:56–63.

Meskill, J., editor. 1965. *The pattern of Chinese history: Cycles, development, or stagnation?* D.C. Heath, Lexington, MA.

Miliukov, P. N. 1990. *Memoirs. Vol. I* (*Vospominaniya. Tom I*). Sovremennik, Moscow.

Miller, D. 1989. Monumental building as indicator of economic trends in northern Rus' in the later Kievan and Mongol periods, 1138–1462. *American Historical Review* 9:360–90.

Miller, E., and J. Hatcher. 1978. *Medieval England: Rural society and economic change, 1086–1348.* Longman, London.

Milov, L. V. 1998. *The great Russian ploughman and the peculiarities of the Russain historical process* (*Velikorusskiy pahar i osobennosti russkogo istoricheskogo protsessa*). ROSSPAN, Moscow.

Mingay, G. E. 1976. *The gentry: The rise and fall of a ruling class.* Longman, London.

Mironov, B. N. 1985. *Grain prices in Russia in the seventeenth and eighteenth centuries* (*Khlebnie tseny v Rossii za dva stoletiya (XVIII–XIX gg.)*), Nauka, Leningrad.

Mironov, B. N. 1985. In search of hidden information. *Social Science History* 9:339–59.

Mironov, B. N. 1990. *The Russian town in 1740–1860: Demographic, social, and economic comparisons* (*Russkii gorod v 1740–1860-x gg.: Demograficheskoe, sotsial'noye i ekonomicheskoe razvitie*). Nauka, Leningrad.

Mironov, B. N. 1992. Consequences of the price revolution in eighteenth-century Russia. *Economic History Review* 45:457–78.

Mironov, B. N. 2000. *A social history of Imperial Russia, 1700–1917.* Westview Press, Boulder, CO.

Mironov, B. N. 2002. "A fed horse is a champ, a hungry one is an orphan": Nutrition, health, and population growth in Russia during the second half of the nineteenth and the beginning of the twentieth century ("Syt kon—bogatyr, goloden—sirota": Pitanie, zdorovie i rost naseleniya Rossii vtoroy poloviny XIX–nachala XX veka). *Otechestvennaya Istoriya* 2:30–43.

Mironov, B. N. 2004. The anthropometric approach to the study of the well-being of the Russian population in the eighteenth century (Antropometricheskii podxod k izucheniyu blagosotoyaniya Rossii v XVIII veke). *Otechestvennaya Istoriya* 6:17–30.

Mitchell, R. E. 1990. *Patricians and plebeians: The origin of the Roman state*. Cornell University Press, Ithaca, NY.

Moorman, J. R. H. 1946. *Church life in England in the thirteenth century*. Cambridge University Press, Cambridge, UK.

Morley, N. 1996. *Metropolis and hinterland: The city of Rome and the Italian economy, 200 B.C–A.D. 200*. Cambridge University Press, Cambridge.

Morley, N. 2001. The transformation of Italy, 225–28 B.C. *Journal of Roman Studies* 91:50–62.

Morris, I. 2005. The collapse and regeneration of complex society in Greece, 1500–500 BC. Princeton/Stanford Working Papers in Classics, Working Paper no. 120510 (Version 1.0, December 2005), Princeton University, Princeton, NJ.

Morris, R. 1979. *Cathedrals and abbeys of England and Wales: The building church, 600–1540*. W. W. Norton, New York.

Mortimer, R. 1994. *Angevin England: 1154–1258*. Blackwell, Oxford.

Mougel, F. 1971. La Fortune des Princes de Bourbon-Conty, revenues et gestion (1655–1791). *Revue d'histoire moderne et contemporaine* 18:30–49.

Nachalo. 1955. *The beginning of the first Russian Revolution: January–March 1905* (*Nachalo pervoy russkoy revolyutsii: Yanvar'–Mart 1905 goda*). Moscow.

Nefedov, S. A. 2006. 1905: Revolution in the context of Westernization (1905 god: revolyutsiya v kontekste vesternizacii). *Uralskii Istoricheskii Vestnik* 15:35–46.

Nefedov, S. 1999. The method of demographic cycles in a study of socioeconomic history of preindustrial society (in Russian). Ph.D. dissertation, Ekaterinburg University, Ekaterinburg, Russia.

Nefedov, S. A. 2002. On the demographic cycles in the history of the medieval Russia (O demograficheskix tsiklax v istorii srednevekovoy Rossii). *Klio* 3: 193–203.

Nefedov, S. A. 2003. On the feasibility of applying the demographic-structural theory to the study of Russian history during the sixteenth century (O vozmozhnosti i primeneniya strukturno-demograficheskoy teorii pri izuchenii istorii Rossii XVI veka). *Otechestvennaya Istoriya* 5:63–72.

Nefedov, S. A. 2005. *A demographic-structural analysis of the socio-economic history of Russia* (*Demograficheski-strukturnii analiz social'no-ekonomicheskoy istorii Rossii*). UGGU, Ekaterinburg, Russia.

Nifontov, A. 1973. *Grain production in Russia in the second half of the nineteenth century* (*Zernovoe proizvodstvo v Rossii vo vtoroy polovine XIX veka*). Nauka, Moscow.

Nikolsky, P. 1910. *The Kirillo-Belozersky Monastery and its organization in the second quarter of the seventeenth century* (*Kirillo-Belozerskii monastyr i ego ustroystvo vo vtoroy chetverti XVII veka*). Vol. I, no. 2. Sinodalnaya Tipografiya, St. Petersburg.

Nohejlova-Pratova, E. 1955. *Nalezy Minci v Cechach, na Morave a ve Slezsku*. Ceskoslovenska Akademie Ved, Prague.

Novosel'sky, A. L. 1945. Economic conditions of runaway peasants in the south of the Muscovite state in the first half of the seventeenth century (K voprosu ob ekonomicheskom sostoyanii beglyx krestian na yuge Moskovskogo gosudarstva v pervoy polovine XVII veka). *Istoricheskie Zapiski* 16:40–49.

Obuhov, V. M. 1927. The dynamics of grain harvests in European Russia between 1883 and 1915 (Dvizhenie urozhaev zernovyh kultur v Evropeyskoy Rossii v period 1883–1915 gg.). Pages 1–160 in V. G. Groman, editor, *The influence of crop failures on people's economy of Russia* (*Vliyanie neurozhaev na narodnoe hozyaystvo Rossii*). Institut Economiki, Moscow.

Oldenburg, S. S. 1992. *The reign of Emperor Nicholas II* (*Tsarstvovanie imperatora Nikolya II*). Terra, Moscow.

Olearius, A. 1980. Description of travels in Muscovy (Opisanie puteshestviya v Moskoviyu). Pages 287–470 in Ju. A. Limonov, editor, *Russia in the eyes of foreigners* (*Rossiya glazami inostrantsev*). Lenizdat, Leningrad.

Orlea, M. 1980. *La Noblesse aux États Généraux de 1576 et de 1588*. Presses Universitaires de France, Paris.

Ormrod, W. M. 1990. *The reign of Edward III: Crown and political society in England 1327–1377*. Yale University Press, New Haven, CT.

Ormrod, W. M. 1999. England in the Middle Ages. Pages 19–52 in R. Bonney, editor, *The rise of the fiscal state in Europe, c.1200–1815*. Oxford University Press, Oxford.

Overton, M. 1996. *Agricultural revolution in England*. Cambridge University Press, Cambridge.

Painter, S. 1943. *Studies in the history of the English feudal barony*. Johns Hopkins University Press, Baltimore.

Palitsin, A. 1955. *The legend of Avramii Palitsin* (*Skazanie Avraama Palitsina*). Publishing House of the Academy of Sciences of the USSR, Moscow and Leningrad.Parsons, J. 2005. Population control and politics. *Population and Environment* 12:355–77.

Pearl, R., and L. J. Reed. 1920. On the rate of growth of the population of the United States since 1790 and its mathematical representation. *Proceedings of the National Academy of Sciences of the USA* 6:275<n>-88.

Peasant History. 1990. *History of the peasantry of the USSR from ancient times to the Great October Socialist Revolution. Vol. II* (*Istoriya krestinastva SSSR s drevneyshih vremen do Velikoy oktyabrskoy socialisticheskoy revolyutsii*). Nauka, Moscow.

Peasant History. 1994. *History of the peasantry of northwestern Russia* (*Istoriya krestianstva Severo-Zapada Rossii*). Nauka, St. Petersburg.

Perroy, E. 1962. Social mobility among the French noblesse in the later Middle Ages. *Past and Present* 21:25–38.

Perroy, E. 1965. *The Hundred Years' War*. Capricorn, New York.

Phelps-Brown, E. H., and S. Hopkins. 1955. Seven centuries of building wages. *Economica* 22.

Phythian-Adams, C. 1979. *Desolation of a city: Coventry and the urban crisis of the late Middle Ages*. Cambridge University Press, Cambridge.

Planhol, X. de. 1994. *An historical geography of France*. Cambridge University Press, Cambridge.

Pogrebinski, A. P. 1953. *The history of finances of pre-revolutionary Russia* (*Ocherki istorii finansov dorevolyutsionnoy Rossii*). Gosfinizdat, Moscow.

Pokrovski, S. A. 1947. *External trade and external trade politics of Russia* (*Vneshnyaya torgovlya i vneshnyaya torgovaya politika Rossii*). Mezhdunarodnaya Kniga, Moscow.

Pollard, A. J. 2000. *Late medieval England: 1399–1509*. Longman, Harlow, UK.

Poos, L. 2004. *Rural society after the Black Death: Essex 1350–1525*. Cambridge University Press, Cambridge.

Poos, L. R. 1985. The rural population of Essex in the later middle ages. *Economic History Review* 38:515–30.

Popper, K. R. 1957. *The poverty of historicism*. Routledge and Kegan Paul, London.

Postan, M. M. 1966. Medieval agrarian society in its prime: England. In M. M. Postan, editor, *Cambridge economic history. Vol. I.* Cambridge University Press, Cambridge.

Postan, M. M. 1973. *Essays on medieval agriculture and general problems of the medieval economy.* Cambridge University Press, Cambridge.

Postan, M. M., and J. Hatcher. 1985. Population and class relations in feudal society. Pages 64–78 in T. H. Aston and C.H.E. Philpin, editors, *The Brenner debate: Agrarian class structure and economic development in pre-industrial Europe*. Cambridge University Press, Cambridge.

Powicke, M. R. 1962. *Military obligation in medieval England.* Oxford University Press, Oxford.

Prokop'eva, L. S. 1967. The "grain budget" of a peasant household in Belozersky Region in the middle of the sixteenth century ("Hlebnii byudzhet" krestianskogo hozyaystva Belozerskogo kraya v seredine XVI v.). Pages 99–110 in N. E. Nosov, editor, *The peasantry and class struggle in feudal Russia* (*Krestianstvo i klassovaya borba v feodalnoy Rossii*). Nauka, Leningrad.

Prokopovich, S. N. 1907. *The agrarian question in numbers* (*Agrarnii vopros v cifrax*). Obshestvennaya Polza, St. Petersburg.

Pugh, T. B. 1972. The magnates, knights and gentry. Pages 86–128 in S. B. Chrimes, C. D. Ross, and R. A. Griffiths, editors, *Fifteenth-century England: 1399–1509*. Manchester University Press, Manchester, UK.

Pushkareva, I. M. 1975. *Russian railroad workers in the bourgeois-democratic revolutions* (*Zheleznodorozhniki Rossii v burzhuazno-demokraticheskih revolyutsiyax*). Nauka, Moscow.

Raaflaub, K. A., editor. 1986. *Social struggles in Archaic Rome: New perspectives on the Conflict of Orders*. University of California Press, Berkeley and Los Angeles.

Raban, S. 2000. *England under Edward I and Edward II: 1259–1327*. Blackwell, Oxford.

Rabochii. 1981. *The working class in the first Russian Revolution of 1905–1907* (*Rabochiy klass v pervoy rossiyskoy revolyutsii 1905–1907 gg.*). Nauka, Moscow.

Rahmatullin, M. A. 1990. *The peasant movement in the Great-Russian rovinces in 1826–1857* (*Krestianskoe dvizhenie v velikorusskix guberniyah v 1826–1857 gg.)*. Nauka, Moscow.

Ramsay, J. H. 1925. *A history of the revenues of the kings of England, 1066–1399*. Oxford University Press, Oxford.

Rashin, A. G. 1956. *Russian population over 100 years* (*Naselenie Rossii za 100 let*). Gosstatizdat, Moscow

Reed, F. E. 1996. CENTENNIA for Windows. Clockwork Software Inc., Chicago.

Reinhard, M. R., A. Armengaud, and J. Dupâquier. 1968. *Histoire Générale de la Population Mondiale*. Editions Montchrestien, Paris.

Reischauer, E. O. 1960. The dynastic cycle. Pages 114–18 in E. O. Reischauer and J. K. Fairbank, editors, *East Asia: The great tradition*. Houghton Mifflin, Boston.

Riazanovsky, N. V. 2000. *A history of Russia*, 6th ed. Oxford University Press, New York.

Ricardo, D. 1817. *On the principles of political economy and taxation.* John Murray, London.

Richardson, L. 1992. *A new topographical dictionary of ancient Rome.* Johns Hopkins University Press, Baltimore.

Robbins, R. G. 1975. *Famine in Russia: 1891–1892.* Columbia University Press, New York.

Robertson, A. S. 2000. *An inventory of Romano-British coin hoards.* Royal Numismatic Society Special Publication 20, London.

Roche, D. 1967. Aperçus sur la fortune et les revenues des princes de Condé à l'aube du XVIIIe siècle. *Revue d'histoire moderne et contemporaine* 14:216–43.

Romano, R. 1967. *I prezzi in Europe dal XIII secolo a oggi.* Giulio Einaudi, Torino.

Rosenstein, N. 2002. Marriage and manpower in the Hannibalic War: Assidui, proletarii and Livy 24.18.7–8. *Historia* 51:163–91.

Rosenstein, N. 2004. *Rome at war: Farms, families, and death in the Middle Republic.* University of North Carolina Press, Chapel Hill.

Rostow, W. W. 1990. *The stages of economic growth: A non-Communist manifesto.* Cambridge University Press, Cambridge.

Roth, R. 2001. Homicide in early modern England 1549–1800: The need for a quantitative synthesis. *Crime, History and Societies* 5:33–67.

Rubinshteyn, N. L. 1957. *The agrarian economy in Russia in the second half of the eighteenth century* (*Selskoe hozyaystvo Rossii vo vtoroj polovine XVIII veka*). Gospolitizdat, Moscow.

Russell, C. 1990. *The causes of the English civil war.* Oxford University Press, Oxford.

Russell, J. C. 1948. *British medieval population.* University of New Mexico Press, Albuquerque.

Saller, R. 2000. Status and patronage. Pages 817–54 in A. K. Bowman, P. Garnsey, and D. Rathbone, editors, *The Cambridge ancient history*, 2nd ed. *Vol. XI.* Cambridge University Press, New York.

Salmon, J.H.M. 1976. *Society in crisis: France in the sixteenth century.* St. Martin's Press, New York.

Saul, N. 1981. *Knights and esquires: The Gloucestershire gentry in the fourteenth century.* Clarendon Press, Oxford.

Schalk, E. 1982. Enoblement in France from 1350 to 1660. *Journal of Social History* 16:101–110.

Scheidel, W., editor. 2001. *Debating Roman demography.* Brill, Leiden, the Netherlands.

Scheidel, W. 2001. Progress and problems in Roman demography. Pages 1–81 in W. Scheidel, editor, *Debating Roman demography.* Brill, Leiden, the Netherlands.

Scheidel, W. 2002. A model of demographic and economic change in Roman Egypt after the Antonine plague. *Journal of Roman Archaeology* 15:97–114.

Scheidel, W. 2004. Human mobility in Roman Italy. I. The free population. *Journal of Roman Studies* 94:1–26.

Scheidel, W. 2005. Human mobility in Roman Italy. II. The slave population. *Journal of Roman Studies* 95:64–79.

Scheidel, W. 2007. A model of real income growth in Roman Italy. *Historia* 56: 322–46.

Schlesinger, A. M. J. 1986. *The cycles of American history.* Houghton Mifflin, Boston.

Schtaden, G. O. 1925. *Moscow of Ivan the Terrible: Memoirs of the German oprichnik (O Moskve Ivana Groznogo: Zapiski nemtsa-oprichnika).* Sabashnikov, Moscow.

Scott, S., and C. Duncan, J. 2001. *Biology of plagues: Evidence from historical populations.* Cambridge University Press, Cambridge.

Seward, D. 1978. *The Hundred Years War: The English in France, 1337–1453.* Atheneaum, New York.

Shahovski, S. I. 2001. The Liberty Union (Soyuz osvobozhdeniya). Pages 526–602 in D. B. Pavlov, editor, *The Liberal Movement in Russia, 1902–1905* (*Liberal'noe dvizhenie v Rossii 1902–1905 gg.*). ROSSPAN, Moscow.

Shapiro, A. L. 1965. The historical role of the peasant wars of the seventeenth–eighteenth centuries in Russia (Ob istoricheskoy roli krestianskih voyn XVII–XVIII vv. v Rossii). *Istoriya SSSR* 5:61–80.

Shapiro, A. L. 1987. *The Russian peasantry before serfdom: fourteenth–sixteenth centuries* (*Russkoe krestiamstvo pered zakreposcheniem: XIV–XVI vv.*). Publishing House of Leningrad University, Leningrad.

Shatsillo, K. F. 1976. The Zemstvo-Liberal Program: Its rise and bankruptcy on the eve of the first Russian Revolution, 1901–1904 (Formirovanie programmy zemskogo liberalizma i ee bankrotstvo nakanune pervoy russkoy revolyutsii, 1901–1904 gg.). *Istoricheskie Zapiski* 97:70–98.

Shatsillo, K. F. 1982. History of the liberation movement in Russia at the beginning of the twentieth century (Iz istorii osvoboditel'nogo dvizheniya v Rossii v nachale XX veka). *Istoriya SSSR* 4: 55–57.

Shatzman, I. 1975. *Senatorial wealth and Roman politics.* Latomus, Brussels.

Shepukova, N. M. 1959. Changes in the relative fraction of privately owned peasants among the population of European Russia, 18th–first half of 19th centuries (Izmenenie udelnogo vesa chastno-vladelcheskih krestian v sostave naseleniya Evropeyskoy Rossii, XVIII–pervaya polovina XIX v.). *Voprosy Istorii* 12:123–36.

Shvatenko, O.A. 1990. *Lay feudal estate in Russia in the first third of the seventeenth century* (*Svetskaya feodalnaya votchina Rossii v pervoy treti XVII veka*). Institut Istorii AN SSSR, Moscow.

Sidorov, A. L. 1960. *The financial conditions of Russia during the World War I, 19143–1917* (*Finansovoe polozhenie Rossii v gody pervoy mirovoy voyny, 1914–1917*). Publishing House of the Academy of Sciences of the USSR, Moscow.

Simiand, F. 1932. *Les fluctuations économiques á longue période et la crise mondiale.* Félix Alcan, Paris.

Skocpol, T. 1979. *States and social revolutions: A comparative analysis of France, Russia, and China.* Cambridge University Press, Cambridge.

Skrynnikov, R. G. 1975. *Russia after oprichnina* (*Rossiya posle oprichniny*). Publishing House of Leningrad University, Leningrad.

Skrynnikov, R. G. 1988. *Russia at the beginning of the seventeenth century: The Time of Troubles* (*Rossiya v nachale XVII veka: Smuta*). Mysl, Moscow.

Skrynnikov, R. G. 1996. *The great prince Ivan Vasilievich the Terrible* (*Velikiy gosudar Ioan Vasilievich Grozniy*). Rusich, Smolensk.

Sladkevich, G. H. 1962. Opposition movements of the nobility during the revolutionary situation. Pages 70–88 in M. V. Nechkina, editor, *The revolutionary situation in Russia in 1859–1861 (Revolyutsionnaya situaciya v Rossii v 1859–1861 gg.)*. Publishing House of the Academy of Sciences of the USSR, Moscow.

Smahtina, M. V. 2003. *The value system of the Russian and the Ukrainian landed gentry in the first half of the nineteenth century (to 1861) (Sistema tsennostey velikorusskogo i malorossiyskogo pomestnogo dvoryanstva v pervoy polovine XIX v. (do 1861 g.))*. Pages 55–72 in *Conferences, colloquia, materials (Konferentsii, diskussii, materially)*. Rossiiski Universitet Druzhby Narodov, Moscow.

Solov'ev, Yu. B. 1979. *The autocracy and the nobility in the end of the nineteenth century (Samoderzhavie i dvorianstvo v kontse XIX veka)*. Nauka, Leningrad.

Soloviev, S. M. 1989. *Collected works (Sochineniya)*. Mysl, Moscow.

Sorokin, P. A. 1937. *Social and cultural dynamics. Vol. III: Fluctuations of social relationships, war, and revolution*. American Book Co., New York.

Startsev. 1984. *February 27, 1917* (27 fevralya 1917 goda). Molodaya Gvardiya, Moscow.

Stearns, P. N. 2001. *The encyclopedia of world history*, 6th ed. Houghton Mifflin, Boston.

Steckel, R. H. 2004. New light on the "Dark Ages": The remarkably tall stature of northern European men during the medieval era. *Social Science History* 28:211–29.

Stone, L. 1965. *The crisis of aristocracy: 1558–1641*. Clarendon Press, Oxford.

Stone, L. 1972. *The causes of the English Revolution: 1529–1642*. Harper and Row, New York.

Stone, L. 1976. Social mobility in England, 1500–1700. Pages 26–71 in P. S. Seaver, editor, *Seventeenth-century England: Society in an age of revolution*. New Viewpoints, New York.

Stone, L., and J.C.F. Stone. 1984. *An open elite? England 1540–1880*. Clarendon Press, Oxford.

Storey, R. L. 1966. *The end of the house of Lancaster*. Stein and Day, New York.

Sumption, J. 1991. *The Hundred Years' War: Trial by battle*. University of Pennsylvania Press, Philadelphia.

Sweezy, P., M. Dobb, K. Takahashi, R. Hilton, C. Hill, G. Lefebvre, G. Procacci, E. Hobsbawm, and J. Merrington. 1976. *The transition from feudalism to capitalism*. NLB, London.

Taagepera, R. 1979. Size and duration of empires: Growth-decline curves, 600 B.C. to 600 A.D. *Social Science History* 3:115–38.

Thirsk, J., editor. 1967. *The agrarian history of England and Wales*. Cambridge University Press, Cambridge.

Thompson, J.D.A. 1956. *Inventory of British coin hoards: A.D. 600–1500*. Royal Numismatic Society, Oxford.

Thomson, J.A.F. 1983. *The transformation of medieval England*. Longman, London.

Thorold Rogers, J. E. 1862. *A history of agriculture and prices in England*, 7 vols. Clarendon Press, Oxford.

Tignor, R., J. Adelman, S. Aron, S. Kotkin, S. Marchand, G. Prakash, and M. Tsin. 2002. *Worlds together, worlds apart: A history of the modern world from the Mongol Empire to the present*. W. W. Norton, New York.

Tihomirov, M. N. 1962. *Russia in the sixteenth century* (*Rossiya v XVI stoletii*). Publishing House of the Academy of Sciences of the USSR, Moscow.

Tihonov, Yu. A. 1966. Russia in the first half of the seventeenth century. Pages 297–321 in B. N. Ponomarev, editor, *Istoriya SSSR, Vol. II*. Nauka, Moscow.

Tihonov, Yu. A. 1974. *Privately owned peasants in Russia: The feudal rent in the seventeenth–beginning of the eighteenth centuries* (*Pomeschichi krestiane: Feodalnaya renta v XVII–nachale XVIII v.*). Nauka, Moscow.

Tilly, C. 1993. *European revolutions: 1492–1992*. Blackwell, Oxford.

Titow, J. Z. 1961. Some evidence of the thirteenth century population increase. *Economic History Review* 14:218–24.

Toynbee, A. J. 1965. *Hannibal's legacy: The Hannibalic War's effects on Roman life*. Oxford University Press, London.

Troitski, S. M. 1968. Spatial distribution of the forms of feudal rent in a large Russian estate in the first quarter of the seventeenth century (Raionirovanie form feodalnoy renty v krupnoy votchine Rossii v pervoy chetvertu XVIII v.). Pages 116–26 in *Almanac of agrarian history of Eastern Europe for 1968* (*Ezhegodnik po agrarnoy istorii Vostochnoy Evropy za 1968 g.*) Nauka, Leningrad

Tuchman, B. W. 1978. *A distant mirror: The calamitous fourteenth century*, 1st ed. Knopf, New York.

Turchin, P. 2003a. *Complex population dynamics: A theoretical/empirical synthesis*. Princeton University Press, Princeton, NJ.

Turchin, P. 2003b. *Historical dynamics: Why states rise and fall*. Princeton University Press, Princeton, NJ.

Turchin, P. 2005. Dynamical feedbacks between population growth and sociopolitical instability in agrarian states. *Structure and Dynamics* 1(1): Article 3.

Turchin, P. 2006. *War and peace and war: The life cycles of imperial nations*. Pi Press, New York.

Turchin, P. 2008. Modeling periodic waves of integration in the Afro-Eurasian world-system. Pages 163–91 in G. Modelski, T. Devezas, and W. R. Thompson, editors, *Globalization as evolutionary process: Modeling global change*. Routledge, London.

Turchin, P., and T. D. Hall. 2003. Spatial synchrony among and within world-systems: Insights from theoretical ecology. *Journal of World Systems Research* 9:37–64.

Usher, D. 1989. The dynastic cycle and the stationary state. *American Economic Review* 79:1031–44.

Usherovich, S. 1933. *Executions in the tsarist Russia* (*Smertnye kazni v tsarskoy Rossii: K istorii kazney po politicheskim processam s 1824 po 1917 god*). Obshchestvo Politkatorzhan i Ssylnoposelentsev, Kharkov.

Utkin, A. I. 1976. *The forgotten tragedy: Russia in World War I* (*Zabytaya tragediya: Rossiya v pervoy mirovoy voyne*). Rusich, Smolensk,

Utkin, A. I. 1987. The numbers and composition of RSDRP in 1905–1907 (K voprosu of chislennosti i sostave RSDRP v 1905–1907 gg.). Pages 8–26 in A. P. Korelin, editor, *Political parties of Russia during the Revolution of 1905–1907: A quantitative analysis* (*Politicheskie partii Rossii v period revolyutsii 1905–1907 gg.: Kolichetcenniy analiz*). Institut Istorii SSSR, Moscow.

Vale, M. G. A. 1986. Seigneurial fortification and private war in later medieval Gascony. Pages 133–49 in M. Jones, editor, *Gentry and lesser nobility in late medieval Europe*. St. Martin's Press, New York.

Valuev, A. P. 1958. Internal conditions of Russia (O vnutrennem sostoyanii Rossii). *Istoricheskii Arkhiv* 1:141–43.

Valuev, A. P. 1961. *The diary of P.A. Valuev, Minister of Internal Affairs, 1861–1864* (*Dnevnik P.A. Valueva, ministra vnutrennih del, 1861–1864*). Publishing House of the Academy of Sciences of the USSR, Moscow.

Vazhinski, V. M. 1963. Grain trade in the south of the Muscovite state during the second half of the seventeenth century (Hlebnaya torgovlya na yuge Moskovskogo gosudarstva vo vtoroy polovine XVII veka). *Uchenye Zapiski Moskovskogo Oblastnogo Pedagogicheskogo Instituta* 127:3–30.

Vazhinski, V. M. 1983. *The agrarian economy in the Black Earth region of Russia in the seventeenth century* (*Selskoe hozyaystvo v chernozemnom tsentre Rossii v XVII veke*). VGPI, Voronezh.

Veselovski, S. 1916. *Soshnoe pismo. Vol. II.* Moscow.

Vodarski, Ya. E. 1966. The numbers and distribution of Russian tradespeople in the second half of the seventeenth century (Chislennost i razmeschenie posadskogo naseleniya v Rossii vo vtoroy polovine XVII v.). Pages 271–96 in V. I. Shunkov, editor, *Villages of feudal Russia* (*Goroda feodalnoy Rossii*). Nauka, Moscow.

Vodarski, Ya. E. 1973. *The population of Russia over 400 years: 16th century–beginning of 20th century* (*Naselenie Rossii za 400 let, XVI–nachalo XX v.)*. Prosveshchenie, Moscow.

Vodarski, Ya. E. 1977. *The population of Russia from the end of the 17th century to the beginning of 18th century* (*Naselenie Rossii v kontse XVII–nachale XVIII v.*). Nauka, Moscow.

Vodarski, Ya. E. 1988. *Noble landownership in Russia in the 17th–first half of the 19th centuries* (*Dvorianskoe zemlevladenie v Rossii XVII–pervoy polovine XIX v.)*. Nauka, Moscow.

Volkov, S. I. 1959. *The peasants of the Crown properties in the Moscow Region in the middle of the eighteenth century* (*Krestiane dvortsovyx vladeniy Podmoskoviya v seredine XVIII v. (30–70-e gody))*. Publishing House of the Academy of Sciences of the USSR, Moscow.

Von Ungern-Sternberg, J. 1986. The end of the Conflict of the Orders. Pages 353–77 in K. A. Raaflaub, editor, *Social struggles in Archaic Rome: New perspectives on the Conflict of the Orders*. University of California Press, Berkeley and Los Angeles.

Vorob'ev, V. M., and A. Ya. Degtyarev. 1986. *Russian feudal landownership from the Time of the Troubles to the end of the Petrine reforms* (*Russkoe zemlevladenie ot Smutnogo Vremeni do kontsa petrovskih reform*). Publishing House of Leningrad University, Leningrad.

Ward, A. M., F. M. Heichelheim, and C. A. Yeo. 2003. *A history of the Roman people*, 4th ed. Prentice Hall, Upper Saddle River, NJ.

Warmington, A. R. 1997. *Civil war, interregnum and restoration in Gloucestershire*. Boydell Press, Woodbridge, Suffolk, UK.

Weary, W. A. 1977. The house of La Tremoille fifteenth through eighteenth centuries: Change and adaptation in a French noble family. *Journal of Modern History* 46:D1001–38.

Wells, C. M. 1992. *The Roman Empire*, 2nd ed. Harvard University Press, Cambridge, MA.

Wheatcroft, S. 1991. *Crises and the condition of the peasantry in late imperial Russia: Peasant economy, culture and politics of European Russia*. Princeton University Press, Princeton, NJ.

White, G. J. 2000. *Restoration and reform, 1153–1165: Recovery from war in England.* Cambridge University Press, Cambridge.

Wickham-Crowley, T. P. 1997. Structural theories of revolution. Pages 38–72 in J. Foran, editor, *Theorizing revolutions*. Routledge, London.

Wickham, C. 1981. *Early medieval Italy: Central power and local society, 400–1000.* Macmillan, London.

Williams, P. 1995. *The later Tudors: England, 1547–1603*. Clarendon Press, Oxford.

Wood, J. B. 1980. *The nobility of the election of Bayeux, 1463–1666*. Princeton University Press, Princeton, NJ.

Wood, J. W. 1998. A theory of preindustrial population dynamics (with discussion). *Current Anthropology* 39:99–135.

Wright, N. 1998. *Knights and peasants: The Hundred Years' War in the French countryside*. Boydell Press, Rochester, NY.

Wrigley, E. A., R. S. Davis, J. E. Oeppen, and R. S. Schofield. 1997. *English population history from family reconstruction: 1580–1837*. Cambridge University Press, Cambridge.

Wrigley, E. A., and R. S. Schofield. 1981. *The population history of England, 1541–1871: A reconstruction*. Harvard University Press, Cambridge, MA.

Yushko, A. A. 1991. *The Moscow Land in the ninth through the fourteenth centuries* (*Moskovskaya zemlya IX–XIV vekov*). Nauka, Moscow.

Zayonchkovski, A. 1938. *The World War of 1914–1918. Vol. II* (*Mirovaya voyna 1914–1918 gg. Tom II*). Gosvoenizdat, Moscow.

Zayonchkovski, P. A. 1963. *Abolition of serfdom in Russia* (*Otmena krepostnogo prava v Rossii*). Prosveshchenie, Moscow.

Zelener, Y. 2003. Smallpox and the disintegration of the Roman economy after 165 AD (Roman Empire). Ph.D. dissertation, Columbia University, New York.

Zhao, W., and S. Z. Xie. 1988. *China's population history* (*Zhongguo ren kou shi*). People's Publisher, Peking.

Zimin, A. A. 1960. *The reforms of Ivan the Terrible* (*Reformy Ivana Groznogo*). Izdatel'stvo Socialno-ekonomicheskoi Literaturi, Moscow.

Zimin, A. A. 1972. *Russia on the threshold of the modern period* (*Rossiya na poroge novogo vremeni*). Nauka, Moscow.

Index

Page numbers in italics refer to tables or figures in the text.

www.ingramcontent.com/pod-product-compliance
Ingram Content Group UK Ltd.
Pitfield, Milton Keynes, MK11 3LW, UK
UKHW031039200125
453888UK00001B/2